Piagetian Psychology
CROSS-CULTURAL CONTRIBUTIONS

Piagetian
Psychology

CROSS-CULTURAL CONTRIBUTIONS

Edited by PIERRE R. DASEN

UNIVERSITY OF GENEVA

Preface by JEAN PIAGET

GARDNER PRESS, INC, NEW YORK

Distributed by Halsted Press

Division of John Wiley & Sons, Inc.

NEW YORK   LONDON   TORONTO   SYDNEY

BF
723
.C5
P55

GARDNER PRESS, INC.
19 Union Square West
New York, New York 10003

Distributed solely by the Halsted Press Division of
John Wiley & Sons, Inc., New York

Library of Congress Cataloging in Publication Data
Main entry under title:

Piagetian psychology.

   1. Cognition (child psychology) 2. Piaget, Jean,
1896–   3. Personality and culture. I. Dasen,
P. R.
BF723.C5P55   155.4'13   76-22199
ISBN 0-470-15186-2

Printed in the United States of America

Preface

This fine collection of studies for which I have the pleasure of writing the Preface presents a rich and instructive body of new documents in the comparative psychology of cognitive structures. This is an area in which there will always be more to explore, but the authors of this collection have succeeded in opening up some new and important sectors. The basic problem dealt with here is whether human reason follows the same course of development in different societies, or whether, as certain social psychologists maintain, we must expect to find great differences, or at least significant variations, in different social environments. If development is similar in different settings, one still must determine to what extent such similarity is due to innate elements, which, in the extreme, would mean that the structuration would be entirely hereditary; and to what extent it can be explained by common mechanisms of equilibration or self-regulation, with leeway for fluctuations due to interactions with the environment.

The two essential results set forth in this work shed light on those difficult questions. The first is that, in general, the developmental stages observed in the societies where our studies were originally conducted have been observed again in very different civilizations. Such a convergence is surely very significant. It would seem to indicate that the laws of psychogenesis of cognitive structures can be compared in their generality with biological epigenesis; the progressive formation of the instruments of human intelligence would be a particular case of this epigenesis. It is especially striking in this regard to note comparable behavior in European children, with certain objects that they are accustomed to, and in children from totally different settings who are handling these objects for the first time.

But a second group of facts brought out by the authors is just as instructive: that there are differences in what we have called the *"décalages"* or time differences among related developments in a child, when one operation, or, more generally, one operational structure is applied to different areas. For example, the operations necessary for solving a problem of conservation are applied more easily, and thus earlier, to a group of discrete objects than to a rather complex continuum (like an area whose shape is changed). Operations depend on the subject's activities, and their development becomes intelligible to psychologists to the extent that there is a common base in the activities of all subjects; this applies even level by level, and to the transitions from one level to another. The time differences, on the other hand, reflect the resistance of the object. Different objects can resist the subject's actions in a multitude of ways that are not necessarily comparable. This means that it is not possible to establish a general theory of time differences, just as in physics there is no universal theory or model of friction effects that disturb certain regularities; rather, each case must be analyzed in itself. This being said, it is of great interest to see that the time differences observed in different social environments studied in this work can vary from one situation to another, according to the customs of the area, and to the cognitive domain being studied—space or discrete collections, speed and time, etc. Where the young subjects have been to school, on the other hand, there seems to be a tendency toward equalization in this regard.

This double finding—relatively general stages, and variable time differences—does not seem easily explained by a theory that sees cognitive mechanisms as innately preformed. Of course, any mental evolution involves elements of heredity and maturation, but this is simply one factor in the functioning and does not imply innateness of mental structures. The progressive construction of these structures would come from a system of self-organization, or equilibration, and would entail the various regulations inherent in such a system—whence the variations in the time differences observed in these studies.

In view of the general results and the richness of specific analyses with which this work abounds, it only remains for us to extend our warm congratulations to its authors, and especially to their coordinator, Pierre Dasen.

J. Piaget

TRANSLATED BY ELEANOR DUCKWORTH

Préface

Le beau recueil d'études que j'ai le plaisir de préfacer fournit un ensemble très riche et très instructif de documents originaux en un domaine que l'on n'aura jamais fini d'explorer mais dont les auteurs ont réussi à défricher de nouveaux et très importants secteurs: celui de la psychologie comparée des structures cognitives. Le problème fondamental ainsi abordé consiste à établir si le développement de la raison humaine s'effectue de façon analogue dans les différentes sociétés ou si comme certaines formes de psychologie sociale ont tendance à le soutenir, il faut s'attendre à de grandes différences, ou tout au moins à de notables variations, selon les milieux. En cas de similitudes entre les divers développements, il reste d'autre part à établir dans quelle mesure elles seraient dues à des facteurs d'innéité, avec pour limite une structuration entièrement héréditaire, ou jusqu'à quel point elles s'expliqueraient par des mécanismes communs d'équilibration ou d'autorégulation, laissant alors une part à des fluctuations dues aux interactions avec le milieu social.

Or les deux résultats essentiels exposés en cet ouvrage projettent une certaine lumière sur ces questions difficiles. Le premier est que, dans les grandes lignes on retrouve en des civilisations très distinctes les stades de développement qui ont été observés dans les sociétés où ont pu être conduites nos études. Une telle convergence est assurément très significative et semble montrer que les lois de la psychogenèse des structures cognitives présentent une généralité comparable à celle de l'épigenèse biologique dont la formation progressive des instruments propres à l'intelligence humaine constituerait aussi un cas particulier. Il est très frappant à cet égard de constater la présence de comportements analogues chez de petits européens, habitués à certains objets coutumiers et chez de jeunes indigènes de milieux tout différents qui les manipulent pour la première fois.

Mais un second groupe de faits relevés par nos auteurs est tout aussi instructif: c'est l'existence des différences dans les "décalages" entres les réussites obtenues. On désigne sous ce nom l'écart temporel qui peut se produire lorsqu'une même opération ou de façon plus générale une même structure opératoire sont appliquées à des domaines différents: par exemple lorsque les opérations nécessaires à la solution d'un problème de conservation s'appliquent plus aisément, et par conséquent plus précocément, à un ensemble d'objets discrets qu'à un continu à variations plus complexes (comme une surface dont on modifie la figure). Tandis que les opérations tiennent aux activités du sujet et que leur développement s'explique plus ou moins rationnellement dans la mesure où l'on peut retrouver en celles-ci un fonds commun à tous les sujets, et cela, de plus, niveau par niveau avec ce que les passages d'un niveau au suivant présentent d'intelligibilité pour le psychologue, les décalages expriment par contre les résistances de l'objet: or les objets, variant de l'un à l'autre, peuvent résister aux actions du sujet de manières multiples et non nécessairement comparables. Il en résulte que l'on ne saurait élaborer une théorie générale des décalages, pas plus qu'en physique on ne possède de théorie ou de modèle universels des frottements qui perturbent certaines régularités mais sont à analyser en chaque cas particulier. Cela dit, il est d'un grand intérêt de constater que les décalages observés dans les différents milieux sociaux étudiés en cet ouvrage, peuvent varier d'une situation à l'autre selon les coutumes de l'ambiance et les domaines cognitifs abordés: espace ou collections discrètes, vitesses et temps, etc. Par contre dans la mesure où les jeunes sujets examinés sont scolarisés il semble y avoir tendance à une égalisation progressive à de tels points de vue.

Or cette union de stades relativement généraux et de décalages variables paraît peu explicable dans l'hypothèse de mécanismes cognitifs préformés en une innéité générale. Bien entendu toute évolution mentale comporte des facteurs d'hérédité et de maturation, mais qui intéressent le fonctionnement comme tel sans que cela implique une innéité des structures. La construction progressive de celles-ci relèverait alors d'un système d'auto-organisation ou d'équilibration avec les régulations variables qu'il comporterait et qui rendraient naturelles les variations observées en ce qui concerne les décalages.

Au vu de ces résultats généraux et de la richesse des analyses particulières dont abonde cet ouvrage, il ne nous reste qu'à en féliciter vivement les auteurs, et spécialement leur coordinateur en la personne de M. Pierre Dasen.

J. Piaget

Contributors

Kwabena Adjei, UNIVERSITY OF GHANA
Salima Al-Fakhri, UNIVERSITY OF BAGHDAD
Carla P. Childs, UNIVERSITY OF PENNSYLVANIA
Pierre R. Dasen, UNIVERSITY OF GENEVA
J. A. Easley, Jr., UNIVERSITY OF ILLINOIS
Ceel Edgerton, UNIVERSITY OF CALIFORNIA, LOS ANGELES
Patricia M. Greenfield, UNIVERSITY OF CALIFORNIA, LOS ANGELES
Ormond W. Hammond, UNIVERSITY OF CALIFORNIA, LOS ANGELES
Allieu I. Kamara, UNIVERSITY OF SIERRA LEONE
Max Kelly, MACQUARIE UNIVERSITY
Ghada A. Khuri, AMMAN, JORDAN
Daniel M. Kiminyo, KENYATTA UNIVERSITY
Lorraine Kirk, UNIVERSITY OF MISSOURI
Monique Laurendeau-Bendavid, UNIVERSITY OF MONTREAL
Sylvia Opper, UNIVERSITY OF MALAYSIA
Douglass Price-Williams, UNIVERSITY OF CALIFORNIA, LOS ANGELES
Gavin N. Seagrim, AUSTRALIAN NATIONAL UNIVERSITY
Michael Walker, UNIVERSITY OF CALIFORNIA, LOS ANGELES
George I. Za'rour, AMERICAN UNIVERSITY, BEIRUT

Contents

Piagetian Psychology
CROSS-CULTURAL CONTRIBUTIONS

INTRODUCTION

BY PIERRE R. DASEN

How universal are the cognitive processes described by Piaget? To what extent is cognitive development determined by cultural variables? Which aspects of Piaget's theory have to be modified to take cultural variations into account?

These and many similar questions are raised in this book. Its purpose, however, is not to provide definitive answers; that would certainly be premature. Cross-cultural Piagetian psychology is a relatively recent development. It has not reached maturity, but is still at the stage of concrete data collection. This book is a reflection of this stage; at the same time its goal is to provide promising leads for future research. Contradiction is the motor of development: presenting the sometimes conflicting viewpoints of several authors in a single volume will, it is hoped, increase the likelihood of development into the next, more formal stage.

In this short introduction, I intend to give some background to the various chapters and express my personal views on some of the questions which are raised. However I do not intend to review all of the relevant information or all of the alternative points of view, for that would fill a book in itself. In the course of this introduction, the rationale for the selection of the chapters and their ordering should become apparent. In editing these contributions, I have been careful not to interfere with the authors' viewpoints; in writing this introduction, I am expressing opinions that may well differ from their own, in some aspects at least.

Cross-cultural psychology enables us to test the hypotheses and theories established on limited and homogeneous populations. Too much of psychology is only the psychology of rats and first-year students. How does it apply in other cultures? A large amount of decentration is necessary to answer these questions, but until we can do so, we are in the situation of the traveller who has a map of New York to find his way through Shanghai.

Similarly, the developmental psychology derived from Piaget's epistemology has been, for a long time, the psychology of the urban, middle-class school child in Geneva, Switzerland, and later in England, Canada, and the U.S.A. To this criticism Piaget would reply that genetic epistemology is not concerned with interindividual or intergroup variations, but with the development of science on the one hand, and the development of scientific concepts in an "epistemic subject" on the other. Developmental psychology, however, is concerned with "real" children, with differences and contextual factors; if it is to be of real value, theoretical or practical, it must eventually apply to all children in all contexts. It is to the attainment of this goal that cross-cultural Piagetian psychology can make an important contribution.

Over the past ten years, there has been a phenomenal increase of cross-cultural studies using the Piagetian framework, an expansion which cannot be matched by up-to-date and critical reviews; at least there is·no single summary that covers the field adequately and completely, and the interested reader will have to browse through several, each having its individual merits and limitations. For example, I may suggest the following: Goodnow (1969a/b), Dasen (1972, 1973), Modgil (1974), Carlson (1975, 1976), Greenfield (1976), and the relevant chapters or sections in Jahoda (1968, 1970), LeVine (1970), Lloyd (1972), Brislin, Lonner & Thorndike (1973), Cole & Scribner (1974), Price-Williams (1975), Glick (1975), and Serpell (1976). Selected readings have appeared in Price-Williams (1969) and Berry & Dasen (1974). This last volume includes a number of previously published or original research reports which reflect the state of the field up to about 1971. The present volume is a follow-up of that reader, but includes only original reports and gives the flavor of research up to about 1975. The gap between the inception of a research project and the eventual publication of its results is unfortunate but inevitable. One attempt to bridge this gap in our limited field is the dissemination of information about planned, ongoing, or as yet unpublished, research projects through the newsletter, *Inventory of Cross-*

Cultural Piagetian Research, which is edited by Seagrim & Dasen and issued approximately once a year.[1] This newsletter was in fact the origin of this book.

The first question I have asked is how universal Piaget's theory is, or what is universal in his theory. Piaget (1974) in fact makes no formal claims in this respect and looks towards cross-cultural, empirical data to provide the answer; in reading between the lines, however, one may notice the expectation that the qualitative aspects of the theory (the basic cognitive processes, the structural properties of the stages, and their hierarchical ordering) should be universal, if not the quantitative aspects (the ages at which children develop through the various levels of the sequence).

Piaget (e.g., 1974, pp. 300–303) distinguishes four factors responsible for cognitive development:

1. Biological factors

First of all there are biological factors linked to the "epigenetic system" (interactions between the genotype and the physical environment during growth), which appear especially in the maturation of the nervous system.

2. Equilibration factors

Individual development is indeed a function of multiple activities, exercising, experiencing or acting upon the environment. Among these actions there arise particular, followed by more and more general, coordinations. This "general co-ordination of actions" presupposes multiple systems of autoregulation or equilibration, which depend upon the environmental circumstances as well as on epigenetic potentialities. The operations of intelligence can be considered as the highest form of these regulations; this shows the importance of the factor of equilibration as well as its relative independence of biological givens. But if the equilibration factors can be hypothesized to be very general and relatively independent of the social environment, this hypothesis requires cross-cultural verification.

3. Social factors of interpersonal coordination

Whether one studies a child in Geneva, Paris, New York or Moscow, or in the mountains of Iran, the centre of Africa or a Pacific island, one finds social changes among children or between children and adults. These operate by themselves, independently of educational transmissions. In any environment individuals ask questions, exchange information, work together, argue, object, etc. This constant interpersonal exchange occurs during the whole of development, according to a socialization process which involves the social life of children among themselves, as well as their relations with elders.

... it is indispensable, in order to discuss the relations between cognitive functions and social factors, to start with opposing the "general coordination of collective actions" and particular cultural transmissions which have crystallized in a different way in each society.

4. Factors of educational and cultural transmission

On the other hand, besides this functional and partly synchronistic (constant or universal) nucleus, one must naturally consider the mainly diachronic (divergent or culturally relative) factor constituted by traditions and the educational transmissions which vary from one culture to another. When one speaks of "social factors," one in fact is usually referring to these differential cultural pressures. In so far as cognitive processes can vary from one culture to another, it is obvious that one ought to consider this group of factors which is distinct from the former. To start with, one could look at the various languages which are likely to have a more or less strong influence, if not on the operations themselves, at least on the detail of the conceptualizations (e.g. content of classifications, relations).

The biological (or hereditary) factors Piaget is referring to are general to the whole human species. Sometimes the importance Piaget attributes to biological determinants of cognitive development is interpreted as an argument for genetic differences between racial groups. This is clearly a misconception: the biological factors posited by Piaget are general systems, such as the existence of *creodes* (necessary paths in development) and *homeorhesis* (dynamic equilibration by which a deviation from the creodes is compensated for by a return to the normal path), which imply a universal sequence of stages. But the second and third factors, the *general coordination of actions* and the *general coordination of interpersonal interactions*, are also hypothesized to be "very general and relatively independent of the social environment," even though Piaget acknowledges that "this hypothesis requires cross-cultural verification." Thus, the first three of Piaget's factors all lead one to predict universality (which explains why cross-cultural studies have not really managed to dissociate them; they constitute the "synchronistic (constant or universal) nucleus." The fourth factor (*educational and cultural transmission*) is implicitly considered to be less important; in particular it is hypothesized to show an influence, if "not on the operations themselves, at least on the detail of the conceptualizations (e.g. content of classifications, relations)." The words "detail" and "content" emphasize the secondary role attributed to this "diachronic (divergent or culturally relative) factor."

How is this universalist hypothesis supported by the data? When I wrote my first two reviews of cross-cultural studies (Dasen, 1972, 1973), the position seemed to be relatively simple: (1) the qualitative aspects of the theory (the sequence of stages, their structural properties, the type of explanations given by the children) have been verified by the vast majority of studies; (2) the *horizontal décalages* (the sequential conservation of quantity, weight, and volume) are usually verified on the average in a population, but not necessarily in each individual; (3) the quantitative aspects (the rate of development through the stages) give rise to considerable cultural variation.

Although I believe that these general conclusions still hold true today, they need to be discussed and qualified, and the situation now appears to be much more complex than was thought at first.

The qualitative universality has recently been challenged, not by empirical data, but on theoretical or ideological grounds. It is especially the last stage in Piaget's sequence, that of formal operations, which has come under attack. Greenfield (1976), for example, in a very thoughtful review paper, speaks of the "paradox of the developmental endpoint":

> Cross-cultural researchers have failed to follow Piaget's own demonstration that, to study development, one must first understand the end-state toward which the developmental process is veering. An implication of Piaget's example for cross-cultural research is to ascertain the characteristics of an ideal type in a non-Western culture.
>
> One major criticism of Piaget's theory of development for cross-cultural research is that his notion of development is really the development of a Western scientist.

Thus, since Western science does not necessarily represent the form of thought valued in other cultures, nor in fact in some subcultures within the West, the Piagetian sequence is likely to be ethnocentric. A similar point is made by Preiswerk (1976, pp. 504, 509):

> For Piaget, science is ipso facto progress: "reason" is intrinsically better than "primitive" thinking. To this one has to object . . . that science can, in certain circumstances, be an obstacle to an adequate understanding of other cultures
>
> Rationalism is a fundamental aspect of Piaget's life work. The belief in decentered reason, in objective science, are elements which can possibly hinder cross-cultural communication.

Buck-Morss (1975) goes even one step further and identifies the Piagetian stages as reflecting specifically the social structure of the industrial and capitalistic West:

> The existence of a "time lag" discovered in the cross-cultural application of Piaget tests may result from a socio-economic bias in Piaget's theory. *Abstract, formal cognition may reflect a particular social structure, embodying the principles of exchange value, reification, and alienation which govern production and exchange in the industrialized West.* (p. 35)

Although some of Piaget's most interesting work has been done in this early (sensory-motor) stage when cognition is still tied to content, he presupposes that the most important thing is not so much what the child can do in this concrete world, as how quickly he can do without it. If the eclectic nature of his concern reflects a socio-economic bias, it is not surprising that he expresses the goal of the sensori-motor stage in strikingly Kantian terms: it is to develop those cognitive skills which "will constitute the substructure of the subsequent, fully achieved ideas of permanent objects, space, time and causality" (Piaget, 1962, p. 122). For Piaget, the first great cognitive leap is the prototypical experience of alienation. It is the ability of the child to divorce subject from object, hence to grasp the building block of Kantian dualism (and of industrial production). (p. 40)

According to Piaget, logical thinking really first begins around age 7 (in a Western child) in what he calls the stage of Concrete Operations. But again, what is remarkable about his tests for this stage is that they do not track concrete thinking at all, not skills of "concrete science" as Lévi-Strauss (1973) has defined it, but progress toward formal abstraction. The actual contents of his conservation and classification tests are only arbitrary. It is their form which is important. They provide the excuse for testing the ability to identify an abstract quality that remains constant despite the diversity of appearance, and it directly parallels the ability to conceptualize commodities and labor in terms of abstract exchange value. (p. 41)

The "reification" of commodities refers to their appearance in the market as things cut off from the transforming activity of their production; they are simply "given," unchanged and unchanging. Piaget's conservation tests have a similar structure: the trick is to see that despite the fact adults have acted on things, the important quality is the one that remains the same. The operational principle of the trick, "reversibility," is that principle of abstract equivalency which cancels out all appearances of difference, which is also the secret of exchange. In contrast, concrete logic is cognitively inferior because its operations go in only one direction. The criterion of "reversibility" thus condemns to inferiority any logic (e.g., dialectical logic) which bases itself on historical reality, for history is indeed irreversible. (p. 42)

Whether Third World countries choose to foster this kind of reasoning is a decision concerning which the issue of "cultural imperialism" need have no bearing: it is a question of national policy toward industrialization, not toward the West. They should be forewarned, however, on the basis of Western experience, of the dangers inherent in this mode of cognition when it becomes more than a tool for technical productivity and begins to dominate all thought, when abstract, formal logic, divorced from social and human considerations, becomes an end in itself and men and women become a tool of technology rather than vice versa. Whether in this regard Communist countries provide a more desirable model for industrialization remains open to debate. (p. 45)

Even though the details of Buck-Morss's reading of Piaget are partly the result of her own historical dialectics, the general criticism of a socioeconomic bias or of the ethnocentrism of Piaget's theory has to be taken seriously and will be part of the debate for some years to come.

Concerning the stage of formal operations, even within Western culture, Piaget has recently revised his position, mentioning that the first results had been "based on a somewhat privileged population" (1972, p. 6). However, he maintains that all individuals reach the stage of formal operations, if not between 11 and 15 years, at least between 15 and 20; ". . . however they reach this stage in different areas according to their aptitudes and their professional specializations" (p. 10). This limitation creates a paradox: the formal operations, which were supposed to be independent of context, are in fact situation-bound.

Extended to the cross-cultural context, this problem area becomes even more complex. The task originally devised by Piaget & Inhelder (1958) as indicators of formal reasoning are clearly reminiscent of typical classroom situations (e.g., experiments in physics) and it is obvious that they would not be meaningful in most other cultural contexts. The few cross-cultural studies of the formal stage have consequently reported negative or ambiguous results (Were, 1968; Kelly, Chapter 5, this volume) or have shown a great dependence on schooling: "school attendance is a necessary but not a sufficient condition for the attainment of formal operations" is one of the conclusions of Laurendeau-Bendavid's study (chapter 4, this volume).

If we turn to other indicators, such as verbal logic problems (e.g., syllogisms), an excellent summary by Scribner (1976 pp. 5–6) also stresses the importance of schooling:

In all cultures, populations designated as "traditional" or "nonliterate" have just somewhat better than a chance solution rate across all types of problem material. . . . Within each culture there is a large discrepancy in performance between schooled and nonschooled. With schooling, there is little between-culture variation in performance for the cultures studied.

However, Scribner goes on to demonstrate that the difficulty with these tasks does not arise from the fact that nonliterate people do not reason logically. But on most occasions they use an "empiric" rather than a "theoretic" approach: instead of accepting the premises as a postulate, they reason logically from real-life knowledge. "Adoption of a particular mode (empiric or theoretic) is influenced in varying degrees by specific features of the material, especially the factual status of the information supplied in the premises" (p. 17). Here again formal reasoning is thus situation-bound, but it is still formal, logical reasoning.

What is lacking (and that is true of all Piagetian psychology, not only of the formal stage, and not only cross-cultural) are studies demonstrating the presence of operational thinking in culturally relevant, real-life situations. Everyone seems to agree that a more "emic" approach (from within the culture; cf. Berry, 1969) is needed, but no one seems to know how to go about it. Chapters 10 and 11 of this volume are among the first viable attempts in the area of kinship concepts.

There remain two difficulties with the universalist position. Even if studies with more adequate experimental situations or studies taking an emic approach were to demonstrate the universal existence of Piaget's last stage (and the same is true of the other stages), the cultural relativists could maintain the following objections:

1. Working from within Piaget's theory, and with the usual methodology linked to it, it seems difficult to find anything but data supporting the theory. The typical research demonstrates either the presence of a certain structure, or its absence (but negative results are conspicuously noninterpretable), and there is little room to find an alternative structure. Preiswerk (1976), for example, doubts the validity of the universal sequence of stages on the following grounds: In the cross-cultural situation, the validity of a finding cannot be judged from its multiple verification. The researchers are all from the same Western macroculture, and even the recent work of their non-Western colleagues suffers from the same induced ethnocentrism.

2. The demonstration that all individuals are able to reason according to a certain structure does not prove that this is their usual or preferred mode of reasoning. In fact we may not be adequately sampling the culturally relevant skills (Berry, 1974). What we may be asking is the question, "How well can *they* do *our* tricks?"; whereas what we should be asking is, "How well can *they* do *their* tricks?" (Wober, 1969, as quoted in Berry, 1974).

In a similar vein, Price-Williams (1975, p. 82), while rejecting Lévy-Bruhl's paradigm of "primitive mentality" as a contrast between Western and non-Western thinking, suggests

> . . . that a mode of thought may exist which does in fact not sharply distinguish intellect and emotion, logic and rhetoric and so forth. It does not follow from this theory that such thought processes are primitive, nor that people who adopt this thinking cannot adopt strict logical criteria when the situation warrants. . . . What seems to be at the bottom of the difficulty of understanding this type of thought is that "logic," "intellect" and "abstraction" are in fact terms which obey certain rules. We like to think that these rules fall along a continuum of development, both phylogenetic and ontogenetic. In addition, this path of development is regarded as unilineal, and any deviation from it perceived as inferior. Some people are now suspecting that parallel lines of development exist: that certain spheres of human activity require one kind of thinking, others demand other kinds of thinking, and each has its own set of rules. The further suspicion arises that what has been hitherto demeaned as "primitive thinking" may indeed be quite sophisticated, and that the reason such thought has been labelled inferior is that we have no understanding of it.

And Price-Williams goes on to demonstrate that there are areas, such as knowledge about altered states of consciousness, in which Western thinking is very primitive (although evolving) compared to that of other cultures. The point is that these other areas, which require a different kind of thinking, may be the ones most valued in a particular culture.

In other words, little is known as yet about the universality or cultural relativism of the "developmental endpoint"; a lot more research and discussion is needed, and the divergence in approaches and points of view is likely to be beneficial until some agreement can be reached. As odd as it may seem, the state of our knowledge about the first stages of development is not much more advanced. It is only very recently that some cross-cultural studies of Piaget's stage of sensorimotor intelligence have been undertaken. In a just completed longitudinal study of rural Baoulé (Ivory Coast) infants aged five to 33 months (Dasen *et al.*, in preparation) we have obtained 259 examinations, using an ordinal scale developed in France by Casati & Lézine (1969)[2]. Almost no adaptation of the test materials was found to be necessary:[3] whereas most of the objects were unknown to the subjects (toys such as plastic cars and dolls, plastic rakes, etc.), they handled these very efficiently. The usual sequential order of stages was found. However, even at this early age, culture was found to influence the rate of development, which was significantly faster than in French babies on some of the tasks. The precocity of motor development in African babies who are raised traditionally had been well studied (Werner, 1972; Warren, 1972; Dasen, 1974b, for reviews); however, Super (1973) has recently demonstrated that there is no over-all precocity, but an early development of those aspects of motor development, that were culturally valued.

Our data suggest a similar heterogeneous precocity in intellectual development. Over and above these quantitative differences, it is, however, the similarities in the sequential organization of the behaviors that are the most striking findings of this research. Similarly, a replication with the same population of an experiment by Inhelder *et al.* (1972), on the emergence of the semiotic function (conventional use of objects and symbolic play), as well as home observations, showed the same sequence of stages in French and in Baoulé children.

Many more cross-cultural studies have been accumulated on the development of Piaget's concrete operational stage, and it would be an enormous task to attempt to summarize them all. Further, this volume is now bringing a wealth of new material. Before we look at it in some detail, I should like to state my personal interpretation of the situation in this field.

1. Cross-cultural Piagetian research has been concerned so far mainly with structures and stages; little discussion has been devoted to processes. This is probably due to the fact that Piaget's notions of "adaptation" (assimilation and accommodation) and "equilibration" are so general that

they do not easily give rise to operational procedures, and more specific process-oriented models are not yet widely known or accepted. It is my contention that future research will show that the basic processes of cognitive development are indeed universal.

2. In the study of cognitive structures, it has become imperative to distinguish between competence and performance (Flavell & Wohlwill, 1969; Heron, 1974; Heron & Dowel, 1973, 1974; Dasen, 1975c). When applying a Piagetian task, intraculturally but even more so cross-culturally, the results represent a "performance level" that may or may not reflect the "competence" for the operations which the task is supposed to measure. A lot of care is needed to insure that the performance level is equivalent to the competence level. Kamara & Easley provide a thorough discussion of this problem in Chapter 1 of this volume. Useful techniques to distinguish performance from competence are additional situational variations (Bovet, 1974; Greenfield, 1976) or training procedures (e.g., Inhelder *et al.*, 1972) which have only recently started to be applied in cross-cultural Piagetian research (Pinard *et al.*, 1973; Dasen, 1975b, in press, and unpublished data).

3. The competence for concrete operational structures is likely to be universal. This hypothesis is based on the finding that, so far, in each culture studied, at least some individuals display a concrete operational performance level when presented with appropriate Piagetian tasks; furthermore, the few studies using training procedures seem to indicate that those individuals who do not spontaneously display a concrete operational performance level are able to do so after training.

I maintain this universalist hypothesis in spite of the recent suggestions of an ethnocentric bias in Piaget's theory. On the other hand, I willingly concede that there are alternative cognitive structures that may be more adaptive in a given environment and more culturally valued. But I am too Geneva-centric and too ignorant of other cultures to imagine what these structures would be, or at least I have not given it enough thought. For the moment, I have to "pass the buck" to the relativists, and ask them to demonstrate what these alternative structures are.

4. Whether or not—and in which way—this competence is used in any given situation (in other words, the "performance") is culturally determined. Cole and his co-workers have reached a similar conclusion in relation to non-Piagetian studies of culture and thought: "We are unlikely to find cultural differences in basic component cognitive processes" (Cole and Scribner, 1974, p. 193); however, cultural differences are found in the way these basic processes combine into "functional cognitive systems" for various purposes. "Cultural differences in cognition reside more in the situations to which particular cognitive processes are applied than in the

existence of a process in one cultural group and its absence in another."
(Cole *et al.*, 1971, p. 233)

This volume contains a number of examples of cultural or subcultural variations in the performance of Piagetian tasks. Significantly, none of these variations appears in the structural aspects of the concepts studied, but they do appear in the rate of development of the concepts, or rather, in the proportion of subjects at any given age displaying a concrete operational performance level (or intermediate levels) on the tasks used.

Another example of a significant cultural variation is my study comparing concrete operational development in three cultures (Dasen, 1975a). According to Berry's (1971, 1975) model of ecological functionalism, it was predicted that nomadic, hunting, subsistence-economy populations would develop spatial concepts more rapidly than would sedentary, agriculturalist groups, whereas the latter would attain concepts of conservation of quantity, weight, and volume more rapidly than would the former. The hypotheses were largely supported by the results of a comparison involving 190 children aged 6 to 14 from three cultural groups: Canadian Eskimos, Australian Aborigines, and Ebrié Africans (Ivory Coast). Of significance to Piaget's theory is the finding that the rates of development are not uniform across different areas of concrete operations. In other words, the "structure d'ensemble" posited for the Genevan child does not hold in different cultures; two concepts that develop congruently in the average Genevan child may develop at very different rates in another culture if one of those concepts is highly valued in that culture (in other words: is culturally more relevant, or, is more adaptive) and the other is not. Similarly, Heron (1974, p. 100) concludes:

And elsewhere (Heron & Dowel, 1974, p. 8):

There seems a good case for not regarding the concrete operations stage as a formal unity: it may be more productive to view it as a set of structures without *necessary* interdependence.

I find myself increasingly inclined to the view that the apparent unity of (the concrete operational) stage has been generated by the cognitively-relevant cultural homogeneity in development of the children serving as subjects in most European and North American studies.

This question of "structure d'ensemble," of structural integration or "domain consistency" needs to be investigated in more detail, keeping the competence/performance distinction in mind. Piaget established the hypothesis on intertask consistency on theoretical grounds and at the competence level; empirical studies at the performance level, however, generally report low intertask correlations (e.g., Tuddenham, 1971). This problem is not only one of cross-cultural research. What is already clear from cross-cultural data, in answer to Cole & Scribner (1975), is that it is indeed not possible, even from a Piagetian point of view, to characterize people "in terms of a single (or even a small set) of processes that organize their thinking in all aspects of their lives."

5. In the previous section, I have interpreted the cultural variations in the performance of Piagetian tasks as real and significant, reflecting cultural "differences," for example, in the values placed on different concepts. However, there are at least two alternative interpretations.

First, in analogy with many of the intracultural, social class comparisons, the results of cross-cultural Piagetian experiments are sometimes interpreted in terms of "cultural deprivation." The development of the Western child is taken as the norm, and the "time-lag" apparent in the development of children in another group is seen as a "deficit" or a "retardation"; the measures are seen as a direct reflection of cognitive competence, and other cultures, for whatever reason (lack of early stimulation, deficient linguistic models, disorganized communities and social interactions, etc.), would be deficient in their ability to foster this cognitive competence. By the same token, according to Cole & Scribner (1974, 1975), one interpretation of cultural differences is to ascribe a childlike status to adults who do not "reach" the final stage on a particular task. Such an interpretation is sometimes seen as implicit in any stage theory, in which ontogenetically later stages are necessarily seen as more "advanced," and therefore "better."

This line of argument is so obviously fallacious that I did not deem it necessary to caution against it in some earlier writings. In order to avoid further ambiguities, I should like to state clearly that I support the difference interpretation and not the deficit interpretation (Cole & Bruner, 1971), or, in the terms of Kearney *et al.* (1973), people from different cultures are *different but equal*. I do not believe that a value system has to be associated with a stage theory. Indeed, the differences we do find beyond the basic universals are the reflection of a truly valuable cultural plurality.

A second interpretation could be phrased in terms of a "Labov effect," namely that the present experiments are inadequate, and their results therefore meaningless. Cole & Bruner (1971) have provided an incisive discussion of Labov's attack on the experimental method as usually applied to the problem of subcultural differences in cognitive capacity, and the same formulations (1971, p. 235) may be applied to cross-cultural studies:

(a) Formal experimental equivalence of operations does not ensure "de facto" equivalence of experimental treatments; (b) different subcultural groups are predisposed to interpret the experimental stimuli (situations) differently; (c) different subcultural groups are motivated by different concerns relevant to the experimental task; (d) in view of the inadequacies of experimentation, inferences about lack of competence among black children are unwarranted.

Thus, the cultural or subcultural differences reported in cross-cultural Piagetian studies may simply reflect methodological problems, for example the fact that the tasks were not "their problem." I do not personally believe that all or most of the results accumulated thus far ought to be discarded on these methodological grounds (cf. Kamara & Easley's critique in Chapter 1, this volume). If we were to follow such an extreme position in the interpretation of the comparison of Australian Aborigines, Eskimos, and Ebrié Africans summarized above (Dasen, 1975a), we would have to assume that the development of spatial and conservation concepts occured congruently in these populations, but that the conservation tasks were inadequate for the Eskimos and Aborigines but not for the Africans, and that the spatial tasks were inadequate for the African but not the Eskimo and Aboriginal children. Whereas this possibility cannot be ruled out, it is definitely not the impression I had when carrying out the study. I believe it is more appropriate to consider the differences found as a true reflection of ecocultural demands, but restrict the conclusions at least momentarily to the performance level. This, I believe, is consistent with Cole & Bruner's position, since they caution against "inferences about lack of *competence*." Finding differences at the performance level is not trivial if we want to know under which circumstances basic competences are expressed in overt behavior.

Thus, whereas I reject a "Labov effect" interpretation in its extreme form, I do not wish to minimize methodological problems. Indeed, I particularly welcome Kamara & Easley's methodological critique as the first chapter of this book.

Kamara and Easley's contribution is certain to make a major impact in the field. However, the first methodological problem they raise seems to me to be less important than the other three. Precise age determination is a problem only in some parts of the world. Kelly, in Chapter 5, gives an example of such problems in Papua New Guinea. He finally "guesstimated" the age of his subjects; however a more precise age determination would certainly have made little difference in the results he is reporting. I did not encounter similar difficulties in my own research with Australian Aborigines and Canadian Eskimos; the few children who did not have accurate birth records were easily removed before the sampling. This is not possible, of course, if the birth records are unreliable (as is still the case in many parts of Africa) or nonexistent. Kirk (1975) has developed an alternative method based on the observation of the exact stage of tooth eruption at each position in the mouth, a technique that produced a correlation of 0.92 between estimated and actual ages within a sample of 131 children in Ghana. The problem is that the method requires pretesting within each group on a subpopulation for which ages are known with accuracy, whereas Kamara & Easley's method can be used even if such a subpopulation does not exist. However, "farm enumeration" is obviously restricted to populations practicing agriculture and shifting cultivation sites, and the "sibling comparison" is likely to be inaccurate since the length of the breast-feeding period is not always constant and much retrospective questioning is involved.

Kamara and Easley's second point is indeed fundamental: to conduct a proper "clinical" interview, the subject and the experimenter must be fluent in the same language, and the experimenter must be acquainted with all the cultural subtleties that enter into the experimental situation. If the child and the investigator are of the same culture, many methodological problems disappear. In this volume, the contributions of Kamara, Kiminyo, Al-Fakhri, Khuri, and Adjei are examples of studies in which the experimenter is a member of the cultural group under study. This fortunate new trend will be expanding in the future, as more psychologists from non-Western countries are trained and show interest in the development of children in their own culture. However, is this the panacea for all methodological problems, and should Western researchers stop working abroad? I do not think so; firstly, the "native" psychologist will still have been trained in the West, or in a local university which reflects Western culture; the theories and methods he has learned will continue to be those of Western psychology. Furthermore, when he carries out a study in a rural, unschooled population, his education and his urban background are likely to make him almost as much of an authority figure, or even a "stranger," as a foreign researcher would be. Only a "native" psychologist can do a truly "emic" study, but the mere fact that he is part of the culture by birth is not a sufficient condition; he will still need a great amount of decentration.

Secondly, there are, in my opinion, a number of worth-while studies carried out by Western researchers, and there are ways to overcome at least some of the communication problems. Opper, Morin (who conducted the Laurendeau–Bendavid investigation in the field), and Kirk, for example, trained local students as experimenters, although they remained present during the experimentation. Furthermore, they had learned the vernacular and were very familiar with the culture through their own lengthy periods of field work.

There are other situations in which it would be difficult to train local experimenters because too few educated people are available; this is the case, for example, in remote parts of Papua New Guinea and Central

Australia. Thus, Kelly and Seagrim had to resort to interpreters or to the use of the English learned at school. With appropriate check items and a few key words of the vernacular, that is sometimes the best that can be done under those circumstances. However, both these authors have an excellent knowledge of the cultures involved, and they are the only ones (not only among the contributors, but among all the researchers I know of in this field) to conduct longitudinal studies. In the study by Price-Williams *et al.*, the researchers, although not Hawaiian, had been familiar to the subjects for several months, and they avoided any formal test situation by carrying out their observations during recreational activities.

Thus the various contributions in this volume are not equally free of Kamara & Easley's second criticism; but, considering that the main thrust in these studies is never simply to make a comparison between Western and non-Western children, I believe they provide important information despite their obvious limitations.

The variety of statistical techniques which the authors have chosen whenever they had to compare two samples over several age-groups illustrates Kamara and Easley's third point. On the basis of these examples, we could start a lengthy discussion on the (in)appropriateness of using parametric statistics with Piagetian data, or on the relative merits and drawbacks of the various nonparametric techniques, or of reducing the data to a single indicator, such as the "age of accession" (and whether to use the 50 per cent or the 75 per cent criterion); this is not the place to do this, but we have to recognize that there is a real problem, and that it would be useful for comparative purposes if a consensus could be reached on the most appropriate method. Kamara & Easley's "combining of p values" over age classes may be a possible candidate for such a method. The problem is that it presupposes that the proportions at any one age level in one of the samples are always greater than (or equal to) the proportions in the other sample; in other words, there can be no "reversals." If reversals do occur, the null hypothesis cannot be rejected if their number is anywhere near one-half of the number of comparisons (k); when only a small fraction of the outcomes constitute reversals, however, a rule-of-thumb that seems to work well is to subtract $1n\ p$ for each reversal, instead of adding it, in computing $\sum 1n\ p_j$, the degrees of freedom of the chi square remaining $2k$. However, no logically founded justification could be found for this practice, and thus the note suggesting it was withdrawn. I mention it here because it may be useful, but my statistical sophistication is not sufficient for me to take responsibility for it.

Alternative statistical methods which had not been applied previously in this field are contained in Laurendeau-Bendavid's chapter, and Kelly uses a multilevel chi square technique which does not require equal cell

cross-cultural studies, for example, space (with some exceptions, e.g., deLemos, 1974; Dasen, 1974a, 1975a, b; Omari, 1972, 1976), geometry and measurement (Page, 1971, 1973), causality, mental imagery (except for some unpublished data collected by Opper, 1971 and by Rioux and Dasen), or Piaget's approach to memory and the more recent work of Piaget's Center of Epistemology (reported in the series "Etudes d'Epistémologie Génétique"). The development of the concepts of time and speed is among those little explored areas (even within Western culture, with the recent exceptions of Montangero, 1974, and Crépault, 1975, and the cross-cultural study by Bovet & Othenin-Girard, 1975). Chapter 6, by Al-Fakhri and Chapter 7, by Za'rour & Khuri are here to start filling this gap.

The enormous amount of research on the concept of "conservation" has created the impression that this concept is of paramount importance in Piaget's theory. No doubt the construction of invariants is an important aspect of concrete operational reasoning, but Piaget sees the attainment of conservation rather as a "symptom," an indicator of more general cognitive structures. These structures should develop in interaction with almost any kind of environment. In line with this conception is the conclusion of Opper's chapter (p. 120):

It seems as if the mental processes develop as a result of general interaction with the environment regardless of the contents of this environment. Intellectual development does not depend upon a specific type of object with which to interact. What is required is an environment containing a variety of objects upon which the internal processes can act. Environments with a degree of diversity are a universal feature, which would explain the apparent universality of certain types of mental operations. . . .

Beyond this general interaction with the environment, certain specific types of activities, manipulations, or experiences, may foster specific skills, but are not expected to generalize to a structure. For example, the handling of clay in pottery-making can be expected to promote the conservation of substance. Price-Williams et al. (1969) found that this was indeed the case in a group of Mexican children who had grown up in pottery-making families. The effect was limited to the conservation of substance in one sample, but was also noticeable on conservation of number, liquid, weight, and volume in another sample.

Adjei, in one part of Chapter 8, takes up this interesting paradigm in his study of the conservation of number, liquid, substance, weight, and volume in rural Ghanaian children and adults, selected according to their occupational experiences: pottery-making, farming, and selling. Pottery-making is found to have a significant effect on the conservation of substance, weight, and volume in the adult group, and on conservation of weight only in the children. These findings are discussed in the light of Adjei's first-hand knowledge of the daily activities prevalent in each subgroup.

No doubt this type of "microscopic" approach will lead to further interesting research. Other specific occupational experiences and skills may be explored, possibly using a greater spectrum of tasks as dependant variables in order to explore more fully the important question of generalization.

The second part of Adjei's chapter, and Chapter 9, by Kirk, provide another lead into a new area of investigation: among the social interactions that foster cognitive development (Piaget's third factor), the style of mother-child interaction may play an important role. Adjei and Kirk provide extremely thorough studies of this question. It will be noticed that Kirk, although she is not Ghanaian, displays an extremely close knowledge of Ga culture.

One of the difficulties in such studies is that the mother-child interaction is assessed during a rather formal situation: the mother has to teach her child how to perform a matching task (Adjei) or how to assemble a puzzle (Kirk). Such formal teaching tasks are certainly far removed from traditional socialization practices in West Africa; in future research, the sampling of mother-child interactions could possibly be done in more natural situations.

This critical remark is not meant to disparage these two very interesting studies, but it draws our attention to the fact that many of our experimental situations, and the "Piagetian tasks" in particular, may be "out of context" in most cross-cultural situations. I have mentioned such methodological difficulties several times during this introduction, and many others before me have pleaded for a more "emic" approach. Greenfield (1976), for example, specifically states: "In conclusion, if Piaget has, in the past, led the cross-cultural enterprise astray, it is because researchers have followed his procedures rather than his theory."

Price-Williams and Greenfield were among the first to explore Piaget's theory cross-culturally; in Chapters 10 and 11 they are now the first, with their co-authors, to suggest how this departure from the traditional procedures could be made. In their study of kinship concepts, they stay close to Piaget's study of the logic of relations, but they explore this in a context which is both familiar and important to their subjects. It is to be hoped that this type of "emic" research will serve as an example for the study of other content areas.

From the point of view of developmental theory, I believe that this collection of research reports provides an abundance of interesting results, if not many definitive generalizations. In this field of investigation, it is too early, I feel, to reach conclusions with a sufficient degree of confidence. This is not necessarily a negative statement. A premature confidence in "definitive" conclusions would only hinder further fruitful research along divergent lines. What I hope this book will provide is a number of leads into new domains of exploration.

If it is too early to speak of definitive generalizations, it may also be premature to speak of the practical applications of these findings. As Kelly states in his conclusion of Chapter 5: "It is too early yet to attempt a formulation of theory derived from this work although education must proceed as if theory were consolidated." It is only in recent years that education in Western countries has started to take Piaget's formulations seriously into account; may it take less time for cross-cultural psychology to become useful to education in non-Western countries. If our tentative formulations are true, there are basic cognitive competences which are universal; however, the curriculum cannot build on these unless it incorporates ways to translate such competences into performance. Sufficient differences on the performance level have been described to caution against the mere exploration of an educational system from one culture to another. In each case, the choice should be guided by a thorough knowledge of child development—not the development of "the child," but the development of the children in each particular context. There is certainly a place for developmental research, whether the educational system is to be copied from the Western model or adapted to local needs and customs.

However, Seagrim, in the last chapter of this book, draws our attention to some of the ethical issues of cross-cultural research and its applications. His examples are drawn from the situation specific to Australia and Papua New Guinea, but his "caveat" has wider implications. In Australian Aborigines, the development of performance on concrete operational tasks is directly proportional to the extent of contact with the dominant culture. When I previously reported such findings (e.g., Dasen, 1974; Dasen, in press; Dasen *et al.*, 1973), I interpreted them as a cultural "difference," and as an indication of the cultural relativity of concrete operations as well as an argument against genetic differences in cognition. But if the application of such a finding is likely to be the planning (or the justification) of a program of cultural assimilation (instead of pluralism), then I can only agree with Seagrim's scepticism about the value of our research. Seagrim warns: "An intellectual homogenization of mankind, on the Western model, is taking place at an exponential rate which, in my opinion, is (an) unmitigated . . . disaster." I think we should consider Seagrim's point very carefully before attempting to devise any "intervention" on the basis of our findings. Too many well-meant "development" programs in the Third World have done more harm than good.

Michael Ogbolu Okonji, one of the foremost African psychologists, had accepted my invitation to write a chapter for this book on the educational applications of cross-cultural Piagetian psychology in Africa. His sudden death, in September 1975, stopped him in this project—a great loss to cross-cultural psychology. May this book be a tribute to Okonji's dedication to cross-cultural psychology.

Fortunately, the subject will receive a thorough treatment in the forth-coming book, "Concept Development in African Children," co-edited by B. Otaala and R. O. Ohuche. There could be no better conclusion to this introduction than announcing this book edited by African psychologists. This is what the editors write about it (personal communication):

At the UNESCO/UNICEF conference[4] held in September, 1974, in Nairobi, it was felt that increasing numbers of investigations were being carried out on various aspects of the development of thought processes in African children and that these efforts were commendable, even if there were still may issues deserving attention. It was strongly suggested that available information should be put together and presented in a manner that any teacher, curriculum worker or other interested person can use. This, it was expressed, should sensitize users to issues associated with concept formation.

The forthcoming book is our humble attempt to meet some of this expressed need. In selecting the articles presented in the book our main concerns have been:
1. Giving teachers, curriculum workers and other persons, information, no matter how limited, on work that has been done in Africa in the area of concept development.
2. Giving illustrations of work done by persons who understand the African environment on some of the cultural activities that affect intellectual development in order especially to inspire future researchers to explore the use of mundane activities of our people as tools for the study of concept formation.
3. Sensitising teachers and teacher educators to the area of concept development so that they may not only be aware of the need to match the subject matter of the curriculum to the level of conceptual development attained by a child at a specific age, but also that they may build on this knowledge at workshops and seminars. . . .

Section one of the book deals with theoretical issues and has five chapters. Chapter one by Professor A. Babs Fafunwa gives a broad coverage of the development of the African child from birth to six years. Chapter two by Professor Ruth Beard discusses the relationship between language and thought. Chapters three and four, by Dr. Barnabas Otaala and Professor Kenneth Lovell, respectively, describe early and later stages of conceptual development as presented in Piagetian theory. Chapter five by Dr. V. Ibikunle Johnson deals with cognitive growth and conceptualisation in science education.

The second section of the book deals with specific selected researches conducted in Africa or with applications of knowledge gained from research to curriculum development or the teaching-learning situation. It contains chapters written by J. Gay, M. Cole, A. I. Kamara, R. O. Ohuche, and R. E. Pearson.

NOTES

1. Current copies of this Newsletter are available to interested scholars, who may also wish to provide abstracts or references of their own work. Write to: T. Ciborowski, Dept. of Psychology, Univ. of Hawaii at Manoa, Honolulu, Hawaii 96822.

2. Similar scales have been developed by Uzgiris & Hunt (1975) and Corman & Escalona (1969).

3. However, the tasks tend to be frustrating, since an object is usually hidden or moved out of reach, and the Baoulé baby frequently tries some nonintellectual scheme to retrieve the object: for example, he is used to being immediately satisfied when he cries. Thus a lot of care has to be taken to create an adequate experimental situation.

4. "The development of science and mathematics concepts in young children in African countries." Report available from Unesco, Paris.

REFERENCES

Berry, J. W. (1969) On cross-cultural comparability. *International Journal of Psychology, 4* (2): 119–28.

———. (1971) Ecological and cultural factors in spatial skill development. *Canadian Journal of Behavioral Science, 3*:324–336 (Reprinted in Berry & Dasen, 1974, pp. 129–40.).

———. (1974) Radical cultural relativism and the concept of intelligence. *In* J. W. Berry & P. R. Dasen (Eds.), *Culture and cognition.* London: Methuen, pp. 225–30.

———. (1975) An ecological approach to cross-cultural psychology. *Nederlands Tijdschrift voor de Psychologie, 30*: 51–84.

———. and Dasen, P. R. (1974) *Culture and cognition: Readings in cross-cultural psychology.* London: Methuen.

Bovet, M. C. (1974) Cognitive processes among illiterate children and adults. In J. W. Berry & P. R. Dasen (Eds.), *Culture and Cognition.* London: Methuen, pp. 311–34.

———. & Othenin-Girard, C. (1975) Etude piagétienne de quelques notions spatio-temporelles dans un milieu africain. *International J. Psychology, 10* (1): 1–17.

Brislin, R. W., Lonner, W. J. & Thorndike, R. M. (1973) *Cross-cultural research methods.* New York: John Wiley.

Buck-Morss, S. (1975) Socio-economic bias in Piaget's theory and its implications for cross-cultural studies. *Human Development, 18*:35–49.

Carlson, J. (1975) Kulturvergleichende Forschung sensu Piaget: einige Perspektiven. *In* H. Walter (Ed.), *Sozialforschung, Band III, Sozialökologie—neue Wege in der Sozialforschung.* Stuttgart: F. Fromman Verlag, pp. 238–312.

———. (1976) Cross-cultural Piagetian research: what can it tell us? *In* K. Riegel &

J. Meacham (Eds.), *The developing individual in a changing world*. The Hague: Mouton.

Casati, I. and Lézine, I. (1968) *Les étapes de l'intelligence sensori-mortrice. Manuel.* Paris: Centre de Psychologie Appliquée.

Cole, M. and Bruner, J. S. (1971) Cultural differences and inferences about psychological processes. *American Psychologist, 26*:867–76. (Reprinted in Berry and Dasen, 1974, pp. 231–46).

———. and Scribner, S. (1974) *Culture and thought: a psychological introduction.* New York: John Wiley.

——— ———. (1975). Developmental theories applied to cross-cultural cognitive research. Paper presented at N.Y.A.S. Conference, "Issues in cross-cultural research."

———. Gay, J., Glick, J. & Sharp, D. W. (1971) *The cultural context of learning and thinking.* New York: Basic Books.

Corman, H. H. & Escalona, S. K. (1969) Stages in sensorimotor development: a replication study. *Merrill-Palmer Quarterly, 15* (4): 351–61.

Crépault, J. (1975) *Contribution à l'étude de la genèse des structures cinématiques. La notion de simultanéité.* Paris: Travaux du Centre d'Etudes des Processus Cognitifs et du Langage, No 5.

Dasen, P. R. (1972) Cross-cultural Piagetian research: a summary. *Journal of Cross-Cultural Psychology, 3* (1): 23–39. (Reprinted in Berry and Dasen, 1974, pp. 409–23.)

———. (1973) Biologie ou culture? La psychologie inter-ethnique d'un point de vue Piagétien. *Psychologie Canadienne, 14* (2): 149–66.

———. (1974a) The influence of ecology, culture and European contact on cognitive development in Australian Aborigines. *In* J. W. Berry and P. R. Dasen (Eds.), *Culture and Cognition.* London: Methuen, pp. 381–408.

———. (1974b) Le développement du jeune enfant africain. *Archives de Psychologie, 41* (164): 341–61.

———. (1975a) Concrete operational development in three cultures. *Journal of Cross-Cultural Psychology, 6* (2): 156–72.

———. (1975b) Le développement des opérations concrètes chez les Esquimaux Canadiens. *International Journal of Psychology, 10* (3): 165–80.

———. (1975c) Cross-cultural cognitive development: the cultural aspects of Piaget's theory. Paper presented at N.Y.A.S. Conference on "Issues in cross-cultural research."

———. (in press) A contribution to cross-cultural Piagetian psychology. *In* N. Warren (Ed.), *Studies in cross-cultural psychology, Vol. 1.* London: Academic Press.

———. deLacey, P. R. & Seagrim, G. N. (1973) An investigation of reasoning ability in adopted and fostered Aboriginal children. *In* G. E. Kearney *et al.* (Eds.), *The psychology of Aboriginal Australians.* Sydney: John Wiley, pp. 97–104.

deLemos, M. M. (1974) The development of spatial concepts in Zulu children. *In* J. W. Berry and P. R. Dasen (Eds.), *Culture and cognition.* London: Methuen, pp. 367–80.

Flavell, J. H. & Wohlwill, J. F. (1969) Formal and functional aspects of cognitive development. *In* D. Elkind & J. H. Flavell (Eds.), *Studies in cognitive development*. New York: Oxford Univ. Press, pp. 67–120.

Glick, J. (1975) Cognitive development in cross-cultural perspective. *In* T. D. Horowitz *et al.* (Eds.), *Review of child development research*. Chicago: Univ. of Chicago Press, pp. 595–654.

Goodnow, J. J. (1969a). Problems in research on culture and thought. *In* D. Elkind and J. H. Flavell (Eds.), *Studies in cognitive development*. New York: Oxford Univ. Press, pp. 439–62.

———. (1969b) Cultural variations in cognitive skills. *In* D. R. Price-Williams (Ed.), *Cross-cultural studies*. London: Penguin, pp. 246–64.

Greenfield, P. M. (1976) Cross-cultural research and Piagetian theory: paradox and progress. *In* K. Riegel & J. Meacham (Eds.), *The developing individual in a changing world*. The Hague: Mouton.

Heron, A. (1974) Cultural determinants of concrete operational behaviour. *In* J. L. M. Dawson and W. J. Lonner (Eds.), *Readings in cross-cultural psychology*. Hong Kong University Press, pp. 94–101.

———. & Dowel, W. (1973) Weight conservation and matrix-solving ability in Papuan children. *Journal of Cross-Cultural Psychology, 4* (2): 207–19.

——— ———. (1974) The questionable unity of the concrete operational stage. *International Journal of Psychology, 9* (1): 1–9.

Inhelder, B., Lézine, I., Sinclair, H. & Stambak, M. (1972) Les débuts de la fonction symbolique. *Archives de Psychologie, 51* (163): 187–243.

———. Sinclair, H. & Bovet, M. (1974). *Learning and the development of cognition*. Cambridge, Mass.: Harvard Univ. Press.

Jahoda, G. (1968) Some research problems in African education. *Journal of Social Issues, 24* (2): 161–75.

———. (1970) A cross-cultural perspective in psychology. *The Advancement of Science, 27* (1): 14.

Kearney, G. E., deLacey, P. R. & Davidson, G. R. (1973) *The psychology of Aboriginal Australians*. Sydney: Wiley.

Kirk, L. (1975) Estimating the ages of children in nonliterate populations: a field method. *Journal of Cross-Cultural Psychology, 6* (2): 238–49.

LeVine, R. A. (1970) Cross-cultural study in child psychology. In P. H. Mussen (Ed.) *Carmichael's manual of child psychology, Vol. II*. New York: John Wiley, pp. 559–612.

Lloyd, B. B. (1972) *Perception and cognition from a cross-cultural perspective*. London: Penguin.

Modgil, S. (1974) *Piagetian research: a handbook of recent studies*. Windsor, Berks.: N.F.E.R.

Montangero, J. (1974) *Le double aspect 'logique' et 'physique' de la notion de durée*. Thèse de doctorat, Univ. de Genève (Neuchâtel: Delachaux et Niestlé, sous presse).

Omari, I. M. (1972) *The development of Piagetian spatial concepts among Pare African children in Tanzania*. Unpublished Ph.D. thesis, Columbia Univ.

———. (1976) Cognitive egocentrism: age and environmental variables in spatial decentration among Tanzanian children. Paper presented at Second Pan-African Conference on Psychology, Nairobi, Dec. 1975—Jan. 1976.

Opper, S. (1971) *Intellectual development in Thai children*. Unpublished Ph.D. thesis, Cornell Univ. Ithaca, N.Y.

Page, H. W. (1971) Locating a point in a two-dimensional space: an experiment with Zulu youths. *Journal of Behaviorial Science, 1* (3): 131–35.

———. (1973) Concepts of length and distance in a study of Zulu youths. *Journal of Social Psychology, 90*:9–16.

Piaget, J. (1972) Intellectual evolution from adolescence to adulthood. *Human development, 15*:1–12.

———. (1974) Need and significance of cross-cultural studies in genetic psychology. *In* J. W. Berry & P. R. Dasen (Eds.), *Culture and Cognition.* London: Methuen, pp. 299–310.

———. and Inhelder, B. (1958) *The growth of logical thinking from childhood to adolescence.* New York: Basic Books.

Pinard, A., Morin, C. & Lefèbvre, M. (1973) Apprentissage de la conservation des quantités liquides chez des enfants rwandais et canadiens-français. *International Journal Psychology, 8* (1): 15–24.

Preiswerk, R. (1976) Jean Piaget et l'étude des relations interculturelles. In G. Busino (Ed.), Les sciences sociales avec et après Jean Piaget. *Revue Européenne des Sciences Sociales, 14* (38–39): 495–511.

Price-Williams, D. R. (1969) *Cross-cultural studies.* London: Penguin.

———. (1975) *Explorations in cross-cultural psychology.* San Francisco: Chandler & Sharp.

———. Gordon, W. & Ramirez, M. (1969) Skill and conservation. *Developmental Psychology, 1* (6): 769. (Reprinted in Berry & Dasen, 1974, pp. 351–52.)

Scribner, S. (1976) Modes of thinking and ways of speaking: culture and logic reconsidered. Unpublished manuscript.

Serpell, R. (1976) *Culture's influence on behaviour.* London: Methuen.

Super, C. M. (1973) Infant care and motor development in rural Kenya: some preliminary data on precocity and deficit. Paper presented at the First IACCP Conference in Africa, Ibadan, Nigeria.

Tuddenham, R. D. (1971) Theoretical regularities and individual idiosyncrasies. *In* D. R. Green *et al.* (Eds.), *Measurement and Piaget.* New York: McGraw-Hill, pp. 64–75.

Uzgiris, I. C. & McV. Hunt, J. (1975) *Assessment in infancy. Ordinal scales of psychological development.* Urbana: Univ. of Illinois Press.

Warren, N. (1972) African infant precocity. *Psychology Bulletin, 78* (5): 353–67.

Were, K. (1968) *A survey of the thought processes of New Guinean secondary students.* Unpublished M.Ed. thesis, Univ. of Adelaide.

Werner, E. E. (1972) Infants around the world: Cross-cultural studies of psychomotor development from birth to two years. *Journal of Cross-Cultural Psychology, 3* (2): 111–34.

Wober, M. (1969) Distinguishing centri-cultural from cross-cultural tests and research. *Perceptual Motor Skills, 28*:488.

1

Is the Rate of Cognitive Development Uniform Across Cultures?—A Methodological Critique with New Evidence from Themne Children

ALLIEU I. KAMARA and J. A. EASLEY, Jr.

In the past decade a small literature has accumulated on the thinking competences that children from non-Western cultures exhibit when confronted with Piaget's conservation tasks. The findings of these studies have been recently reviewed (Dasen, 1972a and 1973) but there has not been any general review of the major methodological issues that must be cleared before any substantive interpretation is defensible. The findings reported by most researchers[1] have appeared to support the prevalent view that children in those societies little influenced by Western culture fall behind middle-class Western children[2] on most if not all tasks by an interval of from two to seven years. A minority of the studies,[3] however, suggests that there may be little or even no appreciable time lag, at least on concrete level tasks. Many of these studies have also supported the view that unschooled children are less advanced in these competences than children of the same age and culture who have attended schools of the Western type.

It is our contention that, because of the methodological criticisms which we shall examine in detail below, no general conclusions are warranted from these studies with respect to the major issue: an alleged retardation attributed to non-Western culture, absence of Western types of schooling, or both. Supported by a few studies of Geneva-trained researchers, Piaget has accepted a time lag of two to four years attributed to the child's cultural milieu as consistent with the social factor in his theory of cognitive development (Piaget, 1966). (See also Inhelder and Piaget, 1958, p. 337.) However, many of the differences between cultures in the ages reported for the first appearance of concrete operations in conservation tasks are so great as to appear to lend support to the much more strongly environmentalist position held by most American psychologists rather than to the biologically oriented developmental theory of Piaget. On the other hand, Cole and Bruner (1971) strongly argue that cultural bias lies behind the retardation interpretation, and Peluffo (1967) interprets the evidence from some of these studies as suggesting cross-cultural universals for all cultures beyond the hunting and fishing level. Greenfield takes another position on the basis of her data from Wolof children from Senegal (1966), suggesting that the important cultural difference lies not so much in the ages at which certain concepts appear as in the types of explanations given by subjects from different cultures. Bovet (1968), Dasen (1973), and Voyat (1970) suggests specific ecological effects of cultural utilization on performance.

What seems important in cross-cultural conservation research is the possibility raised by Piaget's theory that there are some substantive scientific concepts (e.g., certain physical quantities of matter which are invariant over transformations of shape) which have a natural structural basis that emerges on the same timetable in any environment which permits the child interaction with such materials as sand, mud, stones, sticks, and water. The question is whether, for example, children will develop a competence for grasping certain physical quantities with invariance over shape transformations so strongly that once having formulated these conservation beliefs, they will persevere in those beliefs, as Smedslund (1961) suggests, even in the case of apparent evidence against them. Three things are at stake: first, the relationship between competence and training; second, the role of hypothesis testing in belief determination, which in currently popular versions of empiricism is a basic presupposition (it also enters into most psychological and educational theorizing about learning); and, third, the attitude of most Western and non-Western educators concerning the superiority of Western culture for things scientific and technological. If there should be even one fundamental scientific concept which all children in milieus that have not been significantly influenced by Western science develop (to within the reach of clinical interviews) and if they develop it in a manner not dependent on their exposure to direct demonstration or to evidence in the empiricist sense but instead, in a manner which only draws on general manipulative experience in Piaget's sense ("nourishment," activation, the minor accommodation of structures already there, and the steady progressive growth of structures that are capable of growth when actively used), then the fundamental position of empiricism in philosophy, psychology, and education is called into challenge. Empiricism postulates only the most general a priori intellectual capacities (e.g., ability to form associations and logical reasoning) in order for particular environments to teach the organism particular concepts. Structuralism allows that some particular physical competences, as well as general processes like logics, are developed only by the interaction of hereditary codes and an environment generally amenable to being manipulated by the child.

Piaget rests on Darwin's principle, which means here that the long history of natural selection has prepared the human species by adapting it in its detailed adult structures to the world of mud, stones, sticks, and water, in which it frequently lives. The radically nonempiricist thesis of Piaget is that this adaptation consists of a very general capacity to learn, equilibration, and a preprogramming of certain structures, which are subject—like all preprogramming—to the necessary condition of a general environment for nurturing the growth of such structures. The conservative conclusion is that intellectual development is always an accommodation of biology to culture, but the radical educational conclusion is that all humans may, at certain points of their development, be close in their natural intuitions to certain important scientific theories. On this view, if children could be challenged to think and helped to find language for expressing their intuitions, and if their confrontation in schools with the traditional mass of less fundamental—even esoteric—details does not overwhelm these budding competences, those scientific concepts will emerge. While the question of rate of development is secondary to this educational issue, if it should also turn out that the underlying structures for some scientific concepts develop at the same rate in different cultures, then the biological basis of the structuralist's position is even more clearly demonstrated. While some practical-minded educators may be more concerned with the rate of test performance development than with the development of competence, which is more fundamental and more difficult to assess, we argue strongly for the practical need to discover competences. If competence is not yet developed, the pupil's failure to master a concept is a natural and expected consequence. If, however, the competence is there but the desired performance is not, the educator has a clear responsibility to assist in its expression.

The case of structuralism vs. empiricism does not rest only on the experimental questions concerning the development of conservation concepts in cross-cultural perspective. As Thomas Kuhn (1962) and many others have pointed out, scientific revolutions, with their attendant shifts in world view and methodology, are never made by single crucial experiments, but only by a growing crisis caused by the cumbersome load of forced adjustments in the old paradigm. Clearing up the confusion concerning the development of conservation concepts in different cultural milieus will, it seems to us, help scholars take sides on the revolutionary challenge of structuralism, at least in some domain (philosophical, psychological, anthropological, or educational), and help them relate this case more clearly to the educational, cultural, and political tensions in which they live.

Discussions in the literature point to four major methodological problems in this domain of research, each recognized by several writers, but none sufficiently resolved to permit any clear assessment of the fundamental issues. Despite their frequent recognition, their resolution has received very little attention. They are: (1) the failure to give attention to age determination, including a tendency for the age of subjects to be obtained from estimates or from official records, which are notoriously subject to error; (2) the existence in most studies of serious language and cultural barriers between the subjects and the interviewers; (3) the difficulty of making inferences from the data regarding the substantive issue of an alleged retardation because of the lack of an appropriate statistical model; and (4) the tendency for data to be collected through performance tests rather than by clinical interviews, which alone can determine the competences underlying the performance; a practice that reveals a basic misunderstanding of the cognitive structure paradigm and, together with (2) above, systematically distorts cross-cultural comparisons of actual cognitions.

This paper examines the problems raised for the investigator by these four methodological issues as they relate to the general findings of the studies cited above, and reports the attempts to eliminate their distorting effects on data collected by the first author from the Themne tribe of Sierra Leone (Kamara, 1971). It would be somewhat premature to attempt to examine the effects these practices might have in shifting the preponderance of evidence from the negative to the positive answer to our title question. The relevant reporting of procedures is so inadequate in most studies that the effects of these problems on findings could not be guessed. We do have adequate information on these issues for Kamara (1971) and Nyiti (1973); and these studies, while based on relatively small samples, tend to support a more universal view of basic cognitive development. (See Section 3 below.) If the trend in these data is subsequently supported by equally sound replications, we would be able to infer that even Piaget has overestimated the effects of cultural influences on the development of the particular cognitive structures involved in conservation.

1 THE PROBLEM OF AGE DETERMINATION IN THE ABSENCE OF RELIABLE RECORDS

There is hardly a variable that presents more difficulties than those encountered with subjects' ages in societies where records of birth are not kept. Investigators have resorted to a variety of methods, but most of them agree that, at best, such methods provide very rough estimates. The importance of this variable in cross-cultural conservation studies cannot be over-emphasized, because it is a fact beyond dispute that responses to conservation tasks are age dependent, and the major difference between cultures reported in these studies is a retardation of from two to seven years in the estimated average age of acquisition of conservation among children of non-Western cultures. If there are systematic errors in ages reported, the amount of retardation is affected; if there are random errors, the confidence in the difference is affected.

In spite of the recognition of the importance of this problem, it can be observed in many of the reports that it has not been treated with the care that it deserves. Poole (1968) states that "every attempt was made to ensure that the children tested were within the specified age-range," but no indication is given as to what constitutes "every attempt." Prince (1968) claims, without citing any evidence, that "school grades were relatively homogeneous for age." For Price-Williams (1961), "certain children were selected by the teachers as being clearly in each of these age groups," and for the "under sixes" he was compelled to rely on physical characteristics. Heron and Simonsson (1969) state, "For all but a few of the African children it was not possible to obtain a verified age." Greenfield (1966) obtained the ages of her Wolof subjects from the census rolls. De Lemos (1969) simply states that the aboriginal children studied in Australia were aged from 8 to 15 years without giving her basis for age determination.[4] The first author's experience with age determination in Sierra Leone leads us to expect that there will often be serious discrepancies between stated ages as found in school registers and actual ages of the children. Discrepancies between official records and culturally more appropriate methods of age determination were more than a year in the majority of cases in his experience and sometimes amounted to as much as three years. If one realizes the insignificance of counting years and months in a society which does not celebrate birthdays, one can grasp the guessing process that parents go through when asked ages by the census taker and the naturalness of reporting the accepted, official age for starting school when enrolling their child, though he may actually be younger or older by several years. While Lloyd (1971a, 1971b) was able to make use of the growth-study samples for which births have been recorded since 1962 at the Institute of Child Health in the University of Ibadan, Nigeria, such records are not usually available in developing countries.

While it is true that most people have no records of birth in their possession, it is not wholly true that they are unable to describe the ages of children reliably when they have occasion to do so in what is for them a natural way. One interested in determining the children's ages in those societies has to go about it in a more arduous manner— the manner in which they themselves do it—decoding their description into standard quantitative time measures. We describe the field methods Kamara (1971) developed to overcome this problem in the Themne tribe. These methods were also adapted and used by Nyiti (1973) with the Meru people of Tanzania.

In working with the Themne, three methods for determining ages proved most useful: (1) great events, (2) slash-and-burn farm site enumeration, and (3) sibling comparison. Great events are picturesque occasions or important happenings that have taken place either locally or nationally and are well remembered by the people. Often, if one knows where to go, one can find a reliable record of the dates on which such events took place. Such places include the local native administration courts and the district offices. Great local events in the Port Loko district included the death or coronation of a paramount chief, the building of a new school, important bush disputes, the dates of construction of bridges, important initiation ceremonies, and tax strikes. National events in Sierra Leone included important occasions like the visit of the Queen of England to Sierra Leone, general elections which involved the change of a head of state, and the year a census was taken. Great events are especially useful for pinning down a child's age, if the child was born on or about the date on which the event took place. Thus, one woman told the investigator with pride that her son was born the day the Queen visited Port Loko.

Great events are also useful for the purpose of quickly excluding children from the age groups desired for the study. For instance, any child whose parents confirmed that he had been born before, during, or just after Pither's Strike, was automatically excluded from Kamara's study because he would have been at least 14 years old. While great events can be very helpful in age determination, maximizing their usefulness requires that the investigator should have collected in advance a large list of such events and the dates at which they occurred. Armed with this schedule of events, the investigator then proceeds to interview the parents, during which time he appeals to their memories by asking them to recall what event occurred at or near the time the child was born.

The second method Kamara employed in age determination was farm enumeration. The effectiveness of this method originates from the farming practices of the people. Rice farmers employ the practice of shifting cultivation sites every year. A bush site that is at least ten years old is selected each year as a farm site. This selection process heralds the beginning of the farm cycle. About the middle of January, farmers cut down the small trees and the undergrowth with machetes. Then in February the big trees are felled with axes. After felling, the trees are left to dry in the hot months of March and April. In May, the farms are burnt, and the unburnt wood is cleared away from the farms. Ploughing and broadcasting the seed are performed in June after the first rains have fallen; and the farms are weeded in August. September and part of October are slack months, and the only chore that occupies the farmer's attention is bird-scaring—a chore usually relegated to the children. The farms are harvested in November and then allowed to grow up in bush again. To describe his child's age, the farmer enumerates the farms he has laid since the child was born, and then recalls the stage in the farm cycle at which the child was born. The involvement of children in the farm work makes it easy to check against errors.

If farm enumeration is the method of choice among fathers, sibling comparison is the domain of the mothers. More often than not, a question such as "How old is your child?" may be greeted with a response which, literally translated, means "He has called behind three times." This means that he is the oldest of four children, but the sexual mores and the child-rearing practices of the Themne culture make sibling comparison a reasonably accurate method of age determination. Among the Themnes who have not adopted the Western preference for bottle-feeding, children are breast-fed for a minimum period of 18 months. During this period, women are expected not to engage in any sexual intimacy. There are two factors that restrain mothers from doing so. One of these is social pressure, and the other is the belief that if they do their children will be afflicted with diarrhea. Any mother who is suspected to have committed such an "atrocity" during the suckling period is severely reviled by her colleagues. Surprisingly, the women were most cooperative in responding to questions regarding time lapses between weaning one child and the next pregnancy. For example, the question, "How long did it take after weaning before you became pregnant again?" may be met with the answer, "That moon did not leave me" which means that she became pregnant immediately after weaning, i.e., in the same month.

To tell the child's age from the response "he has called behind three times," where the youngest child is still suckling, one adds up the three pregnancy periods since its birth (3×9 months), the three successive suckling periods completed (3×18 months), all the intervals lapsed between weaning and conception (say $2 + 1 + 5$ months), and the age of the youngest child, which can usually be estimated within a month. In other words, this child who has "called behind" three times is $27 + 54 + 8 +$ the age in months of his youngest sibling. If the youngest were 15 months old, then this child who has "called behind three times," is about 104 months old or 8 years and 8 months.

Both sibling comparison and farm site enumeration need to be checked against the list of great events by asking the parents if this child had been born when such and such an event occurred?

From the above description it becomes obvious that these methods of age determination are costly in terms of the investigator's time. They require that individual parents be interviewed, but the rewards of reasonable accuracy derived from such a slow process eliminate most of the doubts that may otherwise be lingering in the mind of the investigator. Among the school children, something that was somewhat of a surprise came out of the parental interviews. There were a considerable number of cases in which the children's ages shown by the school registers were several years in error (mostly younger), even though the parents in some cases had in their possession authentic records such as birth certificates. The lowering of recorded age in school records is probably most often due to the efforts of parents to persuade school officials that a somewhat older child who had been kept out of school was still of official admission age or to make a child who had been kept out of school to help his parents appear closer to the official age for children in his grade. In view of this tendency, the more valid parental interview methods are especially important in milieu studies which address the question raised in the title of this article.

2 THE HANDICAPS OF INTERVIEWERS WHO LACK FLUENCY IN THE SUBJECT'S MOTHER TONGUE

While the presumed necessity for interviewers to be fluent in the subject's native tongue has been indicated by Piaget (1966), only a few studies have managed to meet this criterion. Instead, we note that aboriginal children were examined in English, both in Australia, by de Lemos (1969) and Dasen (1972b), and in New Guinea by Prince (1968). Laurendeau and Pinard interviewed native children of Martinique in French (cited by Piaget, 1966). Piagetian tasks were converted into tests, and after being translated into the subjects' native language, were administered in Hausa by Poole (1968), in Yoruba by Etuk (1967) and in Tiv by Price-Williams (1961). These investigators are evidently not native speakers of the tongue indicated. In other cases (for unschooled children) de Lemos (1969), Prince (1968), and Bovet (1968) used native interpreters from Australia, New Guinea, and Algeria, respectively, in their interviews. Hyde (1959) and Opper (1971) studied Arabic and Thai, respectively, and conducted interviews in these languages with subjects who at least knew them as second languages. Hyde had the assistance of an Arab education officer who observed the interviews in case language problems arose but who did not find it necessary to intervene. Heron and Simonsson (1969) used no language at all in presenting their versions of Piagetian tasks to children in Zambia, or in observing responses to them. We have found reference to eight studies (Kamara, 1971; Kiminyo, 1973; Lloyd, 1971a, 1971b; Nyiti, 1973; Ohuche, 1970; Otaala, 1971; and Pinard et al., 1973) in which the interviews were conducted by native speakers of the children's native tongue. Lloyd (1971a, 1971b) trained two female Yoruba university students to interview the subjects in her study; Ohuche (1970) trained Mende university students at Njala, Sierra Leone, as interviewers for his Mende subjects. Kamara and Nyiti are native speakers of Themne and Tanzanian Meru, respectively, and did their own interviews. Abstracts available of the other studies did not provide sufficient details to permit further classification.

    What we see, except in the last eight studies mentioned, is a situation where one or the other of the two parties involved in the interview, task, or test, is linguistically and culturally handicapped. When the task is presented by an interviewer of a Western culture in his own language, *he* may be at ease, but the subject may be unable to understand and to express himself fully. When the task is presented by a Western interviewer in the child's native language, the subject may be at ease but the interviewer is handicapped in his ability to follow the child's explanations or to follow up on clues spontaneously. When interpreters are used, or no language at all is used, both parties are handicapped in their ability to communicate the subtleties of thought involved in these tasks. It is strange that, in view of the great importance attached to language in current psychology, so little effort has been made to correct these handicaps.

    One of the main reasons why clinical interviews are superior to tests, for Piaget's tasks, is that the interviewer can be alert for and probe into such distinctions as those between the reality perceptions of the child and reliance on social cues, or simply guessing the correct judgment (see Section 4). For interviewers to do this effectively, however, requires not merely competence in the child's most competent language but also a fairly sophisticated knowledge of the child's culture. We might infer that the language and cultural barrier presents an added discouragement against using the clinical method, but the fact that it is never mentioned as the reason suggests that the relationship between Piaget's (1966) demand for "a sufficient ethnological sophistication and a complete knowledge of the language," and the interpretation of the child's own thought, is not generally appreciated. Etuk (1967, p. 33), for example, refers to the advantage of the clinical method in probing further than initial responses and allowing children to express their own ideas. Yet, in adopting a standardized interview schedule, "to allow for comparability from one child to another," she takes great pains to secure an accurate translation (by two Yoruba university lecturers) and, by adopting the procedure of orientation to key words and ideas and the rephrasing of questions, ignores these problems: (1) adults and children have different meanings, (2) listening to the child demands on-the-spot sophistication in his language and culture, and (3) children become experts at guessing the answers adult seek.

In cases where the child has learned the interviewer's language (English, French, Arabic, or Swahili) in school—especially if the child's only contact with it is at school—the retardation observed in the appearance of the task-related concept may be largely attributable to the retardation in mastery of the child's second language as compared with his first language. If one attempts to relieve the child's anxiety concerning the possibility of giving a wrong answer, using the school language provides an added difficulty because its use is probably a signal that invokes the schoolroom set which gives rise to this particular anxiety. When, in order to check for consistency or degree of conviction, the child is asked to explain his answer, working in his second language naturally presents a greater handicap for the child than working in his mother tongue. Handicaps also extend to the interviewer, for who has not experienced some difficulties of communication when conversing in his own language with a nonnative speaker of it? For example, appointments, believed clearly understood by both parties, are often not kept because the details of time and place are understood differently.

When the task is presented in the child's native language, either in a translation prepared in advance or through an interpreter, the interviewer is at a disadvantage if he is not aware of subtle variations of structural significance in the child's answers, and he is handicapped in giving expression to his concerns over the ambiguous cases and cannot accurately probe for greater precision. For example, Goldschmid et al. (1973) mention that Ugandan children's responses were translated into English and then scored, implying that the interviewer was not familiar with the tasks and the theory.

A psychologist who is completely at home in the child's language and culture has a distinct advantage in the validation of the structural significance of responses. Interpreters cannot remove this difficulty unless they are very sensitive to the psychological issues, i.e., they have to be psychologists themselves. When no language at all is used, the standardization of the stimulus presentation that one might expect to occur is quite illusory, since the symbolic meanings attached to various objects, movements, and gestures are not at all standardized across cultures.

All researchers should be expected to find out what sorts of things the children he interviews eat or drink that may resemble the experimental material used in conservation tasks. However, when he is a native of that culture he can more easily cause the actual physical transformations of these substances to evoke familiar transformations performed in daily household activities. It seems significant enough to be reported, for example, that not only were plasticine balls used by Kamara which resembled in texture the rice flour cakes used by Themne families in their sacrificial offerings, but in addition, he called to the subjects' attention the resemblance between the flattening of one of them into a plasticine "pancake" and what is actually done to rice cakes before roasting them, and between breaking the plasticine into pieces and the actual way rice cakes are broken up before boiling them.

Moreover, in this context, certain responses were discovered by Kamara to be artifacts of the child's culture. Consider, for example, the strange explanations many subjects gave after answering questions concerning who would have more rice cake to eat—the subject, or the friend whom he had chosen as the pretended possessor of the second ball of plasticine. (Earlier, both had been judged to have the same amount of rice cake material before one of the balls was transformed.) Some subjects said that their friend would have more and some said less. When pressed for their reasons, many subjects would often say that their friend had more of the rice cake to eat "because he was older," or that he had less to eat "because he was younger." Investigation of such cases by the interviewer revealed that these subjects treated equality as related to fairness, presumably making an analogy to the sharing of rice cakes and other delicacies. But fair distribution of delicacies in Themne culture requires that children who are considered to be older (relative age rankings exist in spite of the problem of determining ages precisely) should get a larger share. Hence, perceived equality of substance was, on second thought, seen as "inequality" from the point of view of the expectation of fair sharing. The original physical context of equality of sharing was thus replaced by a more culturally proper form of sharing as a framework for answering the question. Needless to say, such reasons had to be looked for behind most nonconserving answers before they could be interpreted as nonconservation. (An interview fragment involving conserving responses is presented and analyzed in Section 4.)

It is important to remark that the availability of words in a child's vocabulary for a literal translation of an abstract idea does not guarantee communication, for such words may not be the best choice for expressing that idea. For instance, although words exist in Themne vocabulary for the literal translation of "it must be the same," yet the feeling of necessity which that phrase communicates in English is not well expressed in those words. In fact, the phrase, "it must be the same," when directly translated into Themne sounds ambiguous and awkward. Instead, what we hear in Themne are statements which translate as follows: "One of us cannot have more than the other," "He cannot have more and I cannot have more," "He will not have more than me," and "She cannot have more than I have." All these statements appeal to necessity and imply the necessity of the equality of amounts. The Themne language thus tends to use "cannot" to carry the feeling of necessity rather than "must," and the listener looking for an appeal to necessity would have to recognize this linguistic difference when interpreting and analyzing protocols involving Themne children.

A problem even more subtle than such cultural and linguistic confusions is the matter of the expectations in a given culture as to how children should behave toward adults. Here the advantage does not automatically accrue to the native interviewer, because there is a possibility that his tacit acceptance of cultural norms may blind him to the inhibitions children may have against speaking freely and honestly about conclusions they have reached independently. However, evaluation of this factor requires a cultural sophistication not evident in most of the studies cited. Only by first becoming aware of such cultural norms and then emphatically looking at the interview protocol, so to speak, through the culture of the child, can the structural basis of his judgments of conservation, seriation, or classification be validated.

While cross-cultural researchers cannot be blamed for their lack of fluency in their subjects' native language and their less than intimate acquaintance with their subjects' culture, this situation, where it exists, forces the use of such questionable devices as: standardized questions and checklists for classifying answers, using the children's second languages, and using interpreters. So the results cannot be considered very trustworthy where this condition prevails. The principal solution would seem to be that researchers native to non-Western cultures should be given every encouragement to add to this literature by using their special knowledge of local languages and cultures.

The results of Kamara's study, using more culturally relevant research

Table 1–1
Results of conservation interviews in Sierra Leone (Kamara)
and Geneva (Inhelder and Bang)[**]

		5	6	7	8	9	10	11	12	13
Ages										
Schooled children (Kamara)										
Substance	Nonconservation	3	1	1	0	0	0	0		
	Intermediate	1	1	0	0	0	0	0		
	Conservation	1	3*	4	6	5	5	5		
Weight	Nonconservation	5	3	2	1	0	0	0		
	Intermediate	0	0	1	1	1	0	1		
	Conservation	0	2	2	4*	4	5	4		
Volume	Nonconservation	5	5	5	6	4	2	2		
	Intermediate	0	0	0	0	0	0	0		
	Conservation	0	0	0	0	1	3*	3		
Unschooled children (Kamara)										
Substance	Nonconservation					1	0	0	0	0
	Intermediate					0	0	0	0	0
	Conservation					4*	2	5	3	5
Weight	Nonconservation					4	1	1	0	0
	Intermediate					1	0	0	0	0
	Conservation					0	1	4*	3	5
Volume	Nonconservation					–	–	4	2	3
	Intermediate					–	–	0	0	0
	Conservation					–	–	1	1	2
Schooled children (Inhelder and Bang)										
Substance	Nonconservation	21	17	16	6	3	–	–		
	Intermediate	0	4	1	1	1	–	–		
	Conservation	4	4	8	18*	21	–	–		
Weight	Nonconservation	25	21	19	10	4	4	0		
	Intermediate	0	1	0	2	3	2	1		
	Conservation	0	3	6	13*	18	19	24		
Volume	Nonconservation	25	25	22	11	14	6	4		
	Intermediate	0	0	0	7	3	5	1		
	Conservation	0	0	3	7	8	14*	20		

[**]Entries are numbers of subjects in each task category. Asterisks in the table mark the "youngest" task-age categories in which conserving subjects outnumber the other two categories combined.

approaches, appear to be much more in agreement with Geneva norms than is typical for studies of children in non-Western cultures. Table 1—1 gives the numbers of subjects in each task category. Asterisks mark the appearance of a plurality of conserving subjects. While one may wish for more data, it would appear that conservation of substance appears a year earlier than in Geneva among the Themne schooled children, and conservation of weight and volume appear a year later. Kamara's data for unschooled children suggest a one-year retardation in comparison with schooled children. It should also be noted, however, that the Inhelder-Bang data (Piaget and Inhelder, 1969b)—the only table of Geneva norms we have found—show a plurality in the conservation categories on weight and volume one year younger than the age ranges of 9–10 (weight) and 11–12 (volume) given by Piaget and Inhelder (1969a, p. 99). These ages may be due to the use of 75% as a criterion (Laurendeau and Pinard, 1962, p. 94) or they may be based on other data. A more interesting question, however, is how one would decide whether a statistically significant difference exists between the ages of plurality reported for any two groups. This raises the problem of the next section.

3. THE NEED FOR A SUITABLE STATISTICAL MODEL FOR THE COMPARISON OF SAMPLES.[5]

One of the most common formats for presenting results in the studies reviewed is that of tables of numbers and/or percentages of subjects by age classes and task categories such as those show in Table 1–1. This forms something of an unmentioned convention among researches in Geneva, although in many of Piaget's books, only the approximate age range of stages is given, and Piaget has responded to statistical criticism only by giving the table cited. In some studies the age classes cover two-year intervals instead of one-year intervals, and sometimes the percentages are displayed graphically (e.g., Bruner *et al.*, 1966). Sometimes school grades are used instead of age classes (e.g., Prince, 1968). But these variations all fit conceptually within the same design.[6] This design, however, leaves many researchers dissatisfied. It presents no statistical inference scheme and it provides no summary statistic of a descriptive nature except as it permits a crude estimate of the average age of acquiring conservation, e.g., the lowest age class within which the conservers number 50% or more. In an attempt to circumvent the limitations perceived in simple tables of percentages, a number of investigators have either added or substituted for frequency tables the use of such statistics as chi-square, intercorrelation coefficients, Guttman scale evaluations, and even factor analysis. But if tables of ages vs. task categories are omitted, the reader is left without any possibility of estimating, even crudely, the average age at which subjects acquire conservation in the population studied.

One might assume, for example, that one could test the difference in distribution of frequencies in task vs. age categories by simply computing chi-square. However, what is left unclear by carrying out this kind of chi-square test is the direction of the difference. Simply to test the null hypothesis, thus determining the probability that a random sample of given size from one population would differ so much from a sample of another population, is to ignore the central question of a possible retardation in development which would imply a definite direction of the difference for each cell. One procedure that does appear justified is based on the possibility of combining P values described by Fisher (1946, pp. 99–101).

To investigate the null hypothesis that in two populations for which comparable data exist, the proportion, P_W, of Western children in each âge class who are conservers is not larger than the proportion, P_N, of non-Western children of the same age, we first compute the normally distributed statistic,

$$Z = \frac{P_W - P_N}{\sqrt{PQ\left(\dfrac{1}{N_W} + \dfrac{1}{N_N}\right)}}$$

for each age class separately.[7] N_W and N_N are the numbers of subjects in the age class from the two groups, P is the proportion of conservers in the combined group $(W+N)$ for the same age class, and $Q = 1 - P$.

Having computed Z_j for each of the k age classes $(Z_1, Z_2, \ldots Z_k)$, we find the corresponding one-tailed probabilities $P_1, P_2 \ldots P_k$, for no difference. To combine these probabilities where there are no age classes in which the non-Western conservers form a larger proportion than the Western conservers, we compute

$$V = -2 \sum_{j=1}^{k} \ln P_j,$$

which is distributed as χ^2_{2k} (Fisher, 1946). The combined value P, obtained by looking up V in a chi square table, is the probability that, given the null hypothesis, sampling fluctuations alone would result in the observed differences in proportion.

The next question is, how large a value of P will we accept as reason to reject the null hypothesis; that is, what is our probability criterion level, α? On the standard decision-theoretic paradigm one chooses α on the basis of prior belief—the more dubious one feels about the hypothesis of no difference the larger the value of α the liberal researcher should choose, i.e., if one wishes to minimize the chance of overlooking evidence that could change one's view. One may then also wish to obtain as large samples as possible in order also to reduce the chance of concluding that there is a difference when there isn't. If we had invested as much of our resources of time and money as possible in obtaining a large sample, the basis for choosing α reduces to a matter of relating the hypothesis of the experiment to current theory and to the conservative vs. liberal stance of the researcher.

The three main points of view, it seems to us, are (1) an environmentalist position (e.g., Bruner) which attributes the appearance of conservation to triggering by a Western-type schooling and (2) a biological structuralist position (e.g., Piaget) which emphasizes species-wide genetic-environmental interaction, and (3) a racial heritability position (e.g., Jensen) which attributes general intellectual ability primarily to racially specific genotypes. It seems to us that positions 1 and 3 would have considerable difficulty explaining the null hypothesis, if it were indicated on experimental evidence from an underdeveloped country, position 1 believing that conservation will develop more slowly in environments where Western science has had little impact and position 3 believing that lack of cultural development indicates a shortage of genes for intellectual development. Position 2, however, explains the development of conservation as depending primarily on adequate interaction with physical objects and materials during childhood. Although Piaget himself expects for other reasons to find a retardation in more primitive societies, his theory still leaves us in a position to account for a finding of no difference. So we have a situation where all theorists would be surprised at a finding for the null hypothesis, but where one position could accommodate to it more easily than the other two.

Given this situation, and wanting to interpret Kamara's data, what α value should we adopt? If the null hypothesis were in fact true, but if it were rejected erroneously because we had adopted too large a criterion level (Type 1 error), we would be running the risk of erroneously dropping our basis for challenging these theorists to make an important accommodation of their theories, and missing an opportunity to boost the aspirations of educators in developing countries. On the other hand, erroneously accepting the null hypothesis (a Type 2 error) has less serious consequences for us, because as new data come along, the theoretical accommodation could be easily undone and educators could return to the status quo aspirations. However, other researchers might not accept our liberal desire for a challenge and would countenance greater complacency toward the type 1 error in this case. For example, they may argue that normal science (Kuhn, 1962) requires protecting current theory and would assign a relatively high value to α. Because the null hypothesis represents an uncommon position, we have a turnabout situation in which identification with the major theoretical positions would lead one to the adoption of a relatively large α value, say .10, while the more unconventional position, which interests us, leads us to the adoption of a small value of α, like .01.

When we compare frequencies of conservers in Kamara's samples with the corresponding frequencies in Inhelder and Bang's sample, we get almost total acceptance of the null hypothesis. First of all, in the case of conservation of substance, we find that the frequencies for Themne children are greater than those for Geneva children in every age class for which comparable data are available, i.e., four classes for schooled children and two for unschooled. Next, with respect to conservation of weight, in half of the age classes the frequencies for Themne children are greater than for Geneva children, and vice versa for the other half—three out of six age classes for schooled children and two out of four age classes for unschooled children. Thus, by any applicable test (e.g., a sign test), the null hypothesis must be accepted for these two tasks rather than the time-lag hypothesis. For conservation of substance and weight we accept the null hypothesis and urge theoreticians to reconsider their positions.

For volume, the situation is less clear-cut and we appeal to statistics. Considering Themne schooled children, in five out of six of the age classes the Geneva children showed a higher proportion of conservers, and in one they were equal. Considering Themne unschooled children, in the two comparable age classes Geneva children showed a larger proportion of conservers. When the Z statistic defined above is computed for each age-class comparison and the corresponding P values are combined, neither comparison of Geneva with Themne children (schooled or unschooled) is statistically significant at the .01 level. Table 1–2 shows our results for the

Table 1–2
Group comparisons of Geneva vs. Themne children (conservation of volume)

AGE CLASS i	6–7 1	7–8 2	8–9 3	9–10 4	10–11 5	11–12 6	COMBINED P_i's
Z_i (Geneva vs.							$n = 12$
Themne schooled)	—	.82	1.40	1.60	1.47	0.31	$V = 22.50$
$\quad P_i$ (for above)	.500*	.216	.081	.055	.071	.380	$P < 0.05$
Z_i (Geneva vs.							
Themne							$n = 4$
unschooled)					1.47	1.78	$V = 11.83$
$\quad P_i$ (for above)					.071	.038	$P < 0.02$

*P_1 (6–7) was determined directly, since Z_1 cannot be computed.

conservation of volume comparisons. So we do not reject the null hypothesis for culture difference effects for conservation of volume, and continue to believe in the possible reality of no difference. We note that Opper (1971) and Nyiti (1973) have reported a small time-lag for conservation of volume. But, as we shall see below, we really don't know enough about the development process and the interviews themselves to attach much weight to such conclusions—either ours or theirs—or how to combine our results with theirs.

Some researchers prefer to take a descriptive stance rather than to set up a decision procedure. They refuse to commit themselves to a priori values of α and β, and simply report whatever P values emerge from applying statistical models to their data, using as large a sample as they can reasonably get. While this approach is becoming almost a new convention in social science and appears widely in the cross-cultural literature on cognitive development, a more rational descriptive approach to the cultural retardation issue would be to attempt to describe the observed distributions by fitting mathematical equations to them. The constants of such equations could then provide a basis for making comparisons between samples.

To engage in quantitative research on this problem—whether one prefers decision procedures of descriptive statistics—what is needed is a model of the distribution of conservation categories over children's ages that permits the determination of a parameter (or a set of parameters) whose value(s) capture the essential features of the sample distributions. One such attempt was made by Golshan (1972), who performed a trend analysis of Kamara's data aimed at fitting orthogonal polynomials to his data graphed as scores on tasks vs. age. The nonlinearity of such a graph should be evident from the many studies of the conservation tasks. (See Dasen 1973 for examples of point-to-point graphs from 26 studies on conservation of liquids, and Dasen 1972a for the variety of idealized graphs expected on theoretical grounds.) There is an age range for each task in which the percentage of conservers increases, bounded on the younger and older sides by age ranges with nearly constant percentages which approach zero and 100 percent, respectively.

Golshan found, however, contrary to her expectations, that when she carried through the standard test for nonlinearity, Kamara's data did not support a nonlinear model. His data were mainly collected in the middle range, and given the difficulties of obtaining valid age and stage determinations, there was little reason for him to have extended his observations to younger or older subjects. However, if we extend Kamara's data for six years in each direction, using imaginary cases of younger and older children, a second- or third-degree equation will be required to fit the data—as we verified. That is, if there is no doubt about how younger or older subjects would have performed, there is no doubt about the nonlinearity of the development curves. The question of nonlinearity, approached by applying a test for it, limited to a given investigator's data, thus will be answered differently depending on the particular age range he has chosen. The coefficients of a fitted polynomial are poor descriptive statistics because they depend strongly on prior choices of the most critical ages to be interviewed, and on other design criteria. This argues for a different kind of descriptive statistic and a different approach to a mathematical model. Rather than being applied to the data from an assumed system of equations, a model needs to be developed from the data, ideally from a mechanism derived from detailed observations of the developmental process itself.

The problem of nonlinearity is even greater when one tries to use the standard schemes for statistical inference. While a small variation in age range (say one or two years) does not greatly affect estimates of the median age, it may change the slope of a linear regression line quite markedly. This is especially true if the upper or lower age limit of the sample lies in a region where the percentage of conservation responses on one task is neither very large nor very small. The assumption of linearity does not appear to be a controversial issue, it is not mentioned explicitly. However, researchers using statistical inference designs have invariably made the assumption that the measures of cognitive growth bear a linear relationship to age. It is also typically assumed that the three categories for each task form equidistant points on a continuum. Nyiti (1973), however, employs a fourth category—"undecided"—to eliminate the unwarranted source of error which is due to forcing every interview into one of the three standard categories; and Goldschmid et al. (1973) score responses on a ten-point scale.

Examination of tables such as Table 1–1 and others found in the literature makes it clear that all continuous, linear models yield statistics which are subject to large fluctuations of slope; and these, in turn, are artifacts of the particular scoring method, the age range sampled, and the age class size employed. Consequently, tests of hypotheses about retardation in different populations using conventional statistics will simply be impossible to interpret. However, examination of the raw data in these same tables could help us discover appropriate mathematical models for age distribution of stages and hopefully will lead us toward a new statistical test for these types of experiments.

Ideally, we should like to know the precise age of each subject, since age is the one real continuum we have. However, taking Inhelder's and Bang's data in Table 1–1 (Piaget and Inhelder, 1962, 1969b), we can plot a graph of percentage in one task category vs. the assumed mean age for each age class. (By treating each task category separately, we avoid making assumptions about any continuum underlying them.) The visual appearance of the points suggests that the percent of conservers may be represented by a curve roughly resembling the normal ogive (cumulative areas under the normal frequency distribution). By purely visual, free-hand sketching, we have drawn curves for all three conservation tasks based on Table 1–1. Kamara's two groups were combined for greater stability. (See Figures 1–1, 1–2, and 1–3.) In the same figures we have also graphed data from two other tables given by Piaget and Inhelder (1969b): one based on Elkind (1961); and the other on Lovell and Ogilvie (1960, 1961), also given in Lovell (1961).

Curves of this general type have at least two (and possibly three or four) parameters. Using all the published tables of data, one could, on the standard measurement paradigm, undertake to develop an appropriate mathematical model.[8] A theoretical model of the development mechanism would be an even more difficult task. We shall not attempt here to develop such an equation either on theoretical or empirical grounds. Curves fitted by eye at least have the scientific advantage that they exhibit trends visually and thus serve as a better starting point for making comparisons than force-fitted equations or tables alone. We do note, however, that biologists have come to recognize (having learned it from physicists and chemists, presumably) that population growth theory is enhanced by considering the differential form rather than the conventional integral form (sigmoid curves). The latter form is too insensitive to changes in growth mechanisms, giving the illusion that the growth mechanism is the same. (See Easley, 1967, articles 4 and 5.) For differential growth curves, which are sensitive to variations in the mean age of any class intervals, we would need to have raw age data from several groups. Despite their lack of theoretical basis, the graphs presented make clear the kinds of differences to be found in the data: variations in steepness as well as in relative positions age-wise of the points of greatest curvature, points of inflection, 75th percentile, etc. One wonders whether these differences reflect differences in method of interviewing, language, and age determination, or real differences in cognitive development. We will examine the validity problem in the next section.

In summary of this section, we conclude that the literature we have been reviewing has made no progress toward developing a mathematical model adequate for representing population distributions of conservation competences. Such a model is required for any rational decision procedure to investigate the hypothesis of a cultural origin of conservation. Work is certainly needed on this task, not merely because of the political

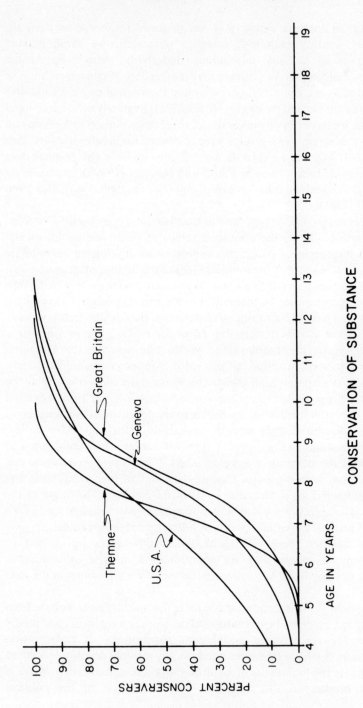

CONSERVATION OF SUBSTANCE

Figure 1–1. Curves showing the development of conservation of substance from four populations, fitted by eye

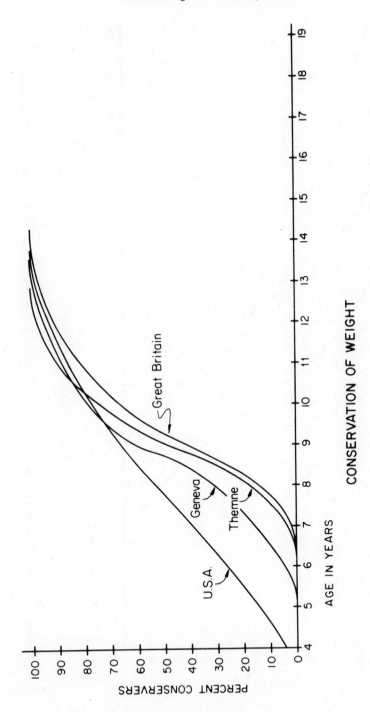

CONSERVATION OF WEIGHT

Figure 1–2. Curves showing the development of conservation of weight from four populations, fitted by eye

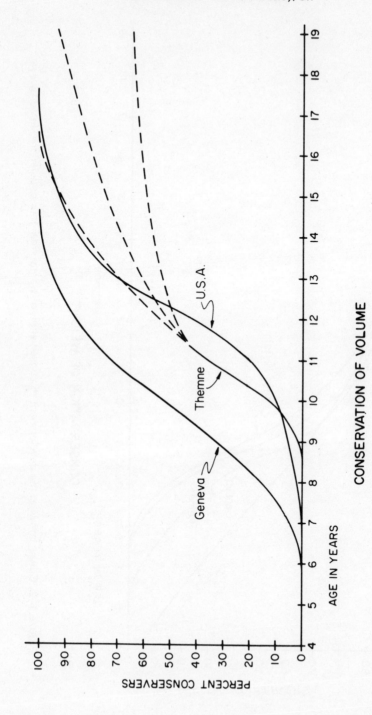

CONSERVATION OF VOLUME

Figure 1–3. Curves showing the development of conservation of volume from three populations, fitted by eye

importance of this research in developing countries, but because researchers continuing these studies in the field need a paradigm to guide their data collection procedures, and help them determine needed sample sizes, age ranges, and age classes.

4. THE DIFFICULTIES OF TREATING PIAGET'S TASKS AS PERFORMANCE TESTS AND THE ALTERNATIVE PARADIGM, STRUCTURAL ANALYSIS[9]

As we noted in section 2, Piaget's objections to the use of tests for determining cognitive structure and process appear to have been largely ignored in most replication studies. We have seen that most of the studies being reviewed have standardized clinical interviews into clinical tests. Piaget pointed out (1929) that tests cannot provide enough information to decide what structures are involved in a child's thinking, and Piaget and Inhelder (1947) characterized tests as giving only the "results of efficiency of mental activity without grasping the psychological operations in themselves" (p. 401). Smedslund (1969) argued that "the constructs involved are anchored neither to distal or proximal physical stimuli, nor to physical response categories, but to the meanings of the subjects' acts."

What is involved in this issue is a conflict between the paradigm for structural analysis (Piaget's approach) and the paradigm for measurement (such as we adopted in the previous section). It has not often been noted that the paradigms for measurement and for structural analysis in science are quite distinct (Harré, 1972, Chapter 3), but those familiar with the appropriate sciences will testify that electrons, benzine rings, fault zones, the jet stream, and DNA are not defined operationally in Bridgman's sense. That is, these concepts are not initially "framed in terms of operations which can be unequivocally performed" (Bridgman, 1938). Furthermore, although there are mathematical models of them, they themselves do not function as variables in multidimensional models. Rather they function as structures in terms of which scientists conceive of many complex phenomena. Cognitive structures in Piaget's sense, and indeed structures underlying phenomena in many other branches of science, cannot be measured or given "operational definitions" in the sense in which Bridgman "defines" length, mass, and other measurable quantities by specifying the operations of measurement. Furthermore, these structures do not clearly define variables and should not be used uncritically in multidimensional models.

In psychology, cognitive structures would correspond to the above-mentioned structures in the natural sciences, and they may be conceived as such in terms of the structural analysis paradigm described by Witz (1970).

One important difference between measurable quantities and underlying structures is that structural elements stand in a many-to-many relation with observable molar events and patterns of events rather than in a one-to-one or a one-to-many relation, as operational definitions of measurable quantities require. Yet, despite the difficulty of directly demonstrating precisely when or where a given structure is present or absent (precise demonstration may block the normal functioning of a structure or even greatly change it), the indirect capacity of structures to explain phenomena has made them the backbone of scientific advance. The researcher's own cognitive processes, organized by structural ideas, enable him to grasp complex phenomena which would not yield to purely mechanical searching for relationships between measurable quantities. This is surely the way in which most important scientific discoveries, including Piaget's operations, were made. The structures are surely not to be replaced by tests, once they have guided the discoverer, so they can be thrown into the hopper with mental age, chronological age, sex, and other variables. They should be understood as structures so that understanding can guide what is done with the data.

As an example of the way in which structures relate to observable phenomena, John Dalton, by thinking of gross properties of matter as expressions of the properties and arrangements of atoms, succeeded in discovering key relations which linked molecular formulas (e.g., HO, HO_2, or H_2O) and atomic weights (e.g., 1 to 8, 1 to 4, or 1 to 16)—both of them aspects of hypothetical structures we call molecules—with the observed combining weight ratio (1 to 8), a measurable quantity. These relations were, of necessity, many-to-many, because there are many combinations of simple formulas and possible atomic weights which are consistent with the combining weight. Thus, it required analysis of a great many compounds, with more than a dozen elements, before the ambiguities between even the simplest structural hypotheses could be eliminated. (See Easley and Tatsuoka, 1968, Chapter 4.) Modern structural chemistry not only started from such a paradigm but continued to employ many-to-many relations in its development, which has made possible today the description of such complex structures as DNA, RNA, and proteins.

Unfortunately, the psychology of cognitive structures is in a very primitive state compared with chemistry, but we can learn from the structural paradigm in the history of the physical and biological sciences. Perhaps the first thing we must recognize from this record is that scientific thought doesn't stop because it is recognized that many different structures can give rise to (be involved in) the same response in an experimental situation, and that many different observations in that situation can spring from (involve) the same structure. On the contrary, the power of structural ideas to guide research and to explain complex phenomena lies in the fact that no single structure acts alone but always in concert with other structures that are present and that are brought into action by the situation, directly or indirectly. This is as true for the structures of complex organisms (cells, tissues, organs, systems) as it is for the atomic and subatomic structures of chemistry, physics, and electronics. If it were not so, no one would be impressed by the explanations they provide. For helpful summaries of the history of scientific structures see Toulmin and Goodfield (1961, 1962) and Harré (1969). Williams' book on Faraday (1965) is also especially valuable.

Historical study may also lead us to reexamine the dominant view that measurement is the basic and most powerful tool for scientific discovery, specifically for the discovery of general laws. Cronbach (1970, p. 25) makes this explicitly the basic goal of psychometrics. In contrast, we note Thomas Kuhn's claim (1961) that, in the history of physical science, measurement rarely has led to theory but on the contrary, qualitative theory has usually preceded and often guided and inspired measurement. It would appear a reasonable interpretation, consistent with Kuhn's view, that insight into structures underlying observed phenomena is needed before we can hope to specify general laws relating measurable quantities that will direct us to experiments, further systematizing our psychological observations and illuminating and refining our ideas about structures. While a few psychometricians have recently been looking to Piaget's tasks as a more unified domain for test construction and to his theory for general orientation to individual differences (e.g., Tuddenham, 1971), Piaget's postulated cognitive structures may require precise description of their dynamic functioning before task-related abilities measurable in tests can be usefully identified. For this we need a clear example of cognitive structures and how they function.

The operationalist point of view is so strong in psychology that there is a temptation to interpret Smedslund's comment, quoted above, as defining structures in terms of common meanings that the psychologist shares with the subject (in the sense either of shared definitions or shared associations). However, Piaget's concept of cognitive structures (especially of "schemes") opens the possibility of interpreting regularities in the subject's behavior in terms of the dynamic functioning of systems of structures, which dictionary definitions and networks of associations don't possess. So we would need a new theory of meaning if we wanted to follow Smedslund's clue. More important, to keep structures in contact with data, we need to learn how to analyze interview protocols in terms of structures which underlie behavior, and how to bring out those structures which do not show in direct-response performance but normally remain as unexpressed competences. Sometimes a brief part of an interview will strikingly suggest a key structure; but to make it more than a guess, other parts of the interview—involving major variations in situations and possibly counter-suggestions—must also be shown to be also accounted for by that same structure. We need an example with a general conception to guide us.

The structural analysis paradigm, according to Witz (1970), relates cognitive structures to observable phenomena in the way that is represented in the diagram in Figure 1–4 (adapted from Witz, 1973). A particular structure, X, is said to assimilate certain aspects of the immediate situation—say p, q, r—for which this structure provides an interpretation or a response and not to assimilate others—l, m, n, o. So the assimilation process yields an important relation. That is, a domain of structures ($W, X, Y, \ldots$) is related to a domain of situational aspects ($l, m, n, \ldots$) in a many-to-many relation, R_1. No structure is uniquely defined by a known set of situational aspects (because in new situations new aspects will be assimilated to old structures), and no aspects observed in a situation can be defined by a given set of structures (because later, new structures will assimilate and thus "redefine" old aspects). Similarly, the overt responses—s, t, u—which the subject makes as a consequence of the activity of structure X, and which thereby give evidence of the involvement of X, form an element of another many-to-many relation—R_2—of situational aspects with cognitive structures (Witz, 1970). This is a relation which, regrettably, Piaget and most Piagetians have failed to develop—or, if some Piagetians have tried to explicate it, they have treated it as a one-to-many or even a one-to-one relation in order to make structures strongly operational, forgetting that structures cannot act alone.

The accommodation of structures to given aspects of the situation, as Piaget stresses, is a second process going on simultaneously with the

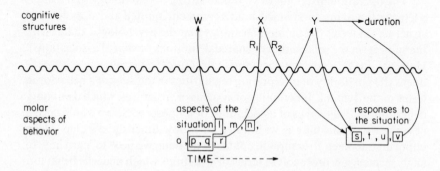

Figure 1–4. Witz's representation of the structural paradigm

assimilation of aspects of the situation to the structures. However, it is not represented in Figure 1–4 but can be added to such diagrams in one of two ways, depending on whether one wants to represent explicitly or implicitly the changes in structures resulting from their accommodation to objects or events of the situation (see Figure 1–5). In the explicit version, on the left, one represents two different structures, X_1 and X_2, before and after accommodation, separated in the time dimension, and the differing aspects assimilated to them. More implicitly, one may represent accommodation by the looped arrow in the right-hand part of the figure (after Furth, 1969, p. 75) which gives an instantaneous representation of the process of accommodation, a process which must be understood as going on simultaneously with the process of assimilation represented by the upward arrow. (The downward arrows for the R_2 relation are omitted in this figure for the sake of clarity.) The need for explicitness in representing accommodation, however, is dependent on the availability of data to give evidence of structural changes. (See Witz, 1971.) We shall follow Witz's convention of leaving out the accommodation arrows altogether in order to emphasize the problem of protocol analysis, i.e., the recognition of structures in recorded aspects of the situation.

To understand how this paradigm can be applied formally in the analysis of protocols of conservation interviews, we consider an excerpt from one of Kamara's interviews, translated into English from Themne (Kamara, 1971). The subject is Amadu, a 9-year-old, unschooled Themne boy, who after several other discussions, was shown two balls of plasticine and then questioned in the manner described by Piaget and Inhelder (1962), with the adaptations to Themne culture and language which we have already described; the plasticine balls represented cakes of bread.

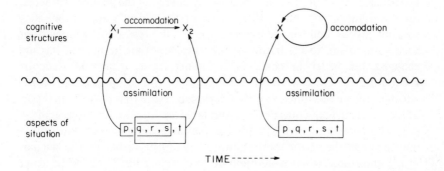

Figure 1–5. Explicit and implicit representation of accommodation

Exp: Which of you would have more bread to eat?

Sub: They are equal, I had shared it equally.

Exp: If Aruna should come, and you tell him that they are both equal, and he denies it, what would you do to convince him?

Sub: [Pauses] . . . He will think that this is more [pancake].

Exp: What would you do to show him that they are equal?

Sub: I will tell him that this looks bigger because it has been flattened, but they are equal.

Exp: What would you do to convince him?

Sub: [Pauses] . . . Then I will gather [ball] this [pancake] and make a ball with it. . . .

The primary question for those convinced of the reality and general usefulness of operational schemes and other structures described by Piaget, is whether the judgment of equality Amadu makes is due to a conservation structure supported by general reversible operations or whether this judgment is due to such low-level perceptual processes as would be involved in recalling the way the plasticine looked before it was flattened, which can cause children to answer as Amadu did, but which Piaget calls "pseudoconservation" (Piaget and Inhelder, 1971, p. 269). Thus the question is uncertain whether the first interaction of experimenter and subject in the first two lines of the protocol should be regarded as true or pseudo conservation. Structurally, it means that the first entry for each person under "observable behavior" in Figure 1–6 could be interpreted as involving a general operational structure or the perceptual structure. This question clearly cannot be answered on the basis of the first interaction alone.

In the second interaction, we have evidence of another structure which appears to be primarily perceptual; we designate it here as a comparison of the surfaces of the ball and the pancake. (Subjects who say that the pancake provides more bread to eat than does the ball often appear to be centering on surface areas, but this is not necessarily "area" in the geometrical sense, for the diameter or some other aspect of the object's appearance may account just as well for the observed behavior.) Amadu attributes some such comparison to his friend Aruna, implying that he himself has not changed his belief in conservation. This means that the structure accounting for conservation is stronger than the comparison structure, which is allowed to function only vicariously. Note that only the first part of the experimenter's question is assimilated by Amadu. An "overload"— due to his being presented with too complex a question to assimilate fully— may in fact be the reason for the pause preceding his response. The last part of the question, "What would you do to convince him?" has to be asked twice more before it is fully assimilated that is, before an object-manipulation scheme is activated that can assimilate "What would you

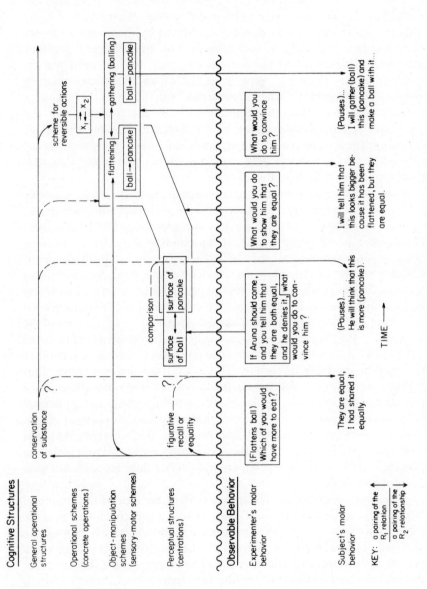

Figure 1–6. Structural analysis of a protocol fragment

do?" as "What motor act will you perform?" rather than as "What will you say to him?"

The next response gives supporting evidence for two structures already mentioned and evidence of one additional structure. (We omit reference to linguistic structures such as would be indicated by the opening phrase, "Tell him that . . .") The second phrase, "this looks bigger," provides additional evidence of the comparison structure, but the third phrase, "because it has flattened,' gives evidence of an object-manipulation structure (a sensorymotor scheme) concerned with flattening the ball into a pancake. This has evidently been activated by the persistence of the questioner and by the perception of the pancake, recalling the act of flattening. The final phrase, "but they are equal," shows the still persistent conservation of substance, suggesting now by its persistence that it is something other than figurative recall.

Clear evidence of a concrete operation relating to the conservation of substance does not emerge, however, until the next repetition of the probe, "What would you do to convince him?" The response to this, which comes after another pause (suggesting a search for another structure to which the question can be assimilated), may be taken, in this context, by Piagetians as evidence of one of the much discussed reversible concrete operational schemes. These are schemes that generate or evoke the reverse of an action in the subject's mind. If one accepts the existence of such operations, the response "I will gather this and make a ball with it" in the context of the question, in the absence of any direct suggestion, and in view of repeated failure to assimilate the question to an action scheme—means a generative structure of reversing the action. This is evidence that the connections between the conservation structure, the scheme for reversible actions, and a related pair of object-manipulation schemes (flattening and gathering) have become active. It is now plausible that conservation of substance is an "operational" competence and not merely a performance. We omit reference to perceptual and kinesthetic structures associated with gathering plasticine—like material (mud balls or balls of rice-flour bread) which have also been at work.

The above discussion is illustrative only of the idea of the structural analysis of interview protocols. If one is to draw a firm conclusion as to the subject's operativity in Piaget's sense, much more data need to be similarly analyzed. That is, the total protocol must be interpretable in terms of a system of structures or competences which the subject uses. The quest for instant reliability represented by the test approach to Piaget's tasks is doomed to involve many errors in the identification of cognitive structures. For one thing, it suffers from a problem of construct validity. For another, reliability is a far from simple concept (Cronbach et al., 1972). Analysis of protocols on the structuralist paradigm is necessarily a slow and nonmechanical procedure. It begins in subjective, but hopefully educated, judgments and moves toward objectivity as it attains completeness of accounting for the total protocol. Witz, in explaining a system of axioms proposed for cognitive structure representations (which he abbreviates as C.S.R.s), says, "In our formulation we emphasize that it is sufficient merely to account for the observed behavior—the short-term dynamics is vague enough to permit many possible accounts, it limits rather than predicts, and an unambiguous picture emerges only when many items of information are considered and more 'overlapping' C.S.R.s come into play." (Witz, 1970, p. 69.) It therefore seems absurd to pretend that one knows how to measure conservation competences by administering standardized lists of questions when no validating clinical interviews—and certainly no explicit structural analyses—have been published. To make advances in public objectivity beyond the highly informal and private discipline of the clinical interview, e.g., as used by Piaget and by Kamara, will require the publication of many deeper analyses of rich behavioral records than have yet been published.

SUMMARY

In summary, we have examined four major methodological problems—deficiencies in most milieu studies on Piaget's conservation tasks—from the point of view of the central question: whether or not there exists a retardation of children's intellectual development in certain non-Western cultures.

1. The age of the subjects becomes a critical factor in this question, and age determination has not been generally given the attention it deserves, being frequently entrusted to records that are notoriously subject to error. Kamara's methods of critical events, farm-site enumeration, and sibling comparison provide a promising approach to the resolution of this problem.

2. Language and culturally specific associations enter into the required clinical interviews in such an important way that a great deal of weight should be given to interviews conducted by researchers who are natives of the children's own culture and who make full use of the language and culture of their subjects in probing to remove ambiguities in responses and in the interpretation of these responses. Full support and encouragement should be given to the emerging group of non-Western scholars interested in and capable of performing such studies. Kamara's data from Sierra Leone were presented as an indication of the possibility that the earlier

evidence of a general lag in intellectual development of children in non-Western cultures, which Piaget and most researchers have accepted, may be suspect. Differences observed by superficial examination of tables of data were not at all impressive.

3. The third methodological difficulty examined was that of experimental design, i.e., methods of relating frequencies of task-response categories to the question of a retardation. A procedure for combining probabilities derived from individual age-class comparisons was explained and applied to data collected by Kamara and by Inhelder and Bang. The result was that only on the conservation of volume was there a nearly consistent—but not significant—lag of Themne children behind Geneva norms. The quest for a more sophisticated and more clearly rational (whether decision theoretic or descriptive) method of analysis was analyzed, pointing out the inadequacies of standard statistical methods. For example, chi-square is typically employed in a way that does not relate to the question, and other statistical tests are sensitive to artifacts of design and often misleading because they make invalid assumptions of a continuous variable and a linear relationship between development and age. Examining the data from typical reports by free-hand graphing illustrated the need for developing a mathematical model more suitable for analysis of data relating to the central issue and for breaking the question down into subquestions, which may some day be related to the mechanisms of development and expression of cognitive competences.

4. Finally, the tendency that many researchers have shown to conduct interviews on conservation tasks as standardized tests instead of by relatively unstructured clinical interviews was criticized in terms of the structural analysis paradigm of Witz. This paradigm helps make explicit what it is that Piaget and Piagetians must keep in mind as they interview children and classify their responses. It also makes possible the discovery of new structures not yet described, which—while not necessarily related to the central issue of cultural retardation—does open the possibility of refining the problem by reinterpreting behaviors that have been interpreted as evidence of retardation.

We conclude that the methodological situation of this area of research is essentially no better today than in 1971, when Piaget commented, "Cross-cultural studies are difficult to carry out because they presuppose a good psychological training in the techniques of operational testing, namely, with free conversation and not standardization in the manner of tests, and all psychologists do not have this training; a sufficient ethnological sophistication and a complete knowledge of the language are also prerequisites. We know of only a few attempts of this quality." (quoted and translated by Dasen, 1972). It is hoped that this important area of research can be developed as a vigorous and rigorous aspect of social science.

NOTES

1. E.g., Almy (1970), Dasen (1972b, 1974), de Lemos (1969, Etuk (1967). Greenfield (1966), Goldschmid *et al.* (1973), Heron and Dowel (1973), Heron and Simonsson (1969), Hyde (1959), Jahoda (1956), Laurendeau and Pinard (cited by Piaget, 1966), Lloyd (1971a, 1971b), Poole (1968), and Prince (1968).

2. Studied, for example, by Piaget and Inhelder (1962), Lovell (1961), and Elkind (1961).

3. E.g., Bovet (1968), Kamara (1971), Nyiti (1973), Ohuche (1970), Opper (1971), Price-Williams (1961), and Voyat (1970).

4. Editor's note: In fact, the age of Australian aboriginal children is usually well documented in mission or government records.

5. The authors are greatly indebted to Maurice Tatsuoka for reading a draft of this section and for suggesting specific procedures and models.

6. We may deplore the lack of clarity about the age classes and other relevant details often omitted in such tables, for this makes it more difficult to assess the retardation hypothesis.

7. For this statistic, see Glass and Stanley (1970), p. 323. We cannot, of course, combine age groups here, for under the null hypothesis, each age group is still a different population.

8. In addition to the normal ogive and orthogonal polynomials, other available candidates for consideration include the logistic curve (Lord and Novick, 1968, chapter 17) and the 4-parameter beta distribution.

9. Some of the material of this section was used in an article, "The structural paradigm in protocol analysis," published in the *Journal of Research in Science Teaching* (Easley, 1974) and is used here with permission of the publishers.

REFERENCES

Almy, Millie (1970) The usefulness of Piagetian methods for studying primary school children in Uganda. In M. Almy, J. L. Duritz, and M. A. White (Eds.), *Studying school children in Uganda.* New York: Teachers College Press, Colombia University.

Bovet, Magali C. (1968) Études interculturelles du développement intellectuel et processus d'apprentissage. *Revue Suisse de Psychologie Pure et Appliquée, 27*:189–199.

Bridgman, P. W. (1938) Operational analysis. *Philosophy of Science, 5*:114–131.

Bruner, J. S., Olver, Rose R., Greenfield, Patricia M., *et al.* (1966) *Studies in cognitive growth.* New York: Wiley.

Cole, M., and Bruner, J. S. (1971) Cultural differences and inferences about psychological processes. *American Psychologist, 26*:867–876.

Cronbach, L. J. (1970) *Essentials of psychological testing* (3rd ed.). New York: Harper.

——. Gleser, Goldine C., Nanda, Harinder, and Rajaratnam, Nageswari. (1972) *The dependability of behavioral measurements.* New York: Wiley.

Dasen, P. R. (1972a) Cross-cultural Piagetian research: A summary. *Journal of Cross-Cultural Psychology, 3*:23–29.

——. (1972b) The development of conservation in aboriginal children, A replication study. *International Journal of Psychology, 7*:78–85.

——. (1973) Biologie ou culture? La psychologie interethnique d'un point de vue Piagétien. *Canadian Psychologist, 14*:149–166.

——. (1974) The influence of ecology, culture and European contact on cognitive development in Australian aborigines. In J. W. Berry and P. R. Dasen (Eds.). *Culture and cognition: Readings in cross-cultural psychology.* London: Methuen. Pp. 381–408.

De Lemos, Marion M. (1969) The development of conservation in aboriginal children. *International Journal of Psychology, 4*:255–269.

Easley, J. A., Jr. (1967) *The uses of mathematics in science teaching.* Final Report NSF contract GW-2252.

——. (1974) The structural paradigm in protocol analysis. *Journal of Research in Sciences Teachings, 11*:281–290.

——. and Tatsuoka, M. M. (1968) *Scientific thought: Cases from classical physics.* Boston: Allyn and Bacon.

Elkind, D. (1961) Children's discovery of the conservation of mass, weight, and volume: Piaget replication study II. *Journal of Genetic Psychology, 98*:219–228.

Etuk, Elizabeth (1967) *The development of number concepts: An examination of Piaget's theory with Yoruba-speaking Nigerian children.* Ed.D. dissertation, Teachers College, Columbia University.

Fisher, R. A. (1946) *Statistical methods for research workers* (10th ed.). New York: Stechert.

Furth, H. (1969) *Piaget and knowledge: Theoretical foundations.* Englewood Cliffs: Prentice-Hall.

Glass, G. V. and Stanley, J. C. (1970) *Statistical methods in education and psychology.* Englewood Cliffs: Prentice-Hall.

Golshan, Mahtash (1972) *A statistical analysis of the study done on cognitive development among school age Themne children of Sierra Leone.* Course paper, Department of Educational Psychology, University of Illinois.

Goldschmid, M. L., Bentler, P. M., Debus, R. L., Rawlinson, R., Kohnstamm, D., Modgil, S., Nicholls, J. G., Reykowski, J., Strupczewska, Barbara, and Warren, N. (1973) A cross-cultural investigation of conservation. *Journal of Cross-Cultural Psychology, 4*:75–88.

Greenfield, Patricia M. (1966) On culture and conservation. *In* J. S. Bruner, *et al. Studies in cognitive growth.* New York: Wiley.

Harré, R. (Ed.) (1969) *Scientific thought 1900–1960*. Oxford: Clarendon Press.

―――. (1972) *The philosophies of science*. Oxford: Oxford University Press.

Heron, A., and Dowel, Wendy (1973) Weight conservation and matrix-solving ability in Papuan children. *Journal of Cross-Cultural Psychology, 4*:207–219.

―――.and Simonsson, Marta (1969) Weight conservation in Zambian children. *International Journal of Psychology, 4*:281–292.

Hyde, Doris M. G. (1959) *An investigation of Piaget's theories of the development of the concept of number*. Ph.D. dissertation, University of London.

Inhelder, Bärbel, and Piaget, J. (1958) *The growth of logical thinking from childhood to adolescence*. New York: Basic Books.

Jahoda, G. (1956) Assessment of abstract behavior in a non-Western culture. *Journal of Abnormal Social Psychology, 53*:237–243.

Kamara, A. I. (1971) *Cognitive development among school-age Themne children of Sierra Leone*. Ph.D. dissertation, University of Illinois.

Kiminyo, D. M. (1973) *A cross-cultural study of the development of conservation of mass, weight, and volume in Kenyan children*. Ph.D. dissertation, University of Alberta.

Kuhn, T. S. (1961) The function of measurement in modern physical science. In H. Woolf (Ed.), *Quantification, A history of the meaning of measurement in the natural and social sciences*. Indianapolis: Bobbs-Merrill.

―――. (1962) *The structure of scientific revolutions*. Chicago: University of Chicago Press.

Laurendeau, Monique, and Pinard, A. (1962) *Casual thinking in the child*. New York: International Universities Press, Inc.

Lloyd, Barbara B. (1971a) Studies of conservation with Yoruba children of differing ages and experience. *Child Development, 42*:415–428.

―――. (1971b) The intellectual development of Yoruba children: A reexamination. *Journal of Cross-Cultural Psychology, 2*:29–38.

Lord, F. M., and Novick, M. R. (1968) *Statistical theories of mental test scores*. Reading, Mass.: Addison-Wesley.

Lovell, K. (1961) *The growth of basic mathematical and scientific concepts in children*. London: University of London Press.

―――. and Ogilvie, E. (1960) A study of the conservation of substance in the junior school child. *Brit. J. Educ. Psych.*, 30, 109–118.

――― ―――. (1961) The growth of the concept of volume in junior school children. *Journal of Child Psychology and Psychiatry, 2*:118–126.

Nyiti, R. (1973) *A study of conservation among Meru children of Tanzania*. Ph.D. dissertation, University of Illinois.

Ohuche, R. O. (1970) *Conservation of quantity and traditional values*. Mimeographed paper: Njala University College, Njala, Sierra Leone.

Opper, Sylvia (1971) *The intellectual development of Thai children*. Unpublished Ph.D. dissertation, Cornell University, Ithaca.

Otaala, B. (1971) *The development of operational thinking in primary school children: An examination of some aspects of Piaget's theory among the Itseo children of Uganda*. Ph.D. dissertation, Teachers College, Columbia University.

Peluffo, N. (1967) Culture and cognitive problems. *International Journal of Psychology,* 2:187–198.

Piaget, J. (1929) *The child's conception of the world.* London: Routledge and Kegan Paul.

——. (1966) Necessité et signification des recherches comparatives en psychologie génétique. *International Journal of Psychology,* 1:3–13. English translation in J. W. Berry and P. R. Dasen (Eds.), *Culture and cognition: Readings in cross-cultural psychology.* London: Methuen, 1974.

——. and Inhelder, Bärbel (1947) Diagnosis of mental operations and theory of the intelligence. *American Journal of Mental Deficiency,* 51:401–406.

—— ——. (1962) *Le développement des quantités physiques chez l'enfant* (deuxième édition augmentée). Neuchâtel: Delachaux et Niestlé.

—— ——. (1969a) *The psychology of the child.* New York: Basic Books.

—— ——. (1969b) Les opérations intellectuelles et leur développement. In P. Fraisse and J. Piaget (Eds.), *Traité de psychologie expérimentale, vol. 7; l'intelligence* (deuxième édition). Paris: Presses Universitaires de France. (Translation: *Experimental psychology: Its scope and method, 7, intelligence.* New York: Basic Books. 1969).

—— ——. (1971) *Mental imagery in the child.* New York: Basic Books.

Pinard, A., Morin, C., and Lefebvre, Monique (1973) Apprentissage de la conservation des quantités liquides chez des enfants Rwandais et Canadiens–Francais. *International Journal of Psychology,* 8:15–23.

Poole, H. E. (1968) The effects of urbanization upon scientific concept attainment among Hausa children in Northern Nigeria. *British Journal of Educational Psychology,* 38:57–63.

Price-Williams, D. R. (1961) A study concerning concepts of conservation of quantities among primitive children. *Acta Psychologica,* 18:297–305.

Prince, J. R. (1968) The effect of western education on science conceputalization in New Guinea. *British Journal of Educational Psychology,* 38:64–74.

Smedslund, J. (1961) The acquisition of conservation of substance and weight in children, III. Extinction of conservation of weight acquired "normally" and by means of empirical controls on a balance. *Scandinavian Journal of Psychology,* 2:85–87.

——. (1969) Psychological diagnostics. *Psychological Bulletin,* 71:237–248.

Toulmin, S., and Goodfield, June (1961) *The fabric of the heavens.* New York: Harper and Row.

—— ——. (1962) *The architecture of matter.* New York: Harper and Row.

Tuddenham, R. D. (1971) Theoretical regularities and individual idiosyncrasies. *In* D. R. Green, M. P. Ford, and G. B. Flamer (Eds.), *Measurement and Piaget.* New York: McGraw-Hill.

Voyat, G. (1970) Cross-cultural study of cognitive development on the Pine Ridge Indian Reservation. *Pine Ridge Research Bulletin,* No. 11. Public Health Service: Indian Health Service Publications.

Williams, L. P. (1965) *Michael Faraday.* London: Chapman and Hall.

Witz, K. G. (1970) Representation of cognitive processes and cognitive structure in children. *Archives de Psychologie, 40*:61–95.

———. (1971) *Structural changes in 4–5 year olds.* Paper presented at the Second Annual Interdisciplinary Meeting on Structural Learning, University of Pennsylvania, Philadelphia, April 2–3, 1971.

———. (1973) Analysis of "frameworks" in young children. *Journal of Children's Mathematical Behavior* (University of Illinois), *1* (2): 44–66.

2
A Cross-Cultural Study of the Development of Conservation of Mass, Weight, and Volume Among Kamba Children

DANIEL M. KIMINYO

INTRODUCTION

Cross-cultural studies in cognitive development are essential in the analysis of factors which are crucial in influencing cognitive development.

Piaget's theory of cognitive development is of special interest to cross-cultural developmental pyschologists because of the important role he has attributed to the unfolding of universal biological functions. The testing of the validity of such universal maturational or developmental sequences can only be done through studying cognitive development of children from different cultural backgrounds.

One of the major concepts of Piaget's theory of cognitive development (and one that has been studied most) is the concept of conservation (the invariance of equality—for instance of substance, weight, or volume—in the face of transformation or deformation) which Piaget considers to be "a necessary condition for all rational activities" (Piaget 1952).

Studies of various types of conservation have shown conflicting results in connection with the effect of schooling on the acquisition of conservation concepts. One of the most detailed cross-cultural conservation studies was done by Greenfield (1966); in this study schooling was found to be a factor crucial in influencing the acquisition of conservation of continuous quantities among the Wolof children in Senegal's urban and rural populations. Recently Ciborowski and Cole (1971) and Dempsey (1971) have supported Greenfield's main finding that schooling has an important role to play in children's cognitive development, especially the conservation concepts.

On the other hand, contrary evidence has been accumulating from studies done by Goodnow and Bethon (1966), and by a great number of cross-cultural studies quoted by Furby (1971).

Similarly, conflicting results have been found concerning the role played by environmental factors on the achievement of conservation concepts. Greenfield, Madiano, and Maccoby (Bruner et al., 1966) have reported differences in conservation scores between rural and urban children within the same cultural background. Other studies have found no such differences in conservation scores while others have asserted that rural children conserve earlier than urban children.

This chapter points out and discusses some of the factors that account for cross-cultural differences in the development of conservation.

RATIONALE

A review of the literature shows general agreement with Piaget's sequential theory of cognitive development among European subjects. But studies in non-European cultures have shown some contradictory results. While the sequential development of mental growth was found to exist among non-European subjects, the predicted "horizontal *décalage*" between the different quantities has not always been confirmed.

There are at least two problems arising from these non-European studies. These problems may be the causes of the contradictory results obtained from the studies.

1. Sociocultural Factors

Piaget (Ripple, 1964) reported that problems are solved relative to the culture in question and that the important fact is the order of appearance of stages. Stages in the development of cognition have been confirmed in non-European cultures (sometimes with a time lag) but what these studies have not investigated conclusively are the types of experience that best help the development of conservation of different quantities. It is the contention of this writer that the most influential types of experiences may be found among those activities within a culture that are useful and vital for survival.

Inhelder (Green et al. 1971) agreed that children who are present on occasions when adults evaluate quantities of goods they wish to buy or sell will develop conservation of mass and weight much earlier than otherwise. Similarly, children whose mothers distribute food in containers of various shapes and sizes may learn to pay more attention to the initial act of distribution than to the perceptual appearance of the containers. Furthermore, children who accompany adults to their daily activities will most likely develop those concepts which are necessary for these activities much faster than others. These seemingly culture-specific experiences may be the causes of the conflicting results obtained by several researchers.

Dasen (1972) cited studies by Goodnow, Goodnow and Bethon, Mermelstein and Shulman, Waddell, Kelly, and Heron reporting no direct relationship between formal schooling and conservation. Conversely, a direct relationship between schooling and conservation was reported by Greenfield (1966), Hendrikz, Prince, and Lloyd (1971), and by Laurendeau-Bendavid in this volume.

2. Lack of Actual Replication

Each and every one of the studies reviewed was a new experiment, dealing with some aspects of one or more European studies. A better way of comparing European and non-European studies would be to replicate actual European studies. In addition, the materials used should be very meaningful and familiar to the subjects. Dasen (1972) emphasized the importance of actual replication. He felt that more cross-cultural studies have shown rather heterogeneous results because each project has been based on different tasks. Cross-cultural research should now concentrate in actual replication of other major studies in the field.

GENERAL HYPOTHESES

The present study addresses itself to the two areas of difficulties, as formulated above.

1. It is an actual replication of Piaget's experiments on conservation of mass, weight and volume (see Piaget and Inhelder, 1941, and Elkind, 1961, in Sigel and Hooper, 1968).
2. It attempts to link conservation to specific experiences. These are the vital and survival activities, which are shared by all the members of a culture.

Urban-rural residence

Urban-rural differences are usually linked to European contacts. Greenfield (1966) found that rural subjects conserved earlier than urban subjects, while Lloyd (1971), found the contrary to be true and Price-Williams (1961) found no difference between the groups.

The Kamba people (from which the sample in the present study was taken) are traditionally small-scale agriculturalists. They provide ample opportunity for the children to watch and participate in adult activities such as weeding, harvesting, selling and buying of produce, and distribution of property such as food and livestock.

Urban children do not have this opportunity to the degree that rural children do because there are few gardens in towns and their parents are workers in factories or shops or are civil servants. Similarly, the introduction of dishes of the same shapes and sizes may influence urban children to pay more attention to perceptual appearance rather than to the initial distribution process.

While it is more likely that urban children will develop other concepts (such as those of geometrical shapes) earlier than rural children because of the familiarity and presence of such concepts in their environment, they would probably develop conservation of mass, weight, and volume later than rural children. These considerations lead to the following hypothesis.

Hypothesis 1

Rural children will give significantly more conserving responses than urban children.

Schooling/Nonschooling

Conservation studies in African cultures dealing with this variable have been very few, but they sometimes reported schooling as one of the principal factors influencing the development of conservation (Greenfield, 1966; Price-Williams, 1961; Lloyd, 1971; Laurendeau-Bendavid, in this volume). This is a very interesting finding because it raises at least two important questions:

1. What do schools provide for children that is missing in informal learning?
2. Are there some variables other than schooling which may be responsible for the high scores on conservation but which have been overlooked?

In response to the first question, the writer's experience with Western education in African settings is that it teaches language skills and rules for performance in examinations. Children in school have little time for the freedom needed for autoregulating experiences which, according to Piaget, are crucial in the development of conservation. Conversely, they are taught ready-made rules to deal with their environmental problems rather than learning them through acting on the environment. Kamii and Derman (Green, *et al*, 1971) reported a disadvantage of this type of schooling. Preoperational children were taught rules for conservation. When tested for conservation, they gave conserving responses, but when they were questioned further they reverted to answers typical of their preoperational development stage. Their answers were illogical and indicated illogical transfer of the concepts they had "learned."

In conclusion, then, it may be said that school children differ from nonschool children mainly in the extent to which they use formal rules.

In reference to question two, three points are in order. First, the quality of the conservation answers among school children may be questionable. Schools in most traditional African cultures have not yet related school life to community life. Children live an entirely different life in schools from their life in the community. Most of the skills and rules learned in schools are never really taken seriously and therefore, never used in real life except for school examinations. Children will clean their school uniforms but fail to clean their bedding and the clothing worn out of school. They are told to boil water before it is used for drinking purposes, but they may never do so. The argument here is that although school children seemingly give more conserving responses than nonschool children (see studies mentioned earlier) they may be using rules and guesswork.

The school subculture teaches children to give responses to every question, regardless of their correctness. This type of teaching encourages guessing on the part of the children.

Secondly, in African cultures (particularly among the Kamba of Kenya) to ask a child the question, Why? after he has made a statement means the statement is wrong and therefore it should be corrected. The child then changes his statement to a new one. This variable may be responsible for the low scores among the nonschool children in the studies mentioned earlier.

The third point to be made concerns the experimenter's rapport with children. The use of local assistant experimenters is risky because they may tell the experimenter what they think he/she wants to know. On the contrary, in learning the local language to conduct the interviewing, the experimenters run even greater risks. In most cases knowledge of local language is not a compensation for cultural and racial differences. Children perform their best when they have good rapport with and confidence in the experimenter. This is rarely the case in most cross-cultural studies in Africa (See Kamara and Easley in this volume).

Among the Kamba people of Kenya, schools deal with language skills and rules. The curriculum contains isolated facts which must be memorized for examinations but of limited use in the local community. While school children spend days in these kinds of experiences, the nonschool children spend theirs in activities related to their real life in the community. This leads to the following hypothesis.

Hypothesis 2

Unschooled children will give significantly more conserving responses than school children.

Sex Differences

Among the adult activities, cooking, sharing food, collecting firewood, and drawing of water are exclusively women's activities.

These are related to conservation of mass, volume, and weight. This leads to Hypothesis 3.

Hypothesis 3

Girls will give significantly more conserving responses than boys.

Type of Quantity and Age

In the original experiments of Piaget and Inhelder (1941) and Elkind (Sigel and Hooper, 1968) it was reported that conservation depends on the type of quantity and the level of age. This leads to Hypotheses 4, 5, and 6.

Hypothesis 4

The number of conserving responses will vary significantly with the type of quantity (mass, weight, and volume).

Hypothesis 5

The number of conserving responses will vary significantly with the age level.

Hypothesis 6

The number of conserving responses will vary significantly, with the type of quantity independent of the age level and with the age level independent of type of quantity.

METHOD

Subjects

One hundred and twenty (120) subjects were tested for this study, of which 60 were taken from a rural area and 60 from an urban area. Similarly, 60 were in school and 60 had never been to school. Subjects chosen were from 7 to 12 years old and those attending school were in grades one through six.

Population

Urban. The urban population from which the sample was taken was about 14,000. Most people worked in the town as laborers and a small number as civil servants. Running water and power were supplied to most residential areas surrounding the town.

Rural. People in the rural areas did not live in villages with houses near each other, each homestead was one to two miles away from the next. The total population of these isolated homes was 3,000. The main differences between urban and rural areas are given below. In the rural area life was characterized by subsistence farming, lack of running water and power, and insufficient public transportation. All rural people worked on their small farms. Children who did not go to school worked with their parents and sometimes served as messengers to the local shops to buy salt and sugar and sell eggs, chicken, fruits, and milk.

PROCEDURE

The subjects were divided into three age groups: 7–8 years old formed group 1; 9–10 year olds group 2; and 11–12 year olds group 3.

Subjects were interviewed individually in a quiet room provided by the headmasters in the two schools, with a table and three chairs.

Each subject was led into the room and asked to sit on a chair opposite the experimenter (E). The assistant experimenter (AE) sat at the corner of the table and recorded verbatim the subject's responses. Before another subject was asked to come in the room the E and AE compared their records to make sure they matched completely. Each subject was tested for conservation of mass (CM), conservation of weight (CW), and for conservation of volume (CV) in this order. A maximum of 45 minutes was taken by the slowest subjects to go through the three tasks.

Conservation of mass

Each subject was given two equal and three unequal balls made from wheat flour. (All subjects were very familiar with local bread of different shapes and sizes made from wheat flour.) Then S was asked to choose— from the five balls—any two that were the same. If S did not find any two balls equal, he was asked to make them equal by taking some pieces away from the larger ball and adding them to the smaller one. After he had ascertained the equality of any two balls the E proceeded in the following manner:

1. Suppose I make this ball here into a pancake, will there be the same amount to eat in the pancake as in that ball or not?
2. Now I am making this ball into a pancake [while the S looks on]. Is there the same amount to eat in the pancake as in the ball, or not?
3. Why do you think so?

Conservation of weight

Ss were asked to weigh two balls on the scale balance provided for them. When they were certain the balls weighed the same, the E asked the following questions:

1. Suppose I make this ball into a pancake; will the weight of the pancake be the same as the weight of this ball, or not?
2. Now I am making this ball into a pancake. Does it now weigh the same as your ball, or not?
3. Why do you think so?

Conservation of volume

Each S was presented with a glass jar filled with some water and asked these questions:

1. Suppose I put this ball into the water in the jar. Will it raise the water to the same point as your ball?
2. Now I am putting my ball into the water. Can you mark the water

level? I am making your ball into a pancake. If I put the pancake in the water will the water come up to the same level, or not?

3. Why do you think so?

ANALYSIS OF DATA

Scores for CM, CW, and CV were analyzed separately using a 4-way analysis of variance. Tests were performed using this design for the following main effects, and their interactions:

(a) Environment

(b) Schooling

(c) Sex

(d) Age level.

1. To test for horizontal *décalage* (the emergence of one type of conservation before another), a single factor experiment with repeated measures was run.

2. The Scheffe multiple comparison of means was carried out to determine differences between means for all conservation quantities.

3. A two-factor analysis of variance with repeated measures on factor A was performed to obtain joint effect of age and type of quantity.

RESULTS

Actual results showing exact number of subjects in each of the three developmental stages (non-conservation, transitional, and conservation) for each conservation task are shown in Table 2–1. For the purpose of detailed data analysis, scores for all subjects were collapsed into the three age groups shown in Table 2–1.

Each conservation task was analyzed separately, using a 4-way analysis of variance design giving comparisons between urban and rural; school vs. unschooled; male vs. female; and age group I vs. II vs. III—and their interactions. The summary of the results (Table 2–2.) showed insignificant differences between urban and rural subjects in CM (MS = 3.36 and 3.26) and CW (MS = 2.58 and 2.48) but a significant difference in their performance in CV in favor of urban subjects. Hypothesis 1 had predicted that rural subjects would score higher than urban subjects. In the light of these results, the hypothesis was rejected in favor of a statement that urban experiences seem to influence the development of conservation as much as rural experiences do.

Table 2–1
Number of subjects in non-conservation (NC) transitional (T), and conservation (C) stages for mass, weight, and volume at successive age groups

Conservation task	7–8 YEARS			Age Groups* 9–10 YEARS			11–12 YEARS		
	NC	T	C	NC	T	C	NC	T	C
Mass									
Pred. Q	11	1	28	3	0	37	0	0	40
Judg. Q	19	1	20	5	2	33	1	0	39
Weight									
Pred. Q	21	0	19	13	0	27	3	0	37
Judg. Q	26	2	12	16	1	23	7	1	32
Volume									
Pred. Q	27	1	12	19	1	20	10	2	28
Judg. Q	30	1	9	21	0	19	8	1	31

*N=40 in each age group.

Table 2–2
A summary showing the effects of environment (A) education (B), age (C), and sex (D) on the acquisition of conservation of mass, weight, and volume

Source	DF	Mass F	Weight F	Volume F
Subject	119			
A	1	0.2474	0.1457	4.6452*
B	1	0.0275	0.7935	0.1290
A vs B	1	2.2268	0.0648	8.9606**
C	2	19.9038**	17.0810**	15.9821**
A vs C	2	0.3299	0.4494	2.9355
D	1	0.1100	1.0364	0.0
A vs D	1	0.1100	1.3117	0.0573
B vs C	2	0.1100	0.3198	1.9677
A vs B vs C	2	3.9588*	1.0486	0.6487
B vs D	1	0.1100	0.7935	3.2258
A vs B vs D	1	0.1100	1.0364	0.1290
C vs D	2	1.1821	1.4615	1.7257
A vs C vs D	2	0.6873	1.9798	2.4122
B vs C vs D	2	1.6770	5.0567**	0.1398
A vs B vs C vs D	2	1.8419	0.1984	1.4301
Error				
A B C D	96			

**Sign. $P < 0.01$
*Sign. $P < 0.05$

Another look at the summaries indicated very insignificant differences between schooled and unschooled subjects in all three conservation tasks. This finding contradicts other studies reported earlier (Greenfield, 1966; Price-Williams, 1961; and Lloyd, 1971), whose results showed schooling as a principal factor in the development of conservation of quantities. It seems evident that schools do not do a better job in providing experiences necessary for conservation development than does informal education. Although the hypothesis must be rejected, that unschooled subjects will give significantly more conserving responses than school subjects, the results of this study show that the causal explanations must come from elsewhere.

The third hypothesis was that female subjects would give significantly more conserving responses than male subjects. Females scored higher than males in CM (MF = 3.40; Mm = 3.13) and exactly the same in CV (MF = 2.03) but slightly lower in CW (MF = 2.40; Mm = 2.66) but the summary showed insignificant difference between them. This finding of no differences in performances on conservation tasks between sexes confirms results obtained in European and non-European cultures.

A different design was used to test for Hypothesis 4, which dealt with horizontal *décalage* (or time lag) between the appearances of CM, CW and CV. A single factor analysis of variance with repeated measures was performed, treating the conservation tasks as the repeated measures. Examination of mean scores for mass, weight, and volume showed the mean score for mass (3.31) was much greater than the mean score for weight (2.53) and volume (2.03), but the mean score for weight was still. larger than the mean score for volume. The summary for this test showed highly significant differences between types of quantity (F = 31.37 p < .01) confirming Piaget's and Inhelder's (1941) original findings, and Elkind's replication study II in Sigel and Hooper, 1968).

A conclusion arrived at from the same studies by Piaget and Elkind was the concern of the fifth hypothesis of the present study: Conservation development was found to be related to the age levels of the subjects. In the present study two tests were performed to obtain main age effects. The 4-way analysis of variance (Table 2–2) gives F ratios which are all highly significant (p < .01).

The probability matrix for Scheffe multiple comparison of means was used to determine any differences between means. Results showed comparisons between means for conservation of mass (M_1 = 2.45; M_2 = 3.55; M_3 = 3.95).

Comparisons between Groups 1 and 2, and between 1 and 3 gave significant differences; but a comparison between Groups 2 and 3 gave a nonsignificant difference. This is what would be expected to happen, because Group 1 has not yet achieved conservation but Groups 2 and 3 have already achieved it.

Similar results for the conservation of weight were observed. The means for the three groups are significantly different ($M_1 = 1.60$; $M_2 = 2.54$; $M_3 = 3.48$). Examination of the raw data showed 22% conservers in Group 1, 50% conservers in group 2, and 77% conservers in group 3.

Comparison of means (1.10; 1.98; 2.03) for conservation of volume showed significant differences only between Groups 1 and 3 and between groups 2 and 3, confirming the expected results that only Group 3 had significantly approached the conservation criterion by having 67% conservers, as compared to 40% in Group 2 and only 12% in Group 1.

The last hypothesis to be tested stated that conserving responses will vary significantly with the type of quantity independent of the age level. In other words, it was predicted that all groups will score highest in mass and lowest in volume tasks, but the same scores will show significant differences between age groups. A two-factor analysis of variance with repeated measures was done on factor A and the results summarized.

The main effect of age was highly significant—($F = 32.8$; $F.99 = 4.79$)—as well as the quantity main effect—$F = 31.26$; $F.99 = 4.61$)—but the interaction was not significant.

GENERAL DISCUSSION

Elkind's "Piaget's Replication Study 2" (Sigel and Hooper, 1968), which was replicated in this study, gives average number of conservation responses for mass as 2.08, the average number given for weight as 1.75, and the average number for volume as 0.25—giving the same order of difficulty as the order that Piaget had observed. The present study obtained the following average numbers of conservation responses for the same quantities: mass 3.31, weight 2.53, and volume 2.03. The fact that the average scores for Kenyan children are higher than those tested by Elkind in the United States should not surprise anyone, since Elkind included 5- and 6-year-olds who for obvious reasons scored much less than the older children. It seems for Kenyan children that the *décalage* between conservation of weight and volume is not as distinctive as it is with the American children. This difference could be attributed to the environmental factors—the subsistence agricultural life that the Kenyan lead, with much practical and concrete use of materials, as opposed to the much more abstract and analytical thinking emphasized by Western education. Elkind confirmed Piaget's observation that other things being equal, conservation responses increased with age. An F for age level was

14.38 and was significant beyond the .01 level. In the present study an F for age level was observed to be 32.8 and significant beyond the .001 level.

Elkind's study showed that differences between age groups appeared as the effect of the type of quantity. It was reported that: (a) for mass, the 5–6 and the 7–11 year groups differed significantly: (b) for weight, the 5–8 and 9–11 year old groups differed significantly; and (c) for volume children 5–10 and the 11-year-old-groups differed significantly from each other in the number of conservation responses given.

In the present study, the use of Scheffe's multiple comparison of means showed that: (a) for mass, the 7–8 and 9–12 groups differed significantly; (b) for weight the 7–8, the 9–10, and the 11–12 groups differed significantly, and (c) for volume, the 7–10 and the 11–12 groups differed significantly from each other in the number of conservation responses given.

Elkind converted the results of his study into percentages for comparison with Piaget's criterion of 75%.

The results of the present study were also converted into percentages for comparison with Elkind's results. Percentages are given in Table 2–4 below. Observation of Elkind's table (Table 2–3) shows that for mass, the 75% criterion was reached at age 9 (86%); for weight it was reached at age 10 (89%), and for volume it was not achieved at age 11 (25%). Similar results are shown for the present study in Table 2–4: mass at age 9 (85%), weight at age 10 (77%); and for volume—seemingly earlier than Elkind had found—at age 12 (82%). In conclusion, the present study, like Elkind's, confirms Piaget's assignment of the conservation of mass to ages 7–8; the conservation of weight to ages 9–10; and the conservation of volume to ages 11–12.

Table 2–3
Elkind's Study **(Sigel et al. 1968, p. 16–17)**
**Percent* of conservation responses for mass,
weight, and volume of successive age levels.
(N = 25 at each age level)**

TYPE OF QUANTITY	AGE LEVEL						
	5	6	7	8	9	10	11
Mass	19	51	70	72	86	94	92
Weight	21	52	51	44	73	89	78
Volume	0	4	0	4	4	19	25

*of 75 possible responses

Table 2-4
Percent* of conservation responses for mass, weight, and volume at successive age levels.
(N = 20 at each age level)

TYPE OF QUANTITY	AGE LEVEL					
	7	8	9	10	11	12
Mass	47	65	85	90	97	100
Weight	40	35	47	77	82	92
Volume	30	22	42	57	67	82

*of 40 possible responses

The Justification Question

American Children

Children's explanations in Elkind's study were categorized in the following manner:

(a) Romancing: "It's more because my uncle said so."
(b) Perceptual: "It's more because it's longer [thinner, thicker, wider narrower, etc.]"
(c) Specific: "You did not add any or take any away." (identity)
"You can roll it back into a ball and it will be the same." (reversibility)
"The hot dog is longer but thinner, so it's the same" (compensation)
(d) General: "It's the same because no matter what shape you make it into that won't change the amount."

Categories (a) and (b) were found to be given by nonconserving children. Elkind reported that romancing and perceptual explanations first increased and then leveled off with age.

Kenyan Children

Explanations given by Kenyan children fitted into three of the four categories given by Elkind, but Kenyan children showed the same patterns in their explanations as reported for the American children.

Perceptual explanations decreased with age, while specific explanations increased with age. Not a single Kenyan child gave a general explanation as defined by Elkind and used in the present experiment. Romancing explanations—"It's the same because my uncle said so"—and "magical explanations" (used by Greenfield, 1966, p. 239)—"It's the same because you have poured or deformed it"—were not many among Kenyan children. There were only eight magical explanations and no romancing explanations. The Greenfield study mentioned above reported that Wolof children achieved conservation through identity rather than reversibility. In the present study only one reversibility explanation was recorded ("You can roll it back into a ball"). All conserving explanations involved the previous identity or equality of the two balls. ("The two balls were equal before; therefore the pancake is the same as the ball") This finding was reported among Wolof children too. ("This and that were equal.") Although perceptual explanations can be used to indicate both nonconservation and conservation explanations, all perceptual explanations given by Kenyan children showed nonconservation.

Greenfield had also found the same thing among the Wolof children. This phenomenon occurs when children pay attention to one instead of two or three dimensions ("The pancake is wider" rather than "The pancake is wider but narrower").

PROBLEMS SPECIFIC TO THE PRESENT STUDY

Conservation of Mass

Table 2–2 shows significant interactions between environment, schooling and age level ($P < .05$). Figures 2–1, 2–2, and 2–3 show these interactions graphically. Figure 2–1 shows clearly that the significant interactions are found only between subjects in the 7–8 group. Schooling seems to be detrimental to urban children in the first age group (7–8). The point has already been made that schooling of the Western type emphasizes analytical perception, which may lead school children to give more perceptual responses—which are in most cases nonconserving. This is more true when the differences between the groups exist only in the nonconserving groups, as they do in this study. The writer's explanation for this phenomenon goes back to the first paragraph of the general hypothesis for this study, in which it was argued that daily experiences in vital activities are responsible for the development of conservation. The unschooled urban children have ample time to go through these experiences, while the school children have limited time to do so. Rural school children help with home activities more often than do urban children. For some urban school children, certain activities are performed by servants; the urban children may lack time to do them (most of their time is given to school work) and they may also refuse to participate in the activities (such as sharing food, drawing water, collecting firewood, or watching adults playing games). Again, some of these activities are no longer necessary in the urban areas, such as drawing water and collecting firewood, most urban homes now have their water and power supplied.

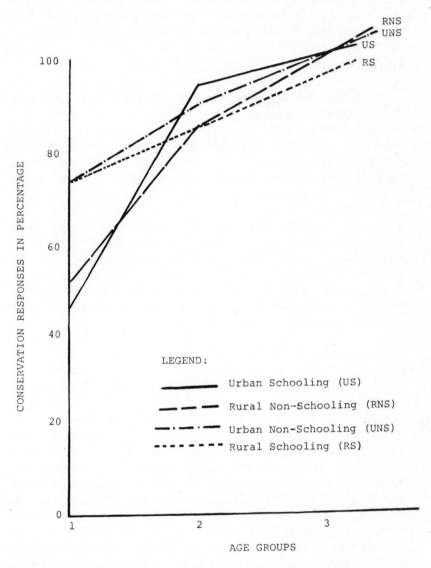

Figure 2–1. 4-way analysis of variance: Summary showing environment vs. schooling interactions on mass

Although schooling may teach children how to think analytically, rural children are more often confronted with reality as they go through concrete experiences in different environments doing their daily work; and therefore they are less likely to give perceptual and nonconservation explanations.

Conservation of Weight

Experiences with weight are rare among the Kamba children because they are related to selling and buying, which go on at the market places rather than at home. In this study, significant differences occurred between female and male subjects and between schooled and unschooled children in conservation responses given for weight (See Figure 2–2).

These differences are difficult to explain, but it is possible that schooled girls conserve weight earlier than unschooled girls because of the practice they receive in weighing articles in school. At the ages 9–10, unschooled girls do not go to the markets alone as boys do, and this may be the explanation as to why unschooled boys did better than schooled girls. On the other hand, schoolboys are separated from girls during handicraft periods and do outdoor work such as brickwork, ropemaking and carpentry, while girls spend their periods in doing housework, which involves weight practice among other activities. This may explain why schoolboys scored more poorly than school girls.

Conservation of Volume

As for the differences in conservation scores for volume, they are found only between urban and rural school children (Figure 2–3). Since the nonschooled urban and rural children showed nonsignifcant differences, it could be that differences in schooling were responsible for the occurrence of significant differences observed between the two groups.

It has been pointed out above that children will develop those concepts which are useful and meaningful earlier than those concepts which are unfamiliar and of no practical use in their lives. Accordingly, it seems that schooling introduces new and unfamiliar concepts and formal rules which interfere with rural children and slow their development of conservation. This interference may not be wholly cognitive, but it may be concrete in the respect that the rural school children find little time to continue experiencing activities as the unschooled children do. The question then is, What happened to urban school children who did so well in comparison with rural school children? Experiences with water seem to be related to conservation of volume. Both schooled and unschooled urban children have plenty of water in or outside their houses. They have the same chances

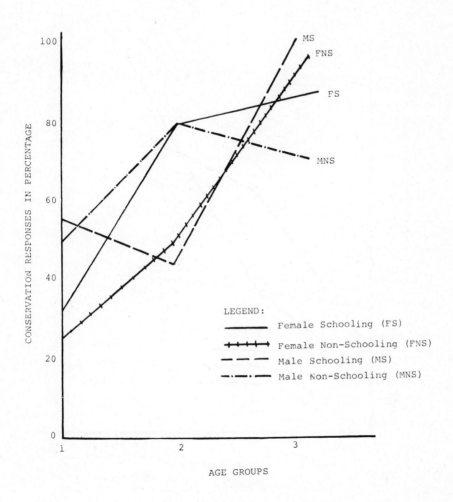

Figure 2–2. 4-way analysis of variance: Summary showing sex vs. schooling interactions on weight

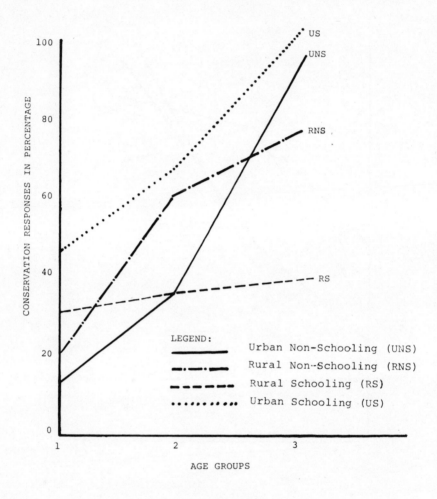

Figure 2–3. 4-way analysis of variance: Summary showing school vs. environment interactions on volume

of learning the concept of conservation of volume. In this case, school experiences must be responsible for the differences, since the syllabus recommends practices in capacity. This brings the problem of why school experiences should enhance conservation of volume in urban children, and fail to do the same in rural children.

The only reason that seems obvious here is that of differences in teaching and in carrying out the recommended exercises in volume and capacity.

Rationale for Leaving Out Justification Question

Conservation studies have repeatedly contended that children's explanations for their answers are crucial in the assessment of the concept of conservation. A number of researchers (Lloyd, 1971; and Smedslund and Dasen, personal communications) have reported some concern about the use of language to determine the presence or absence of conservation. If the child can predict the outcome of deformation before it is carried out, and judge the outcome correctly and consistently in the presence of perceptual inequality, then this may be a sufficient indication of the presence of conservation.

Patterns of responding to the justification question categorize children in the following manner:

(a) Those who give no explanation (NJ).

(b) Those who give inadequate explanations to allow Es to assess conservation.

(c) Those who give adequate explanations and are either classified as conservers or nonconservers.

Children in categories (a) and (b) are usually assigned no points. This seems to be an inadequacy in Es rather than in the children, indicating that Es have failed to design an adequate instrument for measuring the children's concrete operations.

The present study used the following three criteria to measure conservation:

(a) Prediction question (P)
(b) Judgment question (J), and
(c) Justification question (JF).

All children were classified as follows:
1. Those who explained at least one response (80 children).
2. Those who did not explain any of their responses (40 children).

The question that had to be answered at this point was: Were justifiers better than NJ in their performances for P and J tasks (PJ)?

To answer this question, the following analysis was done. Of the 80 justifiers, 52, 42, and 32 children conserved mass, weight, and volume, respectively, and 34, 18, and 17 of the 40 NJ were conservers in the same tasks, respectively, when conservation was measured by PJ criterion.

The mean score for justifiers in PJ was 52 in all three conservation tasks, as compared to 57 for NJ. Up to this point justifiers were not significantly different from NJ in their discovery of conservation when the PJ criterion was the only measure of conservation. Further analysis showed that of the 80 justifiers, 50, 61, and 74, respectively, justified mass, weight and volume. A comparison was made between conservation responses for PJ and PJJ (prediction, judgment, and justification tasks) in percentages. It was found that 62% of all justifiers for mass were conservers when PJJ criterion was used, as compared to 65% conservers when PJ criterion was used alone. The percentages of conservers in weight and volume were 52 and 54, and 40 and 35 for PJ and PJJ respectively. Again the mean score for PJJ was 50 as compared to 52 for PJ.

In conclusion, since the performance for justifiers in PJJ did not differ significantly from their performances in PJ, and since this performance did not differ significantly from the performances of NJ in PJ, and furthermore, since Es have failed to agree on the use of verbal explanation for the discovery of conservation in cross-cultural studies, it was felt that inclusion of the PJJ criterion for conservation had the disadvantage of reducing the total number of subjects by at least one third.

Conversely, using the PJ criterion only did not change the quality of conservation, but it permitted the inclusion of all subjects in the final data analysis. Thus the PJJ criterion was dropped out and PJ was used as a sufficient criterion for the discovery of conservation.

An important point must be made at this stage about the qualitative aspects of this study. Firstly, for those researchers interested in theory building, these results are in order, but for those whose main interest is individual variations, the results are of little interest until further information is given. The individuals in this study are more real than the abstracted group averages.

This statement can hardly be overemphasized in the present study—in which 21 children out of the total of 120 reversed the order of conservation difficulty. Ten children conserved weight before mass, 11 conserved volume before weight, 5 conserved volume before mass, and 2 conserved volume before weight and mass. While conservation of mass was reported to be the easiest in this study, for these children it appears to be most difficult. These individual variations must be taken into account and kept in mind when abstracted average statements are made. Quantitatively, therefore, this study confirmed Piaget's three stages in the development of conservation: (a) non-conservation, (b) transitional, and (c) conservation. Similarly, Lovell and Ogilvie's (1960) finding of "no clear-cut borders between age stages" was strengthened by the results in this study. While there were differences between age groups, it was not possible to predict individual performances according to subject's age, because in some cases young children who were not expected to conserve some quantities *did* conserve, and older ones who were expected to conserve *failed* to conserve. However, this phenomenon has also been reported in conservation studies in the European culture (Fogelman, 1970; Hallam, 1969). This discussion can be ended with an agreement with Roll's (1970) statement that there are more similarities than differences between Kenyan and European children's performances in conservation tasks.

IMPLICATIONS OF THIS STUDY

Specific Implications

1. The first implication is that schools up to the time of this study had not been beneficial to children's cognitive growth and therefore some improvement in content or method of teaching should be effected.

2. Children studied here can benefit from Piagetian diagnostic tests and from Piagetian-oriented curricula which have met with success among European children.

3. Individual (or self-regulatory) experiences account for vast variations found among groups, and among individuals,—although other factors cannot be left out, such as the subject's personality, the experimenter's bias, and familiarity with test materials. It must be at least one of these factors that accounts for Heron and Simonsson's (1969) conclusion that Zambian children reach 55% to 60% after 11 years and then level off— which is obviously contradictory to the findings obtained for conservation of weight in this study.

4 More research is needed—which should include a larger number of subjects, drawn from the same environments but extended to wider areas— before findings of the present study can be taken as factual and real. There has been a tendency for researchers to study one or two of the many tribes in one of the African countries and end up talking about "the African child," as if the Wolof's thinking structure must be the same as the thinking structure of the Zulu child. The results reported in this study should be

generalized to other subjects whose descriptions are the same as the ones in the present study.

Implications for Education

A confirmation of the results of this study would imply changes in curriculum content and teaching methodology, because schools have not measured up to their expectation. Lavatelli (1970) has shown that schools can raise the level of equilibration (self-activity) in children by providing a free choice of activity. She also feels that since early school curricula include classification, number and space, and seriating activities, all teachers should be made aware of the separate thought processes involved in each area, and the order in which they emerge. She continues:

"Awareness of how structures grow will provide guidelines for the teachers in choosing materials and in knowing what to say to children as they use materials." (p. 46)

The results of this study, as of studies in the European cultures, call for a curriculum content that considers the child's developmental status in each concept. In other words, Piagetian tasks should play a large part in schools as diagnostic tests for children's cognitive status to determine grade placement, subject readiness, and remedial instructional programs.

While Piagetian tasks have not correlated significantly with children's performances in school, Carpenter and Lunzer (1955), Feigenbaum (1963) and Bozarth (1968) have reported high correlations between IQ and conservation tasks. Almy *et al.* (1966) noted: "In general, children who are able to conserve at an early age do better in other tests related to mental ability and to beginning reading and arithmetic." (p. 84). Further on Almy reported: "While correlations between progress in conservation and other measures of mental aptitude and school achievement were only moderately high, they were substantial enough and consistent enough to warrant further investigation of conservation." (p. 108)

The point to be emphasized here is that Piagetian tests should not replace other traditional diagnostic tests but should be used along with them. The reason for this emphasis stems from the fact that in some traditional mental tests such as the Stanford-Binet the maximum intercorrelation of one item with all other items has a medium value of .66, with 90% between .45 and .85. Piagetian tests have shown very low intercorrelation of one test with all others except tests on clay and water-pouring, which had a correlation of .66 (Tuddenham, 1971). While these low correlations may be partly due to error, they imply specificity of the measured abilities and therefore these tests may be capable of measuring some cognitive structures that the Stanford-Binet, for instance would not be able to detect.

SUMMARY

The study investigated the effects of schooling, urbanization, and sex on the discovery of conservation of mass, weight, and volume in Kamba children in Kenya.

One hundred and twenty subjects were tested, of whom 60 were chosen from an urban town and 60 from a rural community, 60 miles apart. Both town and rural groups were matched in age, sex, and number of years (from 0 to 6) spent in school. Subjects ranged from 7 to 12 years of age. All subjects were tested individually by the author and an assistant in a quiet room, using the traditional Piagetian tasks for the conservation of mass, weight, and volume.

A detailed analysis of the data indicated no significant differences between: (a) urban and rural, (b) schooling and nonschooling, and (c) male and female subjects in total scores on conservation tasks. Conversely, significant differences were shown to exist between age groups, and between types of conservation tasks. The differences between age groups were similar to those reported from same age groups in European conservation studies. Similarly, the trend of horizontal *décalage* in the present study agrees with that reported in Genevan conservation studies.

The use of verbal explanation as a sufficient criterion for measuring conservation has been questioned, especially in cross-cultural studies. It has been suggested that nonverbal criteria should be designed for assessing conservation. An alternative to verbal explanation as a criterion for conservation has been advanced, namely, the use of the prediction and judgment tasks, because they do not discriminate against subjects who have inadequate language development.

In conclusion, results indicated that Kamba children discovered conservation sequentially and in accordance with Piaget's theory of cognitive development.

REFERENCES

Almy, M., Chittenden, E. and Miller, P. (1966) *Young children's thinking.* New York: Teachers College Press, Columbia University.

Bozarth, J. O. (1968) *The ability to conserve quantity of liquid and its relationship to socioeconomic background and achievement among selected fourth grade pupils.* Tucson: University of Arizona.

Bruner, J. et al (1966) *Studies in cognitive growth.* New York: Wiley.

Carpenter, T. E. and Lunzer, E. A. (1955) A pilot study for quantitative investigation of Jean Piaget's original work on concept formation. *Educational Review, 7,* 142–149.

Ciborowski, T. and Cole, M. (1971) Cultural differences in learning conceptual rules. *International Journal of Psychology, 6* (1), 25–37.

Dasen, P. R. (1972) Cross-cultural Piagetian research: A summary. *Journal of cross-cultural psychology, 3* (1), 23–39.

Dempsey, D. A. (1971) Time conservation across cultures. *International Journal of Psychology, 6* (2), 115–120.

Feigenbaum, K. D. (1963) An evaluation of Piaget's study of the child's development of the concepts of conservation of discontinuous quantities. In Flavell, H. J., *The developmental psychology of Jean Piaget.* New York: Van Nostrand.

Fogelman, R. K. (1970) *Piagetian tests for the primary school.* London: National Foundation of Educational Research in England and Wales.

Furby, L. (1971) A theoretical analysis of cross-cultural research in cognitive development: Piaget's conservation task. *Journal of cross-cultural psychology, 2,* 241–255.

Goodnow, J. J. and Bethon, G. (1966) Piaget's tasks: The effects of schooling and intelligence. *Child Development, 37,* 573–583.

Green, R. D. et al. (1971) *Piaget and measurement.* Montreal: McGraw-Hill.

Greenfield, P. M. (1966) On culture and conservation. In Bruner, J. et al., *Studies in cognitive growth.* New York: Wiley.

Hallam, R. (1969) Piaget and the teaching of history. *Educational Research, 12* (1), 3–12.

Heron, A. and Simonsson, M. (1969) Weight conservation in Zambian children. A non-verbal approach. *International Journal of psychology, 4,* 281–292.

Lavatelli, S. C. (1970) *Piaget's theory applied to an early childhood curriculum.* Boston: A Center for Media Development Inc.

Lloyd, B. B. (1971) Studies of conservation with Yoruba children of differing ages and experience. *Child Development, 42,* 415–428.

Lovell, K. and Ogilvie, E. (1960) A study of the conservation of substance in the junior school child. *British Journal of Education Psychology, 30,* 109–118. (Also reprinted in Sigel and Hooper, 1968.)

Piaget, J. (1952) *The child's conception of number.* New York: Humanities.

Piaget, J. and Inhelder, B. (1941) *Le développement des quantités chez l'enfant.* Neuchâtel: Delachaux et Niestlé.

Price-Williams, D. R. (1961) A study concerning concepts of conservation of quantities among primitive children. *Acta Psychologica, 18* (4), 297–305.

Ripple, E. R. (1964) American cognitive studies: A review. In Ripple, E. R. and Rockcastle, N. V. (Eds.) *Piaget rediscovered. A report of the conference on cognitive studies and curriculum development.* New York: Random House.

Roll, S. (1970) Conservation of number: A comparison between cultures. *Revista interamericana de psicologia, 4* (1):13–18.

Sigel, I. E. and Hooper, H. F. (1968) *Logical thinking in children: Research based on Piaget's theory.* New York: Holt, Rinehart and Winston.

Tuddenham, R. D. (1971) Theoretical regularities and individual idiosyncrasies. In Green, R. D. et al., *Measurement and Piaget.* Montreal: McGraw-Hill.

3
Concept Development in Thai Urban and Rural Children[1]

SYLVIA OPPER

I. INTRODUCTION

During the past decade or so a considerable amount of research has been carried out in different cultures with a view to ascertaining the universality of some aspects of Piaget's theory of intellectual development in children. For the most part the focus of such research has been on questions pertaining to the sequence of the stages of development. Dasen (1972) in his summary of cross-cultural Piagetian research has reported on recent studies, making the important distinction between the four major stages of intellectual development (sensorimotor, preoperational, concrete operational, formal operational) and the sequence of substages found in the development of any particular concept. The latter problem has been investigated by the majority of cross-cultural Piagetian researchers, with the concepts of the concrete operational period being the most popular ones for study. The major objective of such studies was to investigate the sequence of substages and to determine the age of acquisition of a particular concept, or concepts, in the selected culture. Thus considerable attention has been paid to the rate of development of the various concepts.

A further question, on which less work has been done, is that of the optimum level of development in a given culture or society. In other words, do certain groups of persons, considered as a whole, fail to attain one of the major stages of development, and in particular, that of formal operations? Another question that may be raised is what type of mental operations can be subsumed in the different substages. Is it indeed the case, for example, that children not only achieve conservation of liquids at a certain stage of their development, but also use the same types of arguments to support their judgments of conservation, or of non-conservation? If this were found to be the case in a number of different cultures, such a finding would indicate that similar underlying mental structures seem to exist in different societies, and this in turn might suggest the existence of universals in some aspects of intellectual development.

In general, cross-cultural research does tend to support the universality of the sequence of substages in the development of a number of concepts (Vernon, Goodnow, Goodnow and Bethon, Greenfield, Boonsong, de Lemos). One case of a minor and temporary deviation from the overall pattern has been reported (Bovet), in which an initial acquisition of the conservation of liquids was followed by a stage of non-conservation and then by acquisition of the concept some two or three years later. By and large, however, it seems as if some general laws governing the sequence of development for certain aspects of intelligence might be at work in a variety of differing cultures.

There are a number of problems in comparing cross-cultural findings and conclusions which are due to the fact that the various researchers have tended to investigate different concepts and in all likelihood have used different methods of questioning, adopting to a greater or lesser extent the flexible and openended characteristics of the Piagetian "clinical method."

One point made clear by the studies done so far is that the Piagetian tasks seem to be differentially influenced by the various settings. Some of them appear to be fairly insensitive to varying environmental conditions, and similar results are found in a number of different sample populations. For others this does not appear to be the case. Cross-cultural research seems to provide evidence of inconsistencies between the Swiss findings and the results obtained elsewhere. There seems to be no overall lag or retardation noted across all tasks in the different cultures. Rather, it would appear that the results of some tasks follow the Swiss pattern fairly closely, whereas this is not the case with others. Examples of closeness of fit would be the tasks of conservation of solids and weight. Others, like the conservation of length, seem to show greater variability in their results.

The aim of the present research was to investigate the developmental sequence of substages for seven concrete operational tasks, and to identify the types of reasoning used by the children in these tasks, in two samples of children (urban and rural) in Thailand.

II. METHOD AND EXPERIMENTAL PROCEDURES

1. Subjects

Two samples of children, one from the urban capital of Bangkok and the other from the rural district of Bang Pa In, were used as subjects. Each sample was equally divided by sex and included children ranging from 6 to 11 years of age. There were 50 children in the urban sample and 54 children in the rural. The number of children interviewed by age is given in Table 3–1. The characteristics of the two samples were the following:

Table 3–1
Number of children interviewed, by age

AGE	M		F		TOTAL	
	U	R	U	R	U	R
6 Years	5	5	4	5	9	10
7 Years	5	5	6	5	11	10
8 Years	5	5	7	5	12	10
9 Years	5	5	4	5	9	10
10 Years	4	4	2	4	6	8
11 Years	2	3	1	3	3	6
Total	26	27	24	27	50	54

U = Urban   M = Male
R = Rural   F = Female

(a) *Urban* (Bangkok): The children were taken from the demonstration primary school of Bangkok's Prasarnmitr College of Education. Entrance into this demonstration school is very much sought after, and the pupils for the most part come from Thai middle-class and upper middle-class backgrounds, with the parents having generally completed at least secondary school, and very frequently having also completed courses at a teacher-training college or a university. The criteria· of selection of the children for this sample were age, average performance in school as determined by teacher's judgments, and equal distribution of sexes. Bangkok, the capital of Thailand, has a population of over 3 million people, including several thousand foreigners. It is a large city with modern conveniences, and the life of the children of this sample, from the material point of view, would be similar to that of middle-class children in most other large cities of the world.

(b) *Rural* (Bang Pa In): The children were taken from two schools: Wat Chum Pon primary school, covering children from 6 to 10 years, and Bang Pa In advanced primary school, for the children of 11 years. The criteria for selection of the children for this sample were age, average performance in school as determined by teacher's judgments, equal distribution of sexes, and having one (or both) parents engaged in rice farming. Bang Pa In is a typical rural district of the Central Plain rice-growing area of Thailand, and is located some 60 miles north of Bangkok. The language spoken here, as in the above sample, is central Thai, which is the main dialect of the country and the one taught in all schools throughout the country. Although some modern conveniences such as electricity, television, and radio are available, they are generally restricted to the homes of the more affluent members of the community, and the home of the typical peasant child of this sample would be fairly primitive from this point of view.

In summary, the two main samples selected for the research differ essentially in two main dimensions, the one being not entirely independent of the other. On the one hand, they form an urban-rural dichotomy, with all that this implies in differences of environment. On the other, the occupational status of the parents can for the most part be said to consist of middle-class government officials or professionals for the urban sample, and of rice farmers for the rural sample. In other respects, such as age, sex, and average school performance within the framework of a particular group, the samples were similar.

2. Procedures and Tasks

A total of seven Piagetian tasks were given, covering the mental operations of the concrete operational stage.

Partial control for order effects of the tasks was carried out by randomly assigning each child to one of four predetermined orders of presentation, and maintaining this order for each child until he had completed all the tasks. The orders were arranged so that tasks of a similar nature, e.g. conservation of length, using two sticks and several sticks, were separated and were never presented in a single interviewing session. The tasks were: class inclusion—flowers and animals; conservation of length—two sticks and several sticks; conservation of liquids; one-to-one correspondence; and seriation. The procedure for these tasks is given briefly below. A detailed description of the standardized techniques, as well as *in extenso* recording sheets for each concept are reported elsewhere (Opper).

Class Inclusion—Flowers (Piaget, 1952)

The child is presented with a bunch of two kinds of flowers: roses and lotuses (or hibiscus in the case of the urban children). He is then asked a series of questions concerning the relation between roses and flowers (more, less, etc). The purpose is to determine whether the child understands the inclusion system of flowers, whereby roses and lotuses are conceived of as being two subclasses of the same general class—flowers.

Class Inclusion—Animals (Inhelder and Piaget, 1964)

The child is presented with a pile of cards showing pictures of various animals (parrots, birds, water buffalos). He must sort them into different piles and is then asked questions of class inclusion concerning the relations between the subclasses and class of animals (more, less, etc.) The purpose is to determine whether the child understands the relations of subclasses to overall classes in the class inclusion system of animals.

In other words, does the child realize that while all birds are animals, all animals are not necessarily birds, or that while all parrots are birds, not all birds are parrots.

Conservation of Length—Two Sticks (Piaget, Inhelder, and Szeminska, 1960)

The child is presented with two identical sticks, six inches in length, one placed directly underneath the other, and lying horizontal. After he admits to the equality of length, the sticks are moved into various positions where they are no longer exactly underneath each other, and the child is questioned to determine whether he still admits to the equality of length, despite the overlap at the end of the sticks.

Conservation of Length—Several Sticks (Piaget, Inhelder, and Szeminska, 1960)

The child is presented with one stick six inches in length and four sticks each $1\frac{1}{2}$ inches in length, placed end to end so that the four sticks are laid directly underneath the larger one in a horizontal position and with both ends of both sticks coinciding. After the child has admitted to their equality in length, the small sticks are moved into various positions, e.g., in the shape of a W, and the child is questioned to determine whether he still admits to the equality in length between the one long stick and the four short ones.

Conservation of Liquid (Piaget, 1952)

The child is presented with two identical glasses and must pour equal quantities of liquid into each glass. After he admits to the equality of the liquid, one glass is poured consecutively into a longer but thinner glass, a shorter but fatter glass, and four smaller glasses, with a return to the original situation between each pouring of the liquid.

In each situation the child is questioned to determine whether he maintains the equality of the amount of liquid, despite the change of shape and level resulting from the pouring into different containers.

One-to-One Correspondence (Piaget, 1952)

The child is presented with a row of miniature baskets, and he must lay out an equal number of small pineapples (or cars) in a one-to-one correspondence. After the child admits to the equality in number of the two sets, the experimenter bunches up one row of objects. He then tries to determine whether the child still maintains the equality in number of the objects in the two rows. After a return to the original position, the second row is bunched up and the same procedure followed.

Seriation (Piaget, 1952)

The child is presented with a series of 10 small sticks increasing in size from two to six inches. After being shown a model built by the experimenter, which is then removed, the child must construct a seriation (staircase) with the sticks. When he completes this, a second series of sticks ranging from $2\frac{1}{2}$ to 6 inches in length is handed to the child in random order and he must insert the extra sticks correctly, while still maintaining a graded seriation.

All the tasks were pretested and the necessary modifications made to the material and language, prior to the actual interviewing. They were administered by means of a partially standardized version of the clinical method, whereby a portion of each task was fixed, and a further portion left open-ended to allow the experimenter the opportunity to follow other lines of approach, should this be felt necessary in cases where there appeared to be a lack of communication or of understanding on the part of the child.

Each child was interviewed individually, with the number of tasks given in any one session depending upon the age and attention span of each child. In general, the younger the child, the longer it took to administer a task, and hence the greater the total number of sessions required to complete all tasks. No child was kept for more than half an hour at a time, and the interval between each interview session for a particular child was usually one week.

The interviews were given in Thai by two female graduates in educational psychology from Chulalongkorn University of Bangkok.

Before the actual data collection they underwent a course of training that included an introduction to Piaget's theoretical work and considerable acquaintance with the practical application of the clinical method, in the roles of both interviewer and recorder. Throughout the entire period of data collection, close supervision was maintained by the researcher, who also spoke Thai but did not question the children herself.

Scoring

Each task was analyzed separately and the subjects were categorized into one of three developmental substages for each concept: stage 1—clearly no acquisition of the concept or random responses; stage 2—transitional with the beginnings of the concept in some situations only, or insufficient evidence of adequate explanation; stage 3—clear acquisition of the concept, usually accompanied by adequate logical explanations.

In addition to categorizing each subject into a stage of development for a task, the various responses of the children for each item of the tasks were scored for the different types of reasoning used, regardless of the number of times any given type may have been used in the course of the interview. The types of reasoning varied from task to task, and are described in more detail in the section analyzing each separate task. Reliability of coding was obtained by using a second scorer for 20% of the subjects for each task, and comparing the coding of the two scorers.

Reliability was calculated for both the stages and the types of reasoning for each task. An overall average of these different reliability codings for the seven tasks is 96.5%. Since inspection of the data indicated no sex differences in the two samples, the results for both sexes were combined for the various comparisons.

III. ANALYSIS OF DATA

1. Individual tasks

A. Class Inclusion—Flowers

The class inclusion-flowers task was given to 50 urban and 54 rural children. Reliability between the two coders was 100% for the stages, and 95% for the types of reasoning.

(i) Stages

The criteria for categorization into the stages were the following:

Table 3–2
Class inclusion—flowers:
Number of children by stages (percentages in parentheses)*

AGE	N		Stages 1		2		3	
	U	R	U	R	U	R	U	R
6	9	10	6(67)	10(100)	3(33)	—	—	—
7	11	10	4(36)	7(70)	5(45)	3(30)	2(18)	—
8	12	10	2(16)	10(100)	2(16)	—	8(67)	—
9	9	10	2(22)	6(60)	2(22)	3(30)	5(56)	1(10)
10	6	8	1(17)	6(75)	—	1(12)	5(83)	1(12)
11	3	6	—	—	—	2(33)	3(100)	4(67)
Total	50	54	15(30)	39(73)	12(24)	9(16)	23(46)	6(11)

*In all successive tables the figures in parentheses refer to percentages unless otherwise specified

Stage 1: No understanding of inclusion relations. Comparison between discreet subclasses (roses versus lotus), or horizontal comparisons.

Stage 2: Beginning of a framework for inclusion. Some vertical comparisons between subclasses and class, but yet fully articulate. Understanding of inclusion in some situations, but not yet generalized to all.

Stage 3: Correct comparison between subclass and class, or vertical comparisons. Inclusion relations in all situations. The distribution of these children by stages is shown in Table 3–2.

A chi-square comparison (McNemar) between the samples for separate ages shows a significant difference only at 8 years, although the overall distribution between the three stages for all ages combined is significant. This latter finding is probably due to the larger proportion of Stage 3 urban children and of Stage 1 rural children. The 50% criterion of achievement of the concept[2] is reached by the urban sample at 8 years and by the rural sample at 11 years.

(ii) *Types of Reasoning*

A further coding was done for all the responses for the individual items of the task. The system of coding differed from the stages, described above, in which a child was categorized into a single stage. In this analysis the child was coded once for each type of reasoning used. If a child repeatedly used the same type of argument throughout the entire task, only one coding was made. If, on the other hand, a child produced several types of reasoning, he was coded once for each type.

The types of responses found in both samples were the following:

1. *Subjective reasons* (e.g. "I like flowers (or roses)"; "I have already seen them"; etc.)

2. *Reference to characteristics of flowers* (e.g., size, smell, color, etc.)

3. *Naturalistic reasons* (e.g. "They grow"; "people plant them"; etc.)

4. *Tautology* (Answer reproduces the question in slightly different form.) E.g., "Why are there more?" "Because they are more plentiful," or "Because the others are less." Etc.)

5. *Implicit or explicit reference to number or amount of flowers in nonrelational terms*, i.e. with no comparison between subclasses ("Plant is covered with blossoms"; "Flowers are all over the world"; etc.)

6. *Implicit or explicit references to number or amount in relational terms, but only horizontal comparisons between subclasses* (e.g. "More roses"; "More lotuses"; etc.)

7. *Explicit class inclusion with vertical comparisons* (e.g., "Roses are flowers too"; "Roses is a specific name"; etc.)

Inspection of the data shows that the distribution of Types 1 to 5 is similar in both samples, and not used by more than 20% of the children of each sample. Significant differences are found in only two types of responses: Type 6 predominates in the rural sample, while Type 7 responses predominate in the urban one. This may be a reflection of the greater proportion of urban children having achieved the concept when compared with the rural group (46% as against 11%):

To summarize the results on this task, the main differences between the two groups are that the urban children achieve the concept at 8 years and the rural sample at 11 years, thus indicating a slower rate of development on the part of the latter group. Significant differences are found in the overall distribution amongst the three stages and for reasoning Types 6 and 7 (horizontal and vertical comparisons). Both these differences seem to be a reflection of the rural sample's slower pace of development.

B. Class Inclusion—Animals

A second class inclusion task was given to 51 urban and 54 rural children. Reliability between the two coders was 100% for the stages and 92% for the types of reasoning.

(i) Stages:

The criteria for categorization into stages were similar to those for the flowers task, taking into account the different content of animals as against flowers.

The distribution of the urban and rural children by stages is shown in Table 3–3.

Table 3–3
Class inclusion—animals:
number of children by stages

AGE	N		Stages 1		2		3	
	U	R	U	R	U	R	U	R
6	9	10	7(77)	10(100)	1(11)	—	1(11)	—
7	11	10	5(45)	9(90)	5(45)	—	1(10)	1(10)
8	12	10	1(8)	8(80)	8(67)	—	3(25)	2(20)
9	9	10	—	6(60)	5(56)	1(10)	4(44)	3(30)
10	6	8	—	4(50)	3(50)	2(25)	3(50)	2(25)
11	4	6	—	—	1(25)	—	3(75)	6(100)
Total	51	54	13(25)	37(68)	23(45)	3(7)	15(30)	14(25)

Although a Fisher exact probability test (Siegel) shows no significant difference between the two groups at any particular age, the data suggest a difference in the development of this concept. While the urban children move gradually from Stage 1 at 6–7 years, to Stage 2 at 8–9 years, and achieve the concept at 10 years, the rural sample, on the other hand, shows an extremely abrupt passage from an almost total absence of the concept at 6–10 years, to its sudden achievement at 11 years. Only 7% of the rural children are in Stage 2, as compared with 45% of the urban group. There is moreover a significant difference in the overall distribution of the two samples among the three stages.

(ii) *Types of Reasoning:*

The following five types of responses were found in the children of both samples:

1. *Subjective reasons or descriptive reference to elements* (e.g., "Parrots are in cages"; "Birds are in the sky"; "Parrots can talk; birds can't talk"; etc.)

2. *Reference to quantity in general terms* (e.g., "Killed them all"; "They all died"; "If they're killed in the whole world, there aren't any left"; etc.)

3. *Tautology* (e.g., to the question "Why are there more animals than birds?" the child responds: "Because there are many", etc.)

4. *Incorrect comparison between class and subclass, or comparison between subclasses only* (e.g., "Didn't kill parrots, only birds"; "Parrots and birds aren't the same"; etc.)

5. *Correct comparison between class and subclass* (e.g., Birds are animals

too"; "Killed the animals, the birds must die too"; "Only killed the parrots, not the birds"; etc.)

Significant differences were found between the two samples for Types 2, 3, and 5 responses only. Tautology responses are rare among urban children and, with a single exception, not found beyond 8 years. Rural children, however, continue to use this type of response as an argument until 10 years of age. Responses which go beyond the specific context of the task like "all died", or "if one were to kill them all"—which were found to be typical of Stage 1—are significantly more frequent in the rural children, whereas responses which explicitly make the correct comparisons between class and subclass are more frequent in the urban group. These differences no doubt reflect the greater number of urban subjects in Stage 3.

To sum up the results of this task, there is a significant difference between the two groups in the pattern of distribution between the three stages for all ages combined, although this is not the case for any specific age. The three types of reasoning which differ significantly between the samples are those of general reference to number or quantity and tautology (both more frequent amongst rural children) and correct class inclusion comparisons (more frequent amongst urban children). The urban sample acquired the concept at 10 years and the rural one at 11 years. The main problem seems to be that although the Stage 1 child is able to label the different classes and subclasses of animals correctly he cannot discriminate between these subclasses and classes in more complex situations. With development, the child gradually acquires the operations of class inclusion, although not for all situations simultaneously. Generally the inclusion of parrots and birds is acquired first, possibly because of physical similarity, and then—only later—that of birds and animals.

C. Conservation of Length—Two Sticks

The task of conservation of length using two sticks was given to 52 urban and 53 rural children. Reliability between the two coders was 95% for the stages.

(i) *Stages:*

The criteria for categorization into the stages were the following:

Stage 1: No conservation of length. Length is considered equal only when both ends of both sticks coincide. With a change in position, the child believes that the sticks change in length. Concentration on arrival points with no coordination between points of departure and arrival.

Stage 2: Conservation in some cases, but not generalized to all situations.

Stage 3: Conservation in all cases. Evaluation of the interval between the two ends of the sticks.

The distribution of the urban and rural children by stages is shown in Table 3–4.

Table 3–4
Conservation of Length—2 sticks:
number of children by stages

AGE	N		Stages 1		2		3	
	U	R	U	R	U	R	U	R
6	9	10	8(89)	10(100)	1(11)	—	—	—
7	11	10	7(63)	8(80)	1(9)	—	3(27)	2(20)
8	12	10	5(42)	9(90)	1(8)	1(10)	6(50)	—
9	9	10	1(11)	4(40)	—	1(10)	8(89)	5(50)
10	6	7	—	4(57)	—	—	6(100)	3(43)
11	5	6	—	—	—	—	5(100)	6(100)
Total	52	53	21(40)	35(66)	3(6)	2(4)	28(54)	16(30)

Inspection of the data shows that the pattern of development of the two samples is very similar. At 6–7 years the majority of the children of both samples are in Stage 1. At 8 years the urban group achieves the concept, and at 9 years the rural group does so. Furthermore, there is no significant difference in the overall distribution of the two samples.

(ii) *Types of Reasoning*

Very little variation was found in the types of responses given to the different items of this task. Without exception, all the Stage 1 children found that when the two sticks were not aligned, one stick was longer and the other shorter, whereas for the Stage 3 children, the two sticks remained equal in length regardless of changes in position. Three types of arguments were used by the children who had already achieved conservation of length. They were:

1. *Reversibility*: (e.g. "If we put the sticks like they were before, they will be equal, so they must be equal now"; etc.)
2. *Compensation*: (e.g. "This stick is longer at this end, but that stick is longer at the other end"; etc.)
3. *Identity*: (e.g. "They were equal just now and they are the same sticks. You didn't break anything off. You only moved them"; etc.)

Identity arguments were the most widespread amongst both urban and rural children, being used by 89% of the urban conservers and 87% of the rural ones.

To sum up, the development of this concept is very similar in both groups. The urban subjects achieve the concept only one year ahead of the rural children, at 8 and 9 years respectively. One interesting finding is the scarcity of children in Stage 2: generally speaking, either they have the concept or else they do not. The types of responses indicate that in the latter case it is because the children judge length in terms of the points of arrival of the sticks and neglect to focus on the interval or the distance between the two points of departure and arrival. Finally, the majority of conservers use the identity argument in preference to those of compensation or reversibility.

D. Conservation of Length—Several Sticks

A second task of conservation of length, this time using several smaller sticks, was given to 49 urban and 54 rural children. Reliability between the two coders was 95% for the stages.

(i) Stages

The criteria for categorization into the stages were the same as for the previous test of conservation of length.

The distribution of the urban and rural children by stages is given in Table 3–5.

Table 3–5
Conservation of length—several sticks:
number of children by stages

AGE	N		Stages 1		2		3	
	U	R	U	R	U	R	U	R
6	9	10	9(100)	10(100)	—	—	—	—
7	11	10	8(73)	9(90)	2(18)	1(10)	1(9)	—
8	12	10	2(17)	10(100)	4(33)	—	6(50)	—
9	9	10	1(11)	6(60)	2(22)	2(20)	6(67)	2(20)
10	5	8	1(20)	4(50)	1(20)	2(25)	3(60)	2(25)
11	3	6	—	—	—	1(16)	3(100)	5(83)
Total	49	54	21(43)	39(73)	9(18)	6(11)	19(39)	9(16)

The data show that at 6–7 years the majority of the children of both samples are in stage 1. At 8 years the urban sample achieves the concept, whereas the rural children continue to remain predominantly in Stage 1 until 11 years, where there is an abrupt increase in the proportion of Stage 3 children and the concept is acquired. Thus there is a difference of 3 years between the groups in the age of acquisition. The difference in the overall distribution between the three stages is significant.

(ii) *Types of Reasoning*

As in the previous conservation of length task, there was very little variation in the types of reasoning used. The Stage 1 subjects (from 6 to 10 years in both samples) consistently said that the straight stick was longer and that the bent sticks were shorter, whereas the Stage 3 ones (starting at 7 years in the urban sample and 9 years in the rural one) maintained an equality of length between the single straight stick and the four bent ones, regardless of changes in configuration. The same three arguments of reversibility, compensation, and identity as in the previous test were also given by the conservers of the present test. Furthermore, the majority of subjects of both groups used the identity argument (urban 73%; rural 100%) either alone or coupled with one of the other arguments.

In summary, the pattern of development of this concept seems to differ between the two groups. The urban sample acquires the concept by 8 years, whereas the rural group moves abruptly from Stage 1 until 10 years to a majority of children in Stage 3 at 11 years. Similarly to the previous conservation of length task, very few children are in Stage 2. The same types of reasoning are used by both groups, with the identity argument being used the most frequently.

E. Conservation of Liquids

The conservation of liquids task was given to 51 urban and 54 rural subjects. Reliability between the two coders was 100% for the stages and 93% for the types of reasoning.

(i) *Stages*

The criteria for categorization into the stages were the following:

Stage 1: No conservation of liquid. Child finds it natural that a quantity of liquid should vary according to the shape of its container. Concentration on a comparison of the perceptual characteristics of the water, with no coordination of these characteristics.

Stage 2: Progressive elaboration of notion of conservation. Invariance recognized in some situations, but not in others. Beginning of coordination of the relationships involved, but not yet generalized to all situations. Sometimes conservation but with no adequate justifications.

Stage 3: Conservation of liquid. Notion of a total quantity of water remaining constant across all changes in form or shape, supported by adequate justification.

The distribution of the urban and rural subjects by stages is given in Table 3–6.

Table 3–6
Conservation of liquid:
number of children by stages

AGE	N		Stages 1		2		3	
	U	R	U	R	U	R	U	R
6	9	10	3(33)	8(80)	5(55)	2(20)	1(11)	—
7	11	10	3(27)	6(60)	5(46)	2(20)	3(27)	2(20)
8	12	10	1(8)	2(20)	2(16)	7(70)	9(76)	1(10)
9	9	10	—	1(10)	—	6(60)	9(100)	3(30)
10	7	8	—	—	—	2(25)	7(100)	6(75)
11	3	6	—	—	—	1(16)	3(100)	5(84)
Total	51	54	7(13)	17(31)	12(24)	20(38)	32(63)	17(31)

Inspection of the data shows that for the younger ages the pattern of the two samples is fairly similar. By 8 years, however, the urban sample has attained the concept, whereas only one rural subject has reached Stage 3, and it is not until 10 years that the rural group achieves the concept. There is consequently a lag of some two years in the speed of development of the rural group. The overall distribution of the two groups between the three stages differs significantly.

(ii) *Types of Reasoning*

The subjects were also coded for the types of responses given for the various items of the test. These types of reasoning were:

1. *Description of situation* (e.g. "Water is red"; "A lot here, a little here"; "Water is in the glasses"; etc.)

2. *Tautology*

3. *Reference to action of pouring*

4. *Reference to size, shape, or number of glasses*

5. *Reference to water level*

6. *Empirical reversibility* (e.g. "Just now it was equal, and if we pour it back it will be equal, but now it's not equal"; etc.)

7. *Identity* (e.g., "It's the same water. You didn't add any or take any away; etc.)

8. *Reversibility* (e.g. "If you pour the water into the original glass, it will be the same amount"; etc.)

9. *Compensation* (e.g. "It's thin but tall"; "Short but fat"; etc.)

The pattern of types of reasoning is very similar for both samples. Not more than a quarter of the children give Types 1, 2, 3, 5, and 6, whereas Types 4, 7, and 9 occur more frequently. Compensation is the only type of reason that differs significantly between the two groups. This is consistent with the higher proportion of urban subjects reaching Stage 3.

One of Piaget's claims regarding conservation is that this notion is an indicator of the existence of an underlying cognitive structure, consisting of a number of interdependent mental operations that support the notion. Consequently, if a child is able to conserve, he should possess such a structure and thus, in principle, be able to use all the three logical arguments which justify conservation: identity, compensation, and reversibility. In the present task the conserving subjects were always questioned to see whether the presence of one of these logical arguments was concomitant with the two others. It was possible to produce all three arguments in 10 of the 32 urban conserving subjects, and 3 of the 17 rural conserving ones. Two coexisting arguments were produced by 17 of the urban subjects and 9 of the rural ones. The remainder of the children gave only one argument throughout the questioning. Identity and compensation arguments are the most frequent combination for both groups (urban: 12 subjects; rural: 6 subjects). The choice of a single argument is no evidence of lack of competence in the use of the others. It may only indicate that the experimenter was not able to get the child to produce additional arguments without actually suggesting such a course, and suggestions were avoided as much as possible during the questioning. In any event, the majority of the conservers of both groups were able to produce evidence of at least two concomitant arguments (84% for the urban group, 70% for the rural one).

Conservation is not an either/or concept which, when acquired, is at once generalizable to all situations. On the contrary, it seems that some situations are more conducive to its achievement than others. This may be due to varying degrees of difficulty of the respective items. Item 3 of the present task, for instance, involved a comparison between the original glass and four smaller ones, and appeared to be simpler to solve than the other two items where a comparison between two glasses was required. Eleven of the 19 urban and 18 of the 37 rural nonconservers maintained conservation in item 3, but not for the other two items. In general the reversibility argument was used; that is, if one were to pour the four small glasses back into the original one the water would be the same.

That this was not simply an effect of learning because of the position of this item in the testing sequence was shown by repeating Item 1, in most cases where the child had conserved for Item 3, but not initially for Item 1. Despite conservation for Item 3 the children continued to show nonconservation for the repeated Item 1. Something specific to Item 3, therefore, seems to lend itself to a correct understanding of the equal quantity of liquid, which is arrived at sooner than for the other two items of this task. Presumably the requisite mental operations for conservation in this case are easier than those in the situations where a comparison between two glasses is required.

One difference between the two situations is that in the case of the four glasses, the water has been divided up. It is a case of partition rather than a change in shape. Before the child can make a comparison with another quantity, he must first unite or join the small glasses, or rather the liquid contained in them, so as to make a total quantity. The situation forces him to perform operations of addition, since the questions call for a comparison between two total quantities. Moreover, not only is adding necessary in this case; it is also sufficient to insure conservation, since it has restored the original quantity. In the other two situations, however, the operations of addition are not enough to insure conservation, and in fact nothing in these situations requires such additive operations. Instead the child is required to perform operations of multiplication of the two dimensions of the water, and compensate the loss of one with the gain in the other in order to return to the original quantity of liquid. It may be this factor that accounts for the precociousness of conservation in the case of the several glasses, but the point would need further study.

To summarize, the pattern of development by stages is significantly different for the two samples for all ages combined. The urban children are two years ahead of the rural ones in achieving the concept. In general, the presence of one type of logical argument among the conservers is associated with that of at least one and sometimes two other types, with the identity-compensation combination occurring most frequently in both samples. Finally, the item involving a comparison between one large glass and several smaller ones appears to be simpler to solve than the other two items of the task.

F. One-to-One Correspondence

The one-to-one correspondence task was given to 50 urban and 54 rural subjects. Reliability between the two coders was 100% for the stages and 96% for the types of reasoning.

(i) Stages

The criteria for categorization into the stages were the following:

Stage 1: No one-to-one correspondence. Global comparisons with no lasting equivalence between the sets.

Stage 2: Child has one-to-one correspondence in the initial situation, but this is destroyed by the change in configuration. May accept addition (or subtraction) of elements as a means of equalizing the two sets. Has "empirical reversibility"—i.e., accepts that the sets will have an equal number when placed in their original layout, but believes they are not equal when this is changed. Maintains equality in some situations, but not in others.

Stage 3: Maintains equality in all situations.

The distribution of the urban and rural children by stages is given in Table 3–7.

Table 3–7.
One-to-one correspondence:
number of children by stages

AGE	N		Stages 1		2		3	
	U	R	U	R	U	R	U	R
6	9	10	2(23)	9(50)	—	1(10)	7(77)	—
7	11	10	3(27)	7(70)	—	1(10)	8(73)	2(20)
8	12	10	—	6(60)	1(9)	1(10)	11(91)	3(30)
9	9	10	—	1(10)	—	3(30)	9(100)	6(60)
10	6	8	—	—	—	1(12)	6(100)	7(88)
11	3	6	—	—	—	—	3(100)	6(100)
Total	50	54	5(10)	23(42)	1(2)	7(12)	44(88)	24(44)

The urban group already has the concept at 6 years. At 7 years only 3 subjects do not have the concept and at 8 years only one child is still transitional. The rural group, on the other hand, shows a different pattern of development and acquires the concept at 9 years. Thus there is a 3–year difference between the two samples. There is a significant difference between the two groups in their overall distribution between the three stages.

(ii) Types of Reasoning

The subjects were also coded for the following types of responses given for the various items of the test:

1. *Description of situation* (e.g., size of objects; color; action of bunching up; etc.)

2. *Reference to length of lines, either verbally or by gestures* (e.g., long(er) short(er), etc.)

3. *Reference to characteristics of the elements in the lines* (e.g., bunched up, close together, touching, etc.)

4. *Reference to original pairing of objects in two sets.*

5. *Reference to number* (e.g. "Both are seven"; etc.)

6. *Identity* (e.g., "Nothing added nor taken away, only changed the line"; "Just now they were equal, so now they must be equal"; etc.)

Types 2 and 5 are the only ones that differ significantly between the groups. This undoubtedly reflects the lag in the age of acquisition of the concept by the rural group, since a Type 2 response is typical of a Stage 1 child whereas a Type 5 response is typical of the Stage 3 child.

This task, which basically looks into elementary numerical conservation, at the same time provides an opportunity to gain some insight into certain relationships between number and language. This can be done by looking at some of the errors of the younger children, since mistakes in a situation provide an indication of the difficulties encountered in the acquisition of a concept. The following observations are derived mainly from the rural data, due to the fact that the concept developed gradually in these children, whereas the urban group had for the most part already reached stage 3 as early as 6 years.

One main problem seems to be that the word "equal" does not have the same connotation for the younger child as it does for the older one. In many cases the young child knows that the number of cars is equal to that of the baskets. When questioned at the very end of the interview session, after the objects have been removed, he will say immediately that there were seven cars and seven baskets. This information was therefore available to him throughout the entire session. But this knowledge does not prevent him from maintaining that, when one line is bunched up, "there are more cars now because they are shorter." In other words, seven cars become more than seven baskets when they are spread in a longer line. It seems as if the young child treats the word "equal" as being synonymous with "same." For example, when asked whether two sets are equal, he will make a qualitative assessment of the situation and reply, for instance, that they are not equal because the baskets are larger, or because the cars are smaller. He seems to be interpreting the question as being whether the cars and the baskets are the same.

In such a case the most obvious dimension on which to compare sameness would be that of length, all the more so since this is precisely what the experimenter has just changed. So the young child replies "It is not equal, one is longer than the other." The word "equal" seems to initially be interpreted by the child in a fairly stringent sense; in order to fulfil the requirements of equality, everything about the situation must be identical, including the characteristics of the individual objects.

For the child, size and length are concrete characteristics of the objects placed before him. He can easily apprehend these dimensions since all he needs to do is extract this information from the objects themselves. They fall into the category of physical knowledge. Number, however, comes within the heading of logical-mathematical knowledge. For this type of knowledge, the child must do more than just extract information from the objects. He must insert them into his own system of mental operations, which in this case would be the number system, and then extract the required information from this system. Since at this point of development his system is not yet adequate for the situation, he interprets the questions in terms of dimensions which are comprehensible to him. Thus, to a question at one level of abstraction, he replies at another level, that which corresponds to his current understanding. It is not until his number system is sufficiently elaborated, which for the rural subjects occurs at approximately 9 years, that he is able to understand that number is an invariant, despite changes in layout, and that equal number means that one set of elements has neither more nor less elements than another set.

We have here an example of the relationship between language and mental operations. It is not that the child has never heard the words that are used, which in any case are adapted to each child's linguistic level. He himself uses the words adopted by the experimenter, but in an entirely different way from that of the older child or adult. He interprets the words to fit his own mental structures. If these structures do not happen to be adequate for the situation, the connotation of the words is modified to fit his own framework. With the development of his structures comes a change in the connotation of words, which then correspond more to that of the older child or adult.

To summarize the results of this task, the distribution of the children between the three stages differs significantly between the urban and the rural groups. The urban subjects have the concept by 6 years, whereas the rural ones show a gradual transition until they achieve it by 9 years. There is consequently a 3-year lag between the samples. Only Types 2 and 5 reasons differ significantly between the two groups. The main problem encountered seems to be that the Stage 1 child interprets the quantitative aspect of the task in qualitative terms, focusing on such features as the length of the lines, or the size of the individual objects. This different approach is reflected in an apparently different usage of words by children at the various stages of development.

G. Seriation

The seriation task was given to only 32 urban and 54 rural subjects. The reason for the limited number of urban subjects was that the task seemed to present no problems for this sample beyond 8 years and consequently was not given to all the older children.

Reliability between the two coders was 100% for the stages.

(i) *Stages*

The criteria for categorization into the stages were the following:

Stage 1: Failure to construct a complete series. Seriation consists of several short series, or child pays attention only to the top of the sticks, and neglects the baseline. Child has difficulty in inserting the additional set of sticks and either needs to break the whole series to include the new ones, or concentrates on the tops only.

Stage 2: Construction of partially correct series by trial and error. Child can also manage to insert the majority of the additional sticks correctly by trial-and-error method.

Stage 3: Immediate success in construction of series. Use of a system starting with largest (or smallest) stick and moving down (or up) the series methodically. No problem in inserting the additional sticks.

The distribution of the urban and rural subjects by stages is given in Table 3–8.

Table 3–8
Seriation:
number of children by stages

AGE	N		Stages 1		2		3	
	U	R	U	R	U	R	U	R
6	9	10	1(11)	10(100)	4(44)	—	4(44)	—
7	11	10	1(9)	2(20)	4(36)	5(50)	6(54)	3(30)
8	5	10	—	2(20)	—	4(40)	5(100)	4(40)
9	3	10	—	1(10)	—	5(50)	3(100)	4(40)
10	4	8	—	—	—	3(37)	4(100)	5(63)
11	—	6	—	—	—	—	—	6(100)
Total	32	54	2(6)	15(28)	8(25)	17(31)	22(69)	22(40)

This task appeared to be relatively easy for the urban group and was mastered from 8 years onward by all subjects. The rural sample acquire the notion at 10 years: the lag is therefore 2 years behind the urban group.

There is no significant difference in the overall distribution between stages of the two groups. Since this task involved no questions about types of reasoning, no additional coding was done.

2. Overall Comparison of the Tasks

Green's Index of Consistency (Torgerson) was computed to determine whether there existed a consistent order of difficulty in the tasks. For both groups separately the index is not significant (urban: .48; rural: .37), whereas the combined urban and rural data give an index of .62, a significant value, although not a particularly high one. One can assume, therefore, that the tasks form a scale—but not a perfect one—in the following order of difficulty: one-to-one correspondence, seriation, conservation of liquid, conservation of length using two sticks, class inclusion-flowers, class inclusion-animals, and a conservation of length using several sticks.

3. Comparison Between Groups

Table 3–9 shows the percentage of successful subjects of each group for each task, as well as the results of overall comparisons between the two groups. This table indicates that the urban group does markedly better at all tasks, with the exception of conservation of length-two sticks, where the difference is not significant.

Table 3–9
Overall comparison of tasks

		PERCENTAGE OF SUCCESSFUL SUBJECTS		THREE STAGES	
		Urban	Rural		p
Operative Tests					
1.	One-to-one	88	44	21.60	< .001
2.	Seriation	69	40	8.69	< n.s.
		80*		18.35*	.001
3.	Liquid	63	31	10.64	< .01
4.	Length 2 sticks	54	30	7.00	n.s.
5.	Flowers	46	11	16.88	< .001
6.	Animals	30	25	23.80	< .001
7.	Length several sticks	39	16	9.32	< .01

* Since the seriation task appeared to be an extremely simple one and achieved by the totality of the urban subjects beyond 8 years, the interviewing was discontinued for the urban children beyond this age. The figures given in the first instance are those for the sample of 32 children only and consequently not strictly comparable with the other data. If we assume that the older children who were not interviewed were also in Stage 3—and the data suggest that this is a reasonable assumption—the figures would be those marked with an asterisk.

The ages of acquisition of the different concepts by the two groups, together with those of Swiss children are given in Table 3–10.

Table 3–10
Ages of acquisiton for different Tasks

	Thai rural	Thai urban	Swiss
One-to-one	9	6	5*
Seriation	10	7	7**
Liquid	10	8	7**
Length 2 sticks	9	8	8*
Flowers	11	8	8**
Animals	11	10	11*
Length several sticks	11	8	9*

*These figures are derived from notes taken while the author was studying in Geneva in 1966.

**Piaget, J. and Inhelder, B. (1963) Les opérations intellectuelles et leur développement, in *Traité de Psychologie Expérimentale*, Volume 7. Paris: P.U.F.

The findings show that the urban sample is ahead of the rural one in the acquisition of all the concepts, with the advance varying from one to three years.

All types of reasoning seem to occur in both samples for all tasks, the difference lying in the relative proportions for the groups. with some types occurring more frequently in one or other of the samples. In no case, however, does any type of reasoning occur exclusively in a particular group. On the whole, the differences in the incidence of certain types seem to be closely associated with the rate of development. The earlier the age of acquisition of a concept, the higher the proportion of subjects using the type of reasoning associated with success at this task, and the lower the proportion of subjects using the more prelogical types of arguments.

4. Comparison with Geneva results

Table 3–10 indicates that the rate of development of Swiss children and Thai urban children is almost identical. For three of the tasks—seriation, length-two sticks and class inclusion-flowers—the ages of acquisition are the same; for two tasks—one-to-one correspondence and liquid—the Swiss children are one year ahead, and for another two tasks—class inclusion-animals and length-several sticks—the Thai urban children are one year ahead. Moreover the same progression in the acquisition of the tasks can be noted, this suggesting that the order of difficulty of the tasks is the same for both samples. The Swiss children acquire the concepts gradually over time during the period from 5 to 11 years. The Thai urban group acquire the concepts during a 4-year period ranging from 6 to 10 years; the Thai rural group, however, do not start acquiring the concepts until 9 years of age, but within the span of 2 years—by 11 years—they have acquired all the concepts studied in the present research. They seem therefore to have an accelerated rate of acquisition at the older ages, when compared with the two other groups.

IV. DISCUSSION AND CONCLUSIONS

1. Stages

The results show that in all seven tasks the three stages described by Piaget are found in both samples, although in some of them there are very few subjects in Stage 2. This low frequency of Stage 2 subjects may be due to the identical nature of the items of these particular tasks. This provides less opportunity for categorization into Stage 2, which is essentially a transitional one where the child has an understanding in some situations, but not all. For tasks where the various items present a wider range of manipulations, such as class inclusion and liquid conservation, there are also a greater number of Stage 2 subjects. Although all three stages in the development of the various notions are noted in both samples, their relative frequency is not identical, and significant urban-rural differences in the overall patterns of distribution between the stages—for all ages combined—are found in six tasks. The one exception is the conservation of length using two sticks, where the differences are not significant. The major difference observed is that a higher proportion of the total number of rural children is to be found in Stage 1, and a higher proportion of the total number of urban children is to be found in Stage 3. This means that the urban subjects acquire most of the concepts at an earlier age than the rural group. Comparisons at each age, however, indicate that in general there are no significant differences between the two groups for the various tasks. This occurence of the three stages in both groups agrees with Piaget's findings in Swiss children, and with other cross-cultural investigations.

2. Types of Reasoning

The results also indicate that the occurrence of the various types of reasoning is similar for both urban and rural groups, although there are differences in the relative frequency of some types. In general, these differences are a reflection of the higher proportion of the urban subjects in

Stage 3 for all tasks, (using more mature types of reasoning), or conversely the higher proportion of rural subjects in Stage 1, (using a less evolved type of mental processing in their responses to the problems).

The responses observed are on the whole similar to these originally found by Piaget, and in some cases the Thai children use wording equivalent to that of the Swiss children. As with the Swiss findings, the less advanced Stage 1 Thai children tend to base their judgments on the perceptual aspects of the situation and to deal with the information presented in a discrete fashion, without relating it to previous actions or situations. They fail to coordinate all the information into an integrated view that includes both past and present states, in addition to the transformations between the two. This lack of consideration of all the elements leads to a partial, incomplete view with a faulty understanding of the coordination of the factors involved. The more advanced Stage 3 child, on the other hand, integrates all the relevant information into a synthesis of the overall situation which is reflected in an accurate understanding. This replication with Thai children of the types of reasoning found by Piaget in Swiss children is also found by some other cross-cultural researchers using a variety of tasks (Greenfield, 1966; de Lemos, 1969), although less work has been done in the area of types of reasoning than in that of stages.

Two major differences were noted between the Thai and the Swiss samples. The first was a high incidence of "tautological" responses in the class inclusion-flowers task for both Thai groups, that is, answers which say the same thing as the question, but using other words. This phenomenon might, however, be due to the existence in the Thai language of two similar words meaning "a lot," with an almost identical frequency of usage. (They are similar to the English words "much" and "a lot".) Since alternatives are available, the child can respond to a question using "a lot" by merely rephrasing the sentence into answer form, and inserting the equivalent "much." The young child who does this seems to feel satisfied that he has provided an adequate answer to the question as to why there are a lot of flowers, or roses, for example, whereas this might perhaps not be the case if his answer had completely mimicked the question.

The second difference was the occurrence in the liquid conservation task, and to a lesser degree in the one-to-one correspondence task, of what have been termed "action" responses, whereby the nonconserving child justifies the inequality of water (or number) by the previous action of pouring (or of bunching up). No figures are available for the Swiss children on the incidence of this type of reasoning, so comparisons cannot be made. Greenfield, however, has found a similarly large minority of her Senegalese children producing the same type of response, whereas, according to her, American children do not respond in this manner. De Lemos, on the other hand, finds no evidence of this type of response in Australian aboriginal children. Greenfield attributes the occurrence of this type of response in her subjects to what she calls "action magic," that is, to a belief in the magical powers of the authority figure of the experimenter to make water expand or contract at his will.

In principle, this explanation should also apply to the Thai culture, where respect for age, authority, and superior status is carefully cultivated in children from an early age. Teachers, in particular, occupy a very high position in the society's ranking of respect, since they are the possessors and conveyors of knowledge. A child not only respects his teacher for his superior amount of knowledge, but is also grateful to him for transmitting it. The child's attitude toward his teacher is one of respect and belief in the latter's superiority. It is possible that this attitude may have been partially transferred to the experimenters, in their capacity both as adults and as teacher-surrogates, despite the efforts made by the two experimenters not to be identified as teachers.

It is doubtful, however, whether such an explanation, based on "magical thinking," can alone account for the proportion of action responses of the children. If this were the case, then it would seem that a far larger number of children of both urban and rural samples would be thinking along these lines, since respect for teachers is widespread amongst Thai children. But for the liquid conservation task, for instance, only 13% of the urban and 24% of the rural children use this type of reasoning. An alternative explanation might be that these children are merely concentrating on a different aspect of the situation. For example, by looking at the water levels the nonconserving children reach the conclusion of an inequality of quantity. When the experimenter asks for a reason, they refer to the action which led to this unequal situation, that of pouring. In other words, they describe the situation rather than explain it, and the description of the situation in lieu of its explanation seems to be a characteristic of the younger child.

In both class inclusion tasks, there are a number of cases of descriptive responses used as justifications. The "action" responses in the conservation of liquid task might therefore represent only a variant of a descriptive response and the result of a different concept of causality, rather than any attribution of "magical" powers to the experimenter per se. In other words, this type of response might in no way be determined by external factors such as adult pressure, but might simply be the reflection of a different usage of certain intellectual schemes by young children, and of an interpretation of causality different from that of the adult. This question, however, would need further clarification and experimentation before any definitive conclusions could be drawn.

With the exception of the two above differences, it seems that Thai urban and rural children are using the same types of mental processes as the Swiss children and as children in some other parts of the world. Research seems to be accumulating which would suggest the existence of certain cognitive universals in intellectual development within a number of cultures.

3. Patterns of Acquisition

Differences were noted between the two samples in both the speed of development of the concepts—with the urban sample acquiring all seven of them ahead of the rural group—and in the pattern of acquisition. The rural children do not purely and simply show a uniform lag of a certain number of years on the urban sample for all concepts. On the contrary, the lag varies from concept to concept. The urban children appear to acquire the concepts gradually over a protracted period of 5 years, starting at age 6, whereas the rural children do not start acquiring the concepts until 9 years and then very rapidly master them all over a period of only 3 years.

This difference in developmental patterns has a number of important implications. Firstly, from the point of view of adaptation to the environment. If intellectual development consists of the building up of new mental structures on prior existing ones, or on concepts that are already available to the child, then the pace and thus the ages at which such concepts are acquired are crucial. A child of a certain age who already has available a number of concepts enjoys an advantage in adapting to, interpreting, and extending his environment, compared to the child who has fewer concepts at the same age. Since development is particularly rapid during childhood, the former child has a head start on the one who takes two or three more years to reach the same level. He will be making a cumulative gain during this period, building new concepts on his existing base, and thus outstripping the child who is taking longer to acquire the same basic structures. Whether this advance makes much difference in the long run is a moot question, but certainly during childhood and during the schooling years it will most probably affect the quality of a child's interaction with his environment.

Such differences in the pattern of concept acquisition also have important educational implications, particularly for curriculum development. If the basic scientific, logical, and mathematical concepts investigated in the present research are acquired differently by urban and rural children, it is quite likely that others, not studied, are also acquired differently by the two groups. Consequently a single curriculum for schools in the two types of locality might not be appropriate. This question would need more extensive study, but is a point that educators might bear in mind.

4. Urban-Rural Differences

The findings of the present research would seem to indicate, on the one hand, considerable similarity in the types of reasoning used by the urban and rural groups, and on the other, differences in both the speed and the patterns of acquisition of the concepts. Comparisons with the Swiss figures show that the ages of acquisition of the urban group follow the Swiss findings very closely. Other cross-cultural comparisons for the conservation of liquid task—the one that has been used the most extensively in other countries—indicate that in the case of Senegal (Greenfield), the urban children have no lag, but the rural children do. These groups were selected at 2-year intervals, which makes it somewhat difficult to give precise ages. De Lemos finds that Australian aborigines reach the 50% criterion by 12 years. Bovet finds a lag of 2 to 3 years for the Algerian unschooled children, which coincides with the Thai rural findings for the same task. Evidence seems to suggest, therefore, that urban children tend to resemble Genevan ones and that rural, or unschooled, children tend to show a slower rate of development.

This point would need further study. The problem of different patterns of acquisition has not been studied extensively cross-culturally, which makes comparisons difficult at this point.

5. Factors Responsible for the Above Findings

It is evident from the present research that differences exist between the two groups studied, especially in respect to the speed of development, which in turn is related to the pattern of acquisition. A simple conclusion that might be drawn from these findings would be that for some aspects of intelligence urban children develop faster than rural children. The urban-rural dimension, however, is a misleading one, in the sense that it might lead to the assumption that it is locality per se that is the cause of such differences. However, since it is hardly conceivable that locality as such affects intellectual development, it must be something that is regularly associated with a particular type of environment that is reponsible. What then are some of the aspects of the environment that might differ for the rural and urban groups?

Intellectual development occurs as a result of interaction with the environment. This may take the form of either physical interaction with the world of concrete objects, or psychological and social interaction with the world of humans. The following factors which come under the two headings of physical and human interaction are some that might be responsible for the different speed of development noted between the two Thai groups.

First there is the factor of the actual *physical environment*, that is the objects that surround the developing child and with which he interacts in his daily life. In both localities of the present study there is a rich and varied environment, although the types of objects encountered may be different. For instance, the urban Thai child sees more motor vehicles, buildings, and technological instruments such as television sets or radios. The rural child, on the other hand, sees more animals, boats, plants, and agricultural instruments used for the planting and harvesting of crops, particularly rice. The latter environment undoubtedly contains as many and as diverse an assortment of objects as the first environment on which the developing intellectual abilities of the rural child can operate.

Thus it seems as if the two worlds of physical objects, urban and rural, are—not identical—at least equivalent in quantity and variety, and the fact of being in a rural or an urban environment would not seem to affect the quantity of experience for the developing child.

Another factor of a physical nature that might affect the child's performance is *malnutrition*, and its consequent repercussions on health. While it is probably true that the average income of the parents of an urban child of this sample would be considerably higher than that of the parents of a rural child, it seems unlikely that malnutrition is a main determinant of the difference in rate of development. Malnutrition in an extreme form seems to be of rare occurrence in the rural locality chosen—which was, in the fertile rice-growing plain of central Thailand. Rice is readily available for the peasant child; vegetables and fruit are grown in the gardens and fields; fish and prawns are plentiful in the canals and rivers; chickens and ducks are raised for meat and eggs, and in many cases pigs are also kept. Moreover, there seem to be few dietary taboos or restrictions which might act to prevent children from obtaining the necessary intake of proteins or vitamins. The rural child, in all likelihood, would have as adequate a diet as his urban counterpart. For this reason, malnutrition—at any rate in its excessive forms—can be dismissed as a major determinant of the differences noted.

One area that has been receiving a great deal of attention in recent years is *heredity*. The findings of the present research do not present strong evidence in support of the genetic basis of intelligence, in view of the fact that greater similarities were found between the Thai urban and the Swiss urban children than between the Thai urban and rural children.

The varying stages of *industrialization* between urban and rural environments might have an effect on intellectual development, since towns are generally associated with a greater degree of technological advancement than rural localities. One related aspect is the difference in tempo or pace of life between town and village, and consequently the speed of reactions required in order to adapt to the environment. Children growing up in an urban area need to have rapid reactions when crossing streets, catching buses, and watching TV programs. The whole pace of life in a large city is faster than in a village, and this might have repercussions on the pace of intellectual development. At this point, however, very little is known as to the exact relationship between urbanization or industrialization and intellectual development, and to attribute lags in such development to the degree of urbanization without specifying the relevant components of urbanization is to beg the question. This area would need to be studied in far greater detail before any definite assertions could be made.

From the point of view of human interaction, one possible factor that springs to mind is a difference in the effects that the actual *interview situation* might have had on the rural and urban children. It might be, for instance, that the rural children were less familiar with the experience of talking to strangers, one of whom was a foreigner; and thus the interview situation might have intimidated them to the point of depressing their overall performance at the various tasks. While it is true that the rural children, particularly the younger ones, were very shy and reticent about talking during their initial encounters with the interviewers, every effort was made to reduce these feelings of anxiety and to make them feel at ease. This included allowing the rural group to do an easy task before starting with any of the seven in the research. Only if the child seemed at ease after this easy task would the experimenter proceed with the other seven. If he did not seem at ease, she would talk with the child or give him something else to play with, and then return him to the classroom and try again after a lapse of several days. Both experimenters had extremely good rapport with the children and it was found that the rural children rapidly got accustomed to the daily presence of the researcher and her two assistants. Soon many of them would, of their own accord, ask their teachers to allow them to return to the interview sessions; and when they did so, they appeared to be enjoying the tasks, which were always presented in the form of games. It seems, therefore, that after the first week or so in the rural school, and with the exception of some rare individual cases, the effect of the strangeness of the interview situation was no more of a problem for the rural Thai children than for the urban ones.

Another factor might be *language*, although the relationship between language and intellectual development continues to remain an obscure question. Here again it seems unlikely that the Thai urban-rural differences can be interpreted in terms of linguistic deprivation, since both urban and rural Thai society highly esteem ability and skill. In fact, it has always been customary to hold verbal contests on the occasion of village festivals, when teams of men will vie with teams of women in exchanges of repartee and wit. The Thai language contains a wealth of words with double meanings, rhymed words, and many situations where an articulate person can display his mastery of the language. Moreover, such verbal ability is valued in both the urban and rural settings. Therefore, the factor of verbal deprivation for the rural group can be discounted as being of prime importance.

More and more attention is being paid to the relationship between certain *child-rearing practices*, including mother-child interaction in early childhood, and intellectual development. One could speculate that the urban child, who is living in the more competitive world of Bangkok, has one and possibly both parents employed. These parents would be well aware of the need for educational achievement in order to advance in society and would apply more direct or indirect pressure on their children to develop intellectually from an early age. For the child living in a rural community, where competition is less marked, and with one and possibly both parents engaged in growing and harvesting rice, it may be that these parents do not exert quite so much intellectual pressure on their children at the early ages. As a result the rural children present a lag upon entering school and during the early years of schooling when compared with the urban group. With time, however, the pressure of schooling, teachers, and peers helps to promote an acceleration in development at later ages, as noted in the present study. In other words, environmental stimulation and the opportunity for active interaction with the environment are provided outside the home for the rural group. The above hypothesis is purely speculative and was not specifically studied in the present research; consequently no conclusions can be drawn.

Finally, there is the factor of *schooling*, which has both its physical and its human interaction components. It is evident that although the curriculum of all Thai schools is fixed by the Ministry of Education, the type of education at the well-endowed demonstration school of the College of Education in Bangkok would not be the same as that at a primary school in a rural locality, from the point of view of physical facilities, teacher-pupil ratio, materials, and textbooks available, etc. To take but one concrete example, the Prasarnmitr Elementary School in Bangkok possesses a library containing both Thai and English books, where many of the younger children browse during their lunch hour. The rural primary school has no such library, and thus lacks this particular stimulation for improving reading skills. The differences in facilities between the schools in the two localities would lead one to predict an accelerated development on the part of the urban group once they enter school. But curiously enough, the opposite pattern is noted. At the onset of schooling, the urban children are ahead of the rural group in cognitive development and the lag decreases with age. Whatever is responsible for the difference between the two groups seems to have occurred already during the preschool years, and schooling helps to level out this difference with age at the later elementary years.

Cross-cultural findings are ambiguous with regard to this factor of schooling. Greenfield finds more differences between her Senegalese rural schooled and unschooled children than between the rural and urban samples. Goodnow finds that in Hong Kong schooling is more important in the formal tasks than in the concrete ones. Mermelstein and Schulman find in the United States that schooling has no effect on conservation of liquids. In brief, schooling may or may not have an effect, depending upon the task, the age, and the culture. The role of schooling therefore remains unclear, and further research would be needed to ascertain its exact scope of influence.

V. CONCLUSION

In conclusion, the similarities in the sequence of stages and types of reasoning in all tasks point to the existence of similar mental processes underlying the responses of the two groups of Thai children. These would suggest that those environmental factors that are responsible for the development of certain intellectual processes occur for both samples. One conclusion that might be drawn, therefore, is that since there are undoubtedly differences in the environmental contexts of Thai urban and rural children in terms of their surrounding objects, toys, mass media, home amenities, transport, etc, the nature or type of objects is perhaps not so important for intellectual development as the simple fact of their presence.

In other words, it seems as if the mental processes develop as a result of general interaction with the environment regardless of the contents of this environment. Intellectual development does not depend upon a specific type of object with which to interact. What is required is an environment containing a variety of objects upon which the internal processes can act. Environments with a degree of diversity are a universal feature, which would explain the apparent universality of certain types of mental operations described in the present research. It is evident that these are not the only types of processes the intellect is capable of, and that there are others which are more culture-bound. The speed of development of these processes, on the other hand, seems to vary between different cultural and social environments, and might be related to certain specific factors the precise nature of which is still unknown. The home environment and experience of preschool years might be important factors, schooling is possibly another.

Further research is still needed to determine the exact factors responsible for differential rates of intellectual development and the precise mechanisms of interaction between these factors and the intellectually developing child.

NOTES

1. This study was supported by a grant from the Foreign Area Fellowship Program. Thanks are due to Poomrieng Arriyagabutra and Vatana Phumlek for their assistance in collecting the data.

2. This criterion of achievement of 50% of the subjects for any particular age having reached stage 3 is used throughout the present research.

REFERENCES

Boonsong, S. (1968) *The development of conservation of mass, weight, and volume in Thai children.* Unpublished M.Ed. thesis, College of Education, Bangkok.

Bovet, M. C. (1974) Cognitive processes among illiterate children and adults. In *Culture and cognition: Readings in cross-cultural psychology*, J. W. Berry and P. R. Dasen (Eds.). London: Methuen.

Dasen, P. R. (1972) Cross-Cultural Piagetian research: A summary. *Journal of cross-cultural psychology. 3* (1): 23–39.

Goodnow, J. J. (1962) Test of milieu effects with some of Piaget's tasks. *Psychological Monographs, 76* (3, Whole No. 555).

Goodnow, J. J., and Bethon, G. (1966) Piaget's tasks: The effects of schooling and intelligence. *Child Development. 37* (3): 573–582.

Greenfield, P. M. (1966) On culture and conservation. In *Studies in cognitive growth*, J. S. Bruner, R. R. Olver, P. M. Greenfield, et al. (Eds.) New York: Wiley.

Inhelder, B. and Piaget, J. (1964) *The early growth of logic in the child.* New York: Norton.

de Lemos, M. M. (1969) The development of conservation in aboriginal children. *International Journal of Psychology*, 1969, *4* (4): 255–269.

McNemar, Q. (1962) *Psychological statistics.* New York: Wiley.

Mermelstein, E., and Schulman, L. S. (1967) Lack of formal schooling and the acquisition of conservation. *Child development, 38* (1): 39–52.

Opper, S. (1971) *Intellectual development in Thai children.* Unpublished Ph.D. dissertation, Cornell University, Ithaca.

Sylvia Opper

Piaget, J. (1947) *La psychologie de l'intelligence.* Paris: Collection Armand Colin.

Piaget, J. (1952) *The child's conception of number.* New York: Humanities Press.

Piaget, J., and Inhelder, B. (1962) *Le développement des quantités physiques chez l'enfant.* 2nd ed. Neuchâtel: Delachaux and Niestlé.

Piaget, J., Inhelder, B., and Szeminska. A. (1960) *The child's conception of geometry.* New York: Basic Books.

Siegel, S. (1956) *Non-parametric statistics for the behavioral sciences.* New York: McGraw-Hill.

Torgerson, W. S. (1958) *Theory and methods of scaling.* New York: Wiley.

Vernon, P. E. (1965) Environmental handicaps and intellectual development, part 1. *British Journal of Educational Psychology, 35*:9–20.

4

Culture, Schooling, and Cognitive Development: A Comparative Study of Children in French Canada and Rwanda[1]

MONIQUE LAURENDEAU-BENDAVID[2]
TRANSLATED BY HELGA FEIDER

There is already a sizable body of literature in the field of intercultural comparisons of cognitive development, using techniques derived from Piaget's observations. Dasen (1972), in an excellent survey, identifies two main streams in this literature:

The first—and the more prevalent—is mainly of a descriptive nature: it is concerned exclusively with kinds of differences in stages of development, either in the forms in which the stages are manifested, or their order of succession, or their rhythm of development. If one attempts to relate these differences to particular aspects of the cultures compared, in order to arrive at a theoretical explanation, the *a posteriori* character of the explanations made to date becomes obvious: theoretical considerations of this kind have in no way guided the choice of populations or of cognitive tasks to explore.

The second orientation, which Dasen terms "quasi-experimental", goes beyond this level of simple exploration. It first states a set of specific hypotheses concerning the role in the development of cognitive structures played by particular aspects of the cultures concerned—in a variety of content areas. Among the factors so explored, with populations representing traits which are relevent to the stated hypotheses, the most frequently studied are amount of schooling (e.g. Greenfield, 1966; Goodnow and Bethon, 1966; Mermelstein and Shulman, 1967; Okonji, 1971; Prince, 1968), contact with Western civilization (e.g. Dasen 1974; De Lacey, 1971), various ecological factors such as patterns of nomadic and sedentary habits (Dasen, 1974; Dasen, 1975a; Dasen, 1975b; Munroe & Munroe, 1971; Nerlove, Munroe & Munroe, 1972), and occupation and trade (Price-Williams, Gordon & Ramirez, 1969; and Adjei, this book).

The majority of studies demonstrate that marked deviations exist in the acquisition of the different concepts and formal aspects of thinking, when two or more cultural groups are compared. These variations, or *décalages*, are usually in a predictable direction: the greater the extent of education, industrialization, or urbanization in a culture, the faster is the rate of thought development. Furthermore, the studies generally confirm Piaget's observations concerning the order of acquisition and the kinds of responses characteristic of each developmental level. In sum, then, the account of intellectual development given by Piaget seems universally valid, and individual differences never affect the qualitative aspects of this development.

However, the aim of these investigations—to describe specifically what role the environment plays in intellectual development—has not in fact been completely realized, for a variety of reasons. For one, the settings that have been compared differ in so many traits that it is difficult to attribute the *décalages* to specific aspects of these cultures. Furthermore, the aspects of thought studied have in every instance been too few to allow safe conclusions concerning the question whether the *décalages* observed affect development as a whole, or only certain aspects of it. It is difficult to say what conclusions one can draw, from observations so far, about the kinds of intellectual activities that are affected by cultural variables—because of the great variety in the ethnic populations studied, in the methodologies employed, and in the kinds of analyses made. Finally, most of this research is of a simple exploratory nature, making no predictions, and no attempts at causal explanations of the differences. Thus the choice of concepts and of populations has not been aimed to identify the aspects of thinking that are most affected by cultural differences, and those features of the environment which probably determined the differences observed.

As for the studies which Dasen terms quasi-experimental: even though they are relatively free of the usual short-comings of intercultural research, they too have important limitations. Here also it is very difficult to extract a reasonably complete inventory of even the main critical concepts at different stages of cognitive development. Furthermore, it is not easy to distinguish the effects of those elements in the environment which are being studied from the effects of other factors which are not being measured.

In spite of these limits to their scientific import, still these intercultural studies are the only ones available on the question of the universality of operational structures—crucial in Piaget's theory—and also in connection with the more general question of the influence of cultural environment in cognitive development. Certainly it is these questions that explain the present proliferation of intercultural studies using Piagetian constructs, and warrant the planning of further research in the field of comparative psychology, despite the recognized scientific problems. An understanding of the difficulties, however, will justify caution both in the research designs and in the interpretation of results.

AIMS OF THE RESEARCH

The present research is concerned with the question of the universal applicability of Piaget's theory and was done with full awareness of the problems connected with the intercultural approach. Its main goal is to determine the influence of the type of culture and the degree of schooling on the development of certain aspects of thinking, as part of a more general investigation aimed at establishing the developmental implications of the stage concept. In addition to experiments concerned with the influence of culture and education (described in detail below) three sets of studies were carried out to define the real limits of the stage concept. Dagenais (in preparation) attempted to find out if the attainment of a particular operational structure—e.g. the addition of classes—would lead children from two different cultures to generalize in identical ways to the set of related operations (multiplication of classes, addition of relations, etc.). Pinard (1974) and Pinard & Lavoie (1974) have examined the question of whether the relationships between intelligence and perception—which may vary with the stages of intellectual development—are of the same kind in children at identical operational levels but from different cultures. Finally, Pinard, Morin, & Lefebvre (1973) have tried to see if the learning of logical structures will take the same forms in children who are of comparable developmental level, but who live in two very different cultures.

Of all these studies, the one presented here is perhaps the most traditional because it essentially consists of presenting the same tasks to two or more populations which differ in terms of culture or extent of schooling, and then analyzing the differences in performance that result from these variations in culture and education. As distinguished from what is usually done in purely descriptive research, however, the different steps of the experimental method are here directed to the testing of specific hypotheses.

General Hypothesis

The first hypothesis is a general one, in the sense that it makes no specific predictions about the cultural and educational conditions that will eventually be compared, nor about the concept to be studied. The general hypothesis states simply that the succession or the sequence of stages of cognitive development established by Piaget will not be found to differ appreciably from one cultural setting to the next, and will also be independent of the degree of schooling—even though it is expected that differences will turn up in various settings as regards the content of the stages and as regards certain *décalages* in chronological age levels. In other words, it is predicted that the order of succession in levels of mental structuring (the stages characteristic of particular concepts) will be found to show no fundamental modifications in the children of the different environments. Despite the basic homogeneity of development, environmental variations may show themselves (a) in chronological *décalages*, in the sense that the age levels at which particular stages are reached may vary from one population to the other; and (b) in differences with respect to the contents of the stages, in the sense that particular explanations and the response categories typical of a particular stage may also vary with the settings compared. Results of precisely these kinds seem to be indicated in the administration of certain tasks, particularly in the area of precausality, to children from Martinique (Dubreuil and Boisclair, 1961; Boisclair and Dubreuil, 1975).

The statement that the sequence of stages is independent of variations due to cultural setting or degree of schooling—our general hypothesis—is based on Piaget's theory which states: (a) The stage notion itself implies a logical sequence of integrations and successive equilibrations such that any reversal within this sequence would affect the very nature of the stage concept: (b) Mental development has at its basis an ensemble of functional invariants (e.g. assimilation, accommodation, conservation) which by their nature and in their realizations (with respect to space, time, movement, quantity, etc.) are universal and function no matter what objects are involved in the formation of mental structures: (c) The process of adaptation which defines the essence of intellectual functioning rests mainly on the subject's own activity, which imposes a structure on the environment instead of submitting passively to its influence.

On the other hand, insofar as the general hypothesis specifies possible differences in content and chronological variations depending on the populations concerned, it acknowledges two interrelated facts: (a) The postulated invariance in the sequence of stages does not exclude possible variations in age levels of attainment, nor does it necessarily imply that the explanations given at particular stages be completely identical: (b) The prime importance accorded by the theory to the subject and his activity in the process of intelligent adaptation in no way excludes the possibility that the influence of the physical and social environment upon the subject may result in either delays or accelerations in the progression from one developmental level to the next, at the same time affecting the particular kinds of responses characteristic of each stage.

Particular Hypotheses

In addition to the general hypothesis just discussed, a number of specific hypotheses can be formulated concerning the incidence of *décalages* to be expected as a function of cultural variations in degree of schooling and in kinds of cognitive structures.

1. Variations in Cultural Settings

When we vary only the cultural setting, comparing children from different settings but schooled in equivalent ways—one group from an industrial, urbanized society; the other from an agricultural, rural one—the extent of anticipated *décalages* varies with the kinds of cognitive structure considered. It is probable (see Piaget, 1969, pp. 116–119; Inhelder and Piaget, 1955) that these *décalages* will become more and more pronounced as we study structures characterized by the following series of conditions: (a) concrete operations that are supported by perceptual configurations (e.g., seriation of objects according to height); (b) concrete operations that are in conflict with concomitant perceptual configurations (e.g., conservation of physical or spatial quantities in spite of perceptual transformations); (c) concrete operations supported by acquired habits in the use of words or numbers (e.g., conservation of number in a collection of objects in spite of perceptual transformations, where the ability to count is an advantage, though not a necessity); (d) concrete representations with no logical operations in the strict sense (e.g., questioning about certain items susceptible to precausal beliefs, such as animism, dynamism, etc.), which constitute a form of verbal thought which depends on cultural transmissions to a greater extent than do the logical operational aspects of intelligence; (e) formal operations and hypothetical deductive thinking leading to the elaboration of schemes or notions (e.g., proportions, probability concepts, mechanical equilibrium, etc.) which are based on concrete operations and must therefore await the complete achievement of the latter.

2. Variations in Degree of Schooling

When we vary only the degree of schooling, comparing children from identical cultures—one group with a normal degree of schooling, the others only with partial or no school education—the expected *décalages* should vary according to the cognitive structure studied—in the order described above—and according to the degree of schooling: for each of the structures studied, the development should show longer delays the lower the degree of schooling in the subjects. This hypothesis derives from a consideration of the possibilities of social interchange, intellectual exercise and acquisition of knowledge in the school setting.

The *décalages* due to degree of schooling are expected to be so large for the unschooled subjects as to preclude the attainment of the level of formal operational thinking. This prediction is based on Piaget's remarks concerning the necessary but insufficient role of schooling in the elaboration of the structures of formal thought (Inhelder and Piaget, 1955, pp. 299–301; Piaget 1956, pp. 73–74; Piaget 1964, p. 180).

METHOD

The Settings Chosen

To test these different hypotheses, it was necessary to find two cultures which would be opposites in industrial development and urbanization, and in which one of the cultures would contain unschooled population sections or only partially schooled, with neither intellectual factors (e.g., mental deficiency, inability, or school failures) nor social ones (i.e., socioeconomic level of parents) being responsible for variations in the rate of school attendance. The best way to assure that chance would be the main factor in determining the selection of children who either had or did not have schooling was to find a population which was homogeneous, both sociologically and culturally, and in which school attendance had only recently been made compulsory by law, so that not all children had yet been affected. The population of Rwanda, a small country in central Africa, seemed to fulfill these conditions in an almost ideal manner. Its level of technological and industrial.development is still extremely low, and the majority of the people, whether they live in towns or in the hills, make their living by farming. The state of urbanization is still very rudimentary, the only real city being Kigali, the capital city, which has a population of only about 20,000 people and is more like some of the big villages of Western countries than like a real city. Education is far from having reached the total population. Finally, in spite of the ethnic diversity which characterizes Rwanda (there are three different groups: the Tutsi, the Twa, and the Bahutu), the country is homogeneous in respect to social and cultural factors (the Bahutu form about 85% of the population).

In all these respects the population of Rwanda contrasted perfectly with that of French Canada in Montreal, which was to be the other cultural context for this research. The children of the city of Montreal grow up in an environment which is strictly urban and highly industrialized, legislation to make school attendance compulsory for children between the ages of 6 and 16 has been implemented rigorously for a long time.

The matter of cultural differences having thus been satisfactorily taken care of, there was still a second reason favoring the choice of Rwanda's population for comparison with that of Montreal. This was the relationship its school system bears to that of French Canada: Not only do their respective curricula from year to year contain educational material almost identical in content, but furthermore, in both cases the language of instruction is French[3], and the cultural values transmitted in each case are therefore those of the French culture.

Finally, a few practical considerations argued in favor of Rwanda as a research field rather than certain other African countries which offer similar conditions: a marked degree of political stability, which is necessary for a project of some duration; the official status of the French language, which facilitated contacts with—and the training of—testing personnel, who were able to communicate in the language of the subjects; Rwanda's small size, reducing the distances to be traveled to reach all the different populations; and the complete and positive cooperation of the country's university.[4]

Testing Instruments

Since the experimental hypotheses predict *décalages*, the extent of which is likely to vary as a function of the five types of cognitive structures distinguished above, care had to be taken that each of the instruments chosen should correspond to a well-defined type of cognitive structure. Furthermore, it was necessary that the vocabulary and the material used in each of the tests should be adapted to the population, both in Rwanda and in French Canada. In addition, the testing instruments, while using the clinical method to allow an analysis of the subjects' thinking which was not entirely superficial, had to be semistandardized so that assistants from Rwanda could administer them without an excessively long training schedule. Finally, the substantial number of subjects required—as well as the difficulties inherent in an experimentation with a population from various geographically separated sites—made it necessary to keep to a minimum the number of test instruments used. Taking account of all these factors, six testing instruments were constructed or adapted for the purposes of this investigation, so that each of the cognitive structures specified in the hypotheses was measured by a single task—except from the category of mental representations, which were to be assessed by two instruments: the movement of clouds task and the concept of life task.

1. Seriation and Intercalation

The seriation and intercalation task consists of two parts. In the first, the subject is asked to seriate 10 sticks increasing in length from 9.0 to 13.5 cm (intervals being of the order of 0.5 cm). In the second part, the subject has to insert into the series so constructed—with or without help from the experimenter—a second set of four sticks with length values interspersed between certain points of the first series (10.25 cm, 10.75 cm, 11.25 cm, and 11.75 cm).

2. Conservation of Surface

In the conservation of surfaces task [usually called "conservation of area"—Editor.] the subject is required to understand that, if from two areas of equal size (i.e., two rectangular green cartons, 23.0 cm × 30.5 cm, representing two fields of grass) two equal amounts of area are taken away, but under different conditions of distribution over the fields (houses of 2.5 cm^3 which cover up portions of the grass and which are either set side by side in rows or scattered over the fields, depending on the conditions), the remaining surface areas are still equal despite perceptual disparity (i.e., cows eating grass still have the same amount to eat on each field). The task has 16 problems, eight of which are classical conservation problems which include a series of subtractions of surface units increasing progressively in magnitude (1, 2, 3, 4, 5, 6, 8, and 12 houses); the eight other problems are designed to probe the limits of the subjects' comprehension and include either an obvious numerical inequality in the number of units subtracted (1 vs. 0, 2 vs. 1, 3 vs. 2), supported by a perceptual disparity, or a numerical equality supported by an identical spatial disposition of elements (1 vs. 1, 2 vs. 2, 3 vs. 3), or finally, a more subtle numerical inequality of area subtractions in the face of an equal number of units placed on the fields (two or four of the 12 units placed on one of the areas are superimposed one over another).

3. Conservation of Number

In the conservation of number task, each of the three sections begins with the presentation of two equal rows of tokens arranged in one-to-one correspondence (7 vs. 7, 12 vs. 12, 25 vs. 25), followed by the transformation of one of the rows, or even of both at once, where the transformations performed never affect the number, but only the spatial distribution of the elements which initially were in visual correspondence across rows. After each of the two or three transformations that constitute the three sections of the task, the subject has to judge whether or not the number of elements has changed, and, depending on his answer, he has to suggest a way to modify or to reestablish the initial equality.

4. Movement of Clouds

In the movement of clouds task, the subject is asked to give an explanation of what he thinks makes the clouds shift. This task had already been used by Laurendeau and Pinard (1962) in a study of precausal thinking. It contains several questions divided into three main sections: the first two were designed to explore possible beliefs of a superstitious, artificialist, phenomenist, or similar nature, and the third was constructed so as to allow the subject, if necessary, to give explanations of a more strictly physical nature, making reference to the wind, the rotation of the earth, etc.

5. Concept of Life

The concept of life task, which also had already been used by Laurendeau and Pinard (1962), contains twenty-two questions concerning some object, the subject having to decide whether it is alive or not, and why. The list of objects contains animals (six); plants (two); and inanimate objects of diverse categories: natural objects (sun, rain, fire) or manufactured ones (a bicycle, a lamp, a bell); mobile objects (an airplane, a car) or immobile ones (a mountain, a lamp); etc. The range of objects to which subjects attribute or fail to attribute life, as well as the justifications they give in each case, make it possible to specify the extension and the sense a given subject has of the concept of life.

6. Quantification of Probabilities

The quantification of probabilities task is concerned with the development of the notions of chance and proportion. It does not require complicated materials, but yet the subject has to reason at the level of formal thought. In each problem, two collections of red and green marbles are given (e.g., 1/2 vs. 1/3; 1/2 vs. 2/3; 1/2 vs. 2/4; 2/3 vs. 3/5). The subject has to decide each time in which of the two collections he would have the greater chance of picking a red marble at the first try, without looking. This task has 21 problems in all. The first five are used as an introduction, presenting pairs of collections with probabilities of one or zero only (e.g., 2/2 vs. 0/2; 2/2 vs. 1/1). In the six problems which follow there are an equal number of favorable or of unfavorable cases in the two collections (e.g. 2/4 vs. 2/5; 2/3 vs. 3/4). In the remaining 10 problems there are unequal numbers of favorable and unfavorable cases in each of the two collections.

Subjects

1. Age and Schooling

Chronological age and amount of schooling were the two main criteria for dividing the subjects into groups. In both Montreal and Rwanda, all children tested were between 5 and 17 years of age. Within these limits, the subjects were divided into age levels spaced two years apart, so that at each level ages varied by at most one year (i.e., six months at either end). Even though in Rwanda it was not always possible to obtain the precise birth date of the subjects, the information received (parents' identification cards, school files, church registers, verbal information coming from the teachers) were sufficient to guarantee approximations to within a few months. The possible error margin is at most three months, and it diminishes as ages decrease.

In respect to schooling, two corresponding groups with normal amount of schooling were formed, in Montreal (Mtl) and in Rwanda (Rs), respectively, each made up of 5-year-olds who were below school age,[5] and of children between 7 and 17 years who were in classes considered normal for their age. In Rwanda, three further groups of subjects were set up: two groups made up of partially schooled subjects, one group that had left school after the sixth year (R6), the other after the third year (R3), plus one group of subjects completely unschooled comprising those subjects who had never attended a school at all (R0). In these three groups, the chronological age range was necessarily more restricted than with the normally schooled subjects, that is, the minimum age of the nonschooled group was 7 years, and that of the partially schooled ones was 11 or 13 years, depending on whether they had left school after the third or the sixth school years.

2. Number of Subjects

The divisions among the three main variables—cultural setting, chronological age, and amount of schooling—thus led to the formation of 27 subgroups, to which a sufficient number of subjects had to be assigned to ensure a minimum of validity to the results, while still keeping the number of subjects needed at a realizable level. The aim was, then, to have 20 subjects per group, where in fact this aim was slightly surpassed in some of the subgroups, and not quite reached in others, depending on the conditions being favorable or not. Table 4–1 reports the exact numbers of subjects examined in each of the subgroups.

Table 4–1
Number of subjects tested in each subgroup, constituted according to cultural setting, chronological age, and degree of schooling

Age	Mtl	RS	R6	R3	RO	Total
	CULTURAL SETTING AND SCHOOLING					
5	19	19	—	—	—	38
7	20	23	—	—	20	63
9	20	21	—	—	20	61
11	20	22	—	20	20	82
13	20	21	19	20	25	105
15	20	22	20	21	21	104
17	20	20	26	20	20	106
Total	139	148	65	81	126	559

3. Other Characteristics

Each subgroup comprises an approximately equal proportion of girls and boys. In Montreal, the subjects are all from medium levels of socioeconomic status and, in Rwanda, all the subjects were taken from the region of Butare, an area almost exclusively rural, where electricity and telephone are for all practical purposes nonexistent and where the children never travel outside the limits set by their home and their school, and thus have almost no contact with an industrial, technological civilization—for example, a good number of the children have never seen an automobile or an airplane. The fact that a very large majority of the population in this zone is agricultural—whether or not the children go to school—made it unnecessary to include direct controls of a socioeconomic nature.

Experimental Conditions

1. Content of Testing Sessions

All subjects were given the six tasks planned in the investigation, with the exception of the 15- to 17-year-old Montreal subjects and the 17-year-old schooled subjects from Rwanda, who did not get the seriation and intercalation, conservation of surfaces, and conservation of number tasks—these three tasks being definitely too easy to be given profitably to subjects of these advanced age levels. The six tasks were administered in two different sessions, and the order of administration was held constant for all subjects, Montrealers and Rwandese. During the first session, the tasks were seriation and intercalation, movement of clouds, and conservation of surfaces; and in the second session, conservation of number, concept of life, and quantification of probabilities.

2. Test Language

The subjects in Montreal were tested in French and the children from Rwanda in the vernacular of the country—Kinyaruanda, with the exception of some of the schooled subjects between 15 and 17 years who chose to be examined in French, because they felt that they were better able to express their thinking in that language. Thus all the tasks were translated into Kinyaruanda and the children's answers were retranslated into French by skilled translators.

3. Testers

In Montreal, the testers were students from the department of psychology, and in Rwanda, they were students and bilingual teachers of the schools, the teachers' college, and the university. All testers were first given intensive training in this type of semistandardized examining procedure. Detailed response forms made it possible for the testers to transcribe verbatim the subjects' answers and their own observations and thus to avoid the many inconveniences of using recording equipment.

4. Place of Testing

In Montreal, all the subjects were tested in their schools, during the regular class periods. In Rwanda, the schooled subjects were tested in their schools or at home and the nonschooled subjects were seen in their homes or at their places of work. As far as possible, the examinations were done under favorable conditions of privacy, necessary for concentration.[6]

Scoring

The answers given in the various tasks were evaluated in terms of stages. First, a stage scale was defined for each task through analysis of the protocols of the children in Montreal, and then these scales were used in the scoring of the protocols of the Rwandese children, with the proviso that certain modifications or even additions of response categories were used if necessary. From four to six levels were determined for each task, and the transitivity of each scale was ascertained: significant differences were found between the age distributions of subjects at each successive level or stage (by the Kolmogorov-Smirnov test).

1. Seriation and Intercalation

In the seriation and intercalation task, the classification of a subject's level depends not so much on a correct solution to the problem as the method used by the subject. Thus, if a child proceeds in a random fashion— i.e., his method does not seem to follow any recognizable system—he is classed as belonging to Stage 0. If, on the other hand, he makes at least partial comparisons between the sticks in his series, by whatever method he chooses, he is classed at Stage 1a or at Stage 1b, depending on whether he ends up with juxtapositions of couples, triplets, etc., or with a completely ordered series but arrived at by trial and error with many corrections. In all of these cases, the insertion problems usually give rise to nonsystematic comparisons between the sticks to be placed and those that are already in position (e.g., the subject makes comparisons first with stick 1, then 8, then 6, then 2, etc.), or to uneconomical comparisons without transitivity (e.g., the subject first making a comparison with the smaller sticks, then with the larger ones)—in which methods do not necessarily exclude the correct solution to all the problems. It sometimes even happens that a child uses a method which appears like an operational one in respect to one or two of the intercalation problems. (For example, he may use a systematic comparison, beginning with one end of the series and stopping at exactly the point where the new stick has to be inserted. However, the fact that he does not use this method in the solution of all the problems suggests that the subject is guided mainly by a favorable perceptual configuration.)

At Stage 2, the subject has recourse, in the seriation part of the test, to an operational method: he looks first for the longest (or the shortest) of the series, then for the longest (or shortest) of those that remain, etc., but this method is still used without sufficient control (e.g., without proper alignment at the lower ends of the sticks when effecting a comparison or an insertion) to result in correct seriation. In the intercalation problems, the subjects of Stage 2 do not progress beyond the level where they only occasionally employ an operational method.

At Stage 3a, the seriation part is solved correctly and always by operational methods, while the intercalation problems still give rise to the use of more primitive methods. Finally, at Stage 3b, both seriation and intercalation are solved by operational methods.

2. Conservation of Surface

Stage 0 of the conservation of surface task represents those subjects who do not grasp the relevant data in the problem, this being most obvious from the fact that they fail even to answer questions correctly where the equality or inequality of the surface areas is accompanied by corresponding perceptual configurations. Stage 1 includes all those subjects who deny conservation in all cases where the numerical equality is not accompanied by an identical spatial distribution of the elements subtracted. At Stage 2, conservation is sometimes admitted for logical reasons and sometimes denied for perceptual reasons. Finally, Stage 3, conservation is always admitted in the classical situations, but the problems in which the inequality of the remaining surface areas results from the superposition of several elements still lead to incorrect solutions in some children (Substage 3a) but are correctly solved by others (Substage 3b).

3. Conservation of Number

The subjects are classified at Stage 0 of the conservation of number task if their responses betray complete lack of comprehension of the questions. However, they are classified at Stage 1 as soon as they grasp at least some of the questions asked, but when their answers consist in denying conservation of numerical equality as soon as the visual correspondence is destroyed. Stage 1 is further subdivided into three sublevels to differentiate between subjects whose answers show a lack of comprehension in a good number of the questions (Substage 1a), those who systematically deny conservation throughout the entire task (Substage 1b), and those subjects who admit conservation on one single item: only if the perceptual configuration suggests in no way a numerical inequality, that is, when the rows remain of exactly the same lengths, one row simply being moved to the other end of the table (Substage 1c). Stage 2 comprises all those kinds of behaviors that belong to an intermediate level: those that consist of discovering the principle of conservation in the course of the interrogation only, as well as those which show constant oscillation between conservation responses that are logically justified and nonconservation responses motivated by perceptual preoccupations. Finally, at Stage 3, conservation is asserted right from the beginning of the test and for all problems, and the arguments given are consistently logical.

4. Movement of Clouds

Stage 0 of the movement of clouds task is the stage of incomprehension, fabulation, and admission of ignorance. Stage 1 is the stage at which exclusively precausal explanations are given, the most frequent forms being artificialism and phenomenism. At Stage 2, the explanations show the beginnings of causal thinking of a physical nature; most often, other celestial bodies (earth, sun, etc.) are mentioned as being responsible for the movement of the clouds. Aside from the fact that this form of causality is still very rudimentary, it is almost always contaminated with beliefs of a finalistic, animistic, artificialistic, or phenomenistic nature. At Stage 3, finally, the wind is thought to be the only element responsible for the motion of the clouds, or else the motion itself is seen as an illusion, which arises because of the earth's rotation. For some of the subjects, those classified as belonging to Substage 3a, these explanations still tolerate some forms of precausal thinking, in particular, finalism and phenomenalism, while for others, classified under Substage 3b, the explanations are given exclusively in terms of physical elements.

5. The Concept of Life

At Stage 0 of the concept of life task, the subjects have no precise definition of the life concept, and thus respond at random or in a fanciful manner, either without justifying their responses or doing so in a contradictory fashion (using the same argument both for attribution and non-attribution of life). At Stage 1, life is seen as related to movement, to utility, or to the possession of anthropomorphic traits. Depending on the criterion used, the child overextends or limits too severely the list of living things. At Stage 2, self-generated locomotion becomes one of the criteria for life, sometimes even the only criterion. However, errors of classification do occur, either because several criteria are used, not all of them equally good, or because the subject falsely attributes autonomy of motion to certain objects. At Stage 3, life is attributed only to plants and animals, sometimes only to animals. Aside from autonomy of motion, it is usually the possession of biological characteristics (e.g., respiration, growth) which serves to distinguish living from nonliving things.

6. Quantification of Probabilities

At Stage 0 of the quantification of probabilities task, the subjects manifest various kinds of incomprehension: preservation (i.e., always choosing the same side), alternation, random and unjustified choices, pointing to both collections as soon as each contains at least one marble of the color to be chosen, etc.

At Stage 1, there are several strategies but there is never simultaneous consideration of favorable and unfavorable cases, Thus, the children choose either that collection that contains the greater number of favorable cases, the lesser number of unfavorable cases, or the smaller (sometimes even the larger) number of marbles in total. Sometimes it happens that a child alternates between these different strategies, and in these cases, the changes are determined either in chance fashion or by the salience of certain elements in the perceptual array.

At Stage 2, the subject begins to take into consideration simultaneously both favorable and unfavorable cases, but he never succeeds in doing so efficiently except when one of these complementary aspects is held constant in the two collections. Systematically, the subject chooses according to the number of favorable cases when the number of unfavorable cases is the same in the two collections, and vice versa; sometimes he even succeeds in giving arguments of quite an advanced level (compute the proportions, find a common denominator). As soon as the two complementary aspects vary simultaneously, however, the subject goes back to the strategies of Stage 1 or attempts to calculate the proportions, rarely being successful.

At Stage 3, one notes that subjects begin to relate favorable and unfavorable cases even when the two aspects vary simultaneously. In the majority of cases, the first step in this development of relations is the well-justified solution to those problems where the fractions are equivalent (e.g., 1/2 vs. 2/4, 1/3 vs. 2/6, etc.), while the other problems are approached with strategies typical of preceding stages. In certain rare cases, however, the problems with unequal fractions are all correctly solved, while those with equal ones are failed, wholly or in part. In order to account for important differences observed in the number of problems solved at this level, two sublevels are distinguished: a Substage 3a, when only two or three of the problems with equal fractions are solved, while those with unequal fractions are failed at least in part; and one Substage 3b, which is characterized by successes with at least three of the four problems with equal fractions, while the unequal fractions are still partly failed—or on the other hand, a success with all unequal fractions and at least partial failure with equal fractions.

Finally, Stage 4 includes all those subjects who solve all the problems, and whose solutions—even if this is not always explicitly revealed—are arrived at by means of exact calculations of the proportions.

RESULTS

The general hypothesis underlying the present research predicted that cultural and educational variations could result in differences in the content areas at certain stages of cognitive development, but would not in general affect the order of appearance of the stages. On the other hand, this general hypothesis—further elaborated into two specific hypotheses—predicted variations in the ages at which stages were reached as a function of variations (a) in the culture and (b) in educational level, where the magnitude of these variations would be, in either of the two cases, a direct function of the type of mental structure under study. The analysis of the results is directed towards the aim of finding evidence for or against these three predictions.

Stage Content

In general, the principles of correction and scoring elaborated for the Montreal population were also applied without difficulty in the evaluation of the protocols of the children from Rwanda, whose reactions in the different tests were almost always identical with those of the children in Montreal. In only two of the tasks was it necessary to introduce slight changes in the scoring procedures in order to take account of certain kinds of responses found only in the Rwanda children.

First, in the movement of clouds task, explanations related to phenomenism—explanations which establish causal links between cloud movement and some other purely coincidental phenomena, such as sun, clear skies, bad weather, and rain,—are encountered particularly often in Rwanda, but quite rarely in Montreal. It may be tempting to view these explanations—especially where they mention phenomena like the sun, the wind, or the rain—as the beginnings of objective causality. However, the ages at which these explanations appear correspond (in both the Rwandese and the Montreal children) to those where responses of a strictly precausal character are found, such as artificialism or magic. Taking note of these facts and data already known concerning the primitive character of phenomenistic arguments (Piaget, 1927, 1928), it was considered more realistic to group phenomenistic responses with all precausal explanations as being on the same level, and to simply mention the difference in the relative frequency with which each type appeared in the two groups.

In the concept of life task, further differences were found between the children in Rwanda and in Montreal with respect to certain details in the definition of the concept "life." In general, aside from locomotion and anthropomorphic traits (breathe, speak, have intelligence, etc.) it is the notion of utility which serves to differentiate living from nonliving things, in both the Rwandese and the Montreal children. Yet, whereas Montreal children tend to consider an object as nonliving if the object is not really useful, in Rwanda the children's definition corresponds rather to the idea of actions that are either beneficial or harmful to people; thus certain objects are considered nonliving because they are dangerous or malicious or cause bites, wounds, famines, etc. At the same time, life is often seen by the Rwandese children as related to good health (never to be ill, not to die, not to get hurt), but this was rare in Montreal. These differences are to be seen, in our opinion, merely as outward expressions of modes of thinking that are fundamentally identical. Even though it seems important to mention these differences in order to avoid leaving the impression that the types of responses given in the two groups were completely identical, it is not considered practical to express such differences in the scale of stages (especially since, in Montreal, the protocols at each level already exhibited an impressive variety of definitions).

Besides these two exceptions, the content of the stages is always the same in the different groups studied, and this not only at the upper levels of the stage scales, but at all levels of each scale. This identity in the reactions of children from two groups that are nevertheless very different tends to confirm the universal character of the stages which characterize cognitive development.

One might be tempted to attribute this uniformity to the test instruments themselves, alleging (a) that the problems presented to the children and the response categories that define the stages unduly limit the variability of possible responses, or suggesting (b) that the tasks chosen do not represent well the cultural values characteristic of each population studied. The first part of this argument is easily countered by pointing out that our tasks always allow for a variety of responses, and, in particular, a variety of possible justifications. Furthermore, in evaluating the responses we give more attention to the underlying strategies than to their face values; a great deal of emphasis is placed on the justifications given, rather than merely counting correct and incorrect responses. These conditions are favorable enough to permit differences to appear, provided that such differences do indeed exist. As for the second part of the arguments it simply does not seem relevant. Even assuming that the concepts tested do not correspond to universal cognitive categories but are only part of Western culture (which would have to be demonstrated), the fact remains that the reactions are qualitatively the same in both Western and non-Western populations. It can thus be concluded that the evolution of these concepts is the same everywhere, regardless of their place in the conceptual hierarchies of each culture.

Ordered Sequence of the Stages

Now that we have shown the qualitative equivalence of the stages in the different groups studied, it remains to be seen whether the stages succeed each other in a constant order, this being an essential condition to guarantee the authenticity of the stage concept. In a cross-sectional study, this condition can be tested by calculating the median age of the subjects classified at each stage in each task: If each stage progression is paralleled by a progression in the median age of the subjects, and if, furthermore, the differences in the distribution as a function of age are significant between all the stages of any given scale (Kolmogorov–Smirnov test), then one can conclude that the sequence of stages is always the same.

Table 4–2 reports median ages for the subjects classified at the different stages for each of the tasks and for each of the populations studied. Median ages were not calculated for distributions of 10 subjects or less, in order to avoid exaggerating the relativity of the median age as a stage index. Comparisons were calculated for the age distributions found at each stage (Kolmogorov–Smirnov at the .05 level of confidence) and the results of these analyses are represented by the presence or absence of vertical braces in the following way: Where two or more median ages are connected by a brace, this indicates that the age distributions for subjects grouped at those levels were not significantly different; in all other cases, the differences are significant.

In summarizing the data shown in Table 4–2, several interesting observations come to light. First, for the Montreal and the schooled Rwandese subjects, the median age progression is regular throughout, with only one apparent exception (Substages 3a and 3b of the quantification of probabilities test). However, this does not represent a real inversion in the stage sequence, but a simple absence of progression, since the age distributions for the two levels in this case were practically identical (by Kolmogorov–Smirnov), so that the median ages are in fact not different at all.

Further, still considering the Montreal and the Rwandese schooled subjects, not all the distributions within stages are significantly different from each other. For the Montreal group, however—with sufficient numbers of subjects to perform valid analyses—this occurs only at the upper or the lower ends of a scale, or at least at either the first or the last

Table 4–2
Median ages of subjects assigned to each stage in each of the tasks and in each of the subgroups

Task	Stage	Mtl	RS	Groups R6	R3	RO
Seriation	0	—*	6;10	—	13;0	9;4
	1A	5;1	8;8	—	14;8	12;11
	1B	7;1	—	—	—	11;7
	2	—	—	—	—	—
	3a	—	11;4	15;1	13;4	—
	3b	11;6	13;6	14;11	13;6	—
Surface	0	—	5;2	—	—	—
	1	6;10	7;5	15;0	13;5	12;8
	2	7;0	9;3	15;2	13;2	12;11
	3a	9;6	11;5	15;6	—	12;9
	3b	11;1	13;4	15;4	14;10	—
Number	0	—	5;2	—	—	10;8
	1a	5;5	—	—	—	11;3
	1b	6;9	7;1	—	—	9;2
	1c	—	—	—	—	—
	2	9;4	10;10	15;1	14;7	13;6
	3	11;4	13;2	15;3	14;8	13;0
Clouds	0	5;1	—	—	—	—
	1	7;2	7;6	15;3	13;6	12;7
	2	—	—	—	—	—
	3a	9;3	14;7	—	13;4	12;11
	3b	13;5	14;9	15;2	—	—
Life	0	5;2	5;3	—	—	7;6
	1	7;5	8;8	15;1	14;8	12;7
	2	11;3	13;6	15;4	14;8	13;6
	3	12;9	14;8	—	13;2	—
Quantification	0	5;2	—	—	—	—
	1	6;9	8;10	15;1	13;6	10;11
	2	9;2	10;7	15;4	13;6	13;0
	3A	13;1	14;11	—	—	—
	3B	14;9	14;9	—	—	—
	4	—	—	—	—	—

A dash (—) indicates that there are less than 10 subjects

stage. It is well known that if the sample of subjects tested does not include all the age levels during which a particular notion develops, it follows automatically that the distributions at the extreme ends of the scale are truncated; one would have only to add younger as well as older subjects in order to see differences in median age and age distributions at these particular stages, in comparison with those that immediately follow or precede them. Keeping in mind these considerations, it may be concluded that—at least for the Montreal children—the stages are perfectly transitive and correspond to developmental levels that are sufficiently distinct to serve as descriptions for children at progressively higher age levels.

Among the schooled Rwandese, transitivity of stages is similarly found in all comparisons, except for the conservation of surface task, where no significant differences were found between the Stages 1 and 2, nor between 2 and 3a; however, such differences did appear between Stages 1 and 3a and between 2 and 3b, and, in general, the median age increased monotonically over all levels. In this task, the stages do not seem to delimit developmental phases that are as well differentiated for the schooled Rwandese as for the Montreal group.

Among the partially schooled and unschooled Rwandese, however, the results are very different. There is no regular monotonic progression of median ages, which are always very close, often even inverted from one stage to the next; yet these reversals are only apparent, since the differences in the distributions at different stages are rarely significant, even up to the two extreme ends of a scale. Among the partially schooled Rwandese, there are no significant differences at all, and among the unschooled ones there are only three. In general, then, it can be concluded that the development described by the stage scales is not supported by a chronological age progression among the partially schooled and unschooled subjects, and the proportions of younger and older children are about equal at all levels of each scale.

These results seem to jeopardize seriously the very notion of stage, since the condition of transitivity is not fulfilled in three of the five groups of subjects tested. Before rejecting the stage theory, one must try to understand the reason why the behaviors described in the various scales do not follow each other in a regular order among the partially schooled and unschooled subjects. Such results can be explained in at least two ways, only one of which would constitute an argument leading to the rejection of the stage theory: If the lack of transitivity is a reflection of a completely random sequence of strategies—a sequence including various regressions of the kind observed by Bovet (1968) in illiterate subjects—there would be every reason to believe that the stages do not correspond to real and universal steps in cognitive development. On the other hand, if what appears as lack of transitivity is only a reflection of an extremely slow pace of intellectual development (where the subjects, at the very first age levels tested, reach a stage which is more or less advanced but never surpassed thereafter), there would be no reason to discard the principle of stages.

The existing data do not permit us really to decide to which of the two possible causes the observed results should be attributed. In fact, only longitudinal research can eventually answer this question. There are some indications in the data, however, that seem to go in favor of the hypothesis that a slow intellectual development is responsible. In particular, it is to be remembered that among the partially schooled subjects, the youngest ones were already 11 or 13 years old—ages at which mental development, especially when no longer stimulated by the school environment, may very well be—if not totally arrested—at least reduced to a very slow rate. This argument is perhaps somewhat harder to accept in the case of the unschooled subjects; these were tested from the age of 7 onwards, that is, at a point in time where intellectual progress should not normally be interrupted. But if one then considers the levels of response in the partially schooled and the unschooled subjects, it appears that the unschooled subjects restrict themselves almost entirely to inferior or intermediate strategies, while the partially schooled ones rather adopt intermediate or superior strategies. Yet, the group of unschooled subjects includes as many older subjects as do the two partially schooled groups. There is apparent evidence that school attendance is an essential factor in stimulating intellectual development, and perhaps even necessary for attaining the level of concrete operations. If there is no schooling, and if the cultural environment offers no particular challenges of its own, development very rarely reaches the level of concrete operations. It seems that at the age of 7 years, the unschooled subjects have already reached a level which they do not surpass in subsequent years. On the other hand, the strategies that were predicted for the stages on the basis of the Montreal population were quite identical in all groups, even though development appears to be completely unordered as regards chronological age. Assuming that intellectual development does not follow the same laws everywhere, one would expect that any differences would show themselves in the content of behaviors as much as in their sequence. Finally, stage transitivity was indeed substantiated—it must be remembered—in two of the five groups tested; and these two groups were otherwise very different in their cultural aspects and—as will become apparent immediately—in their developmental rhythm. With these reservations, and until the assumptions are proven false, it appears justified to consider the stages as a valid instrument of analysis for the intellectual development of all the groups of subjects considered in this research.

Décalages as a Function of Cultural Setting

The next question to examine is that of *décalages* observed in the developmental rhythm of the subjects from different cultural environments—*décalages* that according to the predictions made should vary in magnitude with the type of mental structures studied. In the present paragraph, only those differences that are due to the cultural setting as such will be treated, and thus only the two groups that were educated in equivalent ways in Montreal and Rwanda will be considered. Further comparisons will include the three other groups in connection with an examination of the *décalages* that are due to the "degree of schooling" factor.

There are several ways in which one can establish the presence and the magnitude of *décalages*, in comparing two populations. One is to consider only the accession to the final stages in the development of each notion, and another is to consider all the stages together, from the most elementary to the most advanced types of strategies.

1. The Age of Accession to the Final Stages

The age at which the most advanced stage appears in the development of a particular concept is the index most frequently employed in evaluating *décalages*. Developmental curves, tracing the percentages of subjects at each age level who were found to have reached the final stage, make it possible to give an estimate of the accession age: It is that age level where, for the first time, 50% of children—other authors prefer 75%—have reached the last stage. Since the precise determination of the accession age is sensitive to the distance between age levels and to the number of subjects in each of the age groups, it is always necessary to test whether the variation in accession age of a population for different notions is significant— McNemar test—or if on the contrary, in spite of fairly substantial variations, the task difficulty is essentially the same for all concepts tested.

Table 4–3
Ages at which the last stage is attained in each of the tasks by two groups—the Montreal children and the schooled Rwandese— and differences between the ages

Task	Mtl	RS	Differences
Seriation	8;6	13;0	4;6
Surface	9;0	13;6	4;6
Number	9;8	12;5	2;9
Clouds	10;6	12;1	1;7
Life	10;4	12;7	2;3
Quantification	—	—	—

Table 4–3 reports the results of these analyses for the Montreal and the Rwandese schooled children. In both groups, it was possible to determine

the accession ages for five of the six tasks, but for the last stage of the quantification of probabilities task the accession rate was always below 50%, even in the 17-year-olds. It so happens that in spite of the marked variations in the accession ages observed in both groups of subjects, to the last stages in the different tests, application of the McNemar test indicates that very few of the tasks are indeed significantly different from each other in difficulty (at the .05 level of confidence). For the Montreal group, the seriation and intercalation task is the easiest of all, and quantification of probabilities the most difficult, while the four remaining ones are of equal difficulty; in Rwanda, however, five of the six tasks are of equal difficulty, and only quantification of probabilities is more difficult than the others.

If, in evaluating the variation between the two groups, one is satisfied with calculating the difference in accession age observed between them for each test (see Table 4-3, under "difference"), one must conclude that the results seem to invalidate the hypothesis, since the magnitude of these differences is pretty nearly the opposite of what was predicted. But taking into consideration what has been said about the relative difficulty of the tests, it becomes immediately clear that these results and the conclusions to be drawn from them have to be viewed with extreme caution. In fact, since the difference in difficulty between tasks is not significant, in spite of great differences in accession ages (up to 18 months), it is clear that it would not be quite correct to attribute an absolute value to these accession ages, nor—therefore—to the differences calculated on these ages.

In sum, because of the distance between the successive age levels (two years) and the relatively restricted number of subjects (about 20) in each age group, the accession ages calculated were not sufficiently precise to permit a reliable evaluation of the relative magnitudes of the observed variations.

2. Number of Subjects Classified at the Final Stage

Another way to evaluate the variations between the two groups is to see if the number of subjects classified as belonging to the last stage of each scale is significantly greater (X^2 test) in either of the groups as compared to the other. Supposing that this is so and that the differences always favor one of the groups as long as the comparison involves identical age levels in the two groups, then extending the age difference between groups from 0 to 2 and then to 4 years and performing the same analysis one can discover within which age limits the population differences cited are maintained, and where they begin to show reversals. The results of this analysis are reported in Table 4-4, which gives the number of subjects from Montreal and from Rwanda who were classified as having reached the most advanced stage for each of the tasks and at each age level. The asterisk indicates the presence of a significant difference (at the .05 level of confidence): an asterisk to the left means a significant difference in favor of the Montreal group, to the right in favor of the Rwanda group. Only in the quantification of probabilities task was it not possible to carry out this analysis because of the small number of subjects who were found to have reached the criterion level in this task; however, in order to arrive at some estimate of the difference between groups with respect to the number of subjects approaching formal operational thinking, an analysis was performed on the number of subjects classed at Stage 3a or higher: subjects who appeared to give some indication of formal thinking (understanding of proportions when the fractions are equal).

The results show that in all the tasks employed the Rwandese children reach the criterion stages later than the Montreal children. Three levels of intergroup differences (*décalages*) can be discérned. The conservation of

Table 4–4
Number of Montreal and schooled Rwandese subjects at the last stage of each task when the Rwandese are 0, 2 or 4 years older than the Montreal comparison subjects

Task	Diff. in ages com-pared	AGE OF MONTREAL CHILDREN							
		5	7	9	11	13	15	17	Total
Seriation	0	0–0	2–0	*12–0	*19–8	19–10	—	—	*52–18
	2	0–0	2–0	12–8	*19–10	19–18	—	—	*52–36
	4	0–0	2–8	12–10	19–18	—	—	—	33–36
Surface	0	0–0	2–0	*10–3	*14–4	14–10	—	—	*40–17
	2	0–0	2–3	*10–4	14–10	14–13	—	—	40–30
	4	0–3	2–4	10–10	14–13	—	—	—	26–30
Number	0	0–0	1–3	* 9–3	12–7	17–12	—	—	*29–25
	2	0–3	1–3	9–7	12–12	17–16	—	—	39–41
	4	0–3	1–7*	9–12	12–16	—	—	—	22–38*
Clouds	0	0–0	*4–0	4–2	12–7	*18–14	*17–12	18–17	*73–52
	2	0–0	4–2	4–7	12–14	*18–12	17–17	—	55–52
	4	0–2	4–7	4–14*	12–12	18–17	—	—	38–52
Life	0	0–2	*9–0	* 8–0	*11–5	13–12	13–13	12–10	*66–42
	2	0–0	*9–0	8–5	11–12	13–13	13–10	—	*54–40
	4	0–0	9–5	8–12	11–13	13–10	—	—	41–40
Quantifi-cation (3A, 3B, 4)	0	0–0	1–0	* 4–0	*12–5	12–9	16–12	17–14	*62–40
	2	0–0	1–0	4–5	12–9	12–12	16–14	—	45–40
	4	0–0	1–5	4–9	12–12	12–14	—	—	29–40

number task shows the smallest amount of difference; the superiority of the Montreal group disappears where the group from Rwanda is two years older, and reverses in favor of the Rwanda group when children four years older than Montreal children are considered. The three tasks conservation of surface, movement of clouds, and quantification of probabilities show an intermediate degree of *décalage*: When the Rwandese are two years older, again the intergroup differences disappear; but even when four years older, the Rwandese children are still not superior to the Montreal children. Finally, the greatest amount of intergroup difference is found for the tasks on seriation and intercalation and concept of life, in both of which a difference of four years is necessary before the Montreal group ceases to be superior.

This analysis may not be as refined as one might wish; however it certainly provides evidence against the initial hypothesis: The order among the tasks in terms of age variations observed (*décalages*) does not in any way conform to the predictions made. The seriation and intercalation task should have been the least affected; yet it is here that the greatest amount of variations was observed between the groups. The conservation of number task, on the other hand, was expected to be—among the three measures of concrete operational structures—the one with the greatest amount of *décalage*, yet it shows the least. Furthermore, the two tasks implicating mental representations of a verbal kind—concept of life and movement of clouds—do not give rise to comparable population differences, in spite of the fact that they deal with mental structures of the same category. Finally, the prediction that greater variations are to be found in the development of formal thinking than in concrete operations were not confirmed. In sum, the magnitude of intergroup variations (*décalages*) does not appear to derive from any specifiable law—at least not from the principles used in the formulation of the hypotheses.

3. The Number of Subjects Classified at Each Stage and Substage

Before interpreting these results, a further supportive analysis will be given to enhance their reliability. This analysis takes account of all levels in the development scale and thus allows an assessment of intergroup differences throughout the entire range in the development of a concept, not just at the last stage. Again using the principle of comparing successively wider age distances (from 0 to 2 and to 4), this time applied to the distributions over the whole range of stages and substages (Kolmogorov–Smirnov test), one can then determine the age span necessary for group differences to become obliterated, and this age span is taken as an index of intergroup differences in the rate of mental development.

Table 4–5
Differences in favor of the Montreal children (M), of the schooled Rwandese (R), or neither (=) when the entire distributions are compared for each task, and when the Rwandese children are 0, 2, or 4 years older than the Montreal comparison children

Task	Difference in ages compared	AGE OF MONTREAL CHILDREN							
		5	7	9	11	13	15	17	Total
Seriation	0	M	M	M	M	M			M
	2	M	=	=	M	=			M
	4	=	=	=	=				=
Surface	0	=	=	=	M	=			M
	2	=	=	=	=	=			=
	4	R	=	=	=				=
Number	0	=	=	=	=	=			=
	2	R	=	R	=	=			=
	4	R	R	R	=				R
Clouds	0	R	M	M	M	=	=	=	M
	2	R	=	=	=	=	=		M
	4	R	=	R	=	=			=
Life	0	=	M	M	M	=	=	=	M
	2	R	M	M	=	=	=		M
	4	=	=	=	=	=			=
Quantification	0	=	=	M	=	=	=	=	M
	2	=	=	=	=	=	=		=
	4	=	=	=	=	=			=

Table 4–5 summarizes the results of this analysis performed on the same subjects and tests as before; the cell entries indicate the presence of significant differences (at the .05 level of confidence), favoring either the Montreal children (M) or the Rwandese children (R), or the absence of a significant difference (=).

These additional data on the whole confirm the results described before. The order of the magnitudes of developmental lags for the three operational structures is exactly the opposite of what was predicted by the hypothesis. Neither does the acquisition of formal operations show *décalages* of greater magnitude than does the acquisition of certain concrete operations. The only new element arising from this analysis has to do with the concept of life and movement of clouds tasks, for which—in accordance with the hypothesis—the *décalages* are of the same order of magnitude; and both tasks rank among those where the *décalages* are greatest.

There is thus sufficient evidence to show that cultural factors produce different rates of cognitive development. However, these differences do not conform to the predictions based on a theoretical analysis of factors such as perceptual configurations, linguistic systems, or factors of cultural or educational transmission, which may be either facilitating or retarding with respect to different mental structures. This is true of those groups with no schooling deficit. But precisely because we are dealing here with fully schooled subjects and because the different notions presented in the tests are not tied to the school subjects in identical ways, it may be supposed— and this remains to be examined in the following paragraph—that the *décalages* observed with the schooled Rwandese subjects depend directly on the relationship between what is taught in the schools and the notions contained in the tasks; in the nonschooled subjects, *décalages* would instead be tied to the type of cognitive structure embodied in each of the tasks. The present results seem to support at least the first part of this supposition, since the three tasks where the *décalages* are the least accentuated concern those concepts that are systematically taught in school (number, surface area, proportions) while the remaining ones are not specifically taught (seriation, cloud movement, and life concept). It remains to be seen if the second part of the supposition will turn out to be true for the non-schooled Rwandese.

Décalages as a Function of Degree of Schooling

The hypotheses formulated at the start stated that variations in the degree of schooling would entail differences in the rate of development and in the attainment of formal thinking; the relative magnitude of the *décalages*, however, should depend only on the kind of cognitive structure and not on the degree of schooling. Four groups of subjects were examined to test these hypotheses; all are from Rwanda and thus from the same cultural setting: one group with a normal degree of schooling (RS), two others partially schooled—one with six years of schooling (R6) and one with three years (R3), and the last group with no schooling whatsoever (R0).

The results obtained with these four groups of subjects are reported in Figure 4–1. It shows, for each of the tasks and for each age group, the distributions of subjects—in percentages—classified at the various levels on the stage scale. Certain aspects of these results deserve to be emphasized in advance of a detailed discussion of each hypothesis, since they determine to a certain extent the choice of methods to be used in their verification. The first thing to be noted is that only the normally schooled subjects reach the final stage of each scale in sufficient numbers to permit the age of accession

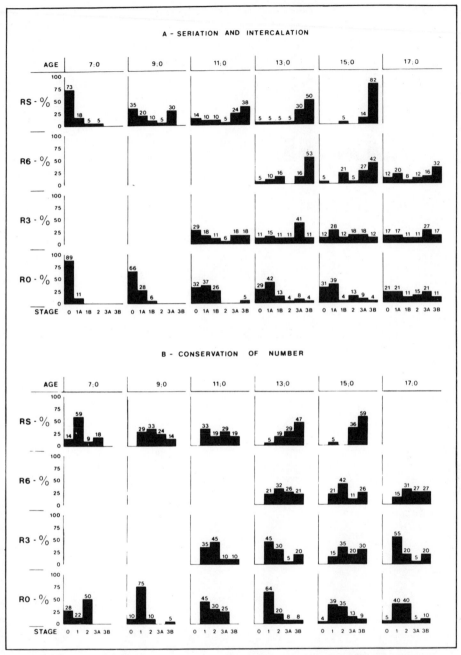

Figure 4–1. Distribution of subjects (in percentages) at each age level for the Rwandese groups (RS, R6, R3, R0), within the scale of stages in the tasks *seriation and intercalation* (A), *conservation of number* (B), *conservation of area* (C), *movement of clouds* (D), *concept of life* (E), and *quantification of probabilities* (F)

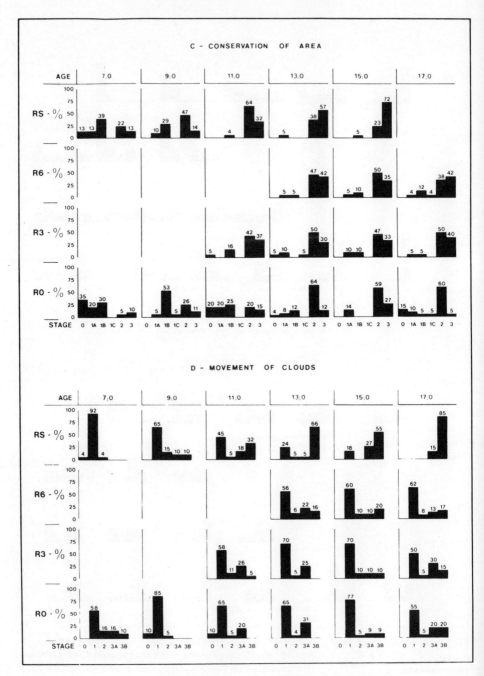

Figure 4–1. (continuation).

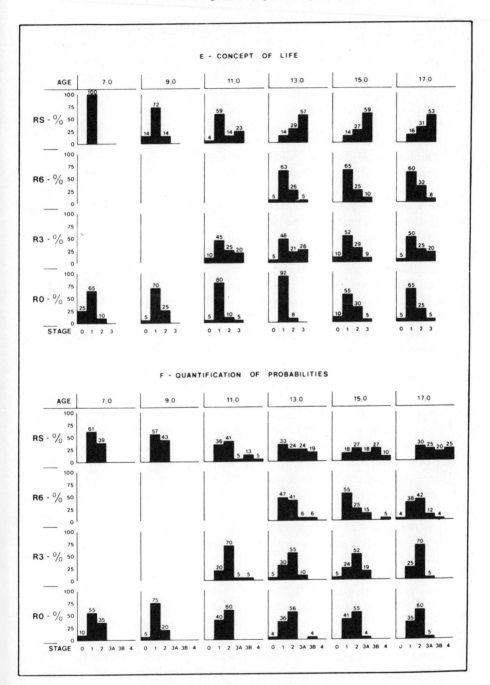

Figure 4–1. (continuation and end).

to this stage to be stated. Nowhere except for the seriation and intercalation test at the age of 13 years does this proportion reach the 50% required for accession. Aside from giving an indication of the accessibility of operational modes of thinking to partially schooled or unschooled subjects, the results lead immediately to the exclusion of any kind of analysis based on comparisons of accession ages or even of the number of subjects reaching the last stages, since they are almost everywhere too small in number. If differences exist between groups with different degrees of schooling, these must be found at levels preceding the criterion level for operational thinking, so that in order for these differences to be revealed, it becomes necessary to perform comparisons over the whole distribution.

A second aspect of the results which becomes immediately evident concerns the almost complete lack of evolution in the partially schooled or unschooled subjects, within the age limits encompassed by the experiment. Some advances or even some small regressions can be noted, but these variations are rarely significant. Thus, in the partially schooled children, the distributions relative to each test do not differ significantly (by Kolmogorov–Smirnov test) between 13 and 17 years in the R6 group, and between 11 and 17 years in the R3 group. And even in the unschooled children, where a wider range of ages was sampled, the differences between distributions do not attain levels nearer significance. In four out of the six tasks, none of the distributions differ significantly from one another for the age range from 7 to 17 years. In the remaining two tasks, there are a very few significant differences, all of them marking a progression: In the seriation and intercalation test, the 7- and 9-year-old children are thus less advanced than those 11 to 17 years old, and in the conservation of number test, three successive levels of performance are recognizable corresponding respectively to the ages 7, 9, and 11, and 13 to 17 years. In sum, it appears that school instruction in and by itself, whether present or partially or totally absent, not only affects the rate of development, but even seems to be a necessary condition for development to occur, at least within the age limits examined here. It remains to be seen if the subjects who did have a limited amount of school experience—the groups R6 and R3—were able to attain levels of reasoning which, although not yet operational even at 17 years, are nevertheless more advanced than those reached by the children who have never attended a school.

One final remark concerning the initial equivalence of the comparison groups. In all the tests, the youngest subjects tested in the groups R6, R3, and R0 obtain results comparable to the results of those subjects of the group RS whose years of school attendance they match. Thus, the R6 of 13 years obtain results in all points equivalent to those of the RS subjects of 11 years, that is, results equivalent to those of children whose age they were at the time they left school. The same is true for the R3 group of 11 years with respect to the RS of 9. As for the R0 group at 7 years, their results are comparable to those of RS 7 as well as RS 5, since there are no real differences at any point between these two groups of subjects. These facts, while arguing in favor of the assumption that factors other than mental aptitude are responsible for the length of time the children stay in school or whether they go to school at all, also seem to allay any concerns about systematic bias in sampling the populations. And since the same sampling technique was used for all subgroups, it may be stipulated that all children tested were initially of similar mental aptitude and that the differences observed over the years in the performance of the children are due mainly to the length of their school attendance. With such data in hand, it now becomes possible to consider each of the specific hypotheses concerning the effects of school attendance.

1. Schooling and Accession to Formal Operations

One hypothesis stated that formal operational thinking will not be reached by the unschooled subjects. This prediction, even though it is supported by the actual data, must be qualified as having been far too conservative. On the one hand, the unschooled subjects are not the only ones not to have reached the stage of formal thinking; and, on the other, school attendance appears to be a condition favorable not only to the development of formal operations, but of concrete operations as well.

As to the first of these two statements, it will be recalled that in comparison of the Montreal subjects with the normally schooled Rwandese subjects, the accession age for the last stage of the quantification of probabilities task was impossible to ascertain for either of the two groups, since in the 17-year-old subjects the success rate was well below the 50% criterion. In the partially schooled or unschooled subjects, successes at the formal level are still less frequent, as is to be expected; in fact, only one of those subjects reached the last stage of this scale (group R6, 15 years). Within the frame of reference of these group performances, and as long as only the last stage of the scale is taken into account, it may be said that school attendance is not a factor that guarantees the acquisition of formal thinking. In some cases, school attendance does indeed contribute to this acquisition, but only if it is pursued past the sixth year—perhaps even well beyond that, since it is only at the age of seventeen years, in the Montreal as well as in the schooled Rwanda groups, that there is a sufficient number of subjects (25% of subjects examined in each of the groups) so that they can no longer be counted as mere exceptions. However, if one lowers the criterion for formal thinking to include the first manifestations of this form of reasoning (Stage 3a), the influence of schooling appears in a new form. The children with normal schooling reach this level, as a group, at about 14 years. The partially schooled subjects, who all left school at the age of 13 years, do not reach this level as a group; only some of them do, and in proportions (up to 20%) which make it difficult to consider them simple exceptions. However, the nonschooled subjects never reach this level as a group (only one case did, apparently very atypical); they do not even reach the first steps toward formal thinking. In sum, no matter which criterion is used, the role of schooling seems to be a necessary but not sufficient condition for the development of formal thinking. Depending on the criterion used, however—whether the earliest manifestations are included or only the final stage in the definition of formal operations—the kind of schooling required is different: In the former case, only a minimal amount of schooling is required—schooling may be interrupted at between the third and the sixth years—while in the latter, school completion is required; but it is not until the age of 17 that its effects are really noticeable.

As for the second statement, this describes a situation which is even less expected than the one just discussed: School experience seems, in certain ways, to be necessary even for an attainment of concrete operational thinking and objective causal reasoning. In the five tasks that concern these two types of cognitive structures, the Rwandese without schooling do not as a group (using the 50% criterion) ever reach the last stage in the developmental scale—at least not between 7 and 17 years. A few individual children do so, however; and even if their number is never very considerable (between 5% and 15% per age level), the phenomenon repeats itself often enough to suggest that these cases, even if they are rare, are not mere accidents. In the conservation of number task, at any rate, the proportion of such cases is as high as 27%—not a negligible proportion. School experience is thus not a necessary condition for the appearance of concrete operational thinking, but certainly it is a facilitating one. This is easy to deduce by comparing the four groups of Rwandese subjects with different degrees of schooling. At the ages of 13 and 15 years (the only ones that are common to all four groups) the proportions of subjects reaching the final level in the three tasks of logical operations taken together (as can be seen from Figure 4–1) are 61%, 37%, 23%, and 11%—for the subjects with complete school experience, those with six and three years of school experience, and those without school experience, respectively. In the area of causal reasoning, the relationship between amount of school experience and the attainment of objective thinking is less precise but still evident, the proportions being 59%, 13% 11% and 4%. In sum, as far as the concrete structures are concerned, their development seems to be facilitated by school experience, although not necessarily following from it.

2. School Experience and Level of Development

The results described in the previous section already furnish some evidence in favor of the relationship—stipulated in the hypotheses—between amount of school experience and rate of development. Considering the different tasks together and using as an index of development the attainment of the last stage of each scale, it can be seen that the higher the level of schooling, the greater the proportion of subjects who attain the criterion stage at the ages of 13 and 15 years. It remains to be seen if this relationship holds for each of the cognitive structures represented by the tasks, and if these variations affect the whole range of development, not only the final stage in the development of these structures.

Since the variations in amount of schooling affect the subjects of the different groups at different points in their development, the only way to compare this development is to choose a chronological age common to all the groups and high enough so that the variations can produce their effects. The levels reached in each group relative to the others will thus indirectly provide information concerning the rate of the development which occurs from the very beginning of school age—when it is assumed, the children of the different groups are all equivalent. The only ages common to all groups and in all of the tests are the ages of 13 and 15 years. Since nowhere (in none of the tasks) were there any differences between the 13- and the 15-year-old subjects of the same group, these two age levels can be grouped together and comparisons effected on the distributions of subjects of the different groups over the scale of stages in each of the tasks; and the Kolmogorov–Smirnov test can be applied to see if the distributions

Table 4–6
Differences found significant (>) or not (=)
in applying the Kolmogorov–Smirnov test in
an intergroup comparison of the Rwandese
subjects' distributions of stages in each task
(ages: 13 and 15 years)

Tasks	RS/ R6	RS/ R3	RS/ RO	R6/ R3	R6/ RO	R3/ RO
Seriation	=	>	>	>	>	>
Surface	>	>	>	=	>	=
Number	=	>	>	=	=	=
Clouds	>	>	>	=	=	=
Life	>	>	>	=	=	=
Quantification	>	>	>	=	=	=

observed differ significantly (at the .05 level of significance) between the groups. Table 4–6 reports the results of these calculations and shows, for each test and each group comparison, where differences were found significant ($>$) or not ($=$). Considering the results as a whole, it appears that the seriation and intercalation task is the one that is the most affected by variations in amount of schooling: At 13 and 15 years, the subjects who have never attended school are less advanced than those who have been in school for three years and who, in turn, are less advanced than those with six years of school experience. After the sixth year, however, school experience no longer produces significant changes, since subjects who at 13 and at 15 years are still in school achieve no better results than those who left school after their sixth year. In the two other concrete operational tasks, there is likewise apparent, some effect of school experience, but the relationship between level of schooling and performance is not as tight. Thus in the conservation of surface task, the fully schooled subjects are superior to all the other groups; but among the partially schooled or unschooled subjects the differences are not large enough to be detected from one group to the next (R0 vs. R3 and R3 vs. R6), although large enough to appear as significant advances from one extreme to the other (R0 vs. R6). In the conservation of number task, the partially schooled subjects show no superiority over the unschooled ones, but the subjects who left school after the sixth year are still somewhat better than the others, since they are the only ones who are not inferior to the fully schooled subjects. Finally, in the three other tasks concerning causal reasoning and formal thinking, only the fully schooled subjects appear more advanced than all the others, and there is no difference between any of the partially schooled and unschooled groups. In sum, variations in degree of schooling do not affect the different cognitive structures in a uniform manner: Some structures prove sensitive to the influence of schooling from the first years on, while others do not seem to benefit from its influence until much later.

Surprisingly however, and contrary to what was suggested by the analysis of the *décalages* between the Montreal children and the Rwandese children with complete schooling, it is not the case that those concepts that are most closely related to the school's instructional context are the most influenced by variations in the degree of schooling. On the contrary, it is the seriation and intercalation task which is the most affected by these differences, and it is the same task, it will be remembered, which revealed the greatest amount of *décalage* in the comparison of the Montreal subjects with the schooled Rwandes subjects. These new results lead to a rejection of the explanation of the observed *décalages* proposed earlier, namely, that perhaps the cognitive development of the Rwandese children might be more directly determined by school influences than that of the Montreal children. But since, as is known by now, schooling influences the development of concepts in very similar ways whether or not they are directly related to school content, the *décalages* observed between the Montreal and the schooled Rwandese subjects must be attributed to factors other than the school itself. Nor could the amount of *décalage* found be related to the ordering established by the theoretical analysis of the structures involved in each task. However, before abandoning entirely the hypothesis of a link between the type of cognitive structure and the relative amount of *décalage*, one needs to examine the question whether such a link can be detected in the partially or unschooled Rwandese subjects, or whether there, too, the *décalages* have no connection with the characteristics of the structures.

3. Schooling and *Décalages* as a Function of Type of Structures

In order to be able to evaluate lags and chronological *décalages* in development, one needs to have a standard measure of the normal rate of development. This standard is not derivable theoretically; even if it is possible in certain cases to establish a theoretical hierarchy of structures, it may happen that the manner of presentation of the tasks (the wording of the questions and the explanations required) will bring about a lack of agreement between the actual acquisiton age and the theoretical hierarchy of difficulties. In the absence of an absolute standard, only a relative standard can be adopted, derived from the performance of a group in which the conditions of development are normal with respect to the factors whose effects one wants to specify. Since the interest here is in determining the effects of a complete lack, or a reduction, of school experience on the rate of development of different cognitive structures, the group that is to serve as a reference must be one which belongs to the same cultural setting as the partially or unschooled subjects, but which has undergone the effects of normal schooling. Therefore, it is the data from the group RS to which will be compared the data from the three other groups in succession, the two partially schooled groups (R6 and R3) and the unschooled group (R0).

In actual fact, because of the somewhat special character of the results obtained, it is not easy to establish precisely the amount of *décalage* between the populations concerned. There can be no question, for example, of calculating the differences between accession ages to different cognitive structures; nor is it possible to compare the numbers of subjects classified at the last stage of each scale, since in none of the groups that have incomplete schooling are there enough subjects that reach the last stage of the scales. One way to obviate this difficulty may be to calculate and to compare the accession ages or the number of subjects, not at the last stage, but at intermediate levels, where there are in almost all cases enough subjects to permit valid analyses. In fact, this alternative is no solution: Whereas one can be certain that the last stages of the development scales represent levels of structuring that are fairly comparable from one task to the next, it is indeed not very likely that this would be so at intermediate levels, which vary considerably in number from one task to the next; these differences are further substantiated by the descriptions of behaviors typical of each stage. If it is not possible to equate the behaviors to be compared, what can be the value of an analysis of *décalages* observed with different tasks, when there is a chance that the order of *décalages* reflects only variations in the degree of structuration achieved at the different levels of development compared?

Under these circumstances, the only possible analyses left are those that involve simultaneously all the stages of each concept. This means that the last type of analysis which was used in the comparison of the Montreal and the schooled Rwandese children will be applied again. As a first step in this analysis, those age levels will be determined, for each task and each of the subgroups, where the schooled subjects show equivalent distributions (by the Kolmogorov–Smirnov test, at the .05 level of confidence). Following this, one simply computes the age differences between the schooled Rwandese and the remaining groups having identical performance levels to obtain estimates of the approximate *décalages* in the different groups.

Table 4–7 summarizes the results of the first part of this analysis; for each task and each age level of R0, R3, and R6 groups, this table contains the ages of schooled Rwandese whose distributions were found

Table 4–7
Ages of RS subjects with distributions found equivalent to those among the R0, R3, and R6 subjects at each level and for each task

Age	Seriation	Surface	Number	Clouds	Life	Quantification
R0 7	5–7	5–7–9	5–7	5–7–9–11	5–7–9–11	5–7–9–11
9	5–7–9	7–	7–9	5–7–9	5–7–9–11	5–7–9
11	7–9	7–9–11	5–7–9	5–7–9–11	5–7–9–11	5–7–9–11
13	9	7–9–11	9–11	5–7–9–11	7–9–11	5–7–9–11–13
15	9	7–9–11	9–11–13	5–7–9–11	5–7–9–11	5–7–9–11–13
17	9–11	7–9–11	7–9–11	5–7–9–11	5–7–9–11	5–7–9–11–13
R3 11	9–11–13	7–9–11	9–11–13–15	5–7–9–11	5–9–11–13–15–17	5–7–9–11–13
13	9–11–13	7–9–11	9–11–13–15	5–7–9–11	5–9–11–13–15–17	5–7–9–11–13
15	9–11	9–11–13	9–11–13–15	5–7–9–11	5–7–9–11	5–7–9–11–13–15
17	9–11	7–9–11	9–11–13–15	5–9–11–15	5–9–11–13–15–17	5–7–9–11–13
R6 13	11–13–15	9–11–13	9–11–13–15	5–7–9–11	5–7–9–11	5–7–9–11–13
15	11–13–15	9–11–13	9–11–13–15	5–7–9–11	5–7–9–11	5–7–9–11–13
17	9–11–13	9–11–13	9–11–13–15	5–7–9–11	9–11	5–7–9–11–13

comparable. It can be seen, for example, that in the seriation and intercalation task, the results obtained with the R0 group of seven years are similar to those of the RS of 5 and of 7, while, in the conservation of surface task, the results for the same subjects are similar to those of the RS of 5, 7, and 9 years. And so forth.

The results of this first analysis illustrate again, and in a new way, the fact that there is almost no evolution of cognitive ability in the RO subjects, and virtually none in the R3 and the R6 groups. This is true at least for the age ranges here considered. In the results reported in Table 4–7, the slow rate of development in the RS group appears in the fact that the performance of one age level, for example that of the R0 group at 7 years, frequently corresponds to several successive ones in the Rwanese schooled subjects.

On the other hand, the almost complete absence of any kind of development in schooled and unschooled Rwandese emerges from the fact that their performance as observed at several, if not all successive age levels, are always comparable to those of the RS of similar age levels.

These two facts, particularly the second—the slow rate of development in the RS subjects—causes difficulties for the second phase of the analysis, which is designed to establish the age differences between the RS and the other groups for equivalent performance profiles. If, as is the case, the performance of the RS subjects is similar at several successive age levels, which one should be chosen to calculate the chronological *décalage* between this and each of the other groups? Three possibilities may be envisioned, only one of which leads to unambiguous results.

One possibility would be to use as a reference point the upper age limit in the RS group in between-group comparisons. Such a choice would obviously be motivated by the wish to describe only the minimum number of group differences. But differences calculated in this way at each level for the partially schooled and the unschooled groups would frequently indicate differences in favor of the latter groups, because the performance of the RS group, just like that of the other groups, remains constant over a wide range of age levels. In general, a test performance equivalent to that of an advanced age in the RS group may be interpreted in a variety of ways, depending on whether the performance level of the RS group itself is still primitive or more advanced. Unfortunately, the results of comparisons based on age maxima is incapable of revealing these fine differences.

Using the mean age of the RS subjects with comparable performance to the other groups does not provide a better reference point than using age maxima. While they are influenced by the dispersion found in the age levels, mean ages do not describe these dispersions. However, this is a necessary requirement, since the dispersions are in themselves an expression of the speed with which a given concept develops in the reference group, and determines the interpretation to be given to the differences calculated.

It would certainly be possible to think of various mathematical solutions to represent simultaneously the mean age and the variability in age levels. But aside from the fact that these different weighing techniques would be essentially arbitrary, they would not account for the strength of *décalages* in as simple nor as direct a manner as the third possibility. This consists in using as a reference point the minimum age of the RS group with distributions corresponding to those found in the three comparison groups. Comparing this minimum age and the age of a particular subject yields then a maximal chronological *décalage*, within the age limits sampled, between the points in time at which a given performance appears in the RS and in the subjects of the other groups. Table 4–8 reports the results of these analyses applied to the actual data for each test and each age level in the R0,

Table 4–8

Differences (in years) observed for each age level and each of the tasks, between the true ages of the R0, the R3, and the R6 subjects and the minimum age of the RS subjects with equivalent performances

	Age	Seriation	Surface	Number	Clouds	Life	Quantification
R0	7	2	2	2	2	2	2
	9	4	2	2	4	4	4
	11	4	4	6	6	6	6
	13	4	6	4	8	6	8
	15	6	8	6	10	10	10
	17	8	10	10	12	12	12
Total		(28)	(32)	(30)	(42)	(40)	(42)
R3	11	2	4	2	6	6	6
	13	4	6	4	8	8	8
	15	6	6	6	10	10	10
	17	8	10	8	12	12	12
Total		(20)	(26)	(20)	(36)	(36)	(36)
R6	13	2	4	4	8	8	8
	15	4	6	6	10	10	10
	17	8	8	8	12	8	12
Total		(14)	(18)	(18)	(30)	(26)	(30)

R3, and R6 groups; in addition, a global index is given: the sum of all the differences observed in each subgroup for each of the tests. A general conclusion to emerge from these data is that variations in the degree of schooling seem to affect to a lesser degree the development of concrete operational structures than that of verbal representations and formal operations. Among the concrete operational structures, however, there is no appreciable difference in the effect of schooling—whether the operations are supported by perceptual configurations, whether they are in conflict with these, or whether they are supported by verbal habits. This means that the predictions made on the basis of a theoretical analysis of the different structures have again been disconfirmed, except for the very general trichotomy which sets apart concrete operations, mental representations of a verbal nature, and formal operations. With respect to the first category, it appears that lack of schooling does not prevent the development of these structures between the ages of 7 and 17, even though what progress occurs is mainly confined to the preoperational levels. For the second and third categories, no progress at all is perceptible between the ages of 7 and 17 years. It appears that complete absence of schooling does not affect the acquisition of these notions any more seriously than does a partial lack of schooling only, including that with six years of schooling; in fact, the *décalages* observed at 13, at 15, and at 17 years are of the same order of magnitude in the R0, the R3, and the R6 subjects.

SUMMARY AND CONCLUSIONS

Five different groups of subjects were given the same set of cognitive tasks. Two of these groups were made up of normally schooled children from two different cultures representing extreme opposites in level of industrial and urban development. Four of these groups comprised children from the same culture but different in terms of degree of schooling. Performance differences due to these cultural and educational variations were discussed with respect to three hypotheses derived from theoretical views concerning the kind of influence such factors might have on the development of different cognitive structures. According to this view, in its most general terms, sociocultural factors may have a supporting role, but not a decisive one. The cultural or educational environment may in fact help to speed up or to slow mental development whatever the case may be; it may even be that such effects are particularly apparent for certain structures— those which appeal to verbal representations or are reinforced by conventionalized modes of verbal expression—and are for this reason more subject to cultural influence than are other structures, which rely mainly on the child's acting on concrete objects. In neither case, however, can cultural influence extend so far as to change the very nature of development, which always exhibits the same steps and stages, and these always follow each other in the same order.

The hypotheses derived from these principles predicted therefore that the sequence of stages as established by Piaget would be essentially the same in all of the groups studied, and only superficial differences in content might characterize the overt expression of modes of reasoning that are basically equivalent. However, variations of culture and degree of schooling should be reflected in different rates of development for the various structures involved in the solution of each task, and the magnitude of these differences in rate of development should depend on the particular character of each of these structures. Thus, it was postulated that concrete operations should be less affected by sociocultural conditions than the verbal forms of precausal reasoning, and the latter less so than formal operations. Furthermore, among the concrete operations, it was expected that *décalages* should vary in magnitude depending on whether the associated figurative or conventional linguistic factors were favorable or unfavorable to a solution.

The results obtained lend unequivocal support to the first of these hypotheses. The six tasks used yielded essentially the same response categories in all of the groups studied. The response categories also seem to correspond well to true stages in the development of each structure, since they follow identical ordered patterns, at least in the Montreal and the schooled group from Rwanda where the transitivity conditions are fulfilled at the group level. In the partially and the unschooled Rwandese, the absence of any kind of evolution, at least at the group level and within the age limits considered here, made it impossible to verify the transitivity condition; in these cases, only a longitudinal study could provide a satisfactory answer. As far as the contents of the stages and the categories of responses are concerned, these are completely identical from one group to the other, except for the two tasks dealing with precausal thought, where there are differences of detail with respect to the relative frequency of phenomenistic reasoning (among other elementary forms of causal thinking), and with respect to the role assigned to the utility criterion in the distinction between living and nonliving entities. The only appreciable differences, then, involve the two tasks of verbal thinking, which by definition have the greatest chance of being affected by sociocultural factors—but only at the level of overt expression. The homogeneity of response categories is all the more noteworthy since the methods employed in the analysis of the results place a strong emphasis on the strategies used and on the justification given, and therefore allow ample opportunity for cultural differences to appear.

The analysis of *décalages* as a function of cultural setting, on the other hand, has led to quite unforeseen results, which are very difficult to interpret within the framework of an intercultural study of an essentially macroscopic kind. When the tasks were ordered as a function of magnitude of *décalages* observed between children from Montreal and the schooled Rwandese, this ordering in no way corresponded to the predictions generated from the theoretical analysis of the structures.

First, the *décalages* relative to the three concrete operational concepts show a rank order exactly opposite to what had been predicted. Further, there was no proportional increase in *décalages* in the development of formal operations when compared to that of certain concrete operations or that of verbal expressions of pre-causal thinking. Finally, the latter do not exhibit greater *décalages* than do certain tasks of concrete operational thinking. In fact, when rank-ordering the tasks according to increasing size of *décalages*, the first three ranks are taken up by the three tasks which, even though they are not directly taught in the schools, concern concepts— number, surface, and proportion—which do have a place in formal school instruction. In other words, the rate of development in the schooled Rwandese is more like that in the Montreal children when the concepts explored have a relationship to subjects taught as part of the school curriculum than when they do not.

Against these observations, however, are those found in the *décalages* as a function of level of schooling. Here it was found that school attendance not only has an effect on the development of concepts related to school subjects, but accelerates the development as a whole. What is even more unexpected is that the one concept which is the most affected by a reduction or lack of schooling is one that is never taught in school. In fact, the schooled Rwandese children demonstrate a significantly faster rate of development, for all of the tasks, than the partially schooled and the unschooled children; they are the only group that as a group reach the level of concrete operations or of objective causal representations, and they are the only ones who show a few examples of formal reasoning. When schooling is lacking or is interrupted at some point, it appears that this slows development to such a degree that no evolution can be detected between the age of school termination and the upper age limit used (17 years). In sum, school attendance appears to be a facilitating rather than a necessary condition for the attainment of concrete operations and objective causal representations, since some of the children without any schooling do attain these. On the other hand, school attendance is a necessary but not a sufficient condition for the attainment of formal operations, since only subjects with full school experience—and only a few of these—were found to have reached this level.

To be precise, however, schooling or its absence does not affect all structures to the same degree: While the *décalages* between the schooled, the partially schooled, and the unschooled Rwandese are less pronounced for the concrete operations than for the causal representations and the formal operations, it is the seriation task, among the concrete operations, which—though it is never directly or indirectly taught in school—is the most affected by variations in degree of schooling. In fact, it is the only task where differences appear between the group with no schooling, the one with three years of school experience, and the one that had six years of school. In all the other tasks, the three groups were found to be equivalent, though clearly less advanced than the Rwandese with full school attendance.

Even though the effects of variations in school experience are more consonant with the predictions than are those of cultural variations—in the respect that the concrete structures are clearly less affected than the causal representations or the formal structures—they too pose problems of interpretation, problems similar to those involving the effects of cultural variation. In particular, it is difficult to understand why it is the seriation task that is the most affected by these two classes of variables, when there is nothing in this task which is either directly or indirectly taught in the schools, and when, furthermore, the characteristics of its structure lead one to suppose that schooling and cultural factors would play a lesser role here.

To conclude, this research, much like most of the cross-cultural literature, has raised more questions than it has provided answers to. This is likely due to the complexity of the phenomena investigated, in contrast to the simplicity of the techniques used to explore them.

NOTES

1. This project was supported by grants from the Canada Council, the Quebec Department of Education, and the International Union of Scientific Psychology (with the assistance of Unesco: 1973 AG/3.2/41/78).

2. We are grateful to our colleagues who have assisted us in various ways: Adrien Pinard, Cécile Boisclair, and Yvon Dagenais, who have contributed their skills in the design and implementation of the experiments; Claude Morin, who supervised the experimentation in Rwanda, assisted by Rwandese students Sylvain Baseké, José Kagabo, J. M. Vianney Maniramo, J. Bosco Mugabo, Joseph Mugabo, J. Leonard Munyankiko, Faustin Munyeshyaka, François Nanayo, Simon Nyilimanzi, Daniel Nzigyie, and Gaetan Rwamjkwaya; and Claude Charbonneau, who helped in the compilation and analysis of the data.

3. It should be pointed out that, in Rwanda, the teaching of subjects other than French, during the first three years of schooling, is carried out in Kinyrwanda, the language commonly used in the country. At the time when French is introduced as language of instruction, the children have learned French well enough to insure that the transition can be made without causing delays or special learning problems.

4. We are particularly indebted to Reverend Georges-H. Lévesque and to

Reverend Jean-P. Crépeau, rector and vice-rector, respectively, at the National University of Rwanda at the time of the experimentation.

5. The 5-year-old Montreal children were attending a kindergarten class, but, since they were tested at the beginning of the school year, they can still be considered unschooled.

6. We would like to thank the Department of Education of Rwanda, the administration of the school district of Butare, the national University of Rwanda, and the Montreal Catholic School Commission for their excellent collaboration.

REFERENCES

Adjei, K. (1977) Influence of specific maternal occupation and behavior on Piagetian cognitive development. Chapter 8 in this book.

Boisclair, Cécile, and Dubreuil, G. (1975) La pensée précausale chez un groupe d'enfants martiniquais. In Jean Benoist (Ed.): *Les sociétés antillaises* (4e édition revue et augmentée). Université de Montréal: Centre de recherches caraïbes.

Bovet, Magali C. (1968) Etudes interculturelles du développement intellectuel et processus d'apprentissage. *Revue Suisse de Psychologie Pure et Appliquée, 27*:189–199.

———, (1974) Cognitive processes among illiterate children and adults. In J. W. Berry and P. R. Dasen (Eds.), *Culture and Cognition*. London: Methuen, pp. 311–334.

Dagenais, Y. (in preparation) Etude interculturelle de la généralisation des opérations.

Dasen, P. R. (1972) Cross-cultural Piagetian research: A summary. *Journal of Cross-Cultural Psychology, 3* (1): 23–39.

———, (1974) The influence of ecology, culture and European contact on cognitive development in Australian aborigenes. In J. W. Berry and P. R. Dasen (Eds), *Culture and cognition: Readings in cross-cultural psychology*. London: Methuen, pp. 381–408.

———, (1975a) Concrete operational development in three cultures. *Journal of Cross-Cultural Psychology, 6* (2): 156–172.

———, (1975b) Le développement des opérations concrètes chez les esquimaux canadiens. *International Journal of Psychology, 10* (3): 165–180.

de Lacey, P. R. (1971) Classificatory ability and verbal intelligence among high contact aboriginal and low socioeconomic white Australian children. *Journal of Cross-Cultural Psychology, 2* (4): 393–396.

Dubreuil, G., and Boisclair, Cécile (1961) Le réalisme enfantin à la Martinique et au Canada français: Étude génétique et expérimentale. In *Thought from the learned societies of Canada 1960*. Toronto: Gage. Pp. 83–95.

Goodnow, Jacqueline, and Bethon, Gloria (1966) Piaget's tasks: The effects of schooling and intelligence. *Child Development, 37* (3): 573–582.

Greenfield, Patricia M. (1966) On culture and conservation. *In* J. S. Bruner *et al.*, *Studies in cognitive growth*. New York: Wiley. Pp. 225–256.

Inhelder, B., and Piaget, J. (1955) *De la logique de l'enfant à la logique de l'adolescent*. Paris: Presses Universitaires de France.

Laurendeau, Monique, and Pinard, A. (1962) *La pensée causale*. Paris: Presses Universitaires de France.

Mermelstein, E., and Shulman, L. S. (1967) Lack of formal schooling and the acquisition of conservation. *Child Development, 38* (1), 39–52.

Munroe, R. L., and Munroe, Ruth H. (1971) Effects of environmental experience on spatial ability in an East African society. *Journal of Social Psychology, 83* (1): 15–23.

Nerlove, Sara B., Munroe, Ruth H., and Munroe, R. L. (1972) Effect of environmental experience on spatial ability: A replication. *Journal of Social Psychology, 84* (1): 3–10.

Okonji, M. O. (1971) Culture and children's understanding of geometry. *International Journal of Psychology, 6* (2): 121–8.

Piaget, J. (1927) *La causalité physique chez l'enfant*. Paris: Alcan.

———. (1928) La causalité chez l'enfant. *British Journal of Psychology* (general section), *18*:276–301.

———. (1956) Discussion entre les rapporteurs. In P. Osterrieth *et al., Le problème des stades en psychologie de l'enfant*. Paris: Presses Universitaires de France. Pp. 50–75.

———. (1960) The definition of stages of development. In J. M. Tanner and Bärbel Inhelder (Eds.),: *Discussions on child development*. London: Tavistock.

———. (1964) Development and learning. *Journal of Research in Science Teaching, 2* (3): 176–86.

Pinard, A. (1974) Le développement de la conservation des longueurs de deux horizontales décalées: Étude comparée d'enfants Canadiens-Français et Rwandais. *Journal International de Psychologie, 9* (3): 195–203.

Pinard, A., and Lavoie, G. (1974) Perception and conservation of length: Comparative study of Rwandese and French–Canadian children. *Perceptual and Motor Skills, 39*:363–368.

Pinard, A., Morin, C., and Lefebvre, Monique (1973) Apprentissage de la conservation des quantités liquides chez des enfants Rwandais et Canadiens-Français. *Journal International de Psychologie, 8* (1): 15–23.

Price-Williams, D., Gordon, W., and Ramirez, M. (1969) Skill and conservation: a study of pottery-making children. *Developmental Psychology, 1* (6, pt.1), 769.

Prince, J. R. (1968) The effect of Western education on science conceptualization in New Guinea. *British Journal of Educational Psychology, 38* (1): 64–74.

5
Papua New Guinea and Piaget— An Eight-year Study

MAX KELLY

The research described in this chapter was carried out in Papua New Guinea and is still continuing at the time of writing (1975). It began in 1968 and has been carried out by the author mainly in collaboration with colleagues at Macquarie University, notably Professor Hugh Philp. A list of acknowledgements appears at the chapter's end.

Three stages of the work are described. The first stage (1968, 1969) surveys achievements of children in two kinds of task: one kind is concerned with getting the "correct" answer, the other with how the answer (correct or not) was derived. These two types of task will be termed "product" and "process." This stage has been replicated as closely as possible in three other cultures: "old" Australians (European descent, English-speaking); non-English-speaking migrants to Australia; and Central Javanese in Indonesia. Papua New Guinea, "old" Australian, and migrant Australian results are broadly reported in Philp and Kelly (1974). The second stage (1972, 1973) was concerned with attempting to disentangle some of the important sources of variance in the survey data; and the third (now continuing) is attempting intervention techniques, at the request of the Department of Education of Papua New Guinea, to change some of the characteristics of Papua New Guinea children relevant to those variables.

It should be noted that the political or national entity called Papua New Guinea simply does not exist as an ethnic group. There are over 700 identifiable language and cultural groups within the boundaries of the emerging nation (Ward and Lea, 1970). As a practical exercise in economics and time, it is impossible to produce a "representative" sample of Papua New Guinea children, and it is stressed that no attempt should be made to generalize the findings here reported beyond the confines of the areas sampled. Three areas were used for the first stage, and one of these has become the centre for the operation of stages two and three. The three areas were chosen for two main reasons. The first was that they had marked, observable differences in language and culture (as well as a number of similarities), and the second was pure expediency. Since the sample was intended to include children with and without primary school experience, up to and including the sixth grade of primary school, as well as children of both sexes, the areas chosen needed to have a school established long enough to provide children with six years of school experience, but not long enough to contaminate a significant number of village children with some—or minimal—time spent in school. In addition, the logistics of an operation which called for lengthy field trips requiring stores, equipment, and camping gear required that access to the areas be obtainable by transport of at least the order of a dugout canoe. While numbers of the areas recently opened up satisfied the conditions for school experience, few could provide girl subjects at the sixth grade level. Education for girls in Papua New Guinea follows an unusual pattern of enrolments and would provide the topic for an interesting essay in anthropology all by itself. Finally, then—with all these constraints—three areas were chosen and marked on the line map (Figure 5–1).

The first was in the Nyausa area of the Sepik River, which empties into the sea on the northwest coast. These people lived in fairly close settlement (for Papua New Guinea) on a peninsula formed by a long 170-degree bend in the river about 360 miles from its mouth, which became inundated at least once a year. The second area chosen was in the great river valley of the Wahgi in the West Highlands of New Guinea, with an average height above sea level of 5,300 feet. The people were of Melpa-speaking clans and the area, while populous, does not foster close settlements. It was the area on which later research has centered. The third was an area of the Goilala district in the foothils of the Owen Stanley ranges. It was the most environmentally inhospitable area used, with an average difference in elevation—from "valley" floor to peak—of 3,000 feet and with little flat land. Some general characteristics of the three groups of people follow:

PAPUA NEW GUINEA MAINLAND

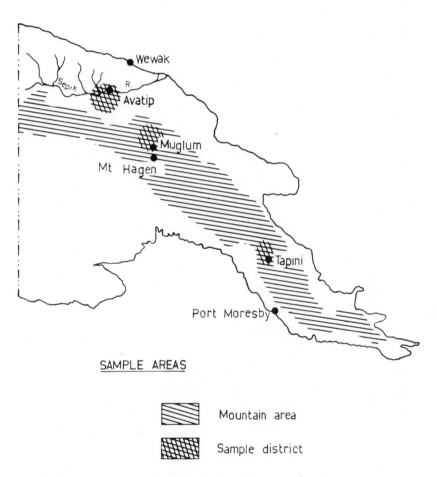

SAMPLE AREAS

Figure 5–1. 1969 sample areas of Papua New Guinea for baseline survey

1. THE NYAUSA LANGUAGE GROUP, EAST SEPIK: THE PEOPLE OF AVATIP.

Avatip is situated in the Ambunti subdistrict, Upper Sepik census division; this division had a population of 2,657 distributed over 350 square miles, at the time of printing of the 1968 Village Directory. Avatip is surrounded by swampy land which supports an unbelievable population of mosquitoes. The main food supplies came from the gardens slashed from the jungle along the river bank and tended by the women and girls. Kaukau, taro, and yam were the staples and varieties of banana, corn, pineapple and pawpaw were also grown. In season fish were caught and smoked to a brown crumbly state, and birds were caught when possible in the surrounding jungle. Some produce was sold at market in Ambunti, four hours paddle upriver, but there was little possibility of earning cash in the village itself, though it had a cooperative trade store in which tobacco, tinned fish, kerosene, and similar trade goods were sold for cash for a period of each day. The people seemed very much interested in obtaining an education for their children, through the origins of their motivation were obscure (Cf. Lawrence, 1969).

The language of the Avatip people has a quite advanced counting system, and words from one to one thousand were recorded. When counting goods the Avatip used a kind of continuous adding process which effected multiplication, and behaved as if they had a number concept, in Western terms. They did not rely on one-to-one correspondence. European contact in the village itself was obtained through the irregular but systematic visits of the patrol officer, the relatively regular visits of the mission "mothercraft" nurse who ran a pre-- and postnatal clinic, and irregular visits by mission workers for religious instruction at the school. The village viewed the Macquarie project with interest and pleasure, though it seemed to be regarded mainly as a status symbol. As the education officer in Wewak pointed out, "Nobody ever goes to Avatip". This was something of an exaggeration, for district inspectors, skin buyers, and other itinerant workers drifted in from time to time. Sorcery was still a force in the village, and during the course of this project a child's body was left undisposed of for two days because it was believed that the death was the result of magic. The nearest center is Ambunti, a settlement consisting of a subdistrict office and associated buildings and staff, a school, two trade stores, an airstrip, a post office and a branch of the Department of Agriculture, Stock, and Fisheries. When "on show" or off to Ambunti, most of the people wore European dress of one kind or another. When working around the village or in the gardens they often reverted to brief lap-laps, though these were now nearly all made of imported cloth rather than woven bark. The school buildings were constructed by the villagers and the materials paid for by the village, as were the teachers' houses. These were built largely of local materials and in local style. The Department of Education had built a house for the head teacher and a one-classroom building from sawn timber and fibro-cement. Unfortunately, this classroom was at ground level and subject to occasional flooding.

In summary, by local standards, the people were relatively healthy and relatively adequately fed and seemed to be cooperating with the administration (then Australian colonial) to the advantage of both parties.

2. THE MELPA LANGUAGE GROUP, WEST HIGHLANDS: THE PEOPLE OF MUGLUM DISTRICT AND KELTIGA.

The center, for the project was the council school at Muglum. This school had been built by the local council from local funds using largely European materials, though there were several houses of native materials on the site. The school grounds were well kept and attractive, with gardens and green playing fields maintained in general by unpaid workers from the villages (mostly women). "Volunteer labor" is hardly an appropriate term, for considerable pressure is brought to bear by councilors and other local officials to get the people to care for the school grounds as well as to maintain the roads and to work for the mission, if the people in question claim membership of one of the sects in operation there.

The people in this part of the highlands did not live in large villages, as did the Sepiks of this sample. Indeed, children were drawn from only one village of any size—Moga—and Moga was quite small compared with Avatip. The village of Muglum, associated with the Muglum school, consisted of eight huts in 1969. By 1974 five more had been added and a patrol post with living quarters for police had also appeared. The huts were much smaller than those of the Sepik sample and appeared to house only the nuclear family. The extended family, or "line," often lived in an "extended" relationship: a line of huts along a track.

The areas from which the original sample was drawn embraced at least 20 "villages" or "lines," all within the Hagen subdistrict, from an area which has a population of 48,226 distributed over 490 square miles, as revealed by the 1968 directory. In the main the sampled people lived on the gently undulating country which forms the Wahgi valley floor. The climate is pleasant to European tastes, though the nights are cold enough to make one wonder why the native people did not develop more clothing than the leaves they wear behind the lower body and the bark net they wear in front. Agriculture was still mainly of the slash-and-burn subsistence kind, kaukau, and some taro being the main crops. Pineapples, European vegetables (potato, bean, tomato) and passion fruit were common and often formed a cash crop. Some coffee stands were native-owned, but big plantations were run by Europeans and supplied opportunities for cash earnings for those who were able to work tending the coffee. Pigs formed an important part of the social scene as bride-wealth, as status objects, and as the main dish at feasts. Anthropological literature abounds on the customs and social organization of the highland peoples. The area sampled was supplied with roads passable to four-wheel-drive vehicles and many "lines" owned a motor vehicle for the carriage of passengers and produce. There were many small trade stores, native-owned, though the income from them did not appear to be high. Thus there were many more opportunities for earning cash than were available on the Sepik, and travel was easier. Further, the center of Mount Hagen lay a mean distance of only 14 miles from the sample area, and Hagen is much larger and more developed than Ambunti. On the other hand, although the population density was greater, the highlands still had fewer school places per head than other parts of the country.

All the sample spoke the Melpa language, which had an adequate counting system to the base eight. All the children had a similar social background, and they were often related in one way or another. There was no difficulty in filling the village sample, but the villagers were unwilling to let the older girls leave the garden work in order to be tested.

Both men and women were more heavily built than the Sepiks and were probably a little taller on the average. They were a happy, lovable people; and in their traditional finery they must surely be among the most colorful in the world. Reports of sorcery and ritual killings are still frequent, as are "pay-back" killings. Two pay-back killings took place during the time of this project within 10 miles of the test center. The social environment appeared to be changing rapidly, at least at the superficial level, because of the increasing "Europeanization" of the area.

Both the subsample group parents welcomed the study and showed intense interest in it, often to an embarrassing degree. Cooperation was all that could have been desired. In conclusion the groups seemed relatively healthy, adequately nourished, and to be advancing rapidly to westernization.

3. THE GOILALA PEOPLE, OWEN STANLEY RANGES: THE PEOPLE OF TAWAUDI AND KUNIMAIPA.

In may ways the Goilala area must be among the most inhospitable in all the country. Though the scenery is spectacular, the areas of flat ground are small and the villages therefore cling to the spurs of the range wherever a relatively gentle slope can be found. The small size of these and the resultingly small area for cultivation of basic foods kept the size of the villages below those of even the settlement clusters of the highlands. The houses were small, at ground level or on piles rising ever higher as the ground dropped away; and were thatched with kunai or pandanus fronds, and walled with pit-pit mats or slabs of wood. While most agriculture is of the subsistence type, kau-kau being the main staple, many European vegetables were grown and much of the produce grown within striking distance of Tapini airstrip was flown to Port Moresby for sale. This commerce was carried out through a small number of wholesalers who bought from the small growers and arranged the airfreighting. Bananas were also an important crop. Little opportunity existed for employment except around the station itself, and few jobs were offered there.

Although the population of the sampled area—5,455 people distributed over 759 square miles—was denser than that of the Sepik area, the small size of the settlements and the difficult walking conditions were combined with the lack of flat land with the result that only one administration school then existed in the Goilala—at Tapini. Apart from the short roads which served this station, only the road linking Tapini with the patrol post at Guari was of any length and significance. In any case, there were few vehicles in the whole subdistrict. The foot trails which wound around the flanks and up and over the steep slopes of the area necessitated spending a great deal of time getting between two points which were separated by only a few minutes of flying time. The Tapini school therefore had a boarding section run by the local council; and the number of children able to attend school was heavily restricted. It has already been noted that two main groups of children commonly attended Tapini school, the Tawaudi and the Kunimaipa. The villages surrounding Tapini, however, were Tawaudi. Considering that even the Tawaudi subjects from some villages had to walk for a week to get to the test situation, it is scarcely surprising that considerable moral persuasion had to be exercised to get village subjects in at all, and accommodation had to be found for them overnight. Consequently, though the station people showed interest and acceptance of the study—they being non-Goilala—the indigenes of the area "cooperated" unwillingly, though the children, once started, seemed pleased enough to work at the tasks. Fears of sorcery were very strong in this area, and during the course of the project (much shorter than any of the other three situations) a sorcery scare was caused by one boarder's cutting hair from another's head. The Goilala were feared by the native population of Port Moresby as troublemakers—with (one must admit) some cause.

One of the Catholic missionaries who had worked in the area a long time told tales of the attacks on baggage and supply columns coming in from the coast in disturbingly recent times, and the district magistrate claimed an incredible proportion of the men of some of the villages were in jail for murder. The Tawaudi were slight, small, and dark. They wore European clothes in the main, perhaps because of the long term mission influence over much of the area. (Perhaps modesty *is* more important than murder.)

If we use the counting words in the language as a standard of comparison, the Kunimaipa were much in advance of the Tawaudi. The Kunimaipa, like the Melpa, used an eight base system. The Tawaudi appeared to use only "one," "one plus," and "many." Certainly the Tawaudi traded and sold garden produce by a literal one-to-one correspondence of object to object. The Tawaudi language also appeared to have only one possible form of question, approximated in English by adding "Isn't it?" to a statement.

It is very hard to give any useful indication of the degree of European involvement in the lives of the Goilala people. On the one hand, they had been in contact for a long time. On the other, they had a relatively small subdistrict station and were isolated from this to some extent by difficulties of travel. Yet the station was served by running water and 240-volt hydroelectric power. Though the terrain was unhelpful, numbers of Goilala walked to Moresby and some stayed there for long periods. It was an area of some contradictions, and apparent "progress" was slow. Perhaps the development of Tapini as a tourist attraction for Papua New Guinea residents and visitors alike will alter the situation.

STAGE 1 STUDIES

The Sample

The sample for stage one was stratified for sex, years of school experience, "age," and language culture groups. It was originally designed to sample by age. Recorded ages in Papua New Guinea proved to be extremely unreliable. Malcolm (1969) describes a method of estimating ages in Papua New Guinea by the eruption of teeth, but rests some of his justification on the work of Gates (1964). When the Gates data are examined, however, the age range for the eruption of—for example—a tooth designated as "upper 1" is from 5 years 9 months to 8 years in females. Since there is no evidence that the range of ages for the eruption of a given tooth in Papua New Guinea children differs materially from that of the New South Wales children described by Gates, it must be concluded that Malcolm's medical knowledge exceeds his statistical sophistication. Because of the unreliability of the age data it was decided to fall back on years of school experience as a baseline to compare children across cultures, which was the original aim of this stage of the research. School records were reliable. The strata used were one, four, and six years of school on the first day of January of the year of testing. The "ages" of the school sample were estimated by the writer and children with no school experience chosen from the same age groups. Since physical development as estimated was a major criterion for the "guesstimated" age, the chronological developmental trend is confused by individual differences in growth rate and nourishment. The subjects were chosen randomly within the strata to overcome some of the more obvious criticisms of a sampling method with any resemblance to "matching"—even when these criticisms are applied somewhat speciously (e.g., Brislin, 1974).

Table 5–1
Planned Sample Papua New Guinea Stage One.
for each language/culture group.

	YEARS OF SCHOOLING				
	1	4	6	0	Σ
Male	12	12	12	36	72
Female	12	12	12	36	72
	24	24	24	72	144

Since there were three language cultures groups chosen, the total sample was 216 school children, plus 216 "village" children with no school experience but of an age distribution similar to that of the school sample. In the field, it proved impossible to fill the cells for the Avatip village sample. The Sepik was running strongly and the village men were unwilling to waste effort (as they thought of it) paddling upstream to secure subjects uncontaminated by school experience when children who did not now go to school (but had gone) existed in numbers in the central village. Only two males and eight females were available. The balance of 62 village children were drawn from Keltiga in the West Highlands. Cross-group comparisons therefore must be made with this fact in mind. It should also be noted that the Goilala "school" sample contained both Kunimaipa and Tawaudi children, while the "village" sample was mainly Tawaudi. The sample was therefore far from ideal. However, it is argued that this is a difficulty of interpretive—rather than absolute—validity. Field research in distant places cannot be quite the same as that carried out in the laboratories of large urban universities. All tests were given on one day, with rest periods; and the average total testing time was about two hours. Thus, with transport problems, the sample as described occupied one researcher and one assistant for seven months.

The Tests

Only those tasks which were based on the work of Piaget are described. The process tasks from Bruner, can be found in Philp and Kelly (1974). It has been pointed out earlier in this chapter that the sample was chosen from children of typical primary school age, because of the relative universality of primary education as compared with secondary education. Consequently, the tasks chosen were those which would be expected to span the ages of primary school in the society in which they were devised. These were:

1. Conservation of Quantity, using rice.
2. Conservation of Length, using sticks.
3. Formal operations using the pendulum task with a tin can, stones, and bark string.
4. A three-dimensional three by three wooden block matrix which increased in length on one dimension and in thickness on the other.

In detail:

1. Conservation of Quantity

Water was not used because of the inherent "messiness" and the pragmatic observation that bright children often say "No, it is not the same, because there are drops still in there". Rice is generally used throughout all the cultures intended for study, and even the Sepik and Goilala children seemed quite familiar with it, though it was too expensive to be a staple. Dry rice is more manageable than a liquid, yet maintains most of the qualities of the liquid if tipped to make it settle after each transformation. The containers used were cylinders of Perspex, the standards being 5 cm in diameter and 15 cm in height and the transformation cylinders being 3 cm × 22 cm and 10 cm × 8 cm respectively. An initial equation of the two standards was obtained; then the tall transformation was presented; then came a return to the standard, the wide-low transformation, and a final return to the standard. After each response the child was asked to give a reason.

2. Conservation of Length

Sticks of pit-pit (a reed commonly used in Papua New Guinea) about 15 cm long were used. There was an initial equation, a displacement of 1/3 with the two sticks in juxtaposition, a return to the initial position, a displacement of 1/3 with the stick about 15 cm apart, a return to the central position, a construction of the inverted T optical illusion, and a return to the initial position. As with quantity, the child was asked to give a reason after each response.

Note: This was a survey, not a normative exercise or a clinical pursuit in depth. It was therefore not concerned with horizontal décalage. Particularly in respect to length, children may have been classed as "conservers" on the task as it was given, though they failed to conserve length on other parts of the task.

3. Formal Operations

The children were presented with three lengths of bark-twist string whose ends had been made into knotted loops. The lengths were 45 cm, 60 cm and 75 cm. They were also shown a container made from an empty "pike-mackerel" can (Pike mackerel is a very common imported food) with a wire hook on top, and five stones, each about 50 g in weight. The median-length string was attached to a nail in the wall, the can and two stones hung on the end, and the pendulum allowed to oscillate from a chalked mark. The children were asked to find out what they could do to make the pendulum go backward and forward more often than a standard pendulum, which was also an empty fish can on a 60 cm string. The standard pendulum was used because there was no other way of dissociating *speed* from *frequency* of oscillation.

Note: Achievement with this task was so disappointing and the task so time-consuming that the later two thirds of the sample were tested with it only if the subject had been classed as a conserver of length.

4. Two-dimensional Matrix

The wooden blocks were arranged as below, with A equaling 5 cm, B equaling 10 cm, and C 15 cm in height, while 1 equaled 2.5 cm × 2.5 cm in thickness, 2 equaled 4 cm × 4 cm, and 3 equaled 5.5 cm × 5.5 cm.

subject

C1	B1	A1
C2	B2	A2
C3	B3	A3

tester

The child was asked to look at the way the blocks were arranged. Then (a) A1, A2, and A3 were removed and the child asked to replace them as before. If a mistake was made, the tester corrected it and the child was asked again to look at the way the blocks were arranged. The same procedure was followed for four more subtasks: (a) C2, B2, A2 removed; (b) all but C3 removed; (c) all blocks removed; (d) C3 placed where A1 originally fitted, all others removed.

Scoring

    1. Both conservation tasks were scored for:
(a) achievement of conservation behavior and acceptable reason
(b) achievement of conservation behavior only
(c) no conservation, or doubtful
2. The formal operations task was scored for:
(a) evidence of combinatorial thinking
(b) success
3. The matrix task was finally scored for correct or incorrect placement of blocks for each of the five subtasks. Initially an attempt was made to describe the type of error, but this soon appeared to be a meaningless exercise.

Language used in the Test Situation

    Because of the aim of the study, the emphasis was on communication. In later follow-up work other considerations dictated the language used in the test situation. In Stage 1, the fourth- and sixth-class school children were tested in English, the language of instruction of the school, and the first-class school children, like all the village children, were tested in their vernacular using sixth-class subjects who had already been tested as interpreters. The following precautions were adopted to minimize errors due to this proceedure.

    1. The form of questions asked was checked by the use of quadruple translation techniques.
    2. The tester learned key vernacular terms for question and response.
    3. Interpreters were changed daily and chosen randomly from the available pool.
    4. Female subjects were checked for possible marriage and associated taboos with the current interpreter.
    5. Children were tested out of earshot, but in full view of waiting subjects.
    6. Check questions were frequently interpolated, e.g., with the length-conservation inverted T illusion, "Which one looks longer?"

General Procedure

The subjects were tested individually in a face-to-face situation, in two sessions. The first used the product tasks described above. The second session, of about the same length, used process tasks. Each child was rewarded with chewing gum and tobacco after each session and given a break of roughly an hour between sessions. It is interesting to note that by the 1972 follow-up series, the highlands children were asking for money as well as sweets and/or tobacco, as a reward for "working for you."

Analysis of Results

Results for Stage 1 are presented in three forms. The first is purely descriptive and in essence is simply the percentage of children in various categories and combinations of categories of the sample who achieved success in the tasks as defined. The second form is concerned with developmental trends for success. The third is concerned with interactions between the independent variables—sex, age, school experience, and language/culture group—and the given dependent variable. It must be stressed that this type of research can really provide nothing but frequency counts in cells of a matrix of variables which are themselves categorized. Although early reports (Kelly, 1971a, 1971b) attempted to use covariance analyses, the writer contends that this is an approach of dubious validity. Forcing data into an analysis of variance or covariance form may have been of use when techniques for nonparametric analysis or factorial designs were not possible. To this end, the program of multilevel chi-square analysis developed by R. Mitchell of Macquarie University was used. This program can handle five factors, each with five levels, and presents the main effects (second-, third-, and fourth-order interactions of the independent variables) on the dependent; but makes no assumptions regarding type of scale in the scoring or distribution of the variable under assessment. Thus neither the analysis concerned with association of one dependent with another, nor, the interaction of independent variables, uses parametric statistics.

Age distribution of sample

Table 5–1 set out the sample as planned, based on years of schooling and equivalent "age" for village children. It was pointed out that recorded ages in Papua New Guinea were unreliable, and that all subjects had their age "guesstimated" by the writer as a guide. The final sample characteristics for "age" are set out in Table 5–2.

Table 5–2
Distribution of guessed ages (in years) from school and village sample

	Range	Mean	Mode
School	6 to 19	10;8	11
Village	6 to 19	11;3	10

The presence of children in the 12-plus age group was due to the comparative recency of the establishment of the school. In later follow-up studies the "bulge" of children markedly older than "normal" had passed through the system, and the mean age of each grade more nearly approached that of a developed country. It is therefore stressed once more that the results of the first survey are not to be thought of as representative of anything except the sample as it was drawn. The age distributions were not different to a degree approaching statistical significance.

Tables 5–3 and 5–4 set out the gross percentages of children in the various subsamples who achieved success in the tasks as listed. Table 5–3 presents achievement of success in conservation of quantity, conservation of length, and formal operations while Table 5–4 is confined to the five sub-tasks of the classification matrix. The gross results have been broken down by language/culture group, school experience versus no school experience, and sex. (M = male, F = female). It must be remembered that the group labeled "Avatip Village" in fact comprises 10 Sepik village children and 62 highlanders.

Table 5–3
Percentage of children in listed subsamples achieving success in tasks.

	Avatip				Muglum				Goilala			
	SCHOOL N = 72		VILLAGE N = 72		SCHOOL N = 72		VILLAGE N = 72		SCHOOL N = 72		VILLAGE N = 72	
	M	F	M	F	M	F	M	F	M	F	M	F
Conservation of quantity*	39	28	44	0	55	53	57	35	28	26	9	0
Conservation of length*	19	6	8	0	17	11	14	7	11	6	6	3
Formal operations	0	0	0	0	0	0	0	0	0	0	0	0

*1. Percentages are rounded
 2. Criterion for success in conservation tables here is behavior with acceptable reason.

Two points come immediately to mind from an inspection of Table 5–3. The first is that no child achieved success in the formal operations task. This is in marked contrast with children from sixth grade in New South Wales (Australia) schools were some 66% of boys and 44% of girls succeed to criterion (Philp and Kelly, 1974) and with children from central Java, whose level of success is similar to that of Australian children (Kelly and Limson, 1976). The second is the striking variation between sub-sample cells in percentage of success. It is worth noting that the order of task difficulty as evidenced by frequency of success is the same as in other countries where these tasks have been used.

This table (5–3) can be read in conjunction with Table 5–7, which presents significance levels for main effects of and interactions between the independent variables.

Where the school and village samples are directly comparable—the Muglum sample of Melpa-speaking people—school experience has no discernible effect on ability to conserve either quantity or length for males, though there is an effect for females. The result for males is in keeping with Piaget's often-repeated statement that the structures which he describes are not affected to any material extent by school. The lower success rate of village female is repeated in the Avatip and Goilala samples. The Avatip village sample was overwhelmingly composed of highlanders—superficially, at least, similar to the Muglum highlanders—while the Goilala village sample was mostly of the Tawaundi people, though the Goilala school sample comprised a significant proportion of the Kunimaipa, who are ostensibly more able than the Tawaudi in performing Western tasks. This finding raises some interesting questions. Firstly, one might ask why the Keltiga village females (added to the Avatip Sepik sample) achieve significantly less well than the Muglum village females when they have so many similarities in life-style and environment. The fact that females achieve less well than males is of itself not a contradiction of Piaget's position. There are observable differences in the village education—i.e., experiences—system across the sexes. It would appear, however, that school has a marked effect on achievement of this kind for females, even when the shortcomings of sampling are considered. The school environment for males and females is much more similar than is the village environment, and the similarities between teaching methods, curriculum, and even teachers' ethnic origins is more similar from one area to another than are the village life styles. This probably accounts for the "levelling" effect of school experience. Paradoxically enough, in the field of the process tasks the same levelling effect is apparent—but in the other direction: the village females are "superior" to the males and are brought closer to them in the school situation as the school males "improve" compared with their village cousins, and as the school females "regress." (Kelly, 1971c).

The lower rate of success in conservation of length and the total failure in the formal operations task are both worthy of comment. In considering the result in formal operations the first causal force was thought to be lack of understanding of the task, which was rather alien to the needs of the children sampled, as they perceived them. Indeed, even now the writer is not certain that communication took place. Nevertheless, follow-up work carried out by Jones of the Papua New Guinea University Educational Research Unit (Jones, 1974) supports the validity of the finding. The pendulum task was abandoned, in the replication of this survey with other cultures, in favor of an electrical analog of the four-chemical test. The correlation between results on the analog and results using the actual four chemicals are of the order of .88. Jones used the same analog, together with other tests he had developed in Malawi, and found extremely low levels of success even with final-year high school students (sixth form) and first-year university students. One suggestion has been that the basic value systems of the children are inimical to the easy development of hypothetic-deductive reasoning. This is currently being explored in relation to cognitive tasks.

The conservation of length results are harder to explain. Two possible explanations present themselves. The first is based on language and will be explored more fully when the 1972 replication study is discussed. It is not easy to ask the Piagetian question regarding length conservation in any Papua New Guinea dialect familiar to the writer. In addition, compensation reasons are easier to give than reversibility. While the writer does not wish to espouse the position of Whorf, or even of Vigotskij, it does seem that the possession of syntactical structures and verbal labels in the language facilitates behavior in related areas, and this seems true in Papua New Guinea for reversibility. Of course this does not solve the chicken-and-egg problem. As has been noted, the Tawaudi people appear to lack counting words, and barter by one-to-one correspondence. But is it a lack of need for counting that has inhibited language development, or has a lack of words inhibited thought? Considering the flexibility of living languages, it is difficult to see why words for "threeness," "fourness," etc., would not be invented on need. Yet later evidence suggests that bilingual school children alter their behavior depending on the language used in the test situation (either the language of instruction or the vernacular). (Kelly and Philp, 1975). The second explanation relates to logical necessity. There is much mensuration in village life—in house construction, for example. This is normally carried out by matching length A to position B or by measuring by some *ad hoc* unit. It was not usual for a man to argue that because X fitted somewhere before, it must fit there again. Thus the mensuration is empirical, pragmatic, and *ad hoc*. No universal units of measurement appear to be involved, and there seems to be a powerful connection between the ability to handle measurement and the achievement of conservation of length (especially in bilinguals) (Kelly, Philp, and Lewis, 1976).

Table 5–4.
Percentage of children in listed subsamples achieving success in the named subtasks, for two-dimensional matrix.

| | | Avatip | | | Mulgum | | | | Goilala | | | |
| | | SCHOOL N = 72 | | VILLAGE N = 72 | | SCHOOL N = 72 | | VILLAGE N = 72 | | SCHOOL N = 72 | | VILLAGE N = 72 | |
		M	F	M	F	M	F	M	F	M	F	M	F
1.	Width only varied	85	83	85	77	92	94	89	64	92	94	71	76
2.	Height only varied	69	69	88	77	86	92	86	71	94	91	62	50
3.	Block C3 remains	50	39	54	29	53	64	29	58	58	58	29	24
4.	All removed	47	53	44	32	54	59	52	29	72	55	29	29
5.	Block C3 reflected	42	39	29	23	56	39	41	14	64	31	9	11

Again let us note that the order of difficulty is similar to that found in other cultures (Philp and Kelly, 1974). The village females tend to do less well than either the school females or the village males, except in the Goilala sample. Here both village groups do markedly less well than the school groups. It has already been noted that the ethnic composition of the Goilala school groups differs from that of the village groups; with respect to ability in Western tasks the school groups do better. Marked differences begin to occur when the criteria for classification change from one only (height or width) or two simultaneously. There are few differences between Subtasks 3 and 4. The task involving reflection of the matrix (Task 5) is considerably more difficult for most subgroups.

Age Trends over Tasks

Because of the "guesstimation" of ages in the samples, the distribution has been divided into three sections: 9 years and below, 10 to 12 years, and over 12 years. Table 5–5 presents grouped ages for all males and all females for conservation of quantity (CQ), conservation of length (CL), Matrix Subtask 2 (height only varied), Matrix Subtask 3 (block C3 remains only), and Matrix Subtask 5 (block C3 reflected).

Table 5–5

Percentage of children in tasks listed achieving success by age groups and sex

Age	Sex	CQ	CL	M2	M3	M5
1	M	17	5	71	32	18
	F	21	4	74	38	17
2	M	43	8	89	57	42
	F	11	3	84	44	33
3	M	55	20	97	65	59
	F	34	8	90	42	30

Note: Formal operations task is not included.

In general there is a trend for percentage of success to rise as age increases. This is always true of males but not of females. Percentage of successes for Conservation of Quantity in the middle of the three age groups falls off markedly for females, while there is little difference between the middle group of females and the oldest when the Matrix 3 and Matrix 5 tasks are compared. In other words, development as measured by these tasks proceeds for males much as it does in any other culture where testing has been carried out, albeit more slowly. Females show irregularities and significant deviations from the male pattern, the absolute level of achievement being markedly lower. It has already been noted that in "process" type tasks it is the females in these samples who do better than the males. (Kelly 1971c). Further breakdowns into language/culture groups are interesting, but are more powerfully and more economically presented using the multilevel chi-square technique previously mentioned. Table 5–6 presents all data from the application of the program to the tasks selected. The key is as follows:

Age: Membership in one of three age groups; 9 and below, 10 to 12, and over 12.

School: Belonging either to the sample with school experience (1, 4, or 6 years) or that with no school experience, called "village."

Sex: Male or female.

Language: Membership in a particular language/culture group. It is necessary to point out again that language/culture group number one consisted of a homogeneous group of Nyausa *school* children along with a mixed group of Nyausa and Melpa *village* children, whereas group three was relatively homogeneous as regards village children (Tawaudi), while the school sample was of mixed Tawaudi and Kunimaipa children.

Standard methods are used to denote statistical significance. One asterisk denotes the .05 level of confidence, two the .01 and three the .001 level. As with Table 5–5, CQ = conservation of quantity; CL = conservation of length; and two matrix Subtasks are used: 2, where height alone varies, and 5, where the tallest, thickest block is reflected across the diagonal and all others are removed.

Table 5–6
Main effects and interactions for multilevel chi-square program for age, sex, school experience, and language/culture groups, applied across tasks as listed

Factor	CQ	CL	M2	M5
Age	***	*	***	***
Sex	***	*	—	**
School	**	—	**	***
Language/culture	***	—	—	***
Age × sex	**	—	—	*
Age × school	***	*	—	—
Age × language/culture	—	—	—	—
Sex × school	*	—	—	—
Sex × language/culture	—	—	—	—
School × language/culture	—	—	*	*
Age × sex × school	—	—	—	—
Age × sex × language/culture	—	—	—	—
sex × school × language/culture	—	—	—	—
Age × school × language/culture	—	—	—	—
Age × sex × school × language/culture	—	—	—	—

As one would expect, age is a significant main effect across all variables. The lower level of significance for conservation of length (as will all conservation of length effects and interactions) is due to the low level of achievement generally in this task. An examination of the earlier tables suggests that sex also is an expected main effect, with the females achieving less well than the males, the difference becoming more marked as age increases; hence the significant age and sex interaction for conservation of quantity and the reflected matrix task. School as a main effect owes its force almost entirely to the differences between school females and village females. Less obvious, but interesting, is the contribution of membership of the language/culture group. This is a significant main effect for conservation of quantity and obtains most of its variance from the disproportionate distribution of Melpa speakers for the Muglum district (a "pure" subsample) and the distribution of Goilala children.

Language/culture also provides a significant interaction with school experience in the matrix Subtasks 2 and 5. There are, indeed material differences for language/culture group membership in all the reported tasks, but none of the other Piaget-based tasks achieves significance at the .05 level or better.

FOLLOW-UP STUDIES

Only those follow-up studies based on Piagetian theory are described. These formed a relatively small part of the total series of follow-up efforts. Decisions as to the course to be pursued therefore were made on grounds other than the results of the Piagetian tasks alone, though the same methodology was used across all follow-up tasks.

The first of these which involved Piagetian variables attempted to disentangle the effects of the linguistic area of culture from the non-linguistic. By "linguistic" we here mean "verbal".

The decision to use language and culture as important variables arose because the total 1969 study, involving 126 measures, demonstrated membership of the language/culture group as an important main effect or interaction in over 100 of them.

Sample (General)

All samples for this and later follow-up studies were drawn from the Melpa-speaking area around Mount Hagen. All samples were either from the Muglum district, or from the similar Keltiga one; and these have been described in some detail earlier in this chapter. However, by the time of the main testing to be described, the constitution of the school population in all three of the primary schools used had changed in two ways: One of the criteria for selection of schools for the 1969 study was availability of males and females of relevant ages with and without school experience. Of necessity, the schools chosen had not been established for more than six or seven years, six being the minimum for provision of the older sixth-grade pupils. Because the schools were new, the composition of the first few preparatory and grade one classes was unusual. Other children—especially the children of important village families—were found in abundance, and the 1969 grade-six "children" included several judged as 20 years old. By 1972 this "teething" bulge had passed through and the age distributions, even though guessed at, began to approach those for which the schools had originally been planned. One would imagine that this would have a material effect on the test results, and indeed, conservation of length in 1972 produced quite different results from those derived with older siblings during 1969. The comparison with some discussion, is offered in and following Table 5–9.

The second difference related to the availability of females with school experience. Initially the primary school principals, almost exclusively expatriate, had brought considerable pressure to bear on parents to enroll girls as well as boys, and to keep them at school. By 1972 two things had happened: One was that with the weakening of the Australian "raj" the parents were less likely to enroll girls anyway, or to keep them enrolled. The second had to do with experience of nonpayment of bride-wealth for educated girls and the observable non-advantage of keeping girls in school and out of the productive gardening in a district oversupplied with "trained" labor. Consequently the school population was both younger and less balanced sexually than in 1969.

Follow-up Study 1

Tasks

As already stated, the 1972 follow-up contained many elements. Some were from the affective area and some were from cognitive positions other than the Piagetian which are reported here. Conservation of Length was repeated using the same techniques as in 1969 (though with language of testing varied by subsample) in order to give some baseline on which to base comparisons. The second task chosen was a form of class inclusion. Pilot studies in 1971 suggested that the building of hierarchies of classification was not a feature of many Papua New Guinea languages or cultural behaviors. Two questions arose: "What *could* the children do if pressed?" and "What *would* they do if relatively unconstrained?" The Melpa "world view" was analyzed, checked with tribal elders, and rechecked with anthropologists. It appeared that Figure 5–2 fairly represents the way in which the language and culture viewed the world.

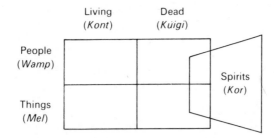

Figure 5–2. Melpa world view classification system

Of the four main boxes, living things contained the greatest variety of classes. However, the classes tend to arrange themselves like the ribs of an umbrella, with *mel kont* ("living things") as the handle. Typical classes include *kim* ("leaf vegetable") *okka* ("sweet potato"), *dey* ("trees"), and *keri* ("birds"). These are often subdivided with a second "noun" and perhaps an adjective. Thus *kim kun pombra* is the green variety of the *kun* kind of leaf vegetable. Many of the classes included in *mel kont* were, of course, foodstuffs. One term, *rung*, cut across many classes and included them, though being subsumed by *mel kont*. However, *rung* (food) is not the inclusive term that the word "food" can be in English, and is more like the difference between "prepared for eating" (usually cooked) and "potentially eatable". It was, however, possible to construct a hierarchy of inclusiveness using two kinds of *kim* in combination as *kim*, adding *okka* to combine with *kim* as rung, and adding *dey* ("trees") to combine with *okka* and *kim* as *mel kont* ("living things").

This system made possible three kinds of questions:

1. Would the children divide objects according to these designations if asked to separate them into piles and then reseparate?
2. Could the children combine the objects in the designated way?
3. Could they accept that the term *kim* was more inclusive than *kun* or *kimpi* (another kind of leaf vegetable), the term *rung* more inclusive than *kim* or *okka*, and the term *dey* more inclusive than either *kim* or *okka*?

In effect the hierarchy can be diagramed as in Figure 5–3.

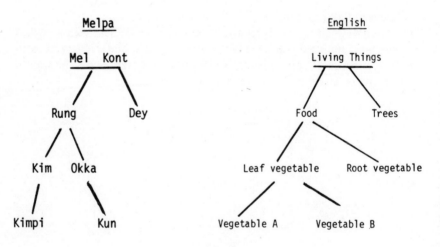

Figure 5–3.

Sample

Three groups of children were tested. Two groups were drawn from the school population and one from the nonschool population. All three subsamples were matched for age and sex, and in addition the two school samples were matched for school experience both in terms of years of schooling and in terms of classes (i.e. having the same teacher). All the children spoke Melpa as their vernacular and the school children in addition, spoke English—the language of instruction used in the school. One school subsample and the nonschool (village) subsample were tested in the vernacular, Melpa. The other school subsample was tested in English. In effect, this was an attempt to hold culture constant while varying language by comparing the results of the two "school" samples; and to hold language constant while varying culture by comparing the results of the two samples tested in the vernacular—one "school" and one "village". It must be stressed that the two samples of school children should have been equally able in their knowledge of English, in whatever skills were taught by the school, and in Melpa, the vernacular. There is no reason to suppose that all three subsamples were not equally able in the vernacular but it was assumed that the different experiences of the school children vis-à-vis the village children would make a "cultural" difference. No conclusions are being drawn about the sampled populations and thus the classic objections to matching do not apply. The scoring was based on behavior; and all language used in the test situation was consistently English or Malpa, depending on subsample as designed.

Table 5–7 sets out the numbers in the cells for the total sample.

Table 5–7
Numbers of subjects used in 1972 follow-up study by age, sex, school experience, and language used in testing

		YEARS OF SCHOOLING			
		4	6	0 (village children)	N
Tested in	M	12	12	0	24
English	F	12	12	0	24
Tested in	M	12	12	24	48
Melpa	F	12	12	24	48
		48	48	48	144

Materials

The tasks used Polaroid color photographs of instances of the classes diagramed earlier. It had been established that Papua New Guinea children did not behave differently when classifying color photographs than when classifying real objects of which the photographs were a depiction, (Kelly, 1971b, and Philp and Kelly, 1974), though there were differences when colored drawings prepared by a Western artist were used. The set comprised:

1. 2 trees (*dey*): one used for firewood, and the other for "tobacco" (though the wood was sometimes burned).
2. 2 varieties of sweet potato (*okka*)
3. 2 instances of leaf vegetable A (*kim pompa*)
4. 4 instances of leaf vegetable B (*kim kimpi*)

Method

Each child was given two forms of the task in a split-half design.

1. All photographs were laid before him. He was asked to identify each, and then asked to sort them into two piles.

The larger pile was indicated and he was asked to sort this pile into two piles.

Again the large pile was indicated and he was asked to sort the numbers into two piles.

Scoring was based on the predetermined hierarchy: the first sort was correct if the trees were separated from the food pictures; the second if the root vegetables were separated from the leaf vegetables; and the third if the *kimpi* were separated from the *pompa*.

2. The six leaf vegetables were laid before the child, who was asked to identify them and to indicate if they were all *kim*.

He was then asked, "Are there more *pompa* than *kimpi*? Are there more *kimpi* than *pompa*? Are there more *pompa* than *kim*? Are there more *kimpi* than *kim*?" Then the two root vegetables were added and the same procedure followed, using *rung* as the class word and *okka* and *kim* as the subset classes. Finally the two trees were added and the procedure again followed, using *mel kont* as the class term.

Results

A. Conservation of Length.

It has been noted that this was a replication of the task used in the first survey and used identical materials ("pit-pit" sticks) and identical method. (The method was reported earlier.) Two sets of results are offered. The first, in Table 5–8, sets out the results from the follow-up study divided with reference to school experience and sex. The second, in Table 5–9, compares these with the earlier findings for the Melpa group only.

Table 5–8
Conservation of length, percentage succeeding by school experience and language of testing: 1972 follow-up.

	LANGUAGE OF TESTING		
	School English (N = 48)	*School Melpa (N = 48)*	*Village Melpa (N = 48)*
Correct with or without reason	45.8	37.33	20.8
Correct with acceptable reason	37:5	27.0	10.4

Table 5–9
Conservation of length. Comparison of comparable school and village groups, correct with reason, for Melpa children in 1969 and 1972 (four and six years of school only).

	School (English)	*Village (Melpa)*
1969 N = 72	21	10.5
1972 N = 48	37.5	10.4

From Table 5–8 it is obvious that the trend in success is school English > school Melpa > village Melpa whether the criterion is behavior or behavior with reason. The difference between school children tested in English and school children tested in Melpa is not statistically significant, but the comparison between school and village children tested in the vernacular, Melpa, is highly so ($p < .01$). School seems to make a difference to the capacity to conserve length. It is also worth noting that the proportions of children able to "give a reason" for conservation, compared with the total able to succeed in the task "with or without reason," decreases significantly from "school English" (.82) to "school Melpa" (.72) to "village Melpa" (.50). It is easy in the Melpa language to express a reason for conservation based on compensation (e.g., "The bit sticking out on that end is the same as the bit at the other end"). It is quite difficult, without circumlocution, to express reversibility because of the lack of a conditional mood. While this may have bearing on the different results "with reason," it does not explain the greater success of the school children compared with the village children. On a number of occasions Piaget has noted that the structures he describes are not taught in school. However, he is talking of Western European societies. One may infer that the conditions under which length conservation schemes develop are not common in the village environment of Papua New Guinea and that they are more common in the school environment, while in the Western European society these conditions are indeed found in the out-of-school situation, and school factors are therefore redundant.

Table 5–9 provides some interesting comparisons. *The proportion of village children achieving conservation changes virtually not at all from 1969 to 1972.* There is, however, a material rise among the comparable school group over the same period (21% to 37.5%). The composition of the two samples was highly similar in all respects but age, as was the method of testing, etc. It has been noted that the "teething bulge" of older children who enrolled in the early classes when the school first opened had passed through the system by 1972, though in 1969 they heavily seeded Class 6 and to some degree Class 4. Considering that this is the only apparent difference in the two samples and that the village samples did not show differences over the two years, one may infer that exposure to the conditions necessary for development of conservation schemes available in school but not out of it, is less effective as the child increases in age upon first exposure to them.

B. Class Inclusion

1. The task was given in two forms. The first—a possible division—was designed simply to see if the children *would* divide the stimulus set in the predetermined way. While efforts had been made to make the hierarchy stimulus set accord with Melpa possibilities this did not of itself imply that children would use these when the task was in a relatively free situation. Table 5–10 gives the percentage of each subgroup of the 1972 sample who did sort the pictures into the predetermined piles.

Table 5–10
Percentage of subjects in each subsample whose classification matched the set one

School English	50.0
School Melpa	45.8
Village Melpa	16.6

Two findings emerge from this table: The first is that not all children do, as a matter of course, follow the class system inherent in their vernacular. The second is that school experience has a highly significant effect on ability to divide classes of objects, even when the classes are made up from the vernacular.

The main aim of this task was of course the test for *class inclusion.* Results appear in Table 5–11.

Table 5–11
Hierarchy of class inclusion—per cent succeeding by subsample

	Success at "Kim" inclusion point	Success at "rung" inclusion point	Success at "mel kont" inclusion point
School English	81.2	43.7	58.3
School Melpa	70.8	22.9	52.0
Village Melpa	60.48	31.2	41.6

The only comparison between criterion subsamples which reaches statistical significance lies between school English and school Melpa at the *rung* inclusion point, though the general trend is school English > school Melpa > village Melpa. It should be noted that the words *kim* and *mel kont* like the English equivalents "leaf vegetable" and "living things" are terms which have a clear inclusion/exclusion denotation. The term *rung*—which is normally translated as "food"—unlike its English equivalent, is not as precise in demarcation since it is more properly thought of in common usage as "prepared for eating" or "cooked." However, it is also used in the sense of "can be prepared for eating" and in this sense it is a reasonable parallel to the English "food". The data do not imply in what sense the children thought of *rung,* but the language used in the test situation is clearly related to successful behavior at the *rung* inclusion point.

It is of some interest to note that the level of success in the class inclusion task is quite high for all groups at the lowest level of the hierarchy. There is no comparable result from West European samples, to the writer's knowledge, but Richardson and Kelly (1972) using brass and steel nuts with second-year fitting and machine apprentices (17 years of age) report 5% failure in a similar task.

Follow-up studies 2 and 3

Two further studies are reported. The first was carried out later in 1972 and is interesting in a negative way. It was an attempt to delineate some areas of cognitive development in preschoolers in New Guinea. The preschool "movement" had developed sporadically and spasmodically in some large urban centers, mostly for the children of expatriates and the comparatively affluent. The setting used for this small study was Goroka, the chief town of the East Highlands, about twenty minutes flight (by F-27) from Mount Hagen. Thirty preschoolers were tested, aged 4 to 6 years, and 30 of the same age and sex were drawn from the non-preschool population of the villages surrounding Goroka. No ethnically based comparison can be made because the village children were all of the Gorohoku tribe whereas the school children came from all over Papua New Guinea except Gorohoku. Eight tasks were administered in any language which would serve to communicate (i.e. Melanesian, vernacular, or English). Three of these tasks were based on Piaget's work. These were (1) conservation of quantity, using rice (see 1969 study procedure), (2) matrix classification Subtasks 1, 2, and 5 (see 1969 procedure); (3a) a "staircase" of seven sticks differing in length by 2 cm each, from 4 cm upward; (3b) three sticks which had to be inserted in appropriate places. These sticks were 7, 12, and 15 cm respectively.

The results are set out in Table 5–12, divided by school experience and sex.

Table 5–12
Preschool/village sample. Percent achievement success in the listed tasks. (Percentages to nearest whole.) (Sample age range approximately 4–6.)

| | SCHOOL | | VILLAGE | |
	Male $N = 15$	*Female* $N = 15$	*Male* $N = 15$	*Female* $N = 15$
Conservation of quantity	0	0	0	0
Matrix 1	53	66	53	53
2	20	0	6	6
5	0	0	0	0
Ordinal relations, basic set (a)	40	33	26	60
Insertions (b)	0	6	0	0

It would seem that the only tasks within the capacity of all subsamples were the two easy block replacement tasks and ordering the basic set of seven sticks in the staircase form. The numbers in the sample cells are too small for statistical significance or to have any valid implications. Table 5–12 is presented as an indicator of the lower cutoff point (or beginning point) for the development of Piagetian structures in some Papua New Guinea children. Clearly common attribute grouping (matrix) and simple ordering have begun to appear in a sample with a mean age of 5. Conservation of Quantity is quite absent and only one child (school female) succeeded in entering intermediate length sticks in the ordered set of seven. It is quite conceivable that more sensitive indicators of Piagetian structures are needed if it is desired to explore the cognitive development of children of this age group.

The second of the two further studies offers more positive results. It was carried out in 1973 with secondary children from Mount Hagen High school from Form 3. The age range for the 79 children tested was reported from school records as 16 to 19. All the subjects had won a place at the high school at the terminal examination following seven years of primary school, and had survived $2\frac{1}{2}$ years of secondary school when tested. They could be called the "academic cream" of the West Highlands. The subjects fell into three groups:

1. Melpa children, whose environment had already been described;

2. Enga children. These people are a very large language group whose land borders on the Melpa tribes' ground. Their way of life is quite similar in most respects to that of the Melpas, though an anthropologist would be quick to point out differences—with some heat one suspects.

3. "Urban" children. There were the children of teachers, warders, policemen, etc. from many parts of the country who were currently stationed at Mount Hagen.

In the main the children from Groups 1 and 2 grew up in villages, while Group 3 spent much more time in towns and hamlets—or at least they did not grow up in an environment where the prime work of their parents was agriculture.

Tasks

Two tasks are reported here. The first is Conservation of Length, the second Conservation of Area.

1. Conservation of Length
  (a) The procedure using sticks as described earlier.
  (b) A similar procedure using two shoelaces. These were equated, and then one was "distorted" in random ways before returning to the straight position, parallel with the other, for a final equation.

2. Conservation of Area
  (a) A sheet of quarto paper was equated with a second sheet. Ten 1 cm

wooden cubes were placed on each sheet, arranged in a pattern 2 cm by 5 cm at the top left-hand corner. The areas left uncovered were equated. One group of ten blocks was then scattered at random across the paper and the "equation of area" question was asked. The original pattern was re-formed and a final equation sought.

(b) Two sheets of paper represented a tribe's ground. Wooden block "huts" 1 cm × 1 cm at base were used in different arrangements to simulate villages. Eight huts were used for each sheet of paper. The pattern again was equation deformation of one set, and equation. Care was taken to make sure the idea of paths or tracks (which are not used for gardens) did not confuse the issue. Some village arrangements use more ground for tracks than others.

Sample

Table 5–13 sets out the sample composition which comprised the whole of Form 3 for 1973.

Table 5–13
Sample Composition

	Melpa	Enga	"Urban"
Male	30	18	9
Female	1	2	6

Results

1. Conservation of Length: all children succeeded in both parts of the Conservation of Length task.
2. Conservation of area: Table 5–14 sets out the results for Conservation of Area, parts (a) and (b).

Table 5–14
Conservation of Area: success with reason

(Percentages in brackets)

	MELPA		ENGA		"URBAN"		TOTAL	
	M	F	M	F	M	F	M	F
Part a	14	0	7	0	5	5	26	5
	(46)	(0)	(38)	(0)	(55)	(83)	(45)	(55)
Part b	14	0	7	0	4	5	25	5
	(46)	(0)	(38)	(0)	(44)	(83)	(43)	(55)

All children were able to conserve length in both forms. Conservation of area results are rather different. The attempts to split the sample derived from a hunch that the urban children would not suffer from the interference of cultural measurement differences which might mitigate against the rural children's acquiring conservation of area. The cell numbers are small, admittedly, but an appropriate test does not show any statistically significant differences. Looking at the totals, and disregarding the females, who number only nine, it is noteworthy that 100% of the "educationally creamed-off" children, using a Western educational criterion, succeed in length by form 3. Equally noteworthy is the finding that less than half conserve area. This fits well with the teachers' reports that problems involving area and/or volume cause much trouble for secondary pupils. However it is at variance with the finding of Jones (1974), a summary of which appears in Table 5–15.

Table 5–15
Jones's result for length and area (percentages)

	A N = 16	B N = 44	C N = 59
Conservation of length	56	73	64
Conservation of area	81	75	51

A = Preliminary students, University of Papua New Guinea
B = Senior High School form 5
C = High School form 4

Unfortunately, at this period of knowledge, there is no apparent reason for the Jones data. There are more students in both groups A and B who conserve area than there are students who conserve length. Since Piaget argues a logical necessity for length conservation before area conservation, it would seem that Jones's subjects are of a very different kind from those in the Mount Hagen high school sample, and indeed from any others yet reported. Perhaps this highlights our lack of real knowledge of these phenomena and is an appropriate point to cease description of data and to begin some sort of summing up.

At several points in this chapter it has been noted that the tasks reported were but a part of the total framework of Papua New Guinean research within which they were located. Naturally, in this volume, tasks outside the Piagetian framework are not relevant and are not included. The Piagetian research was not the major part of the total program. This is because the primary aim was to provide assistance to the education authority in the achievement of its stated aims. The process of change, or the identification of the underlying factors responsible for the results, was of major concern. Whether or not the enormously detailed and logical descriptions of development provided by the Piagetian school are universal to all mankind is, in this context, a moot question. Yet it does seem certain that where a culture displays skill in Western European science and technology, there are found the structures described by Piaget. The government of now independent Papua New Guinea wishes to train at least some of its people in the skills of Western science and technology. This is our justification for the educational changes we have suggested (and seen adopted) to achieve a higher rate of success in Piagetian tasks. We think, however, that the basic intellectual structures to be developed in Papua New Guinean children in realization of this aim are those concerned with "hierarchilization," or the power to construct lattices of increasing class inclusiveness. The presence or absence of these lattices (of the Melpa "umbrella" structure) seems to correlate with success in the current Western-style school system. It may be that this is an intellectual structure more basic to humans than that which surfaces in European children in the way that Piaget has described. Or it may be that this is a necessary condition for development through the Piagetian stages.

Currently we have set up a ten-year program in Papua New Guinea teachers' colleges to train student teachers in the recognition of vernacular class structures and their interrelationships. These will then form the basis for domino and card games for children beginning school. The games are designed in the hope that children will be led as follows:

1. to an awareness of the basic structures of their own language/culture.

2. towards a facility in grouping "foreign" objects in ways congruent with their own basic structures,

3. to a grouping of familiar objects in foreign structures,

4. and finally to facility in grouping "foreign" objects in "foreign" structures in a really meaningful way.

After this the Dienes style of mathematical learning may have the success it has lacked until now. Already pilot studies have demonstrated success in "transfer." With the Mount Hagen high school students described circa Table 5–15, training in their own cultural method of measuring perimeter and area has resulted in "spontaneous" conservation of area in the Piagetian form. This had persisted for six months when last tested. Other pilot studies concerned with methods of coding and retrieval of information, and training in these methods, indicates transfer to success in Piagetian tasks. It is too early yet to attempt a formulation of theory derived from this work, but education must proceed as if theory were consolidated. The emphasis on process in the research has paid dividends. An exploration of levels of success à la Piaget, we would argue, is sterile description, if factors promoting change are ignored. We look forward to a time when the relationships between the major theoretical divisions are understood. In the meantime, empirical and *ad hoc* formulations are the only tools the educator has.

ACKNOWLEDGMENTS

The work described in this chapter has been carried out by the author in collaboration with the following:
1. For the great majority of the work, Professor Hugh Philp, Macquarie University, Australia.
2. For the main line Papua New Guinea survey, Kipling Uiari, then of Psychological Services, Papua New Guinea, now Secretary of State for Finance.
3. For the preschool study, David Harris, also of Macquarie University.

REFERENCES

Brislin, R. (1974) Methodology of Cognitive Studies. Paper to meeting of the *Australian Institute of Aboriginal Studies*, Canberra. May 1974.

Department of District Administration, Papua New Guinea (1968) *Village Directory*. Port Moresby: G. Read. Acting Government Printer.

Gates, R. E. (1964) Eruption of permanent teeth of N.S.W. school children. Part I—Ages of eruption. *Australian Dental Journal*, 3:211–218.

Jones, J. (1974) Educational Research Unit, University of Papua New Guinea, Report 1974. Port Moresby: University of Papua New Guinea.

Kelly, M. R. (1971a) Some aspects of conservation of quantity and length in Papua New Guinea in relation to language, sex and years at school. *Papua New Guinea Journal of Education*, 7: 55–60.

———, (1971b) A two-criteria classification matrix with some Papua and New Guinea children. *Papua New Guinea Journal of Education*, 7:46–49.

———, (1971c) The validity of Bruner's concepts of modes of representation of reality with a sample of Papua and New Guinea children. *Papua New Guinea Journal of Education*, 7:33–37.

———,(1971d) *Some comparative results on Piaget and Bruner measures from the four-culture study on cognitive development*. Paper to 43rd ANZAAS Congress, Brisbane, May, 1971.

———, and Limson, U.S. (1976) *Urban Children of Central Java and Piagetian Measures*. Indonesian Ministry of Education. In press.

————, and Philp, H. (1975) Vernacular test instructions in relation to cognitive task behaviour among highland children of Papua New Guinea. *British Journal of Education Psychology, 45*:189–197.

————, Philp, H. and Lewis J. (1976) Conservation of length, concepts of measurement, and language hierarchies. In press.

Lawrence, P. (1969) *Road belong cargo*. Manchester: Manchester University Press.

Malcolm, L. (1969) Growth and development of the New Guinea child. *Papua New Guinea Journal of Education, 6*:23–37.

Philp, H. and Kelly, M. (1974) Product and process in cognitive development: Some comparative data on the performance of school-age children in different cultures. *British Journal of Educational Psychology, 44*:248–265.

Richardson, E. and Kelly, M. (1970) Some factors affecting the success of craft students in technical education. *The vocational aspect of education, 24*:73–78.

Ward, R. and Lea, D. (1970) *An atlas of Papua and New Guinea*. Glasgow: Collins and Longman.

6
The Development of the Concept of Speed Among Iraqi Children

SALIMA AL-FAKHRI

INTRODUCTION

After the work of Piaget attracted the attention of psychologists around the world, the cross-cultural movement started the replicating of his studies, using different methods. A number of basic facts have been discovered regarding the mental development of children. The sequence of stages revealed in most of the studies is similar all over the world; however, differences have been noted in the onset of each stage in the various cultures.

Studies conducted in a number of places, such as Aden, Algeria, Iran, Lebanon, Martinique, and Somalia, showed that children in these areas exhibit a lag of one to four years in the onset of each stage as compared to children in the West, although the sequence of stages is the same.

Recent Soviet studies by Galperin (1971) and by Proskura (1971) (in Al-Hamdani), based on the seminal work of Vygotsky (1966), reveal however a very important fact: that mental development is determined by the child's interaction with the objects and members of his society. This supports the idea that a child's thinking is influenced by cultural patterns. His thinking may also depend on the nature of his interaction with the elements and determinants of his culture.

Mentchinskaia (1966) shows that learning influences the development of thought, on the basis of Vygotsky's theory that learning should lead development and not lag behind it.

We conducted a number of studies following the Piagetian developmental approach among children from Baghdad, as a preliminary survey of the development of reasoning among Iraqi children. These studies include:

1. Conservation of liquids.
2. Logical composition of classes (class inclusion).
3. The conservation of length.
4. Spatial coordinate system (horizontality and verticality).
5. Measurement of length: subdividing a straight line.
6. Concept formation on dissolution. (Al-Fakhri, 1972–4)

Other Iraqi psychologists studied the conservation of quantity (substance, weight, and volume), the conservation of length (Al-Shaikh, 1973), and seriation and serial correspondence (Safar, 1974), on samples of children from Baghdad, following standardized experimental procedures. All of these studies, irrespective of the procedure used and the concept studied, agreed in showing a lag ranging from two to four years behind the Western child. The sequence of the stages was the same.

The present study deals with the development of the concept of speed. It differs from the above-mentioned studies in that the formation of the concept of speed requires the formation of the concept of time and length as constituents: because the concept of speed depends on the relationship between time and space. The child is not able to form the concept of speed unless he understands the conservation of time (irrespective of the events taking place during the time interval and irrespective of the synchronization of these events, and in spite of the fact that these events may be different in quality and quantity), and unless he understands the conservation of length.

Previous studies on the conservation of length amongst Iraqi children have shown that the concept lags behind about two years (Al-Fakhri, 1973c) to four years (Al-Shaikh, 1974) when compared with the European child. Thus the Iraqi child can be expected to lag behind at least as much in the formation of the concept of speed.

THE PROBLEM

The following three goals were set for the study:

1. To study the thinking processes of Iraqi children of various ages as they watch similar events occurring simultaneously, and ending with the same result.

2. To study the thinking processes of the child on this task when the child cannot directly compare the equality of distance.

3. To discover the thinking processes of the child when the time required for the events is the same but the action completed is different.

The author derived most of her ideas from Piaget's studies. However, the study described here is not an exact replica of Piaget's (1969, 1970) studies. The writer chose simplified situations that can be considered elementary in the formation of the concept of speed.

SAMPLE

The sample used in this study consisted of 267 children, distributed about evenly between the sexes and among the ages. The subject's ages ranged between 4 and 13 years.

Preschool children (ages 4 and 5) were taken from a kindergarden in a middle-class section of Baghdad. School children (ages 6–13) were taken from three primary schools in a predominantly working-class area of Baghdad. An overwhelming majority of the subjects' parents were illiterates. Table 6–1 gives details of the sample.

Table 6–1
Sample of children

Ages	Females	Males	Total
4	12	15	27
5	14	14	28
6	12	14	26
7	14	13	27
8	12	11	23
9	12	14	26
10	15	14	29
11	13	11	24
12	14	13	27
13	14	16	30
Total	132	135	267

METHOD

Subjects were taken one at a time. Three tasks were given to each child; after each task a dialogue was started with the subject regarding his judgment of the issues involved.

The procedures used can be divided into three separate steps:

1. A. Two roads made of cardboard, each 2.5 meters long and similar in their other dimensions, are laid down parallel to each other. Both roads end with a barrier.

B. Two small cars of equal size and of different colors are used. These cars move with a speed that can be predetermined by the experimenter.

C. The cars are put at the starting point. When the child gives the signal, both cars are started moving at once, and they reach the barrier simultaneously.

2. The same materials used above are used—but with a difference: the roads are not parallel but form an angle at the starting point.

3. The roads are laid down parallel. Two cars of different sizes with different speeds start together, but one car (the larger one) runs at a slower speed than the other, so that by the time the small, fast car reaches the end of the road, the large, slow car has completed only three-fourths of the road.

PROCEDURE

1. The child is requested to compare the two roads in regard to their length. If he doubts their equality, he (she) is requested to place one over the other to verify their equality.

2. When the child gives the signal, the two cars start together; he (she) is then requested to note their arrival at the barriers and decides whether they arrive at the same time.

The experimenter tries to make certain, through dialogue with the child, that the child has arrived at the concepts of speed (faster/slower) distance, and the relationship between speed and distance and time.

At the second stage of the experiment the whole procedure is repeated—but with one difference: the child is asked whether the roads are still equal in length after their position is changed. If the child answers that their length has changed, an attempt is made to find out how the child has arrived at this conclusion. In any case the experiment proceeds.

3. The experiment is repeated, with parallel roads and the same

duration but with the cars traveling at different speeds, and an attempt is made to be sure that the child has arrived at a formulation of the concepts of time, distance, and speed.

The children's responses are recorded verbatim and any other behavioral manifestations are taken note of.

ANALYSIS OF THE RESULTS

The results were analyzed by calculating the frequencies and percentages of the responses of various types. These seem to follow a specific pattern corresponding to age, quite similar to the pattern discovered by Piaget.

The following stages were discovered:

Stage 1

The first stage is characterized by two types of responses:

A. The child does not seem to understand the questions asked. Instead, he (she) takes the cars and plays with them, not paying attention to what he is asked to do.

B. The child denies that the two cars have arrived simultaneously. Sometimes, the child even denies that they have started at the same time. He maintains that the speed, distance, and time either increase together or decrease together. The fast car is the car that has taken more time and traveled a longer distance. The child thus denies conservation of distance and time.

Both types of responses are found mostly among children whose ages range between 4 and 7. It is to be noted that about two-thirds of the children 4 years of age and about half of the children 5 years of age did not respond to the experiment and seemed unable to understand what they were requested to do.

The child at this age seems to watch the simultaneous arrival of the two cars, but still remains hesitant as to which one of them arrived first. He is liable to change his opinion several times.

Other children refuse to admit that the cars arrived simultaneously and insist that one of the cars arrived earlier, but the car that "won" the race took more time and traveled a longer distance (in spite of the fact that he agrees to begin with that the roads are of equal length). This type of response was found in about 50% of the children 6 years of age. The frequency of this response decreases gradually with age. Example: "The blue car won. It traveled more. Its road is longer, and takes more time. It is faster".

But since the child had agreed to begin with that the two roads were equal and then denied it later on, his (her) attention was drawn to what he (she) had maintained before—that the roads were equal in length. After some thinking the child responded, "The road has become longer".

The child does not find it difficult to change his (her) position; thus he may maintain that the car that arrived earlier, after starting at the same time and traveling a road of equal length, has *not* moved faster.

Example: "The blue one arrived first, the white one traveled more. The blue one took more time. The white car won. The white car took more time. The white car is faster".

When the roads were laid down at an angle, the position of the second road was in itself sufficient to allow some children to deny the equivalence of the two roads. Of the children 7 years of age, 93% maintained that the roads were not equal. This type of response decreased gradually and systematically with age. Yet it did not disappear completely. Of the children 13 years of age, 20% maintained that the roads were not equal when their position was changed. When children were reminded that they had formerly pointed out that the two roads were equal, and requested to explain the difference, (since nothing was taken from either road nor added to it) most of the children said that the road had become oblique, and the oblique road was therefore longer.

Conservation of length was found to be lacking among 56% of the children 9 years of age. It seems that even some children who have arrived at the end of primary school (6 years of schooling and 12 years of age), and have studied measurement in arithmetic, still do not form the concept of conservation of length.

Example from a 12-year-old child: "The faster car needs more time. The car moves by the kilometer. The kilometers of the blue car are more than the kilometers of the white car. Each car has its own kilometer; this means that each kilometer has a different length."

It is evident from this response that the meaning of the unit of measurement is not clear to the child. The child has no concept of the constancy of the unit of measurement.

It was also noticed that 61% of the children at age 6 formulate a direct relationship between distance, time, and speed. Example: "The small car won; the small one traveled more. The small car took more time. The small car is faster."

When asked why the faster car needs more time, the answer given was,

"Because it travels faster. If you travel faster you need more time; when you travel slowly you need little time.

"The small one took a lot of time, its road became longer, the smaller car is faster and the faster takes more time and its road becomes longer. If you travel slowly you take less time and your road becomes shorter."

After the age of 7, the percentage of such responses decreases.

Stage 2

The child of this stage conceives of the relationship between speed and time, a mental process that requires establishing relationships between events, which differs from the mental process evident in the first stage.

Explanations given by the subject show that he (she) is able to link the events together but, lacking reversibility, he cannot retrace the course of the events and is therefore unable to construct the system of "co-displacements" which constitutes operational time (Piaget, 1970).

Example: "The roads are equal; the white car is faster; the white car traveled more. The blue car has a longer road; the blue car took more time. The blue car won. The blue car traveled more. The white car needs more time but the road is the same."

The subject can perceive the simultaneity of arrival, but fails to perceive synchronization. In spite of the fact that the child perceives the simultaneous starting time and the simultaneous arrival of the two cars, he refuses to accept that the two cars spent equal time on the road. This leads the child to contradict what he has already declared: he judges the two roads to be unequal; and in his mind the time has become unequal as well, and the speed has become unequal too. The child is unable to see the contradiction however, and reverts to a direct relationship between time, distance and speed, which is contrary to what he had arrived at before. This leads to his hesitation and his denial of the equality of the roads, after previously declaring that they were equal; or he may deny the cars arrived simultaneously and insist later that one of the cars "won."

Example: "The two roads are equal; they have become both of them equal. The blue one won, the blue one traveled more, the blue one took more time, the blue one is faster. The white one has a longer road to travel, because the blue one overtook it by far."

When the child is reminded that the two roads are equal, he maintains "Now it has become a little longer."

Another example shows a different line of thought. The child maintains the simultaneity of starting and arrival, the equality of the roads in length, and the time taken by the two cars; then he contradicts himself and maintains that one of them is faster.

Example: "The two roads are of equal length, they arrived together, they won together; but the blue one is faster, the blue one traveled more."

The same type of response was found in the second experiment.

Example: "The two roads are the same. Both started together, both won, both of them took the same amount of time. The oblique road is longer, the car traveling on the oblique road is faster, and no car won because they arrived together. The car that has more petrol wins, the one that wins needs more time, because they have put more petrol in it."

In the third experiment—where the smaller car is the faster car and covers the whole road while the large one completes only three fourths of the road, the children at this stage are quite hesitant.

Example: "The small car won. The small car traveled more. The big one took more time. The small one has a longer road, but the big one traveled more, because the small car won the race."

Another example: "The small car won, the small car took more time. The big one traveled more because it is not fast. The fast car travels less, which means that its road is shorter and takes less time. The car that travels slowly takes more time, and the big one traveled more."

It is obvious here that distance is still linked to time and the child does not differentiate between them. He is unable to face two events which differ in their end results although taking the same time. He fails, therefore, to synchronize the end of the activity. Time varies directly with speed, and the faster the event, the more distance has been covered.

This type of response appeared first at the age of 5 and increased until age 8, where 58% of the subjects responded this way. Later this type of response decreased gradually as children arrived at the proper concept.

In the second experiment, this type of response appeared a bit later and still reached its peak at the age of 8, where it was given by 46% of the children. However, after that age it did not decline sharply, and was present until—at the age of 12–13—40% of the children used this mental process. This stage of mental development was found to be prevalent among children whose ages ranged between 7 and 10.

Stage 3

The criterion used in this study for the attainment of the concept of speed was the following: The child had to relate the equality of distances with the simultaneous arrival of the two cars, and then conclude that their speed was equal. This conclusion was reached by a number of children at the age of 6. The proportion of children who met the criterion was very small indeed: it did not exceed 11% for the first task and 4% for the second. The percentage increased with age, but the highest one ever reached was

54% for the first task and 38% for the second task, where the roads were not parallel. As to the third task, about three fourths of the children 12 years of age were able to understand the negative relationship between distance and time.

Example: "The two cars arrive together. Time is equal. Speed is equal. They traveled together."

As to the second task the predominant response given by the children was similar to that cited earlier in the second stage. A little more than one third of the children did however, give the correct answer.

"The roads are equal. They arrive together. The two cars traveled together. The two cars are of the same speed because the road is the same."

Table 6–2
The distribution of Iraqi children's answers in percentages, classified according to stages and tasks, and conservation of length

Ages	FIRST TASK			SECOND TASK			CONSERVERS OF LENGTH	THIRD TASK	
	Stage 1	Stage 2	Stage 3	Stage 1	Stage 2	Stage3		Negative relation	Positive relation
4	92	4	4	96	4	—	—	82	18
5	90	10	—	97	3	—	—	83	17
6	65	23	12	88	8	4	7	62	38
7	67	18	15	92	4	4	19	48	52
8	65	9	26	52	26	22	7	43	57
9	58	23	19	36	32	32	43	58	42
10	52	17	31	28	34	38	44	45	55
11	21	25	54	42	29	29	65	37	63
12	18	30	52	22	41	37	63	26	74
13	27	23	50	23	40	37	80	10	90

Table 6–2 shows the frequency of the answers given by the child in each of the experiments. It is evident from the results that changing the position of one of the roads in the second task resulted in the failure of the children to attain conservation of length. This made the majority of the children unable to display the concept of speed properly; only 37% of the children were able to reach the level of operational thinking.

Since the concept of speed is considered to be formed when the child can give the correct answers for all three tasks, and since only 37% of the children were able to accomplish this, it may be assumed that children in our sample were unable to form the concept of speed at this age (12–13). This is borne out by the fact that 20% of these children showed that they have not developed conservation of length which is a requirement for the formation of the concept of speed.

The fact that 52% of the children 12–13 were able to accomplish the first task may be considered an indication that the concept is perhaps formed later.

DISCUSSION

It is evident from the results shown above that a few of the children reach the concept of speed at the age of 6 and the number of such children increases with age in a gradual manner.

It is also evident that there are three stages through which children develop. The first is distinguished by the fact that the concept is not formed. The second is a transitional stage where the child understands some of the relations, but is unable to relate them to one another. The third stage is distinguished by the formation of the concept of speed and the appearance of operational thinking.

If we use the 50% criterion for concept formation, and success in the first of the three tasks only, it can be seen from the table that the concept is formed at the age of 12 (52%). If the roads are not parallel, however, only about a third of the children display the concept, which means that the concept is not truly acquired.

The experiment did not proceed further, to enable us to show when the concept is formed for all variations of the positions of the roads. The appearance of the three consecutive stages is in accordance with the findings of Piaget and those who followed him. The thinking processes displayed by Iraqi children in the various stages are quite similar to those described by Piaget. As a matter of fact, some of the answers given by the Iraqi children were exactly the same as those cited by Piaget (1970), if we disregard the age and take the mental stage of development as criterion.

The first stage that was found is preoperational: the child is able to perceive all the relevant factors, but is unable to relate them to one another. He (she) concentrates on one factor only and neglects the rest, which Piaget calls "centration." Thus the child arrives at conclusions such as the idea that "shorter" means "finished first," therefore "traveled faster."

The second stage is characterized by the mastery of the relationship between time and distance. However, the duration of the event is not fully comprehended by the child.

The third stage, that of concrete operations, shows reversible mental operations in all the relevant factors and the coordination of successive events.

The difference between our results and Piaget's was in the onset and duration of the stages. Piaget's sample formed the concept at the age of 9, whereas amongst the Iraqi children the concept was not completely formed at the age of 12–13. The results of this study are similar to the results found by Za'rour and Khuri (1977) conducted in a nearby Arab culture (Jordan).

These results also confirm Dasen's conclusion that the formation of the concept of speed and time lags more in children from developing countries (Dasen, 1972). This seems to be due to the fact that the concept itself is more complex and depends on conservation concepts that need to be formed and are prerequisite to the formation of the concept of speed.

This study also confirms the results of studies conducted in Iraq on other concepts. Thus Al-Shaikh (1974) found that conservation of matter and conservation of length lag about two to four years behind the European child. Safar (1974), also found that the concepts of seriation and serial correspondence lag about three years. Za'rour (1971) arrived at similar results in a nearby Arab culture (Lebanon) with regard to the conservation of quantity (liquid) and number. It is to be noted that these studies used experimental procedures and did not follow Piaget's clinical approach, yet the same results were noted with regard to the sequence of stages and the lag of the Arab children as compared with the European and American child.

Since the present study did not take children beyond the age of 13, it is not possible at the present time to ascertain the age at which the concept is formed among the Iraqi children (insofar as the concept of speed is concerned in all three tasks).

The present study shows that the development curve for the concept of speed is asymptotic (curve "d" in Dasen, 1972), whereas the results of previous studies on other concepts show only a time lag (curve "c").

This lag may be attributed partially to the educational system in Iraq, which seems to emphasize rote learning (Al-Omar, 1973; Bahri, 1973; Fernandes and Issa, 1972; Al-Nasser, 1973); and textbooks seem to be bent on the explicit dictation of values by the authors and passive reception by the children (Al-Khatib, 1974). All in all, there seems to be little emphasis on the development of mental operations. Using special methods of training, where the child participates in the process, leads to the transfer of children from the transitional stage to the formation of the concept (Safar, 1974). The influence of the environment in general cannot be underestimated, either. Children suffer a great deal from cultural deprivation. These factors may contribute to the lag evidenced in this study and other studies cited previously.

It is to be noted again that the sample used in this study, comes from a low socioeconomic background; they are also schooled children, and they may for this reason, be different from children who did not go to school. Thus further studies are needed along these lines to cover higher social strata as well as unschooled children.

These studies have used so far as an explanation for differences in concept formation the blanket term "culture;" it is evident that the term "culture" is very broad and covers a large number of factors. It seems to the author that if we want to reach a better understanding of the nature of the effects of "culture" on concept formation, it is necessary to have a better description of how cultural factors act in retarding or speeding up concept formation.

Some indices are already available as to the role of the educational system; however, other cultural factors need to be looked into, such as parent-child relationships, child-rearing practices, and the educational level of the parents.

REFERENCES

Bahri, M. (1973) *Evaluation of teacher-made tests for fourth-year primary school grammar.* Baghdad: Center of Psychological and Educational Research, University of Baghdad. In Arabic.

Dasen, P. R. (1972) Cross-cultural Piagetian research: A summary. *Journal of Cross-Cultural Psychology, 3* (1), 23–39.

Al-Fakhri, S. (1972a) *Concept formation among Iraqi children: Dissolution.* Baghdad: Center of Psychological and Educational Research, University of Baghdad. In Arabic.

Al-Fakhri, S. (1972b) *Development of the concept of speed among Iraqi children.* Baghdad: Center of Psychological and Educational Research, University of Baghdad. In Arabic.

Al-Fakhri, S. (1973a) *Children's discovery of liquid conservation.* Baghdad: Center of Psychological and Educational Research, University of Baghdad. In Arabic.

Al-Fakhri, S. (1973b) *Logical composition of classes in children (class inclusion).* Baghdad: Center of Psychological and Educational Research, University of Baghdad. In Arabic.

Al-Fakhri, S. (1973c) *The conservation of length in children.* Baghdad: Center of Psychological and Educational Research, University of Baghdad. In Arabic.

Al-Fakhri, S. (1973d) *Measurement of length: subdividing a straight line.* Baghdad: Center of Psychological and Educational Research, University of Baghdad. In Arabic.

Al-Fakhri, S. (1974) *Spatial coordinate system; concepts of horizontality and verticality.* Baghdad: Center of Psychological and Educational Research, University of Baghdad. In Arabic.

Fernandes, H. J. and Issa, M. (1972) *Evaluation of annual English classroom tests in grade V of primary schools.* Baghdad: Center of Psychological and Educational Research, University of Baghdad. Unpublished.

Galperin, P. Y. (1971) A method, facts, and theories in the psychology of mental actions and concepts formation (Symposium 24. 48. 58). In Al-Hamdani, M. *Psychological Studies from Socialist Countries*, Baghdad: Ministry of Information, pp. 105–115.

Al-Khatib, H. (1974) *Transformations in the value-orientation of primary school readers 1957–1972*. Unpublished M.A. thesis, Baghdad University.

Mentchinskaia, N. E. (1966) Développement de la pensée au cours du processus d'enseignement scolaire. In *Recherches Psychologiques en U.R.S.S.*, Moscow: Edition du Progrès, pp. 347–389.

Al-Nasser, P. V. (1973) *An analytical study of the baccalaureate examination for the primary school level*. Baghdad: Center of Psychological and Educational Research, University of Baghdad. Unpublished.

Al-Omar, N. (1973) *Evaluation of teacher tests for fourth year primary school science*. Baghdad: Center of Psychological and Educational Research, University of Baghdad. Unpublished.

Piaget, J. (1969) *The child's conception of time.* London: Routledge and Kegan Paul.

Piaget, J. (1970) *The child's conception of movement and speed.* London: Routledge and Kegan Paul.

Proskura, E. V. (1971) Teaching and formation of serial orders by preschool children (Symposium 32. 184. 186). In Al-Hamdani, M., *Psychological Studies from Socialist Countries.* Baghdad: Ministry of Information, pp. 124–127.

Safar, S. (1974) *The formation of the concepts of seriation and serial correspondences among Iraqi children.* Unpublished M.A. thesis, Baghdad University.

Al-Shaikh, A. A. (1974) *The conservation of length among Iraqi children*, Unpublished.

Vygotsky, L. S. (1966) Development of the higher mental function. In *Psychological Research in U.S.S.R.* Moscow: Progress Publishers, pp. 44–45.

Za'rour, G. I. (1971) The conservation of number and liquid by Lebanese school children in Beirut. *Journal of Cross-Cultural Psychology, 2*:165–172.

Za'rour, G. I. and Khuri, G. A. (1977) The development of the concept of speed by Jordanian school children in Amman. This book.

7
The Development of the Concept of Speed by Jordanian School Children in Amman

GEORGE I. ZA'ROUR and GHADA A. KHURI

The concepts of time and speed constitute an important part of the mathematics and general science curricula. These two concepts are basic to the understanding of other concepts such as acceleration, Newton's three laws, distance-time graphs, and velocity-time graphs. But the relationship of the concepts of time and speed are often taught through routine memorization of formulae without attention to the underlying logic.

Piaget's studies (1969, 1970) of the growth of the child's understanding of time and speed are particular applications of his general theory of intellectual development. He suggests that the two concepts of time and speed grow gradually through the formation of logical operations. Piaget (1970, pp. 185–186) maintains that two types of operations are distinguishable: operations of a qualitative nature and operations of a quantitative nature. Operations of the latter type include proportions and grasp of the relationships between distance, speed, and time. Piaget (1970) has also used four main stages to describe the development of the concept of speed as a time-distance function. In the progression of these stages, the child's reasoning is influenced by perception, and gradually develops to a stage in which he is able to abstract and generalize. The stages will be described and classified later as part of the section on procedure.

Few studies investigating the developmental ability of children in attaining the concepts of time and speed have been carried out after Piaget. Lovell's studies (1960, 1962) support Piaget's findings concerning both time and speed concepts.

As reported in Chapter 6 of this volume, Al-Fakhri found that the types of responses of Iraqi children follow a specific pattern similar to that discovered by Piaget. However, she points out that there is a time lag in the attainment of the concepts. Bovet and Othenin-Girard (1975) studied a group of adults who have never been to school, as well as schooled and unschooled adolescents in the Ivory Coast. Their results suggest that schooling in the case of adolescents, and sex in the case of adults who have never been to school, seem to influence the attainment of the concepts of duration, speed and distance.

Dempsey (1971) carried out a study to investigate the effect of culture on the ability to conserve certain aspects of the concept of time. He detected some similarities and differences among five different Indian tribes. As for the importance of the speed concept to other scientific concepts such as acceleration, Raven's study (1972) revealed that the acquisition of the speed tasks should come prior to the acquisition of the acceleration tasks.

The present study was carried out to investigate how the concept of speed is achieved and used by Jordanian school children in Amman. Specifically, it attempted to answer the following questions:

1. Are the stages of development described by Piaget identifiable in the Jordanian school children of Amman?

2. Is there any relationship between the attainment of the concept of time and the intuition of speed?

3. Do children understand the various tasks of the concept of speed equally?

4. Is there any relationship between the ability to develop the concept of speed and the variables of sex, age, and scholastic level?

METHOD

Materials

The following set of materials, similar to those described by Piaget (1969 and 1970) were used:

1. Two cardboard tunnels numbered 1 and 2, of the lengths 100 cm and 127 cm, respectively.

2. Three small cars of different colors, operated by means of batteries and supplied with a speed control button.

3. Two cardboard roads, each having a length of 100 cm.

Subjects

The subjects of this study were 151 Jordanian elementary and intermediate school children living in Amman. Except for Intermediate 1 (7th grade) they were drawn from six age groups, 8 through 13, corresponding to six school grades from 3rd to 8th, inclusive. As there were not enough 7th graders aged 12, some of the Ss (subjects) of this group were slightly younger or older.

The Ss, all of whom attended a private school in Amman, were judged to be heterogeneous with respect to socioeconomic status, but they all were of Jordanian nationality and spoke Arabic as a native language. As for scholastic levels, the subjects in the sample were placed in three categories (top, average, and bottom achievement groups) according to their grades and the evaluation of their respective teachers. **Table** 7–1 provides descriptive data about the subjects.

Table 7–1
Descriptive data about the subjects

GRADE	FREQUENCY		AGE		SCHOLASTIC LEVEL		
	M	F	X	s	Top	Average	Bottom
3	13	13	8;5	3.1	13	8	5
4	14	14	9;5	3.2	16	7	5
5	13	13	10;6	3.0	10	10	6
6	13	14	11;4	3.2	9	11	7
7	13	13	12;4	6.4	11	11	4
8	9	9	13;4	2.0	7	4	7

M refers to males; F refers to females.
X refers to the mean chronological age at time of interview in years and months.
s = Standard deviation in months.

Procedure

The data were collected through individual interviews conducted in colloquial Arabic. The experiment consisted of five tasks, taken mainly from Piaget's studies on the time and speed concepts (1969, 1970). Each task was followed by a set of questions concerning time and speed. The tasks were used to assess the child's understanding of various aspects of the speed concept. **Three** of the five tasks dealt with the intuition of speed qualitatively and the remaining two dealt with the concept of speed quantitatively. The procedure in questioning the subjects was similar to that used by Lovell (1962). The questions were administered to all the students of the sample and when no sensible answers were given by the subjects, the questions were asked again after the task was performed in front of the subjects. Questions were repeated when necessary to clarify any language misunderstanding.

Task 1. Simultaneous-synchronous times, unequal speeds, and unequal distances

The subject was shown two cardboard tunnels of different lengths (100 and 127 cm long) numbered 1 and 2, and two cars. The investigator told the subject that the two cars would start moving at the same time and come out at the same time. The subject was then asked: "Did the two cars travel the same distance?" "Did one car travel for a longer time?" If the answer was yes, he was asked: "Which one? Why do you think so?" and "Did the two cars travel at the same speed or at different speeds?" If the subject answered that the cars went at different speeds, he was asked: "Which car went faster? Why do you think so?"

Task 2. Simultaneous-synchronous times, equal speeds and equal distances

The subject was shown two cardboard roads of equal lengths (100 cm each) and two cars. The investigator told the subject that the two cars would start traveling at the same time so that they would reach the end of the two roads at the same time. The subject was then asked the same questions as in Task 1.

Task 3. Partly synchronous times, unequal speeds, and equal distances

The subject was shown two equal cardboard roads and two cars made to proceed with different speeds at unequal intervals. The subject was then asked the same questions as in Task 1.

Tasks 4 and 5. Speeds of movements in succession traveling unequal distances in unequal times (equal speeds in Task 4 and different speeds in Task 5).

The subject was shown a moving car made to travel along a path 4 cm long in 2 seconds (6 cm in 2 seconds in Task 5). This was then repeated with another car, traveling along a parallel straight line 8 cm long in 4 seconds (12 cm in 3 seconds in Task 5). The paths were sketched and their lengths and required number of seconds recorded beside each. The subject was asked if the two cars traveled at the same speed or at different speeds. If the subject answered that they traveled at different speeds, he was asked which one went faster and why he thought so.

Piaget (1970) claims that in attaining a correct intuition of speed, children pass through four main sequential stages. In Stage 1, the child perceives speed as one car overtaking another, or even judges speed merely from the stopping points. For example, if the two moving objects reach the same place at the same time, their speeds are judged to be equal, ignoring the distances covered and the time of departure. In Stage 2, the child's reactions are considered as midway between intuition centered on one factor, and logical correlation: the child's reasoning vacillates between wrong and correct after further questioning. This stage marks a beginning of progressive decentration of intuitions, but the operational level is not attained.

In Stage 3, the child conceives speed as a distance-time relation. He admits that two objects travel for an equal duration of time with the object covering the longer distance being the faster. Temporal order (before and after) is differentiated from spatial order (right and left). However, at this stage only concrete operations are attained. When the same movements that are being compared are made in succession, new operations are required—formal or hypothetico-deductive operations. In this case, the child has to coordinate the two movements in his mind.

Thus, Stage 3 is divided into two substages:

First there is Substage 3a, in which the child understands speed at the level of concrete operations but is unable to compare two successive movements. For example, the child would say that the moving object taking 4t to travel a distance of 8d is either quicker or slower than the object taking 2t to travel a distance of 4d; children either consider distances and neglect times or consider times and neglect distances.

In Substage 3b the child starts a gradual construction of proportions. The child succeeds in questions on equal times and unequal distances (or vice versa) but fails on questions where both times and distances are different. The child is still influenced by perception, since he thinks either of time or of distance alone without being able to unite them in a single ratio.

In Stage 4, formal operations are achieved. Again, two substages are distinguished: Substage 4a, in which the child solves by means of trial and error the problems of proportions, although he has already attained formal operations; and Substage 4b, in which the child tends to follow a systematic procedure (Piaget, 1970, p. 202).

The attainment of the concept of speed requires the subject to compare two movements. Comparison may be made between two simultaneous speeds (Tasks 1, 2, and 3) or between two successive speeds (Task 4 and 5). The difficulty with the simultaneous movements lies in the fact that the subject is faced with two problems at the same moment—a time problem and a speed problem. In Tasks 1, 2, and 3, the subject is required to concentrate either on the entirely simultaneous equivalent durations (Tasks 1 and 2) or on the partly synchronous durations (Task 3) of both cars. Before being able to give a correct speed response, the subject must concentrate on the simultaneous difference (Task 1) or on the simultaneous equivalence (Tasks 2 and 3) between the distances traveled by the two cars. However, in the case where the two perceived movements are successive (Tasks 4 and 5), the product of the distance and time relationship of each car should be compared. The subject is required to find ratios between two distances covered and two durations.

Treatment of the data

Both the judgment and the type of reasoning provided by the subject in each of the administered tasks were taken into consideration in classifying the Ss into stages or categories. A criterion of threequarters of correct responses was used to determine the age level of operational responses. An operational response was attained whenever a subject gave a correct judgment supported by logical reasoning. The effect of age and scholastic level was measured through the use of chi-square tests, and sex differences were evaluated by testing differences between two proportions.

RESULTS

The intuition of speed (Tasks 1, 2, and 3)

The results of these tasks supported Piaget's findings that a correct intuition of speed as a distance-time function develops with age and passes through the different sequential stages. A chi-square test analyzing the frequencies with which the Ss at various age levels fell under the different developmental stages was significant beyond the 0.001 level. Table 7–2 shows the percentage of children who were able to give a correct response (both a correct judgment and a logical explanation in Tasks 1, 2, and 3.) It also shows that roughly three quarters of correct responses were reached in Task 3 at age 11.

The majority of the Ss 8, 9, and 10 years old either gave wrong responses (and sometimes wrong reasons) or changed their opinions after further questioning or after performing the experiment. Considering the Ss who gave no correct judgment and/or logical reasoning even after performing the experiment, 44% in Task 1, 79% in Task 2, and 42% in Task 3 indicated that the two cars traveled at the same speed because they reached the same spot in space at the same time. From the point of view of the concept of

Table 7–2
Percentage of Ss at each age level giving operational responses in three tasks involving the intuition of speed

Mean age level (years and months)	Task 1	Task 2	Task 3
8;5	00.0	00.0	00.0
9;5	14.3	32.1	46.4
10;6	26.9	42.3	50.0
11;4	59.2	70.4	81.5
12;4	84.6	84.6	88.5
13;4	88.9	88.9	100.0

time, it was found that a total of 128 Ss could conserve the synchronous durations in Task 1. Of these, 73% were able to give a correct judgment of the question of speed. Of those who could not conserve synchronous durations, 21.7% gave correct judgments. As for Task 2, all the subjects admitted the equality of synchronous durations. However, the percentage of those who gave an abstract explanation in terms of the equality of both time and distance increased from a low of 20% at age 8 to 61%, 62%, 78%, 88%, and 89% at the successive age levels, respectively. These results show that, in general, conserving durations is reached ahead of the intuition of speed and that conserving synchronous durations leads to a gradual development of the speed concept.

Comparing Two Successive Movements (Tasks 4 and 5)

No responses were found at the 3a stage as defined by Piaget to these tasks. Table 7–3 shows three identified stages corresponding to Piaget's substages 3b, 4a, and 4b. A chi-square test analyzing the frequencies with which the Ss at various age levels fell under the different developmental stages was significant beyond the 0.001 level. It may be deduced that the formal operational stage was attained at the age of 13.

Table 7–3
Percentage of Ss revealing various stages of development in tasks 4 and 5

Mean age level (years and months)	Stage 3b Concrete operational (Task 4 correct)	Stage 4a Transitional (Task 5 solved by trial and error)	Stage 4b Formal operational (Tasks 4 and 5 correct)
8;5	00.0	00.0	00.0
9;5	17.8	00.0	00.0
10;6	15.4	07.7	07.7
11;4	33.1	15.0	18.5
12;4	15.4	30.8	34.6
13;4	05.6	11.1	77.8

The explanations of the Ss who gave wrong responses in Tasks 4 and 5 consisted mostly of the following statements: shorter distance and/or less time, greater speed (53% in Task 4 and 54% in Task 5); and longer distance and/or more time, greater speed (27% in Task 4 and 19% in Task 5).

Sex and Scholastic Level

No significant sex differences at the 0.05 level were detected. As for the scholastic level, the chi-square test showed that differences among the three categories (top, average, and bottom achievement sections) were significant beyond the 0.05 level in the attainment of speed tasks demanding concrete operations (Task 2, $X^2 = 8.00$, df = 2; Task 3, $X^2 = 6.80$, df = 2) for the 11–13 age groups, and in the attainment of speed tasks demanding formal operations (Tasks 4 and 5, $X^2 = 9.90$, df = 2) for the 8–10 age groups. These significant differences were in favor of the top achievement section.

DISCUSSION

Comparing Two Simultaneously Perceived Movements

The results of Tasks 1, 2, and 3 supported Piaget's (1970) and Lovell's (1962) findings that young children judge speed from the point of arrival of objects, irrespective of distances traveled and even of starting times. This is illustrated by the reasons of subjects at Stage 1. At this stage, the subject's attention is fixed on one factor only (the arrival points), ignoring the others (distance traveled and departure time). This act of centration diminishes gradually until the subject becomes able to consider both the distance traveled and the times of departure. This is illustrated by the reasons given by Stage 4 subjects. The present study showed that not until the age of 9 years—in agreement with Lovell (1960)—do more than 75% of the subjects equate two synchronous movements, and not until the age of 11–12 do subjects give correct speed judgment. This suggests that equality of synchronous durations is attained ahead of an intuition of speed, and a correct speed judgment is attained after conserving time. The question of speed is not simply a problem of perceiving both the intervals and distances defined by the starting and finishing points, but additionally, a problem of correlating the two.

Comparing Two Successive Movements

The results of Tasks 4 and 5 also support Piaget's findings and the findings of Tasks 1, 2, and 3 concerning the mechanism followed in the developmental processes. Young children either considered distances and neglected times or considered times and neglected distances, as illustrated by the responses of Stages 1 and 2 subjects (concrete stages). When the Ss were reminded of the neglected factor, two types of reasons were distinguished. In one of these, time and distance were taken to be inversely proportional to speed—the moving object taking 2t to travel a distance of 4d is quicker than that taking 4t to travel a distance of 8d (Task 4). In the other type of reason, time and distance are considered directly proportional to speed and hence the car moving the 8d in 4t is quicker than that moving the 4d in 2t and so on. As the child's thinking develops, it frees itself from centration and the child becomes able to discover simple proportions correctly at stage 3. He can then construct rather than discover proportions. This was illustrated by the responses of Stage 4 subjects. Typical answers of this stage were: "The car moving a distance of 12d in 3t is quicker than the car moving 6d in 2t, because if the second car moves another 6d keeping its speed constant, it will need another 2t. Thus, it consumes more time than the first in covering the same distance". It is clear that this type of reasoning requires more advanced thinking than is required in the case of simultaneously perceived movements. Operations of this latter type of motion are intensive (Tasks 1, 2, and 3) while operations of the successively perceived motions (Tasks 4 and 5) are extensive (Piaget, 1970, chapter 9). Thus, it is not surprising to find that the extensive operations are attained at a later stage than the intensive operations of Tasks 1, 2, and 3. The fact that all subjects of stage 3 were able to discover the simple ratios of Tasks 4 (1 to 2) does not agree with Piaget's findings that there is a time lag between the attainment of the concepts in Tasks 1, 2, and 3 on the one hand, and Task 4 on the other (Piaget's Substage 3a). This may be a result of any delay in attaining the concept of speed in the first three tasks compared to Piaget's findings. In addition, the type of schooling might be another intervening factor in the process of cognitive development.

Age, Sex and Scholastic Level

In agreement with the findings of Piaget (1970), Lovell et al. (1962), and Al-Fakhri (1977), the findings of the present study revealed that age is a significant factor in the development of the speed concept. However, the age at which the concept of speed was found to be attained was different among the subjects of the various studies. The present study, in close agreement with Al-Fakhri's (1977), showed that an understanding of speed was found to come between age 11 and 12 in the case of concrete operational tasks. Formal operational tasks were attained at the age of 13 in this study. If lagging behind Western subjects is established, it suggests that culture might be a major variable influencing the child's cognitive development.

As for sex, none of the previous studies on speed development have tested differences between girls and boys. In the present study, sex differences were found not to be significant.

Regarding scholastic level, the results suggest that achievement at school as well as age are significant factors in the child's cognitive development. Needless to say, achievement at school is a function of a multitude of variables, an important one of which is the child's mental ability.

The findings of this study have a number of implications. Knowing the characteristics of each stage of development suggests that content as well as learning situations should be selected for the elementary curriculum to help the child overcome the deficiencies of each stage and to facilitate the development of logical thought that appears in later stages. In the specific case of speed, time, and distance relationships, the importance of sequencing concepts and of placing them at appropriate age levels should be realized. A pupil who does not attain a well-developed concept of speed cannot employ operational thinking to a more complicated situation in this field (problem solving) or to a more advanced concept such as acceleration. Moreover, the developmental theory suggests that formal and abstract expressions of speed should be reserved for later stages. Finally, more studies seem to be needed to investigate whether teaching and training accelerate the attainment of the concept of speed.

REFERENCES

Al-Fakhri, Salima (1977) *The development of the concept of speed among Iraqi children*. Chapter 6 in this book.

Bovet, M. and Othenin-Girard, C. (1975) Étude Piagétienne de quelques notions spatio-temporelles dans un milieu africain. *International Journal of Psychology, 10*, 1–17.

Dempsey, D. A. (1971) Time conservation across cultures. *International Journal of Psychology, 6*, 115–120.

Lovell, K. and Slater, A. (1960) The growth of the concept of time: A comparative study. *Journal of Child Psychology and Psychiatry, 1*, 179–190.

Lovell, K., Kellet, V. L., and Moorhouse, E. (1962) The growth of the concept of speed: A comparative study. *Journal of Child Psychology and Psychiatry, 3*, 101–110.

Piaget, J. (1969) *The child's conception of time*. London: Routledge and Kegan Paul.

Piaget, J. (1970) *The child's conception of movement and speed.* London: Routledge and Kegan Paul.

Raven, R. J. (1972) The development of the concept of acceleration in elementary school children. *Journal of Research in Science Teaching, 9,* 201–206.

8
Influence of Specific Maternal Occupation and Behavior on Piagetian Cognitive Development[1]

KWABENA ADJEI

INTRODUCTION

In evaluating the studies undertaken to test and replicate Piaget's cognitive developmental theory, Wohlwill (1962, 1968) observed that the preoccupation of a vast majority of researchers with the effects of age, socioeconomic, and performance variables on cognitive level is of doubtful value to the questions implicitly posed by Piaget's system. Wohlwill's criticisms apply to most Western studies, as well as to some cross-cultural ones. Recently, Piaget (1966) has offered a virtually exhaustive classification of the most essential developmental factors—which the comparative approach has the advantage of delineating—and the most pertinent questions posed by them. According to Piaget, the hierachization of intellectual operations is assisted by the constant and dynamic interaction of the following groups of factors:

1. biological;
2. equilibration or autoregulation;
3. social factors of interpersonal coordination; and
4. cultural and educational transmission.

Equilibration and social factors are of central importance in Piaget's theory. Unfortunately, their relative contributions to cognitive development have received very little rigorous attention in both cross-sectional and comparative studies generally. Apparently, the relatively homogeneous western cultural milieu does not provide adequate methodological opportunities for any effective examination of these factors. On the other hand, the opportunities brought by the utilization of naturally occuring cultural phenomena, especially in relatively heterogeneous non-Western settings, justify the significance Piaget attaches to this approach. A review of contemporary Piagetian research will reveal some of the unfortunate gaps left in our knowledge, with the aim of beginning to fill them.

The first systematic conservation study undertaken to investigate the influence of the biological factor was that of de Lemos (1966, 1969). Selecting "part-blood" and "full-blood" Australian aboriginals, de Lemos found the latter to be significantly inferior to the former on the concepts of quantity, weight, length, and area, while on volume the difference approached significance. The researcher readily attributed the differential pattern of performance of her two groups of subjects to genetic factors. Later, Dasen (1970, 1972b) replicated the study from the same location but failed to verify de Lemos's results. Nor was any evidence of genetic bias found by Vetta (1972), who reanalysed de Lemos's (1969) data. Thus both Dasen and Vetta agree in principle that de Lemos's findings provide no grounds whatsoever for supporting a genetic or biological explanation that researchers have yet to demonstrate.

The majority of the available cross-cultural evidence bears on the relative contribution of such cultural and educational transmission variables as "schooling" (Goodnow, 1962; Goodnow and Bethon, 1966; Greenfield, 1966; Prince, 1968), "urbanization" (Greenfield, 1966; Mohseni, 1966; Peluffo, 1967; Poole, 1968), "social status" (Lloyd, 1971) and "length of European contact" (Waddell, 1968; de Lacey, 1970, 1971, 1972; Dasen, 1970, 1972). Although the results for the school/nonschool and urban/rural differences have not been clear-cut and consistent, all the findings tend to suggest quite clearly that invariably, properties of Western cultural environments appear to be relatively more favorable to the development of Piagetian intellectual operations in non-Western cultures. Implicit in this group of studies is the assumption that biological, equilibration, and social factors are operative in the cognitive developmental process, but differential cultural and educational transmission factors tend to exert a modifying influence and thus predict patterns of operational performance in non-Western groups selected to vary in terms of the experience. However, despite the fact that these studies are subject to Wohlwill's (1968) criticism, they advance a stage beyond noncomparative Western ones in delineating some factors of cultural and educational transmission by exploiting intracultural differences. Unfortunately, the factors delineated are relatively global and do not provide us, in definite terms, with the specific experiential variables involved.

Recently, therefore, considerable emphasis has been placed on the a priori identification of specific cultural and educational experiences in operational development (Goodnow, 1969). Evidence in this connection has, indeed, been scanty. Prince (1968) in New Guinea, and Okonji (1971) in Uganda, have adduced evidence to indicate that quantitative difference in performance may not be due to schooling per se but to some quantitative aspects of it; Price-Williams et al. (1969) have interestingly linked the specific skill of pottery making to the development of conservation in Mexican children. The factors delineated by Prince, Okonji, and Price-Williams et al., involve a number of specific activities in which the individual actively engages. These include exercising, active manipulation, and experiencing. Such activities could conveniently be subsumed under Piaget's equilibration factors. Thus, the microscopic approach not only recognizes the central importance of the mechanism of equilibration or autoregulation in Piaget's cognitive theory but allows the interested researcher to uncover the specific cognitively salient experiences inherent in the indigenous non-Western cultures and those nurtured by Western cultural media. The relative dearth of empirical knowledge on equilibration factors is therefore very unfortunate.

In spite of the recent emphasis placed on the cognitive significance of socialization factors, based on the now widely unquestioned notion that the human organism does not develop in a social vacuum, there has regrettably been no empirical effort dedicated solely to the examination of the possibility of a linkage between social factors and Piagetian operational development. The Witkinian studies in psychological differentiation and cognitive styles have succeeded in pinning down the mother-child interaction correlates at both cross-national (Witkin et al. 1962, 1967; Dyk and Witkin, 1965) and cross-cultural (Dawson, 1963, 1967; Berry, 1966a, 1966b; Okonji, 1968, 1969) levels. Similarly, Hess and Shipman (1965, 1967) have convincingly linked differential family control systems and maternal behaviors to the socialization of the cognitive style dimensions postulated by Kagan, Moss, and Siegel (1963) and Kagan (1964). It is therefore surprising that an elaborate theory like Piaget's should lag behind other cognitive theories in adducing evidence in support of, or against, the importance of social antecedents of cognition. One of the criticisms which had often been leveled at Piaget was that of his initial de-emphasis on psychosocial or sociocultural variables. This is, as explained by Elkind (Piaget, 1969), a result of his (Piaget's) genetic epistemological—rather than developmental—psychological orientation. Ironically, in his *Psychology of Intelligence* (1959, p. 156), Piaget noted that the social environment

even more, in a sense, than the physical environment . . . affects intelligence through the three media of language (signs), the content of interaction (intellectual values) and rules imposed on thought (collective logical or pre-logical norms).

In elaborating on the second medium, Piaget (1966) reiterated that from an early age, cognitive development operates according to a socialization process involving social exchanges among children and adults. These exchanges interact with the process of equilibration to lay down the foundation for the development of logical or logico-mathematical operations. On the basis of Piaget's own formulations and of the relevant literature, it would appear that the social factors occurring in the context of mother-child interactions would be particularly potent in influencing the course of Piagetian intellectual operations, especially logical or logico-mathematical structures, despite the obvious insurmountable methodological problems involved.

Two major issues are, therefore, involved in the present investigation. Stated briefly, they are as follows:

1. The pattern of conservation performance on the concepts of quantity, weight and volume in Ghanaian 7- to 9-year-old school children and rural illiterate adults would vary in terms of the relative amounts of analogous conservation skills nurtured by an occupational experience; and

2. The maternal rates of socially reinforcing, insighting, encouraging, or suggesting behaviors should be positively related to the child's (4–5 years) cognitive scores (on discrimination, intuitive seriation, and number conservation), whereas with the maternal variables of assisting, direct-interfering, participating, intercepting, or directing, the relationship is inverse.

METHOD

1. Subjects

A total of 200 subjects, consisting mostly of mother-child pairs, was selected from populations located in rural and urban areas in Ghana and in lower- and middle-class areas in Glasgow, Scotland.

A. The Rural Subgroup

The rural Ghanaian subgroups were sampled from predominantly farming, selling, and pottery-making groups in locations in the Volta Region of Ghana, some 130 miles north of Accra. Mothers, aged between 25 and 40 years, were illiterate and permanent rural residents. The children were in two age groups: the older one were 7- to 9-year-olds receiving public primary school education in their localities; the younger children, all non-firstborns were non-nursery school 4- to 5-year-olds. For this group of subjects, the existing mode of upbringing adopted by mothers tends to be characterized by a relative lack of verbal stimulation, of approval, of attention, or of encouragement to children to ask questions and explore their surroundings (Ferron, 1964). Apparently, the most utilized family control system tends to be essentially imperative and status normative in character, supplemented by the use of supernatural sanctions as socialization techniques. Besides, partly as a result of the characteristic rural family units, most children tend to experience varied amounts of multiple parental upbringing (Barrington, 1962) and live in multiple occupational environments. The potentially confounding nature of variables in the psychosociological environments of the rural children required that they had lived permanently in their indigenous homes and only with their own parents.

1. *The farming families.* There were 26 mother-child pairs, of whom 19 included children 7 to 9 years old and 7 included children 4 to 5 years old. Living in the adjoining towns of Nkonya Ahenkro, Ntsumuru, and Kadjebi, these dyads were from families in which traditional food-crop farming is essentially a manual activity consisting initially of cutting the bush with cutlasses, followed by burning, clearing, harrowing, sowing or planting, weeding, and finally harvesting. Children from about 4 years of age participate in clearing, sowing or planting, weeding, and harvesting. The Nkonya farmer's child is usually alloted a small plot for tilling. On returning from the fields children carry logs of firewood or big tubers of yam or loads of other foodcrops in basket or bowls for home consumption or for sale.

2. *The selling families.* These consisted of another 26 mother-child pairs of the same dyadic composition and from the same locations as the farmers. Basically, selling is a female activity and in traditional occupational status second only to farming. It involves bargaining and bulk buying of commodities from wholesalers, petty traders, farmers, and fishermen, and subsequent retailing in periodic markets. Loads of commodities are transported to the markets by human porterage and arranged on tables, mats, rags, or bare ground, in circles so that the quantity invariably reflects

the price. Certain commodities like beans, groundnuts, salt, rice, and flour are measured for sale in empty tins of different sizes. Very young children take part in their mothers' selling activities. From the age of about 7 years, children might be required to bargain, bulk-buy, and sell commodities in markets, sometimes all by themselves. Since almost every selling family is also a farming family, it engages in the farming activities described above during off-market periods. It appears, however, that selling mothers and their children are generally more familiar than others with crude measures of quantity and price estimation of given quantities of particular commodities, and thus possess simple numerical or arithmetical skills as compared to their purely farming counterparts.

3. *The pottery-making families.* The 19 pairs consisting of mothers and 7- to 9-year-olds which were selected from this occupational group lived at Kpandu Fesi, located in the same geographic location as Nkonya, seven miles from Ahenkro. While the typical Fesi woman engages simultaneously in farming, selling, and pottery making, she normally sets aside an average of three days per week for her commercial pottery-making business, over and above the pottery making which follows farming and selling activities on other days. Pottery making is a manual activity, which consists initially of collecting and pounding old pottery products, sieving to obtain a very fine clay powder, and mixing in water along with fresh clay dug from the neighborhood. A few days later, the mixture is kneaded by hand to the requisite texture. Subsequently, the mixture is divided into identically shaped quantities, any of which is normally used for the end product. During the process of pottery making, clay is added to or taken away from each of the quantities. Shaping and smoothing then is done. The final steps in the process consist of baking the pots or dishes in a blazing fire and glazing them in covered pits. Finished clay products are normally transported on the head or by "mummy trucks" to the central market at Kpandu (Gabi) for sale. In the Kpandu area, pottery making runs both in families and in villages. The womenfolk in this area of Ghana are reputed for their expertise in the village craft from time immemorial. Children from these families observe their mothers tranforming identical molds of clay into pots and dishes at a very early age. Before the age of 5, they are given pieces of clay to play with. Thus the common form of the child's activity is imitating. At about school age (6–7 years) Fesi children are, as a rule, also sent to fetch broken pieces of pottery and fresh clay from nearby clay dugouts, and to stow away identical molds of clay and end products. The Fesi potter child is therefore afforded considerable visual, manipulative, and proprioceptive experiences, which become more pronounced with the years. Some children are deliberately made to acquire the pottery-making skill, and these home experiences are enhanced and given expression by the

emphasis on clay work at school. By Primary 3, most Fesi potter pupils become capable of making their own products, including pots, dishes, cups, jugs, and ashtrays. According to Price-Williams, et al.—(n.d.)—pottery making is a skill that embodies the elements of conservation of substance and perhaps also of weight. Obviously, pottery making in Fesi appears to nurture specific experiences more relevant to the development of conservation than does farming or selling.

B. The Urban Subgroup

This consisted of a separate group of 13 mother-child pairs including children aged 4–5, and 19 pairs including children 7–9, drawn from the Legon academic elite settlement in urban Accra. While these two age-groups of children submitted to the same sampling requirements as their respective traditional counterparts, they were nevertheless contrasted in terms of their type of schooling. The Legon children 4–5 and 7–9 attended the special University nursery and primary schools, whose standards approximate western ones. That they speak more fluent English both at home and at school places them at an advantage over their more traditionally bred rural peers. Sampled mothers were literate, aged 25–40 years and working full-time as qualified teachers, nurses, bank workers, or secretaries or as self-employed hairdressers and seamstresses. These dyads came from families in which the head or his spouse occupied an academic position in the various faculties of the University of Ghana. Most of these people were educated mainly in British and American universities. Characteristically, they hold master's degrees and doctorates in their disciplines, and earn an annual income ranging from ¢3,400 to ¢7,500 (about £1,200 to £2,680 sterling or $2,400 to $5,000 US $.) As a direct consequence of their educational level, occupation, and income, those elite families enjoy a high status. This can be reckoned in terms of their material possessions, especially status symbols, residences of the Western type, and a distinctive style of life and an outlook which reflect the relative amounts of Westernization they have experienced and continue to experience.

Their sociological and psychological home atmospheres contrast sharply with those of their traditional counterparts (Lloyd, 1966). Essentially this group maintains a nuclear family and both parents take up the upbringing responsibility. In the context of a permissive, relatively free home atmosphere in which role-conforming rigidity and superstitions are deemphasized, the Legon child is actively encouraged to ask questions, to which carefully thought out answers are provided, and to explore his environment through play and imitation and is praised or rewarded for positive behaviors or achievements. Lloyd's conclusion about the Yoruba

Table 8–1
Samples of Ghanian intra-cultural groups—pairs
consisting of mothers and 7- to 9-year-olds

Age	Level of education (in years.)	Urban elite	Rural potter	Rural seller	Rural farmer	total
7	2	5	4	4	4	17
8	2	7	8	7	7	29
9	3	7	7	8	8	30
24–45	Illiterate	—	19	19	19	57
Total number of Ss selected		19	38	38	38	133

elite—that "the orientation and practices of the elite mothers are similar to those of achievement-producing Western middle-class mothers" (p. 178)—finds applicability here.

C. The Scottish Subgroups

Living in class-differentiated areas in Glasgow, Scotland, these subjects also fell into two distinct groups in terms of the index of father's occupational categories, officially arranged and documented by the General Registrar's Office, Edinburgh, in the Population Census of 1961 (Volume 6).

1. *Middle-class.* This consisted of 20 mother-child pairs sampled from the Hillfoot and Bearsden suburbs of Glasgow and belonging to Social Classes 1 and 2. Characteristically, the fathers' occupations can be broadly described as professional and managerial.

2. *Lower-class.* Living in the predominantly working-class areas of Clydebank/Whitecrook and Drumry, this group of 20 mother-child pairs came from families which included skilled, semiskilled, and unskilled workers, classified as Social Classes 3 and 4.

Table 8–2
Samples of Scottish and Ghanaian pairs consisting of mothers and
4- to 5-year-olds, from various socioeconomic backgrounds

Age	Level of education	Scottish groups Middle	Lower	Ghanaian groups Urban Elite	Rural Traditional
4–5	Non-preschool	—	—	—	14
4–5	Play group	20	20	—	—
4–5	Nursery	—	—	13	—
25–45	Illiterate	—	—	—	14
25–40	Literate	20	20	13	—
Total Mother-child pairs		20	20	13	14

In either group, the mothers and their children were between 25–40 years and 4–5 years of age, respectively. The latter were all non-firstborns, had the same sex distribution as the Ghanaians and attended local preschool play groups. On the other hand, the level of education of the middle-class mothers was generally higher than that of their lower-class counterparts. None of the Scottish families employed domestic servants of any kind.

2. Tasks

Three groups of tasks and measures were employed: the adapted miniature situation for cross-cultural sampling of maternal behaviors; the discrimination and appreciation of seriation and of number tests for 4- to 5-year-olds and the conservation of number, substance, liquid, weight, and volume test widely used for 7- to 9-year-olds and illiterate adults cross-culturally. Each group of tasks is culturally translatable (Werner and Campbell, 1970):

A. Miniature situations

Consisted of the "Figure-Craft"—a control measure—and the "drying line" situations.

1. *Figure-Craft.* An interaction situation wherein a child constructed simple or complex shapes/figures of its choice using notched plastic pieces, supervised by its mother. The task lasts for five minutes only and is meant to condition the dyad to the observer's presence in the observation room.

2. *Clothesline.* Specifically contrived by the investigator to elicit preselected maternal behaviors and facilitate recording cross-culturally, it involves a child first in discriminating among a mixed pile of numerous miniature cardboard clothes, in order to solve the puzzle of finding a matching pair, and secondly, in hanging them one above the other on a model drying line having with two parallel lines. Essentially, this task represents a puzzle of such a level of difficulty that an independent solution by a 4- to 5-year-old is virtually impossible. The youngster is forced to solicit help and attention from its mother or to involve her directly in the task, consequently setting up an interaction situation. This task lasts 10 minutes. The maternal behaviors elicited by this technique, and subsequently sampled are:

Socially
reinforcing: verbal conditioning of child by praising, expressing affection, etc. ("That's very good, John").

Insighting: briefing a child, or focusing his attention/thought processes on the cue-giving characteristics of the task situation.

Suggesting: orienting the youngster's attention/thought processes to possible or alternative courses of action, but leaving the final decision making to him (e.g., "Would you . . .").

Assisting: physically aiding the child in the solution of the puzzle.

Direct-inter-
fering: making a firm, matter-of-fact statement which does not however, necessarily imply compliance (e.g. "Don't hang that on, Kofi.").

Distracting: drawing the child's attention to things irrelevant to the task solution (e.g. "This is a quiet room, isn't it?).

Intercepting: taking over completely from the otherwise busy child and thus rendering him temporarily or permanently passive.

Participating: taking direct or active part in the task with the child, thus rendering him less active.

Directing: giving directly phrased command and specifying that the child's activities be carried out in an explicit manner, but without necessarily implying compliance. (e.g. "Hang it up here.").

B. Intuitive Cognitive Tasks: 4- to 5-year-olds

The tasks selected are the Piaget's (1952) discrimination, seriation, and number tasks, which appear to be represented, at least at an intuitive level, in the cognitive capacities of children 4–7 years of age.

1. *Discrimination and seriation* (Elkind, 1964). In the discrimination test—a control measure—the subject was required to discriminate size differences in a random array of three-dimensional wooden blocks; in the seriation task, the subject was to use a chosen number of these three-dimensional blocks to construct a stairway.

2. *Number*. The intuitive conception of number was tested by presenting the subject with two rows of sweets (of the same length but varying in number) and requiring him to select the row which has more sweets and eat them all (Mehler and Bever, 1967). Criticisms against this method as a valid measure of conservation have been raised variously by Piaget (1968), Siegel and Goldstein (1969), Rothenberg and Courtney (1968) and Willoughby and Trachy (1971).

C. Conservation Tasks: 7- to 9-year-olds and Illiterate Adults.

Subjects were required to give equality/inequality judgments as to the invariance of number, quantity (continuous and discontinuous), weight, and volume problems (Piaget, 1952) and to justify their responses accordingly.

3. Materials

With the exception of the Figure-Craft, locally available and familiar materials were used.

A. Figure-Craft

Over 200 pieces of differently colored and shaped pieces of plastic, easily fittable. A commercially available craft (in Britain) recommended for 3- to 8-year-olds.

B. Clothesline

1. *Drying line.* A portable (47.5 cm × 15.5 cm × 3.5 cm) plywood base supporting two posts 18 cm high and 40 cm apart, through which two parallel (upper and lower) steel rods pass, separated by 8 cm of space.

2. *Clothes.* 44 miniature pieces of cardboard clothing, each about 14 sq cm. There were 11 different kinds of clothes (vest, T-shirt, cardigan, jacket, shirt, pullover, jumper, pair of shorts/trousers, skirt, dress), four of each kind, of which two were color duplicates. Nine different color combinations were used on the 44 pieces of clothing so that each color appeared almost the same number of times.

C. Discrimination and seriation (4- to 5-year-olds)

Two sets of nine 3-D wooden blocks, painted white or red. Of the white blocks, the smallest was a cube measuring 25 mm on each side and the remaining eight increased in height by successive steps of 10 mm each. Of the red, the smallest was 25 mm × 25 mm at the base and 20 mm high; the remaining eight increased in height by successive steps of 10 mm.

D. Number (4- to 5-year-olds)

Chocolate "Smarties" (Glaswegian Ss); black and white "Sweeties" (Ghanian Ss). In each case, the stimulus material was of the same color and size.

E. Conservation tests

1. *Substance and weight.* Two standard balls of clay, each 30 mm in diameter; one ball of clay 45 mm in diameter.

2. *Liquid.* Three identical glasses measuring 110 mm high, 50 mm at the base, and 75 mm at the top opening; one tall cylindrical jar 200 mm high, 45 mm at the base; one transparent plastic container measuring 90 mm high, 100 mm in diameter of the base or top opening; and ordinary drinking water.

3. *Volume*. Three balls of clay (same as for substance and weight); three identical glasses (same as for liquid); ordinary drinking water.

4. *Number*. Twenty-six equally sized ripe palm-nut fruits.

4. Procedures and Test Sequence

A. Interaction Situations

Following a 3 to 4 monthly period of preobservation in the sampling locations in Glasgow, or 4 to 6 weeks in Ghana, each mother of the sampled dyads was requested into the observation room alone. Subsequently, the investigator listed her co-operation, and by giving her the responsibility over the whole situation by means of deceptive standard instructions, led her into believing that the focus of observation was the child. To condition the pair still further to the observer's presence, it was required that they interact in an initial five-minute Figure-Craft situation before the ten-minute observation phase proper. Below are the instructions which summarize the procedure:

We are interested in the way your little son/daughter plays when you are with him/her. I have here two sets of playthings for young children: This one (observer shows the Figure-Craft) and these (observer shows the drying line and miniature clothes).Since I would like ——— (name) to feel very relaxed and thus learn to ignore my presence when he/she comes to play, I wish to request you to please ask ——— to make any object or shape he/she wants with these plastic pieces for only five minutes (observer pours the plastic pieces on the table). You will be signalled thus (observer taps the table slightly with a pen) when the five minutes are over.

After that, you will next tell ——— that it is drying time and that he/she is going to hang his/her mummy's washing on a drying line. As you can see, (observer points to the drying line) there are two drying lines and there are four pieces of clothing of each kind (observer spreads the heap of miniature clothes on the table and sorts a few out). All ——— has to do is to search among these clothes, find two that match, thus (observer demonstrates by hanging a pair correctly), and hang them on these lines one above the other. He/she is to hang—on these two lines—the clothes that match in shape and color until the lines are covered from one end to the other. This game takes only ten minutes. You will find that the game is of such a kind that ——— will probably need your attention from the very beginning. You can give whatever attention you wish. Remember that this is just a play situation and all we need is your cooperation in every way, so that I can sit down quietly in the corner and take down a few notes about how ——— plays when he/she is relaxed by your side. Please ignore the fact that I am in this room and do whatever you wish. Thank you.

These instructions were slowly repeated for each mother and any doubt she had of the degree of maternal participation wanted was dispelled by telling her to give whatever attention she wished. The child was then brought in, and the observer immediately started recording the mother's behavior using a notational system.

Cognitive tasks for 4 to 5-year-olds

After the two consecutive sessions, each of the 4 to 5-year-olds was tested on the discrimination, seriation, and number tasks—in that sequence, mainly to control for the motivational effects of the sweets used in the number tasks on the others.

1. *Discrimination*. Subjects were required to find the smallest (shortest) or the biggest (longest) 3-D block from a random array of nine (Elkind, 1964). The positions of the shortest and the longest blocks were reversed in each of the four presentations, to control for perseveration responses.

2. *Seriation*. Subjects were required to build a stairway, beginning with seven of the nine white 3-D blocks preselected and disarrayed on the table. A demonstration of the model was presented by the investigator if the subject's first attempt at constructing the series ended in failure. Should subjects fail still further, a model consisting of only the two shortest white blocks was provided, and the procedure was terminated thereafter if an independent serial ordering by the child failed to take place. Upon successful seriation of seven blocks, however, the seriated blocks were spaced at equal intervals and the subject was encouraged to fit in a randomly preselected set of three red 3-D blocks, etc.

3. *Number*. Two rows each of four "Smarties"/black and white "Sweeties" were arranged in one-to-one correspondence across the length of the table and subjects were required to give equality/unequality responses. Thereafter, two more were added to one row, the length of which was subsequently shortened to three inches while the length of the four-"Sweetie" row was stretched to five inches. (Perseverative and recency responses were minimized by counter-balancing this presentation). The Scottish subjects were instructed, to "Take the line that will give you most Smarties to eat and eat them all." While the Ghanaian subjects were directed to: "Take the toffees that would make you "cheat" your friend and eat them all." For the Scottish and Ghanaian subjects, the words "most" and "cheat," respectively, were employed to take into consideration their relative lack of comprehension of the relational term "more."

C. Conservation tasks

The general procedure was the individual testing of mother and child in consecutive sessions separated by a few minutes during which no communication occurred between mother and child. Initially, elaborate rapport was established in informal conversational—not lasting normally beyond eight minutes. The test sequence followed was substance, liquid, weight, number, and volume.

1. *Substance, liquid, and number.* In view of the ambiguity of relational terms in some non-Western languages—pointed out by Heron (1971) in Zambia, de Lemos (1969) in Australia, and Greenfield (1966) in Sénégal —and the lack of satisfactory equivalents for "same," "more," and "less" (see Adjei, 1973) in Ghanaian languages, these conservation tasks, which are more susceptible to confounding linguistic variables, were presented in sharing terms to insure what Werner and Campbell (1970) have called "cultural translation," or in the terminology of Sechrest et al (1972), "experimental equivalence." Thus basically, the "sharing technique" required the subject to suppose initially that food or water was being shared between himself and another individual. For equality/ unequality judgment, the subject was presented, for example, with one standard ball of clay and then required to make a selection of the ball "which should be given to your friend so that he/she does not cheat you." Upon correct judgment of equality, one of the two standard balls was transformed into a ring or sausage form. Thereafter, the subject was asked: "Would one cheat or not cheat the other?" The response was pursued "Why would one cheat" or "Why would one not cheat?"

2. *Weight.* Subjects were made to suppose that they were weighing *kenkey* (a Ghanaian food made from fermented maize flour). After selecting the two standard balls in the equality judgment and transformation steps (as in substance), subjects were asked whether one was "as heavy as," "heavier than," or "lighter than" the other. The same expressions were employed in demanding an explanation of their responses. (These expressions were employed because there are approximate vernacular equivalents for them.)

3. *Volume.* The procedure consisted first of employing the substance and liquid tests to obtain equality judgments for the two standard balls of clay and glasses each half-filled with water respectively. Thereafter, one ball of clay was dropped into one glass of water and the subject was required to respond to "go up as high as," "go higher than," and "go lower than" questions when the levels in two standard glasses were compared. The same procedure was followed when one of the standard balls of clay was transformed and dropped into one of the half-filled glasses of water. As in the weight problem, responses were pursued accordingly.

5. Scoring and Grading Systems

A. Maternal Behaviors

Recording consisted of noting the frequencies with which the notational codes for each category of behavior occurred during the clothesline observation session. The notation of continuous and rapid occurrence of the same behavior was accomplished by attaching the frequency of occurrence to the code (Hutt and Hutt, 1970, and Lytton, 1971). Frequency counts were then summed up to obtain a total for each code during the 10-minute session.

Inter-observer reliabilities were established on four mother-child pairs in Glasgow. The coefficients (Spearman's Rank Correlation) were .47, .74, .88, and .93 for the first, second, third, and fourth observations respectively. These coefficients were estimated after all the form observations had been completed.

B. Cognitive tasks (4 to 5-year-olds)

On each of the tests, each subject's performance was noted in one of two categories: appreciation of concept (1) and no appreciation of concept (0).

1. *Discrimination.* (1) indicated three or four correct responses; (0) indicated less than three correct responses.

2. *Seriation.* (1) meant successful seriation of at least seven blocks without help; (0) meant serial arrangement of less than seven blocks—with or without help.

3. *Number.* (1) meant taking the row containing six elements; (0) meant taking the row containing four elements.

C. Conservation tasks

Subjects were categorized into conservers (C); non conservers (NC) and transitionals (T).

1. *Conservers.* These gave responses at "not cheat," "go up as high as," or "as heavy as" on the two subtests of number, liquid, substance, volume or weight respectively. Their justifications were classified into *perceptual, direct action* and *transformational* (including identity, reversibility, and correlative action).

2. *Nonconservers.* Consisted of subjects who gave "cheat" responses for number, liquid and substance; "heavier/lighter than" for weight and "go higher/lower than" for volume on both subtests.

3. *Transitionals.* They were the subjects giving NC response on one subtest and C response on the other.

Nonconservers and transitionals could not justify their response with any of the reasons classified previously for conservers.

RESULTS

1. Specific experiences and conservation performance

A. Quantitative Findings

The results reported here were derived by chi-square analyses of the cell frequencies (see Tables 8–3 and 8–4) of any two groups categorized into conservers and nonconservers/transitionals.

Table 8–3
Number and proportion of Ghanaian 7- to 9-year-olds conserving (N = 19)

SUBGROUP	NUMBER		LIQUID		SUBSTANCE		WEIGHT		VOLUME	
	N	Proportion	N	Proportion	N	Proportion	N	Proportion	N	Proportion
Urban elite	19	1.00	16	.84	14	.74	9	.47	10	.53
Rural potter	18	.95	16	.84	15	.79	14	.74	4	.21
Rural farmer	19	1.00	13	.68	11	.58	7	.37	7	.37
Rural seller	16	.84	11	.58	11	.58	4	.21	8	.42

1. 7 to 9-year-olds. No significant differences were found between any two subgroups of the Ghanaian 7 to 9-year-olds on number, liquid, or substance and volume tasks. On weight, however, the rural pottery-making children were significantly superior to their rural counterparts at the .003 and .05 levels respectively. In contrast, nonsignificant differences were evident on weight as between rural farming groups and selling groups, and between any rural groups and the urban elite.

2. *Illiterate Adults.* Table 8–4 revealed the number and liquid tests as relatively insensitive to adult group differences. On the other hand, differences were evident on substance, weight, and volume. On substance, the potters were significantly superior to the sellers at the .05 level but identical to farmers. On weight, the potters were significantly superior to the farmers at the .004 level but identical to the sellers, who in turn tended

Table 8–4
Number and proportion of Ghanaian rural illiterate mothers conserving (N = 19)

SUBGROUP	NUMBER		LIQUID		SUBSTANCE		WEIGHT		VOLUME	
	N	Proportion	N	Proportion	N	Proportion	N	Proportion	N	Proportion
Rural potter	19	1.00	17	.90	19	1.00	18	.95	14	.74
Rural farmer	19	1.00	18	.95	16	.84	9	.47	5	.26
Rural seller	19	1.00	19	1.00	14	.74	16	.84	4	.21

to perform significantly better than the farmers at the .04 level. On volume, the potters were again significantly superior to their farmer and seller counterparts at the .009 and .003 levels, respectively. No significant differences were found between the farmers and sellers on volume.

B. Qualitative findings

Interesting group-related differences were revealed in the distributive pattern of the justifications supplied by the Ghanaian children and adults. For their conserving responses, the rural potter and urban elite children tended to provide a relatively higher percentage of transformational reasons on substance and weight than either of the rural nonpotter groups or a combination of both. There was a tendency for the elite children to supply a relatively higher percentage of transformational reasons on liquid and volume than any 7- to 9-year-old group studied. Of the conserving transformational reasons, the rural potter or urban elite children offered about three times more indirect action (mainly reversibility) reasons than their nonpotter counterparts. And whereas an appreciable percentage (50%) of the potter children's identity reasons were supplemented by direct-action reasons, there were on the whole relatively few identity reasons with perceptual supplement—all of them given by the elite. Finally, the potter and elite groups tended to supply fewer direct-action reasons as independent supports for conserving responses than did their rural non-potter peers.

With regard to the nonconserving responses, the rural potter or urban elite children tended to rely much more heavily on perceptual explanations than the nonpotter groups, and supplied relatively very few or no direct action reasons on each test (except on number, for which the potter children offered 33% nonconserving direct-action reasons) in comparison to the non-potters, for whom the percentage was relatively higher across all the tests.

The group distribution pattern of the justification types supplied by the illiterate mothers for their conserving responses was identical to those described for their children above. There was, however, no difference between adult potters and nonpotters in terms of the reasons supporting their nonconserving reasons.

2. Cognitive Development and Specific Maternal Behaviors

A. Maternal Behavior Dimensions

Group differences and similarities in maternal behavior were determined using the Mann-Whitney U test (Siegel, 1956, pp. 116–127).

Table 8–5
Comparison of Ghanaian elite and rural illiterate mothers: maternal behavior

Maternal behaviour	Urban Elite ($n_1 = 13$) Median	Rural Illiterate ($n_2 = 14$) Median	U
Socially reinforcing	1.0	0.0	35.0**
Insighting	18.0	4.0	21.5**
Encouraging	0.0	0.0	88.0
Suggesting	2.0	1.0	51.0*
Assisting	67.0	98.5	67.0
Direct-interfering	6.0	2.0	31.0**
Participating	14.0	10.0	55.5*
Intercepting	5.0	3.0	69.5
Directing	12.0	16.0	73.0

**p < .01
*p < .05

The maternal distracting behavior dimension was not included in the tables and the analysis because there was virtually no score on it.

1. *Comparison of groups of Scot mothers.* The Mann-Whitney U values revealed nonsignificant social class differences with respect to the socially reinforcing, insighting, suggesting, assisting, direct-interfering, participating, and directing behaviors. On the other hand, the maternal encouraging dimension was the only one which emerged statistically significant ($U = 82.5$, $n_1 = 20$, $n_2 = 20$; $p < .001$) in favor of the Scott middle-class mothers.

2. *Comparison of Ghanaian Groups.* Table 5 reveals the trend of significant differences for the behavior studied.

Table 8–6
Comparison of combined Scot and combined Ghanaian mothers: maternal behavior

Maternal behavior	Ghanaian mothers ($n_1 = 27$) Median	Scot mothers ($n_2 = 40$) Median	Z	p
Socially reinforcing	0.0	5.0	7.14	.00003
Insighting	11.0	15.0	2.11	.01
Encouraging	0.0	1.0	1.17	.12 NS
Suggesting	1.0	4.0	4.54	.00003
Assisting	69.0	48.5	2.25	.01
Direct-interfering	3.0	2.0	1.48	.07 NS
Participating	11.0	5.0	1.78	.04
Intercepting	4.0	1.0	3.22	.0001
Directing	14.0	7.0	3.85	.0001

Table 8–7
Comparison of Scot and Ghanaian elite mothers: maternal behavior revealing intracultural differences in Ghana

Maternal behavior	Scot mothers ($n_1 = 40$) Median	Ghanaian elite mothers ($n_2 = 13$) Median	Z	p
Socially reinforcing	5.0	2.0	1.63	.05
Insighting	15.0	18.0	.89	.19
Suggesting	4.0	2.0	2.52	.006
Direct-interfering	2.0	6.0	3.10	.001
Participating	5.0	14.0	1.98	.02

Obviously, only socially reinforcing, insighting, direct-interfering, and participating maternal dimensions emerged as relatively sensitive to differences in social status.

3. *Comparison of Scots and Ghanaians.* As a result of the pervasive nonsignificant differences between the two Scottish groups, they were combined for cross-cultural comparisons. Table 8–6 compares the combined Scot groups with the combined Ghanaian groups, and Tables 8–7 and 8–8 summarize the results for the Scot mothers compared with the Ghanaian elite and the rural illiterate mothers respectively.

Combining the comparisons undertaken in Tables 8–5, 8–6, 8–7, and 8–8, the following is a summary of the results:

a. On one hand, while the Ghanaian elite and the rural illiterate groups did not differ on the frequencies of their assisting, intercepting, or directing behaviors, they nevertheless differed significantly from the Scots on each of these variables.

b. On the other hand, whereas the Ghanaian elite mothers tended to elicit significantly more socially-reinforcing, insighting, suggesting, direct-interfering, and participating behaviors than did the rural illiterates, either groups tended to be lower on socially reinforcing and suggesting behaviors

Table 8–8
Comparison of Scot and Ghanaian rural illiterate mothers: maternal behaviors revealing intracultural differences in Ghana

Maternal behavior	Scot mothers ($n_1 = 40$) Median	Ghanaian illiterates ($n_2 = 14$) Median	Z	p
Socially reinforcing	5.0	0.0	4.83	.00003
Insighting	15.0	4.0	4.12	.00003
Suggesting	4.0	1.0	4.21	.00003
Direct-interfering	2.0	2.0	.76	.22
Participating	5.0	10.0	.51	.30

than their Scot counterparts. On insighting, however, the Ghanaian elite and the Scots were identical, while the Ghanaian illiterate mothers tended to be lower on this variable than the Scot mothers. But on the maternal variables of direct-interfering and participating, the Ghanaian illiterate and the Scot mothers were identical, whereas the elite tended to be significantly higher on these variables than the Scots.

As far as the encouraging dimension is concerned, the difference between the elite or illiterate Ghanaians and the Scot lower-class mothers was nonsignificant. However, the Scot middle-class mothers tended to elicit significantly more encouraging behaviors than either Ghanaian group $(p < .05)$ when interacting with their children.

B. Relationships Between Maternal Behaviors and Cognitive Development

The correlation coefficients reported in the following tables are point-biserial coefficients (r_b) which determine the degree of relationship between a variable assumed to have an underlying continuous distribution (maternal behavior) and a dichotomous variable (child's cognitive scores).

From Table 8–9, it becomes evident that there is a general tendency for most of the maternal behavior variables of the Scottish mothers to be negatively related to the children's scores in the various cognitive dimensions. Nevertheless, the highest and the most important maternal behavior correlates of the child's cognitive dimensions are the socially reinforcing, insighting, direct-interfering, and directing behaviors. Apart

Table 8–9
Relationships (point-biserial coefficients) between maternal behaviors and the cognitive dimensions of 4- to 5-year-olds: Scot mother-child pairs (N = 36)

	CHILD'S COGNITIVE DIMENSIONS		
Maternal behavior	*Discrimination*	*Seriation*	*Number*
Socially reinforcing	−.35[b]	−.38[b]	−.21
Insighting	−.29[c]	−.34[c]	.09
Encouraging	−.18	.05	−.14
Suggesting	.14	.21	.25
Assisting	−.01	−.18	−.06
Direct-interfering	−.12	−.47[a]	−.36[c]
Participating	−.12	−.07	−.13
Intercepting	−.05	−.09	−.22
Directing	−.04	−.30[c]	−.51[a]

$a = p < .005$
$b = p < .025$
$c = p < .05$

Table 8–10
Relationships (point-biserial coefficients) between maternal behaviors and the cognitive dimensions of 4- to 5-year-olds: Ghanaian mother-child pairs (N = 23)

	CHILD'S COGNITIVE DIMENSIONS		
Maternal behavior	*Discrimination*	*Seriation*	*Number*
Socially reinforcing	−.24	.19	.19
Insighting	.25	.06	.52[a]
Encouraging	.15	−.16	−.12
Suggesting	−.02	−.02	.20
Assisting	.28	.21	.05
Direct-interfering	.15	−.42[b]	.08
Participating	−.06	.10	.27
Intercepting	−.44[a]	.36[c]	.25
Directing	.10	−.41[b]	−.28

a $p < .025$
b $p < .05$
c $.10 > p > .05$

from these, the table indicates a virtual lack of relationships between maternal dimensions of encouraging, assisting, participating, and intercepting and the child's scores on any of the cognitive dimensions. Similarly, the results for the Ghanaian mother-child pairs (as indicated in Table 8–10 did not only show that the relationships were weak but also that they were mostly nonsignificant and indicated inconsistent trends.

There was, however, a general tendency for maternal rates of insighting to relate positively to each cognitive dimension of the child, although this was significant only in the case of number. Maternal direct-interfering,

Table 8–11
Relationships (point-biserial coefficients) between maternal behaviors and the conservation scores of 7- to 9-year-olds: Ghanaian rural illiterate mother-child pairs (N = 12)

	CONSERVATION CONCEPTS			
Maternal behavior	*Substance*	*Liquid*	*Weight*	*Volume*
Insighting	−.06	.01	−.34	.28
Encouraging	−.33	−.08	−.24	.12
Suggesting	.24	.02	.47*	.41*
Assisting	−.24	−.36	.08	−.24
Direct-interfering	−.03	.06	.41*	−.20
Participating	.18	.39*	.27	−.16
Intercepting	.41*	.28	.47*	−.23
Directing	−.36	.05	−.39*	−.16

*p = $.05 < p < .10$

intercepting, and directing behaviors correlated significantly positively with the child's dimensions of seriation, discrimination, and seriation respectively.

To examine these relationships still further, the 12 rural illiterate mother-child pairs on which conservation data were available were used. The summary of results appears in Table 8–11. Although this section of results is not specifically intended to be employed to examine our hypothesis, it will definitely throw light on some of the most important relationships found in the two previous tables.

None of the relationships revealed in Table 8–11 was significant at the .05 level. It is, however, evident that maternal suggesting, direct-interfering, and directing behaviors showed some of the highest relationships with the child's cognitive dimensions in the rural illiterate cultural group at the level of the operational structure tapped.

DISCUSSION

1. Specific Experiences and Conservation

On the whole, the quantitative data on both Ghanaian age groups studied largely support the facilitative effects of the pottery-making experience reported the Mexican investigation of Price-Williams, *et al.*, (1969), and of the urban elite Ghanaian child's background. Similarly, the trends revealed by the qualitative results were correspondingly neat.

With regard to the illiterate adult groups, the significantly higher performance levels of the potters relative to the nonpotters on substance, weight, and volume conservation were in accord with our predictions. However, the 7- to 9-year-olds were significantly superior to their rural counterparts on weight only, and surprisingly but nonsignificantly, were the poorest performers on volume. There is thus clear-cut evidence to suggest that while the adult potters' superiority is attributable to their intensively nurtured pottery-making skill, their children's inconsistent performance is indicative of their acquisition of rudimentary experience resulting from a generally lower level of participation in the craft. Evident from the background information detailed elsewhere in this report is the indication that the Ghanaian potter child's experiences remain considerably more visual than manipulative. Nevertheless, the potter group does appear to have the requisite experiences on the basis of which to perform—in contrast to their nonpotter schooling peers—at a higher level on some of the conservation tasks which have direct experiential counterparts. This, partly at least, explains the statistical departure of our

7- to 9-year-olds' results from those of the San Marcos potter children in Mexico, of Price-Williams, *et al.*

The 7- to 9-year-olds' performance on weight deserves its own discussion. The Fesi potter children selected are exposed to numerable carrying and lifting pottery-related activities. Examples are the carrying of clay from nearby dugouts and stowing away identical molds of clay, or carrying or seeing finished clay products transformed from the raw product. In a typical potter home, then, opportunities are provided for the acquisition of the specific and relevant sort of carrying and lifting activities which predispose the individual to making correct judgment of weight in terms of previously acquired sensory and motor experience. Goodnow (1969, p. 259) explained that such experiences may:

... provide an "action model," a pragmatic model that serves as a landmark, reference point, or mnemonic device for pinning down relationships and holding it in mind.

Evidently, our results on weight tend to show that carrying children (potters) can perform at the same level as noncarrying children (urban elite) but higher than the other carrying children (farming and selling). The reasons for this are obvious. The urban elite in Ghana is a "class in formation." Children belonging to this social status group are never of the carrying variety, because carrying duties are executed by wards. Nevertheless, their concept of weight is likely to develop normally as they encounter appropriate experiences in a rather stimulating Western-type environment. Contrariwise, the typical rural nonpotter child experientially departs from his potter counterpart in terms of the relevant sort of carrying and lifting opportunities nurtured by events in the latter's home. The former is not normally exposed to the carrying or lifting of identically shaped objects the transformation of which they have visually experienced. The typical rural nonpotter (particularly the farmer) child has since very early infancy carried cylindricaly shaped objects—tubers of yam or cassava and logs of firewood—over appreciable distances from the farm, and comparatively flatter and lighter objects—plates, trays—over errand-distances around the neighborhood. Tubelike objects carried over relatively long distances might be pinned down as weighing more than the flatter, obviously lighter objects carried over relatively short distances by the very young child. These carrying experiences could disrupt a child's discovery of the invariance properties of weight through "internalizing" an "action model" (Goodnow, 1969) in terms of which the child can form a generalized but erroneous impression that apparent differences in size of objects must necessarily result in variations in weight.

That this formative impression carries over into adulthood is seen in the significantly contrasting performance of the potter or seller adults on the one hand, and that of their farmer counterparts on the other. As a result of her skill and her carrying experiences since infancy, the adult potter (like her child) must have acquired the experiences relevant to the discovery of the invariance of weight. Similarly, since the adult sellers normally carry their items to the market in bulk and subsequently arrange them in smaller quantities for sale—so that differences in quantity reflected in differences in price—they must realize better than do their own children and adult farmers that the items arranged for sale are equivalent to the bulk they originally carried to the market.

Carrying per se, therefore, is not a sufficient condition for weight conservation. Thus the relative stability of the potters' (adults' and children's) and the adult sellers' weight conservation stems from the fact that they are the beneficiaries of a more adaptive kind of specific carrying experience.

For the adults, it is surprising that the performance of the sellers on weight could not be generalized to substance and volume, since certain aspects of their occupation contain essential parallels to those typical in conservation situations. Possibly, the experience nurtured by the selling occupation is task-specific. In the light of the Mexican data of Price-Williams, et al, however, the potter children's performance on the volume task is indeed astonishing and unexpected. On the tasks of number and liquid, it is likely that the difficulty level of the concepts relative to the children's age range masked any evidence of group difference. It is possible that the use of the "sharing technique"—with its inherent cultural translations and other safeguards against inappropriate verbal communication—made the problems easier for the 7- to 9-year-old subjects studied than would have the classical Genevan testing procedure.

2. Maternal Behavior and Cognitive Development

In this study, the insighting behavior of the Ghanaian mothers showed a significant positive correlation with the child's number performance. Kirk's (1977) results in Ghana (reported in this volume) confirm this finding: The frequency of her Ga mother's reference to similarities or differences, and of reference to relationship—both of which make up the present author's insighting dimension—had a significant positive correlation with a child's aggregate performance of three Piaget tasks and with his performance on the Conservation of Quantity task (clay). With the exception of this single finding, the rather low and nonsignificant relationships which emerged between the maternal socially reinforcing, suggesting, or encouraging dimensions and the child's cognitive performance failed to yield any useful insights. Kirk (1977), on the other hand, found a significant inverse relationship between a Ga mother's attempt to motivate a child and the latter's performance in length conservation.

As regards our Scot mother-child pairs, maternal socially reinforcing or insighting behaviors showed significant inverse relationship with a child's discrimination or seriation task performance. However, like the Ghanaian results, suggesting and encouraging maternal variables failed to predict the child's cognitive status. Therefore, the positive relationships predicted between each of the maternal dimensions (insighting, socially reinforcing, encouraging, or suggesting) and each of the child's cognitive dimensions, were not altogether supported by our results. Instead, there emerged a reversal of relationships in the two cultural groups. In contrast, the inverse relationships predicted between direct-interfering, intercepting, participating, and directing behaviors and the child's cognitive task performances were to some extent supported by our results. Although the data for Ghanaian mother-child pairs tended to suggest that the trend of relationship might depend upon the particular dimensions being correlated, those of the Scots tended to indicate that the overall trend was in accord with our prediction. It is noteworthy from our results that although maternal direct-interfering or directing behavior correlated inversely with the children's cognitive dimensions, the only significant relationships in each cultural groups were those found for direct-interfering or directing and seriation.

In spite of the fact that the Piaget cognitive tasks used by Kirk (1977) appear to differ in content, function, and complexity from our own, it is interesting to observe that Kirk's findings support those of this study. For a Ga mother's emphasis on negative imperatives (which appears synonymous with our "direct-interfering"), and on physical intervention by completing steps in the puzzle (intercepting), was found to have a significant inverse relationship to a child's conservation of clay or to the aggregate of two conservation task performance respectively. Each of Kirk's categories of total maternal involvement and physical maternal involvement also evidenced a consistent but nonsignificant relationship with the child's cognitive dimensions. Evidently, of all the maternal dimensions studied, the insighting, socially reinforcing, direct-interfering, intercepting, participating, and directing behaviors appear to be the best predictors of the child's Piagetian cognitive task performance.

Our results tend to suggest that in the upbringing of the child, the excessive use of such behaviors as the socially reinforcing or insighting— otherwise considered behavioristically to be positive control systems—tend to inhibit cognitive development in much the same way as do direct—interfering and directing. The relationships between social reinforcing or insighting behaviors and the child's cognitive dimension to evidence culturally opposite trends is indicative of the finding that the Ghanaian mothers tended to be significantly lower on these two dimensions than their Scot counterparts. It thus appears that infrequent (possibly intermittent) reinforcements or insighting are more effective in enhancing development of concepts of the Piaget type than their excessive application in upbringing practices.

The views expressed here are consonant with those held by Piaget (1966) on the interaction between social exchanges and the process of equilibration to form logical or logico-mathematical concepts. Excesses of certain exchanges can be seen as limiting a child's independent action, exploration and discovery of the laws of nature. Whether too frequent social reinforcing makes a child complacent and thus discourages his further active exploration or participation in other activities is a question open to future investigation. However, since insighting a child is analogous to centering his cognitive equipment only on the relevant cues in a problem-solving situation, this is likely to prevent the spontaneous discovery and acquisition by the child of certain flexible cognitive strategies such as those required for decentration. On the other hand, explicit restricting, intercepting, or interfering might directly prevent the individual from elaborating his sensory-motor potentialities through exploration and active participation. Finally, directing not only discourages self-initiated action and active participation, but shapes an individual's cognition in accordance with the sanctions, obligations, and norms operative in his society.

Briefly, the quality or extent of a maternal behavior control system can interfere with the equilibration process in various and subtle ways, producing a child with clear cognitive deficiencies which are not directly explainable on the basis of his biological apparatus or his physical environment.

SUMMARY

The major issue involved in this investigation is the examination of the developmental association between specific occupational experiences or maternal behaviors and Piagetian operations. The basic prediction advanced is that these experiences interact with the individual's internalizing mechanisms to produce differential cognitive performance.

In the first group of studies, a total of 133 subjects were selected, comprising comparable groups of Ghanaian rural pottery-making, farming, and selling mother-child pairs and urban elite children. All the mothers (aged 25–45 years) were illiterate and the children (aged 7–9 years) had primary schooling. These subjects were tested on the conservation of number, liquid, substance, weight, and volume. Our results indicated that at the adult level, the potters' superiority on the tests of substance and weight was more distinct that at the 7–9 year level. The potter children were significantly superior to any of the rural groups on weight only, but relatively the poorest of all the groups on volume. It is doubtful whether at the 7–9 year level, the acquired experience of pottery making is sufficient to produce significantly superior performance on all the conservation tests. The results of this first group of studies indicated the relative importance of specific physical experiences (equilibration factors).

The second group of studies dealt with Piagetian cognitive elements in specific maternal behaviors. A total of 67 pairs of mothers and 4-year-olds was sampled, from Scottish and Ghanaian groups. A number of cognitively relevant maternal behaviors were observed and recorded in a specially devised interaction situation. Subsequently, the 4- to 5-year-olds' cognitive concepts—discrimination, seriation, and number—were tested in the same session. Direct-interfering and directing maternal behaviors emerged as significant negative correlates of one or another cognitive dimension of the child, in the two cultural groups. In contrast, socially reinforcing and insighting maternal behaviors showed a significant inverse correlation with the child's discrimination and seriation dimensions in the Scottish group, but showed a generally positive (though mostly non-significant) trend in the Ghanaian group. The only significantly positive relationship observed in the latter group was between insighting and number. In the light of the cross-cultural differences in these behaviors, it was found that whereas maternal direct-interfering and directing would invariably relate to cognitive inhibition, the cognitive product of the socially reinforcing and insighting maternal behaviors might depend on their extent. Some of Kirk's (1977) results were found to support those reported in this study which delineated some of Piaget's (1966) social factors of interpersonal co-ordination in operational development.

NOTE

1. This chapter is adapted from a Ph.D. thesis submitted to the University of Strathclyde in September, 1973, in accordance with the regulations governing the award of the Ph.D. in psychology.

REFERENCES

Adjei, K. (1973) *Maternal Behaviours and Cognitive Development.* Unpublished Ph.D. thesis, University of Strathclyde, Glasgow, 1973.

Barrington, K. (1962) *Bringing up children in Ghana.* London: George Allen and Unwin, Ltd.

Berry, J. W. (1966a) *Cultural determinants of perception.* Unpublished thesis. University of Edinburgh.

――. (1966b) Temne and Eskimo perceptual skills. *International Journal of Psychology, 1* (3): 207–229.

Dasen, P. R. (1970) *Cognitive development in aborigines of Central Australia: Concrete operations and perceptual activities.* Unpublished Ph.D. thesis, Australian National University, Canberra.

――. (1972a) Cross-cultural Piagetian research: a summary. *Journal of Cross-Cultural Psychology, 3* (1): 23–39.

――. (1972b) The development of conservation in aboriginal children: a replication study. *International Journal of Psychology, 7* (2): 75–85.

Dawson, J. L. M. (1963) *Psychological effects of social change in a West African community.* Unpublished Ph.D. thesis, Oxford University.

――. (1967) Cultural and physiological influences upon spatial-perceptual activities in West Africa. Parts 1 and 2. *International Journal of Psychology, 2* (2): 115–128, 171–185.

de Lacey, P. R. (1970) A cross-cultural study of classificatory ability in Australia. *Journal of Cross-Cultural Psychology, 1* (4): 293–304.

――. (1971) Classificatory ability and verbal intelligence among high-contact aboriginal and low-socioeconomic white Australian children. *Journal of Cross-Cultural Psychology, 2* (4): 393–396.

――. (1972) A relationship between classifactory ability and verbal intelligence. *International Journal of Psychology, 7* (4): 243–246.

de Lemos, M. M. (1966) *The development of the concepts of conservation in Australian Aboriginal children.* Unpublished Ph.D. thesis, Australian National University, Canberra.

――. (1969) The development of conservation in Aboriginal children. *International Journal of Psychology, 4*:255–269.

Dyk, R. B., and Witkin, H. A. (1965) Family experiences related to the development of differentiation in children. *Child Development, 30*:21–55.

Elkind, D. (1964) Discrimination, seriation, and numeration of size and dimensional differences in young children: Piaget replication study 6. *Journal of Genetic Psychology, 104*:275–296. Also in I. E. Sigel and F. H. Hooper, (Eds.), *Logical thinking in children.* New York: Holt, Rinehart and Winston, 1968, pp. 56–75.

Ferron, O. (1964) *A study of certain factors affecting the tested intelligence of some groups of West African children.* Unpublished Ph.D. dissertation, London University.

Goodnow, J. J. (1962) A test for milieu effects with some Piaget's tasks. *Psychological Monographs, 76*:1–22, (Whole No. 555).

————. (1969) Cultural variations in cognitive skills. In D. R. Price-Williams (Ed.), *Cross-cultural studies*. Middlesex, England: Penguin.

————. and Bethon G. (1966) Piaget's tasks: The effect of schooling and intelligence. *Child Development, 37*:573–582.

Greenfield, P. M. (1966) On culture and conservation. In J. S. Bruner, *et al.*, *Studies in cognitive growth*. New York: Wiley. Pp. 225–256.

Heron, A. (1971) Concrete operations, 'g' and achievement in Zambian children. *Journal of Cross-Cultural Psychology, 1*:325–336.

Hess, R. D., and Shipman, V. C. (1965) Early experience and the socialization of cognitive modes in children. *Child Development, 36* (4): 869–886.

————. (1967) Cognitive elements in maternal behaviour. In. J. P. Hill (Ed.), *Minnesota Symposia on Child Psychology*. Minneapolis: University of Minnesota Press, *1*:57–81.

Hutt, S. J. and Hutt, C. (1970) *Direct observation and measurement of behavior*. Springfield, Illinois: Charles C. Thomas.

Kagan, J. (1964) Information processing in the child: Significance of analytic and reflective attitudes. *Psychological Monographs, 78*, (Whole No. 578).

————. Moss, H. A. and Siegel, I. E. (1963) Psychological significance of styles of conceptualization. *Monograph of the Society for Research in Child Development, 28* (2).

Lloyd, B. B. (1971) Studies of conservation with Yoruba children of differing ages and experience. *Child Development, 42*:415–428.

Lloyd, P. C. (Ed.) (1966) *The new elites of tropical Africa*. London: Oxford University Press.

Lytton, H. (1971) Observation studies of parent child interaction: A methodological review. *Child Development, 42*:651–684.

Mehler, J. and Bever, T. G. (1967) Cognitive capacity of very young children. *Science, 153*:141–142.

Mohseni, N. (1966) *La comparaison des réactions aux épreuves d'intelligence en Iran et en Europe*. Thèse d'université, Université de Paris.

Okonji, M. O. (1968) *Cultural variables in cognition*. Unpublished Ph.D. Thesis, University of Strathclyde.

————. (1969) The differential effects of rural and urban upbringing on the development of cognitive styles. *International Journal of Psychology, 4* (4): 293–305.

————. (1971) Culture and children's understanding of geometry. *International Journal of Psychology, 6* (2): 121–128.

Peluffo, N. (1967) Culture and cognitive problems. *International Journal of Psychology, 2* (3): 187–198.

Piaget, J. (1952) *The child's conception of number*. London: Routledge and Kegan Paul.

————. (1959) *The psychology of intelligence*. London: Routledge and Kegan Paul Ltd. (Originally published in 1947).

————. (1966) Nécessité et signification des recherches comparatives en psychologie génétique. *International Journal of Psychology, 1*:3–13. English translation in J. W. Berry & P. R. Dasen (Eds.), *Culture and cognition: Readings in cross-cultural psychology*. London: Methuen, 1974.

———. (1968) Quantification, conservation and nativism. *Science, 162*:976–979.

———. (1969) *Six psychological studies*, (D. Elkind, Ed.) London: University of London Press.

Poole, H. E. (1968) The effect of urbanization upon scientific concept attainment among Hausa children in northern Nigeria. *British Journal of Educational Psychology, 38*:57–63.

Price-Williams, D. R., Gordon, W., and Ramirez, M. (1969) Skill and conservation. *Developmental Psychology, 1*:769.

——— ——— ———. (n.d.) *Skill and conservation—extended report: A study of pottery-making children*. Unpublished.

Prince, J. R. (1968) The effect of Western education on science conceptualization in New Guinea. *British Journal of Educational Psychology, 38*:64–74.

Rothenberg, B. B. and Courtney, R. G. (1968) Conservation of number in very young children: a replication of and comparison with Mehler's and Bever's study. *Journal of Psychology, 70*:205–212.

Sechrest, L., Fay, T. L. and Zaidi, S. M. H. (1972) Problems of translation in cross-cultural research. *Journal of Cross-Cultural Psychology, 3*:41–46.

Siegel, L. S. and Goldstein, A. G. (1969) Conservation of number in young children: Recency versus relational response strategies. *Developmental Psychology, 1*:128–130.

Siegel, S. (1956) *Nonparametric statistics for the behavioural sciences*. New York: McGraw-Hill.

Vetta, A. (1972) Conservation in aboriginal children and "genetic hypothesis". *International Journal of Psychology, 7*:247–256.

Waddell, V. (1968) *Some cultural considerations on the development of the concept of conservation*. Unpublished paper presented to a genetic epistemology seminar, Australian National University. October. 1968.

Werner, O. and Campbell, D. T. (1970) Translating, working through interpreters and the problem of decentering. In R. Naroll and R. Cohen (Eds.), *A handbook of method in cultural anthropology*. New York: Natural History Press, 398–420.

Willoughby, R. H. and Trachy, S. (1971) Conservation of number in very young children: A failure to replicate Mehler and Bever. *Merril-Palmer Quarterly, 17* (3): 205–9.

Witkin, H. A. (1967) A cognitive style approach to cross-cultural research. *International Journal of Psychology, 2*:233–250.

———. et al. (1962) *Psychological differentiation*. New York: John Wiley.

Wohlwill, J. F. (1968) From perception to inference: A dimension of cognitive development. *In* I. E. Sigel and F. H. Hooper (Eds.) *Logical thinking in children*. New York: Holt, Rinehart and Winston, Inc., 472–498. Reprinted from *Monograph of the Society for Research in Child Development*, 1962, *27* (2): 87–112.

9
Maternal and Subcultural Correlates of Cognitive Growth Rate: The GA Pattern[*]

LORRAINE KIRK

The intent of this research is to account for differences among children in rate of cognitive development. For the purpose of this study, three Piaget-derived tasks of concept acquisition are administered as measures of cognitive development to Ga children of three subcultures. To account for observed differences in task performance, a series of possible determinants are isolated from the environments of the children. The primary variables considered here are (a) subcultural and (b) maternal. We shall examine these variables for their relationship with cognitive development as measured by the Piaget tasks.

Section 1 of this paper describes the cultures in which this study took place. Section 2 outlines the procedures used in administering the Piaget tasks. Section 3 discusses the patterns which emerge in Piaget task score across subcultural and maternal variables. Finally, Section 4 discusses relationships between task score and a further series of potentially causal environmental variables.

1. ETHNOGRAPHIC BACKGROUND:
THE THREE GA SUBCULTURES

This section presents a brief ethnographic description of the Ga, focusing primarily on the differences among the three subcultures considered in this study. A fuller description of the people can be found in Field (1937; 1940), Kilson (1966), and Fitzgerald [Kirk] (1970). The characterization given here is short and impressionistic; there has been no attempt to quantify or systematize all subcultural variations.

THE GA PEOPLE AS A WHOLE

The Ga traditionally occupy about 500 square miles within and around Accra, Ghana, extending some 30 miles along the coast and up to 20 miles inland. According to the 1960 Population Census (Gil et al. 1964), more than half of the 250,000 Ga live in urban areas, primarily Accra.

The rural Ga population maintains relatively close contact with the six traditional Ga coastal towns. The inland villages were formed as outgrowths of the coastal towns, and the villagers, although they may live their entire lives in the rural areas, still think of themselves as residents of the old towns from which their ancestors emigrated. In the fall of each year large numbers of villagers pour into their coastal towns of origin to celebrate the harvest festival.

Traditionally the Ga live by hoe agriculture and, along the coast, by ocean and lagoon fishing. Small domesticated animals and hunting supplement the diet. Women, especially in the urban areas, are involved in petty trading and have a long tradition of economic independence. The city offers clerical, civil service, driving, and miscellaneous manual labor jobs.

The political system of the Ga was traditionally decentralized. The most important features of social identity and items of property are inherited in the male line, although some smaller items of property and occasionally land are passed in the female line. In the Ga coastal towns residence is largely duolocal (Kilson, 1966; Field, 1937), while in the villages the predominant residence pattern is one in which the nuclear family lives in the house of the husband's father.

The Ga area is outstanding in its amenability to the present study. It provides a number of clear-cut environmental contrasts within a common language and culture. Within such an arena it is possible to achieve systematic variation in a number of environmental variables, and by this means to study the effects on the cognitive development of children of each variable in relative isolation.

There are three distinct life-styles among the Ga: (a) traditional rural, (b) traditional old-town urban (densely populated), and (c) Westernized suburban (urban affluent). These three types of life-style correspond fairly consistently with residential area. Although there is some overlapping of life-style near the boundaries of the areas, it is possible to isolate core areas in which only one of the three life-styles exists, to the almost entire exclusion of the others. By eliminating borderline areas from consideration it is possible to isolate three distinctive life-styles for contrast in this study. Yet, underneath these distinctive subcultures, there remain the constants of a common language, a common macroculture, and a common gene pool. The Ga language is spoken as the mother tongue by Ga in all three areas,[1] although degree of additional fluency in English and other Ghanaian languages varies across the three subcultures. An overall genetic similarity among the Ga of the three subpopulations is maintained over time through movement across subcultural boundaries and through significant cross-fertilization: (a) families tend to be distributed across, rather than within, subcultures and (b) mating occurs frequently across subcultures, especially between rural and old-town urban populations.

The brief ethnographic descriptions which follow are presented to acquaint the reader with some of the more outstanding differences among the three subcultural environments.

THE ENVIRONMENTS OF INLAND RURAL CHILDREN

The approximately 200 inland Ga villages are primarily agricultural; farming is supplemented by the domestication of small animals and occasional hunting. Women do much of the farming, and sometimes small-scale selling on the side.

Population density within village boundaries is intermediate between that in old-town urban and suburban areas. Rooms are generally shared by a number of people, but the crowding is not excessive in comparison with that in the old-town urban areas, and there is ample open space near the house for play. Rural children live in a culturally, linguistically, and occupationally more homogeneous community than do either of the urban groups, although even in the Ga villages the presence of Ewe or Twi minorities is not uncommon. As a result of the relative homogeneity of the village communities, rural children find it least necessary of the three subcultural groups to switch back and forth among diverse systems of behavior, value, and linguistic code.

Village houses are rectangular in shape, usually with an enclosed courtyard in which much of the domestic activity takes place. Most houses support a patrilocal extended family. The Ga villages which were sampled in this study range in size from one to about 150 houses. Larger villages in the area, ranging up to approximately 300 houses, are heavily mixed ethnically, and for this reason were excluded from the sample.

The movements of rural children in a normal day are ordinarily restricted: for younger children, to the house and farm; for older children, to the house, village, farm, school, and road. Play is usually cooperative and rarely independent, occurring in groups of all sizes.

The diet in the rural areas contains considerably less protein and vitamins than that in suburban areas. Western medical facilities available to the villagers are less adequate than those available to suburban and old-town urban children.

Educational materials are sorely lacking in most rural schools. Teachers in rural schools have generally received fewer years of training than have urban or suburban teachers. They tend to emphasize rote memory rather than problem solving and independent activity. The children's first language (Ga) is used most of the time for communication both within and outside of the classroom. Rural schools tend to have higher student-teacher ratios and lack the more permissive, stimulating atmosphere of the more affluent suburban schools. Learning of academic subjects in rural schools progresses at a fairly slow pace. Academic work is interspersed with more physical work (such as hoeing) in rural schools than in urban or suburban schools. More regimented marching also seems to be done in the rural schools. Academic work is of relatively low value in this subculture; children tend to begin school later, attend school less consistently, and quit school earlier than urban or suburban children. Rural children seem subdued and respectful, and far less active in the classroom than either old-town urban children, who roughhouse more, or suburban children, who (with their abundant materials and permissive environment) are very busy in their work and play.

The surroundings of rural children are the least diversified with respect to the products of western technology, but the children are very familiar with the natural environment and with manual farming technology. The absence of electricity in the rural areas severely limits the number of ways in which the evening hours can be used. Evenings can accommodate such activities as drumming, dancing, and story telling, but rural children and adults generally go to sleep early.

At home, rural children are considerably more restrained than are urban or suburban children in speech, exploration, and play. They are expected to conform to traditional norms of modesty, silence, obedience, and respect for elders, and are bound to a heavy work routine imposed by the demands of agricultural life. Such considerations as time, fatigue, health, and space cause rural parents and older siblings to be demanding and minimally permissive toward younger children. Rural children are expected to take responsibilties and to be "grown-up" early. Punishments in the villages appear to be frequent, severe, and physical by comparison with those in the suburban areas, but mild by comparison with those in the old-town urban areas. The parents of village children place little emphasis on elaborate verbalization, excellence in problem solving, independent thought and action, and ability to take initiative, but rote verbal performances are highly valued. Much learning is expected to take place by watching.

Rural communities tend to use a fairly context-bound linguistic code, taking shared implicit meanings relatively for granted. Subjectively, rural speech seems to involve less lexical variety and structural complexity, more repetition and stereotypy, more paralinguistic communication and more silence than does communication in the other subcultures. Fewer loan words from English appear in rural speech.

THE ENVIRONMENTS OF OLD-TOWN URBAN CHILDREN

I shall distinguish here between the relatively traditional old-town urban Ga and the relatively westernized suburban Ga. Within the former category there is also a distinction between the urban old towns and the periurban old towns. Of the six old towns, two of them may be considered fully urban. These are GaMashi and Osu, the core areas of which are the focal points for the old-town urban sample. The following description of the old-town urban subculture is therefore derived from the central areas of these two towns.

The old-town urban communities are comprised predominantly of the traditional, less affluent Ga living within the city of Accra. Urban Ga are basically traditional but are undergoing rapid change, acting within diverse systems of behavior which often prescribe contradictory behavior. The long history of these traditional towns, however, distinguishes the old-town urban population from that so common in many African urban centers, in which there is a great influx to the towns of rural people unacquainted with the urban culture and without means of support. Long-standing operations such as fishing and trading, which are independent of and predate the government and European employers, are still common occupational activities in the old-town areas, and on-going migration from the villages is minimal.

The old towns are located on the coast. GaMashi, from which a majority (65%) of the old town sample was taken, lies within the heart of the Accra business district. Osu is located two miles away from this area, and, unlike GaMashi, is outside the city center. Osu has a slightly lower population density than GaMashi. Otherwise the two areas are very similar.

The urban old towns are involved in ocean and lagoon fishing. Fish are traditionally sold by women who specialize in that trade. Old-town women also frequently engage in other kinds of trading, both in large market places and along the streets. Some old-town urban women do clerical work. Chickens are frequently raised around urban homes. Men not engaged in fishing are frequently employed in semiskilled occupations.

Urban children are in contact with larger numbers of people in the course of the day than are their rural and suburban counterparts. Population density is extreme in the old-town urban areas, far exceeding that of either rural or suburban areas. Some large houses in the urban centers support 50 or more children. Spaces between houses are often limited and crowded, and the streets and passageways usually serve as primary play space. Pedestrian traffic on the streets is heavy, and where sidewalks exist, they are often too small to accommodate all the traffic. In this crowded, composite urban community, children are in contact with a large group of people which is highly heterogeneous with respect to culture, value system, language, race, and occupation. Urban children must be able to do considerable switching among diverse behavior systems, although the demands on them are not as extreme as on suburban children, who are intimately exposed to several non-African systems of behavior, value, and dialect.

Houses are often large and rectangular, with unroofed courtyards in which much domestic activity takes place. One also finds here some older, European-style houses of two stories, and many small structures. Old-town urban houses generally contain fairly large extended families. Residence is usually duolocal; that is, matrilineally related women and small children live together in the women's houses, while patrilineally related men and older boys live together in the men's houses.

With the dense population of the urban old towns, one finds generally poor housing. Public outdoor water faucets supply a city block or so with water to be carried in buckets. Open gutters are the rule for conducting sewage into the sea.

Old-town urban children are intermediate between rural and suburban children in their exposure to both Western and traditional technology. The children of market women are frequently required to accompany their mothers to market in the city center; older children are sometimes expected to sell on their own. Electricity is available for some public areas, such as the more frequented streets and public squares, and can also be found in some of the more affluent homes. The unavailability of electricity in most homes, however, limits the variety of activity which is possible in the house after dark, as it does in the rural areas; but in the old towns there is considerable activity in groups outside the house at night.

The diet of old-town urban children does not contain demonstrably more protein or vitamins than does that of rural children, but contains considerably less of both than does the diet of suburban children. Medical facilities are more readily available here than in the rural areas, but the quality of treatment which old-town people receive is poor compared with that received by their more affluent suburban counterparts.

The availability of educational materials in old-town schools is intermediate between that in rural and suburban schools. Most of the communication in the classroom and during recess takes place in the Ga language. Old-town urban teaching sophistication would appear to be intermediate between that in rural and suburban areas, with respect to the number of years teachers have been trained, the teaching methods used, and the student-teacher ratio. There is some physical work and marching during school hours, but these appear to be stressed somewhat less than in rural areas. There is more roughhousing in the urban schools than in the rural schools, where respect and restraint are more strictly enforced. Children in urban schools do not show as much resourcefulness, independence, and attentiveness in their school work as do children in suburban schools. Urban children seem to receive slightly more pressure to attend and achieve in school than do rural children, although this pressure does not approach that received by suburban children. Although there is still prevalent here a fairly cynical attitude toward education, where concept manipulation does not generate much intrinsic interest, education is more often seen as economically rewarding than in the villages. As with rural children, old-town urban children do not seem to receive much encouragement to be experimental or independent, and learning is often expected to occur by watching. The age at which school is commenced and the length and regularity of attendance is also intermediate between the other residential areas.

In school and at home old-town urban children are encouraged neither to be as elaborate in their verbal reference nor as inventive and independent as are suburban children. Old-town children are rather unrestrained and raucous, manifesting a significant breakdown of the traditional norms of modesty, silence, obedience and respect for elders which are still fairly stable in the rural areas. The observer sees a picture of uncontrolled bedlam in the old towns, marked by noise, rough play, argument, insult, and fighting among the children, and an apparent inability of adults to control the situation. The Western observer would expect the adults to feel harassed at their lack of power to control the large groups of children which move about boisterously and sometimes destructively. This harassment, coupled with a fairly demanding work routine, would seem to induce the impatience and lack of permissiveness seen in the attitudes of old-town urban adults toward children; punishments appear to be more frequent, severe, and physical in the old-town urban areas than in either of the other residential areas.

In the urban old towns one often sees young children being teased. Teasing is done, for instance, by repeatedly holding a desired object within a young child's reach, then withdrawing it; by taking a child's food from him and laughing; by putting a child in a place from which he cannot extricate himself, coming toward him as if to rescue him, then withdrawing; or by deliberately confronting a child with frightening things. Old-town children up to the age of 6 or so are frequently seen in severe temper tantrums in which they lie on the ground alone, rolling and screaming at the tops of their lungs for extended periods of time. This pattern is seen to some extent in all residential areas, but nowhere does it seem to be so extensive and elaborate as in the old towns.

The speech styles of the old-town urban community would seem to lie midway between those of the rural and suburban communities with respect to dependence upon context, structural complexity, lexical variety, and reliance upon paralinguistic communication. English loan words also seem to appear with intermediate frequency. Old-town urban children are exposed to a greater number of languages than are rural children, but have less intimate exposure to English, and read and write less often, than do suburban children.

THE ENVIRONMENTS OF SUBURBAN CHILDREN

The term "suburban" refers here to the more Westernized, affluent Ga who live in modern houses in the more recently developed neighborhoods outside the center of Accra. Generally one or both of the parents in a suburban Ga home are well-educated professional people or government officials. Mothers are often employed.

The population density in the suburban areas is very low relative to the old-town urban and rural areas, approximating the population density of American suburbs. Frequently children have their own bedrooms and playrooms. Most houses have sizeable yards, and children are not forced to play in the streets. The homes are oriented toward a nuclear rather than an extended family; residence is neolocal.

Suburban children are exposed to a culturally, linguistically, occupationally, and racially heterogeneous community. They must switch frequently among several disparate linguistic, value, and social interaction systems.

The range of movement of suburban children in a normal day is geographically wide, but relatively narrow in terms of the numbers of people contacted outside of school each day. Their play is usually either independent or cooperative, with small groups of children or adults. Children are not expected to contribute economically to the family's welfare.

The diet of suburban children is much richer in protein and vitamins than that of the other subcultures. Suburban children are notably taller than children from the other areas. The Western medical attention available to them is qualitatively and quantitatively superior to that available to rural and old-town urban children.

Most suburban Ga children are driven to well-equipped and well-staffed English-speaking private schools with relatively permissive atmospheres; here children are strongly encouraged to be creative, inventive, independent, and busy. Little physical work is done. Academic learning progresses comparatively rapidly here. Suburban children are under considerable pressure from parents to excel in formal study, and many are required to study at home. There is also high peer group competition in and value on school subjects. Formal education is valued in suburbia for more than its economic advantage: There is considerably more emphasis here on the intrinsic interest of school activities and the manipulation of concepts than in other residential areas. Suburban children tend to start school earlier (perhaps as young as 2 or 3 years of age), attend school more consistently, and continue in school much longer than do children from either of the other areas.

At home, suburban children have considerable freedom of action, exploration, and play. The constant access of suburban children to electricity and machinery expands the number of ways in which evening hours can be used. Suburban mothers tend to emphasize independence, elaborate verbalization, reasoning, and excellence in problem solving as opposed to "getting the job done" or strictly rote performances. Learning is expected to be accomplished as much by doing as by watching. Suburban parents and older siblings are relatively lax in punishing violations of many traditional norms. The conformity of suburban children to the traditional norms of modesty, silence, restraint, obedience, and respect for elders is notably less rigid than that expected of rural children. The circumstances of suburban parents with respect to health, energy, space, material conveniences and servants allow them to be fairly permissive with their children. Suburban parents appear to demand less work and responsibility from their children. Children seem to be considered "grown-up" at a later age in suburbia than in the other areas. Punishments seem least frequent, least severe, and least physical in suburbia.

The adult speech to which suburban children are exposed seems to be the least context-bound among the three speech communities. Not only are the fluently spoken languages more diverse here, but spoken suburban Ga is more explicit, shows greater structural complexity and lexical variety, relies less on paralinguistic communication, and incorporates less silence than do rural and old-town urban Ga. More reading and writing of both Ga and English is done here. More English and Twi loan words are used in Ga speech.

2. PROCEDURES FOR DETERMINING VARIATION IN RATE OF COGNITIVE DEVELOPMENT AMONG GA CHILDREN

To assess differences among Ga children in rate of concept growth, three Piaget-derived tasks of concept acquisition were given in the Ga language to a sample of 413 Ga children, 5, 8, and 11 years old from rural, urban, and suburban environments. The tasks were chosen for their general cross-cultural adaptability and the amenability of the task materials and verbal presentation to alterations which would make them comparably meaningful to children of all three Ga subcultures. The number of tasks was limited by the concentration span of the 5-year-olds within the sample. The battery consists of two conservation tasks and a spatial task of egocentricity. The tasks are conservation of quantity (clay), conservation of length, and perspectives (spatial visualization). Task protocols in Ga and English are available in a previous work (Fitzgerald [Kirk], 1970). Two of the tasks had been standardized on an American sample of school children by Read Tuddenham (n.d.).[2] All tasks were derived from Piaget's pilot experiments, but all were conducted in a manner less open-ended than Piaget's in order to render the task scores more amenable to statistical analysis.

The Tasks

Conservation of quantity (clay). The standardized English version of this task was derived by Tuddenham from Piaget's French version (Piaget and Inhelder, 1941, p. 7). In translating the English version into the Ga language, some adjustments in imagery had to be made in order to adapt it to the experiences of Ga children.

Conservation of length. To my knowledge this task has not been standardized on American children. It was developed from Celia Stendler Lavatelli's translation of Piaget's task (1964, pp. 105–116). Two equal lengths of wire were used to represent the paths along which two children walked. One length was segmented into four equal lengths; the other was continuous. When the child agreed that the alternative paths were the same length in parallel orientation, the discontinuous length of wire was taken through a series of transformations. The child was asked after each transformation whether or not the paths represented by the wires were the same length. As in English, the Ga word for "length" (*kɛlɛ*; short form = *kɛ*) is potentially ambiguous, as it can refer to either spatial length or temporal duration. This ambiguity is as unavoidable in Ga as it is in English and French.

Perspectives (spatial visualization). This task was standardized by Tuddenham on American school children and resembles Piaget's task, "The Three Mountains" (Piaget, 1963, pp. 210–213). The scene in Ga was a homestead: a house, a goat, a passenger truck, and a tree. Otherwise, the task materials and verbal presentation remained essentially the same as in Tuddenham's English version.

The Sample

Four hundred and thirteen Ga speaking children of ages 5, 8, and 11 years were sampled randomly from rural, urban, and suburban subcultures within the Ga area. Ages were determined by a dental method outlined in Kirk (1975), which involves observation of the stages of eruption of each tooth in the child's mouth. There was a total of 174 rural children, 132 urban children, and 107 suburban children. The distribution of tested children by estimated age and subculture appears in Table 9–1. Only core residential areas, representing the more extreme forms of each subcultural

Table 9–1
Age and residence of the 413 Ga children
given Piaget tasks*

	ENVIRONMENTAL GROUP			
Age group	Rural	Urban	Suburban	Total sample
4–6 years	65	53	37	155
7–9 years	62	43	37	142
10–12 years	47	35	34	116
Totals	174	131	108	413

*This is the sample of children exposed to the Piaget tasks; the sample Ns which appear in Table 9–5 represent the children who were testable (see Note 5) on a particular task or set of tasks.

life-style, were chosen for sampling, in order to maintain sharp contrasts among the three subcultures. Children were included in the sample only if (a) they spoke the Ga language as fluently as they spoke any other Ghanaian language, (b) at least one of their parents was Ga, and (c) their histories indicated that they had lived most of their lives in that core residential area in which they were found during sampling. The first criterion assured that the children doing the tasks were comparably fluent in the language in which the tasks were given. The second criterion, together with the fact that only villages and urban areas which were predominantly Ga were sampled in the first place, assured that a child would not have a heavily foreign cultural background. The third criterion eliminated the occurrence of cases within the sample which were borderline with respect to the subculture (residential area) in which they grew up. This tended to make contrasts among the three subcultures more valid.

Village (rural) sampling. From those villages of the Accra plains which were predominantly populated by Ga, a random sample of 25 villages was drawn. To select a random sample of children from a village it was necessary to visit the village at least twice. On the first visit, the chief was contacted and the project explained. The chief was asked to set aside part of a day on which all residents of the village would remain at home for sampling. On the second visit the investigator and the Ga examiner went from house to house, asking to see all the children who lived there. From among these children were selected those who fell within the age ranges 4–6, 7–9, and 10–12 years, and who fulfilled the sampling requirements above. If it appeared that a significant proportion of the residents had not remained in the village at the appointed time, a new date was set for sampling. For each child selected, information was recorded on his languages, the ethnic backgrounds of his parents, his residential history, his age, his sex, his school history, and that of his parents. On a third or subsequent visit to the village the child was tested. In smaller villages all houses were visited. In larger villages every *n*th house was visited, for *n*'s ranging from two to ten.

Old-town urban sampling. Old-town urban children were chosen from within two highly populated, traditional Ga urban areas. These were demarcated on a city map beforehand on the basis of a series of criteria, such as life-style and house type, which were felt to characterize the traditional old-town Ga. From these areas, random sampling of city blocks was done, and within these blocks, sampling was done by visiting every *n*th house during off-school hours. All the children present at the time were seen, in order to determine their ages and their linguistic, parental, and residential backgrounds. Information sheets were completed for those who satisfied the criteria for testing. Names were recorded of all children resident in the house who were absent at the time; these children were seen on a subsequent visit. In other respects urban sampling procedures were similar to those in the villages.

Suburban sampling. Unlike village and urban areas, which are fairly homogeneous with respect to tribe, the suburban areas of Accra are more ethnically mixed. Several suburban areas within the outer areas of the city contained a large proportion of Ga. These were sampled door to door, with all Ga houses included in the sample. For the remainder of the suburban sample, it was necessary to consult agencies and individuals for advice on where the more well-to-do Ga lived. In selecting the suburban children who satisfied sampling criteria, it was not necessary to see the children themselves before the testing, as the parents could give reliable birth dates and other essential information.

Testing Procedures

All 413 children in the sample were tested by the same Ga examiner in order to maintain comparability. The Ga examiner was Samuel Nii Dodoo, a university freshman at the time of the study. The American investigator was present during testing but—together with other adults and children—remained clear of the immediate testing area. The testing area in the villages was usually the shade of a large tree at the edge of the village or a neighborhood school or church. In the urban areas testing was usually done in a large open space within a block or so of the child's house, or in a neighborhood school or church. In the suburban areas testing was generally done in a spare room of the house or in the yard. Testing in all three residential areas took place on the ground. The tasks were sequenced with the conservation of quantity task first, the perspectives task second, and the conservation of length task last.

A major problem in the coordination of large numbers of children for testing was the tendency for information about the tasks to be disseminated, by onlookers or by children already tested, to children who had not yet been tested. Several precautions were taken to minimize the probability that this might occur. It was assumed that the 5-year-olds could not report with much coherence the content of the tasks, and furthermore that older people would not heed them. The 5-year-olds were generally tested first, therefore, and no attempts were made to restrict their communication with others after they had been tested. The 8- and 11-year-olds, however, were gathered together before any of them had been tested. The untested children waited in an area or room set off for them, and they were segregated from the rest of the community until they had been tested. In some areas, where population was high and control was difficult to maintain, the probability of information leakage was further

Lorraine Kirk

minimized by having the children who had already been tested remain in yet another separated area until all testing was complete. In areas where there was no difficulty in segregating the untested children from the community, children were released as soon as they were tested.

As visiting occurs significantly among neighborhoods within rural areas, within urban areas, and within suburban areas, and as children from several neighborhoods frequently go to the same schools, additional precautions were taken to minimize information leakage among the children of different neighborhoods. All children resident in a

Table 9–2
Significance levels for observed subgroup differences

Conservation of quantity (clay) task

Environment	Age	RURAL			URBAN			SUBURBAN		
Environment	Age in years	5	8	11	5	8	11	5	8	11
Rural	5		.02	.001	no	—	—	no	—	—
	8			.001	—	no	—	—	no	—
	11				—	—	.001	—	—	no
Urban	5					.02	.05	no	—	—
	8						no	—	no	—
	11							—	—	.05
Suburban	5								.05	.001
	8									.1
	11									

Conservation of length task

Environment	Age	RURAL			URBAN			SUBURBAN		
Environment	Age in years	5	8	11	5	8	11	5	8	11
Rural	5		no	.02	no	—	—	no	—	—
	8			no	—	no	—	—	no	—
	11				—	—	no	—	—	.1
Urban	5					.05	.01	no	—	—
	8						no	—	no	—
	11							—	—	no
Suburban	5								.05	.001
	8									.02
	11									

Note: (1) Two tailed *t* test of significance were used.
(2) A "no" in the table indicated that the significance level is greater than .1.
(3) Dashed cells represent meaningless comparisons

Table 9–2 (continued)

Perspective task

Environment	Age in years	RURAL 5	RURAL 8	RURAL 11	URBAN 5	URBAN 8	URBAN 11	SUBURBAN 5	SUBURBAN 8	SUBURBAN 11
Environment	**Age**									
Rural	5		no	.001	no	—	—	no	—	—
	8			.02	—	no	—	—	.001	—
	11				—	—	no	—	—	.001
Urban	5					no	.01	no	—	—
	8						.01	—	.001	—
	11							—	—	.05
suburban	5								.001	.001
	8									no
	11									

All tasks combined

Environment	Age in years	RURAL 5	RURAL 8	RURAL 11	URBAN 5	URBAN 8	URBAN 11	SUBURBAN 5	SUBURBAN 8	SUBURBAN 11
Environment	**Age**									
Rural	5		.05	.001	no	—	—	no	—	—
	8			.001	—	no	—	—	.02	—
	11				—	—	no	—	—	.01
Urban	5					.05	.01	no	—	—
	8						no	—	no	—
	11							—	—	.01
Suburban	5								.001	.001
	8									.01
	11									

neighborhood or group of neighborhoods which was likely to have significant intercommunication were tested in sequence, in as short a time span as possible.[3] Sometimes a series of neighborhoods would be tested in sequence early in the morning before any of the children had gone to school, where they might discuss the tasks. Sometimes school and non-school children between the ages of 7 and 12 from one or more neighborhoods were gathered together at a central school for testing, with untested children isolated from all others. Five-year-olds from these areas were usually tested without the above precautions prior to the testing of the older children.

Figure 9–1. *Line graphs of Piaget task score means by age and environment*

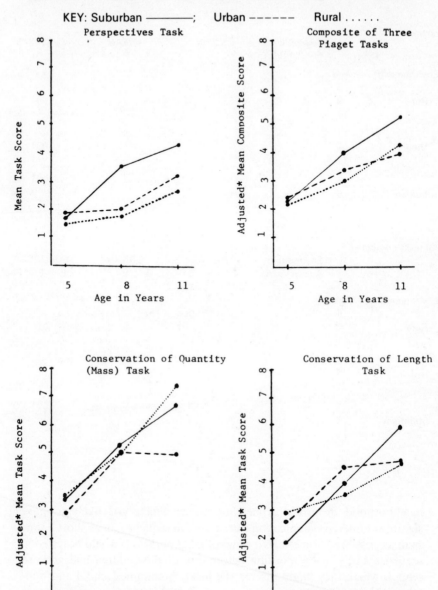

KEY: Suburban ————; Urban ————— Rural ......

*For each of the conservation tasks, the task score means (based on four-point scales) were multiplied by two in order to make them comparable in magnitude to the eight-point scale used with the perspectives task. The mean composite scores were divided by 2 for the same reason.

3. VARIATIONS IN TASK PERFORMANCE ACROSS SUBCULTURE AND MATERNAL BEHAVIOR

This section considers the effects of subculture and maternal behavior on Piaget task performance by observing task score patterns which emerge across environmental contrasts.

Effects of Subculture

There are three subcultural areas under contrast: rural, urban, and suburban. Only children who were raised almost exclusively in one of the three areas are included in the sample; there are no children from transitional or borderline areas. Hence mutually exclusive environmental domains are compared, so that sharp contrasts among the three subcultures is possible.

Task score means. The sample of 413 children was broken down into nine subsamples on the basis of contrasts among (a) the three age groups (4–6 years, 7–9 years, and 10–12 years) and (b) the three environmental groups (rural, urban, and suburban). For each of the three Piaget tasks and for two combinations of tasks (a combination of the two conservation tasks on the one hand and a combination of all three tasks on the other), task score means and standard deviations were computed within each of the nine subsamples, the six marginal samples, and the total sample in Table 9–3, where the number of testable[4] children in each sample is also presented.[5] In these representations of the data, each of the conservation scores has been multiplied by two in order to make them comparable in magnitude to the eight-unit score of the perspectives task. The task score means are also represented graphically in Figure 9–1. Intertask correlations are presented in Table 9–4.

Two-tailed t tests of significance were run on the mean task score differences among children of similar age from contrasting subcultures, and among children of the same subcultures across differences in age. Levels of significance of mean task score differences appear in Table 9–2. The following is a summary of the statistically significant differences in task score by age and subculture.

From Figure 9–1 and Table 9–2 it can be seen that there are no statistically significant differences in task score among subcultures in the 5-year-old group. For all three subcultures and all three tasks there is a statistically significant increase in task score from age 5 to age 11. There are statistically significant increases in task score from age 5 to age 8, except for rural children on the conservation of length task and rural and urban children on the perspectives task. There are significant increases in task

Table 9–3

Tables of Piaget task score means, standard deviations, and sample sizes for each age-environment subsample

Environment	RURAL				URBAN				SUBURBAN				ALL			ALL ALL
Age in years	5	8	11	All	5	8	11	All	5	8	11	All	5	8	11	
Task																
Conservation of quantity (times 2)	3.44	5.06	7.34	5.17	2.90	5.02	4.91	4.38	3.40	5.18	6.64	5.14	3.28	5.08	6.40	4.93
Conservation of length (times 2)	2.89	3.55	4.63	3.68	2.57	4.51	4.62	4.03	1.93	3.89	5.88	4.00	2.53	3.94	5.00	3.87
Perspectives	1.46	1.76	2.60	1.90	1.82	2.00	3.17	2.26	1.66	3.54	4.25	3.15	1.64	2.30	3.24	2.35
Sum of two conservation tasks	3.00	4.28	6.00	4.42	2.77	4.76	4.77	4.25	2.74	4.54	6.26	4.64	2.86	4.50	5.70	4.43
Sum of three Piaget tasks (divided by 2)	2.20	3.02	4.30	3.19	2.38	3.41	3.97	3.34	2.25	4.04	5.25	3.95	2.26	3.41	4.46	3.44

TASK SCORE MEANS

Table 9–3 (continued)

STANDARD DEVIATIONS

Environment Age in years	RURAL				URBAN				SUBURBAN				ALL			
Task	5	8	11	All	5	8	11	All	5	8	11	All	5	8	11	ALL ALL
Conservation of quantity (times 2)	3.54	3.49	1.67	3.45	3.43	3.37	3.71	3.62	3.62	3.55	2.59	3.53	3.54	3.47	2.89	3.54
Conservation of length (times 2)	3.35	3.39	3.27	3.41	3.53	3.55	3.72	3.71	3.12	3.80	2.94	3.68	3.36	3.58	3.37	3.58
Perspectives	1.63	1.86	1.58	1.77	1.80	1.88	1.81	1.92	1.49	2.00	2.25	2.21	1.66	2.05	1.98	2.01
Sum of two conservation Tasks	3.00	2.78	1.81	2.85	3.09	2.75	3.46	3.21	2.95	3.34	2.03	3.15	3.01	2.93	2.56	3.05
Sum of three Piaget tasks (divided by 2)	1.90	1.70	1.32	1.84	1.99	1.72	2.21	2.06	1.47	2.03	1.54	2.09	1.82	1.85	1.77	2.00

Table 9–3 (continued)

Environment Age in years	RURAL				URBAN				SUBURBAN				ALL			ALL ALL
Task	5	8	11	All	5	8	11	All	5	8	11	All	5	8	11	
Conservation of quantity (times 2)	54	60	46	160	31	43	35	109	30	37	34	101	115	140	115	370
Conservation of length (times 2)	47	59	47	153	28	43	35	106	29	37	34	100	104	139	116	359
Perspectives	54	60	46	160	47	42	35	124	33	37	32	102	134	139	113	386
Sum of two conservation tasks	45	59	46	150	27	43	35	105	27	37	34	98	99	139	115	353
Sum of three Piaget tasks (divided by 2)	42	59	46	147	26	42	35	103	26	37	32	95	94	138	113	345

SAMPLE SIZES

*Sample sizes represent the number of testable children on a given task or set of tasks. If a child did not respond to any part of a task or group of tasks, he could not be included in the calculation of those particular task score statistics.

Table 9–4
Intertask correlations for each age-environment subsample

Environment Age in years	RURAL				URBAN				SUBURBAN				ALL
Tasks correlated	5	8	11	All	5	8	11	All	5	8	11	All	ALL
Conservation of quantity with Conservation of length	.53	.30	-.05	.37	.55	.26	.74	.53	.50	.65	.07	.54	.46
Conservation of quantity with Perspectives	.12	.13	.20	.24	.26	.10	.30	.23	-.15	.06	-.09	.13	.19
Conservation of length with Perspectives	.15	-.08	.12	.09	.01	.01	.34	.14	-.28	.12	.09	.20	.14

score from age 8 to age 11, except for urban children on the conservation of quantity task, rural and urban children on the conservation of length task, and suburban children on the perspectives task.

In the composite of the three Piaget tasks, suburban children score significantly higher than urban and rural children, both at age 8 and age 11. Suburban children also score significantly higher than urban and rural children at ages 8 and 11 on the perspectives task. Furthermore, there is a particularly marked divergence at age 8 between suburban and nonsuburban children on the perspectives task, as suburban children increase dramatically in task score from age 5 to age 8, while other children show nonsignificant increase in task score from age 5 to age 8.

Suburban and rural children both score significantly higher than urban children on the conservation of quantity task at age 11. This is because of the fact that the score for urban children actually declines (although the statistical test is not significant) from age 8 to age 11, while the other two groups show a statistically significant increase from age 8 to age 11.[6]

For the conservation of length task, the only statistically significant subcultural difference is that 11-year-old suburban children score higher than 11-year-old rural children (p < .1).

Some of these task score patterns are discussed in greater detail:

1. *Relatively high performance and rapid improvement over time of suburban children on the Piaget tasks.* It has been seen that 5-year-olds of all three subcultures perform at approximately the same level, but that task score improvement generally drops off with age for rural and old-town urban children relative to suburban children. This pattern seems consistent with the hypothesis that suburban children, with their longer and more intensive schooling; their access to diverse and numerous material learning aids; the emphasis placed in their surroundings on concept manipulation, elaborate verbalization, intellectual excellence, and independence; the diversity of their social milieu; their daily geographic mobility; their good health and diet; and their exposure to situations not too dissimilar from the testing situation, should be better equipped for performance on the Piaget tasks, and that this effect should increase in direct proportion to the length of time the children have been exposed to such an environment.

2. *Relative deficiency of rural and urban children on the perspectives task.* There are probably several skills involved in successful response to this task. The first is the "mental reshuffling" (Goodnow, 1969a), or mental reversal of the child's image of the village. This seems to be related to a kind of mechanical egocentricity. A second mental gymnastic involved in this task is the projection of the child's vision into the doll; that is, understanding that he is supposed to try to imagine seeing what the doll

Table 9–5
Correlations between maternal behavior indices and task scores of 5-year-olds
(N = 25)

TASK SCORE	MATERNAL BEHAVIOR INDEX											
	(1) Total Verb Roots	(2) Frequency of "Terminal Sequences"	(3) Frequency of Verb Root Linkage	(4) Frequency of Task-Unrelated Verb Roots	(5) Specificity: Comparison A	(6) Specificity: Comparison B	(7) Frequency of Reference to Function	(8) Frequency of Requests for Verbal Feedback	(9) Emphasis on Negative Imperatives	(10) Frequency of Imperatives	(11) Frequency of Positive Imperatives	(12) Frequency of Dis-agreement or Agreement with Child
1. Conservation of Quantity (Mass) Task	−.38	−.06	.36	−.16	.41C	.33	−.33	.08	−.49C	−.20	−.12	−.45C
2. Conservation of Length Task	−.28	.24	.19	−.21	−.03	−.14	−.19	.27	−.23	−.20	−.16	−.17
3. Perspectives Task	−.07	−.13	−.19	−.30	−.25	−.23	−.14	−.22	.19	.21	.16	.15
4. Aggregate of Two Conservation Tasks	−.40	.10	.31	−.24	.24	.13	−.33	.19	−.41C	−.26	−.19	−.34
5. Aggregate of Three Piaget Tasks	−.42C	.04	.19	−.37	.11	.01	−.38	.09	−.26	−.17	−.14	−.22

Table 9–5 (continued)

TASK SCORE	MATERNAL BEHAVIOR INDEX											
	(13) Frequency of Disagreement with Child	(14) Frequency of Reference to Similarities or Differences	(15) Frequency of Reference to Relationships	(16) Frequency of Attempts to Motivate Child	(17) Frequency of Justifications	(18) Emphasis on Speed	(19) Emphasis on Slow Approach	(20) Emphasis on Accuracy	(21) Proportion of High Frequency Phrase Connectors	(22) Frequency of Phrase Connectors	(23) Frequency of Rare Phrase Connectors	(24) Total Maternal Involvement
1. Conservation of Quantity (Mass) Task	-.46C	.27	.52B	-.17	.44C	-.15	-.23	.19	-.30	.26	.50C	-.06
2. Conservation of Length Task	-.31	.29	.37	-.41C	.22	-.16	-.30	.24	-.20	.12	.21	-.32
3. Perspectives Task	.29	.30	-.03	-.21	.04	-.08	.05	.08	-.31	-.05	-.06	-.32
4. Aggregate of Two Conservation Tasks	-.44C	.30	.51C	-.35	.37	-.19	-.30	.24	-.25	.21	.41C	-.20
5. Aggregate of Three Piaget Tasks	-.28	.40	.46C	-.44C	.35	-.22	-.27	.24	-.33	.16	.34	-.32

Table 9–5 (continued)

MATERNAL BEHAVIOR INDEX

TASK SCORE	(25) Physical Involvement	(26) Frequency of Violation of Cycle 2 Rule Against Touching Puzzle	(27) Physical vs. Verbal Involvement	(28) Verbal Involvement	(29) Frequency of Demonstration by Mother	(30) Physical Intervention by Completing Steps	(31) Physical Intervention by Touching Puzzle	(32) Time in Completion of Cycle 1	(33) Time in Completion of Cycle 2	(34) Increase in Gesture and Physical Contact with Child from Cycle 1 to 2	(35) Composite Index A	(36) Composite Index B
1. Conservation of Quantity (Mass) Task	-.25	.05	-.22	.01	.19	.05	.09	-.24	-.46C	.34	.52B	.54B
2. Conservation of Length Task	-.33	-.23	-.12	-.27	.35	.40	-.08	.05	-.26	.19	.22	.30
3. Perspectives Task	-.02	.12	.22	-.37	-.10	.07	.10	.36	-.04	.28	-.11	.01
4. Aggregate of Two Conservation Tasks	-.35	-.10	-.23	-.13	.32	.24	.01	-.14	-.44C	.35	.42C	.48C
5. Aggregate of Three Piaget Tasks	-.35	-.05	-.15	-.27	.27	.24	.05	.01	-.45C	.48C	.33	.44C

Table 9–5 (continued)

MATERNAL BEHAVIOR INDEX

TASK SCORE	(37) Composite Index C	(38) Composite Index D	(39) Composite Index E	(40) Composite Index F	(41) Composite Index G	(42) Composite Index H	(43) Composite Index I	(44) Composite Index J	(45) Composite Index K	(46) Composite Index L	(47) Composite Index M
1. Conservation of Quantity (Mass) Task	.54B	-.53B	.55B	.51B	.00	.25	.30	.32	.39	.63A	.58B
2. Conservation of Length Task	.22	-.30	.31	.12	-.41C	-.24	.21	.32	.49C	.38	.33
3. Perspectives Task	-.07	.26	-.00	-.08	-.22	-.22	.32	.36	.13	.09	-.05
4. Aggregate of Two Conservation Tasks	.44C	-.47C	.49C	.37	-.20	.04	.26	.35	.50C	.58B	.53B
5. Aggregate of Three Piaget Tasks	.37	-.30	.44C	.30	-.28	-.05	.35	.45C	.52B	.55B	.46C

The significance of the correlations was computed using a two-tailed t test, and is coded by the capital letters following the correlations in the table as follows: A means that $p \leq .001$; B means that $p \leq .01$; and C means that $p \leq .05$. Italic figures are correlation of absolute value of .40 or greater.

sees. This may be related to both social and mechanical egocentricity. A third skill which is most certainly involved in performance on this task is perceptual: the decoding of two-dimensional representations (the color photographs) into three-dimensional images. This is a perceptual skill which children have been observed to lack in cultures in which access to drawings and photographs has been limited, and where two-dimensional representation of reality is not a tradition (Segall, Campbell, and Herskovits, 1965; Sellers, 1941; Hudson, 1960). Among the Ga, experience with two-dimensional representations of three dimensions is limited in rural and old-town urban areas, whereas suburban children have access to great numbers of photographs and picture books from an early age and are repeatedly encouraged to draw and write. A fourth skill which should contribute to quality of performance on the Perspectives Task is linguistic. Decoding of the relatively elaborate explanations and instructions probably requires a great deal of linguistic training. Such constructions in the English versions as "You pick the picture that shows what the doll sees," "The doll is sitting on the same side as you, so she sees things the same way you do," "It couldn't be this one, because the house is on the wrong side," and ". . . because the picture doesn't show the front door of the house" would seem to be a bit hard to decipher for children not accustomed to such context-free speech. Hence perceptual and linguistic differences among the three subcultures may very well confound effects due to differences in egocentricity or the ability to reshuffle mental images. Independent considerations, then, of (a) egocentricity and mental image juggling, (b) perceptual skills, and (c) linguistic skills would each result in the finding that suburban children would do better on the Perspectives Task than children of the other groups.

3. *Relative excellence of rural children on conservation of quantity (clay), in contrast to a relative deficiency of rural children on the other tasks.* As rural Ga children have the least and poorest quality of schooling among the three groups under contrast, and as they have least contact with the various complexities of the city, their relative excellence on the conservation of quantity task is intriguing. This is especially so in view of the fact that rural children have relatively low scores on the other two tasks.

We might try to account for this effect by noting that rural children have considerably more direct contact with the materials and transformations of the conservation of quantity (clay) task than do either of the other two groups. Rural children play and model considerably with clay. Rural children do much carrying of mud, dirt, and clay. Mud is used in a variety of work, such as the building of houses by molding together large earth slabs to produce flat walls, and in the periodic plastering of walls and floors with earth. Farming also involves the moving and packing of earth. In the course of these activities children are frequently witness to and sometimes participant in many operations with earth such as subdividing, measuring, and transforming the shape of earth, mud, or clay. Price-Williams, et al. (1969), in his study of Mexican children of potters and nonpotters, finds that children of potters score substantially higher than do children of nonpotters on the conservation of quantity task using clay, but that potters' children do not excel relatively on other tests of conservation. Adjei (1977), in an article in the present volume, finds that children of rural potters score significantly higher than children of rural nonpotters on a task of conservation of weight, but not on other conservation tasks. It may be that Ga farm children perform no less (perhaps more) of the kinds of operations performed by potters' children in Mexico and in the Volta region of Ghana than do urban or suburban Ga children.

An alternative explanation is provided by Goodnow (1969a), who suggests that the greatest contrasts among cultures might be seen on tests "calling for imaged changes, . . . where the child has to carry out some spatial shuffling or transforming in his head, without the benefit of actually moving the stimulus around." Along this line, she suggests that children who have had least education might be most disadvantaged on this type of task. "Subjects with less formal schooling often impress their highly educated observers as making greater use, even excessive use, of action and direct manipulation of material" (1969a, p. 256). Although the conservation of quantity task, as standardized by Tuddenham in California and as administered among the Ga, does not involve the child's direct manipulation of the materials, the operations performed by the examiner on the clay in the presence of the child involve considerably less mental transformation than do either of the other two tasks. The conservation of length task involves an analogy: The wire paths are spoken of as the paths walked by two children, and the child is asked about the relative lengths of their walks. This seems to be a fairly massive transformation to handle. The perspectives task involves mental image reversals of several kinds, as in visualizing the model village from the opposite side without going around the board to look. However, this kind of analysis focuses exclusively on the role of cognitive deprivation without taking into account the differences in linguistic skill required for good performance on each of the three tasks. The conservation of quantity task requires least verbal skill in understanding the instructions and questions, and the skill required for answering the questions is minimal. The conservation of length and perspectives tasks, on the other hand, both require considerable linguistic sophistication in understanding the import of the tasks, the instructions and the questions. Although Goodnow may, then, be correct in saying that children with least education are most disadvantaged on certain kinds of tasks, the disadvantage may be of a linguistic as well as cognitive nature.

Other investigators have noted that the conservation of quantity task has been one of the most cross-culturally invariant of Piaget's tasks. This generalization is certainly consonant with the present findings among the Ga that children from rural and suburban groups do not test as disparately on the conservation of quantity task as they do on the other tasks.

An additional explanation of the relatively weak performance of rural children on all but the conservation of quantity task might be considered: The conservation of quantity task was presented first; rural children might be expected to tolerate the testing least well and hence fatigue most rapidly, because of differential unfamiliarity with the materials, operations, and social relationships of the testing situation.

Effects of Maternal Behavior

To the extent that variation in Piaget task scores cannot be adequately accounted for by subcultural variation, how else can the task score variance found in the Ga population at large be accounted for? One type of environmental input to examine as a possible source of cognitive differences in children is the behavior of the children's mothers. Mothers are with their children extensively, and in all three subcultures studied, mothers are primarily responsible for training their young children. It is therefore reasonable to hypothesize that the cognitive growth of a child depends to a large extent upon the mother.

In this section we will outline the ways in which task performance differs across differences in maternal behavior. In order to determine the nature of the mother's role in the cognitive development of the child, a controlled sample of mother-child interaction was taken, using 5-year-olds from each of the three subcultures, to whom the Piaget tasks had previously been administered. Sampling of mother-child interaction was done under controlled conditions in which mothers taught their children to assemble a puzzle. Elements of maternal behavior that seemed relevant to the child's cognitive functioning were correlated with the task performance of the children. The 47 indices of maternal behavior utilized in this analysis are described in detail in Kirk (1976) and Fitzgerald [Kirk], (1970), together with procedures used in the mother-child interaction experiment and some observed patterns of variation in maternal behavior across subculture and several other environmental factors.

The data presented in Table 9–5 indicate that children's performance on the Piaget tasks may be a function of the ways in which the children's mothers behave in interaction with them. That is, we can predict on the average that children will do well on particular tasks of cognitive development if their mothers relate to them in certain ways. From the statistically significant correlations in Rows 1 through 3 of Table 9–5 it is seen that of the three tasks, performance on the conservation of quantity task is by far the easiest to predict from the maternal behavior indices. The indices have less predictive value for the conservation of length task score and virtually no predictive value for the perspectives task score.

1. Predicting Conservation Task Score

Rows 1, 2, and 3 of Table 9–5 deal with correlations between maternal behavior indices and conservation task score. Rows 1 and 2 indicate the strengths of relationship between maternal behavior and each of the two individual tasks for conservation. Rows 4 indicate the strengths of relationship between maternal behavior and the cumulative conservation score. The predictive abilities of each of these three sets of data are discussed below:

Predictions of the conservation of quantity task score is possible from Rows 1 of Table 9–5. The best single predictors of the conservation of quantity task score are the composite indices. The highest correlation is found between task score and composite index L[#46], which is a linear combination of the following simple indices:

#15 (the frequency with which the mother explicitly makes statements or asks questions about relationships among parts or structures of the puzzle);

#23 (the frequency with which the mother uses rare phrase connectors in her speech); and

#21 (the proportion of common phrase connectors in the mother's speech).

This composite index shows a correlation of .63 with the conservation of quantity task score. The three factors involved (simple indices #15, #23 and #21) correlate individually with the conservation of quantity task score .52, .50 and −.30, respectively.

Several other composite indices—A[#35], B[#36], C[#37], D[#38], E[#39], F[#40] and M[#47]—show correlations with the conservation of quantity task score of ±.51 to ±.58.

Setting aside the composite indices, there are eight simple indices which, individually, show statistically significant correlations with the conservation of quantity task score:

#15 (frequency of specific reference to relationships)	r = .52
#23 (frequency of rare phrase connectors)	r = .50
#9 (emphasis on negative imperative)	r = −.49
#13 (frequency of disagreement with child)	r = −.46

#33 (time in completion of a second session of teaching in which the mother was asked to refrain from touching the puzzle)   r = −.46

#12 (frequency of agreement or disagreement with child) r = −.45

#17 (frequency of justification and explanation)   r =   .44

#5 (semantic specificity)   r =   .41

Among these indices, only #5, #15, #17 and #23 can be considered nonspurious in their causal implications; in other words, the causal relationships between only these indices and task score can be assumed to be unidirectional.[7]

Prediction of the conservation of length task score is possible from Rows 2 of Table 9–5. The best single nonspurious predictor of the conservation of length task score is Composite Index K[#45], which is a linear combination of the two simple indices:

#15 (the frequency with which the mother explicitly makes statements or asks questions about relationships among parts or structures of the puzzle) and

#5 (the degree to which the mother is specific in referring to parts or structures of the puzzle [comparison A]).

This composite index shows a correlation of .49 with the conservation of length task score. A second composite index which shows a significant correlation (r = −.41) with the conservation of length task score is G[#41]. This index is a linear combination derived by factor analysis of seven of the simple indices:

#3 (the frequency with which verb roots occur linked to more than minimal semantic content);

#5 (the degree to which the mother is specific in referring to parts, structures or positions on the puzzle);

#14 (the frequency with which the mother makes reference to similarities or differences among puzzle parts or structures);

#15 (the frequency with which the mother explicitly makes statements or asks questions about relationships among parts or structures of puzzle);

#17 (the frequency with which the mother justifies or explains the actions necessary);

#21 (the proportion of high frequency phrase connectors used by the mother); and

#23 (the frequency with which the mother uses rare phrase connectors).

Aside from the composite indices, there are only two simple indices which have correlations of .40 or greater with conservation of length task score:

#16 (the frequency with which the mother attempts to motivate the child); and   r = −.41

#30 (the frequency with which the mother intervenes physically by completing a step).   r =   .40

Prediction of aggregate conservation task score is possible from Rows 4 of Table 9–5. The statistically significant relationships seen here between several maternal behavior indices and the aggregate conservation task score indicate that there are specific kinds of maternal behavior which affect children's ability to perform well on tasks of conservation. Composite Indices L[#46], M[#47] and K[#45] correlate .58, .53 and .50, respectively, with the aggregate conservation score. The aggregate conservation task score correlates less strongly (although significantly) with Indices #9, #13, #23, #33, #35, #36, #37, #38 and #39.

The patterns of correlation between Columns 1 and 2 of Table 9–5 are similar, but in most cases the indices have stronger correlations with conservation of quantity task score than with conservation of length task score. There are a few indices of maternal behavior which correlate strongly with conservation of length task score but not with conservation of quantity task score. Maternal behavior associated with more sophisticated performance on the conservation tasks might be characterized as cognitively complex or abstract.

2. Predicting Perspectives Task Score

No maternal behavior indices, simple or composite, show statistically significant correlations with the perspectives task score, even though the perspectives task score does show significant variation across subculture. This is consistent with our speculation that performance on the perspectives task might be heavily influenced by the degree to which children are routinely exposed to pictures. Other characteristics of the mothers' behavior may have significant impact on the ability of the child to achieve high scores on the perspectives task, but no such hypothetical characteristic is tapped by any of the 47 indices utilized here.

3. Predicting Aggregate Piaget Task Score

Since cognitive abilities do not necessarily develop evenly along all dimensions, it is probably meaningful to look at correlations of the aggregate Piaget task score with the maternal behavior indices (Rows 5 of Table 9–5). We find that the indices which bear the strongest relationships with the aggregate Piaget task score are K[#45] and L[#46], showing correlations of .52 and .55, respectively. Among the simple indices, the aggregate Piaget task score shows the strongest relationship (r = .48) with Index #34 (a measure of the degree to which the mother, when asked not to touch the puzzle, increases her rate of gesture and/or physical contact with the child). This factor also shows a positive but very modest relationship with each of the three individual tasks.

4. The Importance of Index #15

Index #15 (the frequency with which the mother points out relationships among puzzle parts or structures) appears to have particular importance both theoretically and statistically. It appears frequently throughout the analysis as a relevant feature of maternal behavior. It is the only simple index to show a correlation above .50 with any individual measure of the child's cognitive ability (r = .52 with the conservation of quantity task score). Although it does not show a correlation significant at the .05 level with the conservation of length task score in and of itself (r = .37), it shows a higher correlation (r = .51, p ≤ .05) than any other simple index with the aggregate score of the conservation tasks. Even among all indices— composite and simple—it shows one of the highest correlations both with the aggregate conservation score and with the aggregate score for all three Piaget tasks. It contributes heavily to those composite indices which correlate most highly with the task scores. It is considered a nonspurious index, with maternal behavior assumed to be the causal factor in the relationships observed. Index #15, along with the Index #5 and Index #17, taps what might be called maternal communicative specificity, a factor also found associated with the child's rate of cognitive growth in a similar study among the Kikuyu of Kenya (Kirk and Burton, 1976).

The extreme visibility of Index #15 is theoretically important in light of the frequent observations of other investigators that precision in relational thinking is crucial to cognitive performance. Piaget emphasizes this factor in his discussion of cognitive growth (1947). Performance of the concrete operations which he postulates, for example, requires an ability in the child to see and manipulate relationships between two or more elements. The Miller Analogies Test, a device for predicting ability to perform well in graduate school, specifically taps this ability. Also tapping the ability to hold two or more concepts in mind at once is the Verbal Association subtest of the Illinois Test of Psycholinguistic Abilities (S. A. Kirk, et al. 1969). This test correlates highly with the Stanford-Binet and the Wechsler Intelligence Scale for Children (Huizinga, 1971), and all three tests are used to predict school performance. These observations, together with the consistent relationships observed here between the mother's frequency of reference to relationships and the child's rate of cognitive development, suggest that training in sensitivity to relationships may be a vital environmental variable in cognitive development, not only in Western cultures, but among Africans as well.

A further strong relationship, not altogether easy to interpret theoretically, exists between Index # 15 and the age of the mother (also between Index # 15 and the position of the child in the birth sequence, a variable inevitably highly correlated with the age of the mother). It seems that the older the mother and/or the later born the child, the more likely the mother is to point out relationships to her 5-year-old child within the task-teaching situation.

4. CORRELATION OF TASK SCORE WITH EDUCATION AND SOME OTHER ENVIRONMENTAL VARIABLES

A series of other environmental variables were examined for their associations with task score. These variables included the number of years a child and his parents had attended school, the relative ease of transport between the child's community and the capital city, the size of the child's community, the degree of multilingualism of the child and the ethnic origins of the child's mother and father. Controlling for the age of the child, none of the correlations between any of these variables and task score showed consistent statistical significance, with the exception of the ease of transport between the child's community and the capital city (recorded for rural children only), which correlated $-.20$ ($p < .05$) with the conservation of length task score. A more detailed treatment of the associations of these and other variables with task score can be found in Fitzgerald [Kirk] (1970).

5. CONCLUSIONS

This study attempts to isolate environmental variables that might account for differences in rate of cognitive development among Ga children. In pursuit of this objective, it assesses strengths of relationship (a) between subculture and rate of cognitive development and (b) between maternal behavior and rate of cognitive development. The major conclusions appear below.

1. Subcultural membership is associated with the child's rate of cognitive development as measured by one of the Piaget tasks.

Rural, old-town urban and suburban Ga children of ages 5, 8 and 11 years were given three Piaget-derived tasks of concept acquisition. These tasks were conservation of quantity (clay), conservation of length, and perspectives (spatial visualization). The results of the testing indicate the following trends:

A. Although 5-year-olds from the three subcultures perform at approximately the same level on the tasks, there is a considerably lower rate of improvement with age among rural and old-town urban children than among suburban children and, accordingly, suburban children perform relatively well on all tasks by age 11. Task score divergence across subculture increases with age, occurring earliest on the perspectives task and latest on the conservation of quantity task.

B. An exception to this pattern is found on the conservation of quantity task. Here rural children perform as well as suburban children at all ages, whereas the rate of improvement and level of performance of rural children on the other two tasks is relatively low. Subcultural differences in score on the conservation of quantity task are not significant at 5 and 8 years of age.

C. Suburban children at ages 8 and 11 have a clearly significant advantage over both other subcultural groups on the perspectives task. Differences between rural and old-town urban children are insignificant at all ages on this task.

D. Task scores show a patterned and significant increase with increasing age. There is a notable break in this pattern, however, among old-town urban 11-year-olds on conservation, where there is negligible improvement in task score from the 8- to the 11-year level.[8]

In spite of these trends in the relationships between subcultural membership and task performance, we find consistent and statistically significant associations only for the perspectives task.

2. A number of features of maternal behavior are associated with the child's rate of cognitive development as measured by the conservation tasks.

A. *The conservation tasks.* Both of the two conservation tasks show some statistically significant relationships with maternal behavior, and the patterns of association between maternal behavior and each of the two conservation tasks are similar.

Strong relationships are observed between a number of maternal behavior variables and the *conservation of quantity (clay) task* scores of the children. Specific features of maternal behavior which show statistically significant positive correlations with this task include: (a) the mother's specificity of reference (Index #5), (b) her frequency of reference to relationships (Index #15), (c) her frequency of justification and explanation (Index #17), (d) her frequency of use of rare phrase connectors (Index #23), (e) her infrequency of use of negative imperatives (Index #9) and (f) her infrequency of agreement or disagreement with the actions of the child (Index #12). Only among the first four of these can it be confidently inferred that the maternal behavior, rather than the cognitive skill of the child, is the causal factor in the relationship observed.

The composite indices, constructed from the simple indices #1 through #34, and taking advantage of cumulative effects of several features of maternal behavior, are the best predictors of the conservation of quantity task scores (e.g., r = .63 with Composite Index L[#46]).

In general, mothers of children who achieve conservation of quantity early seem to be more creative, verbal, precise, and concerned with explanation, relationship and the manipulation of concepts; in short, they seem more cognitively complex.

Children's scores on the conservation of length task, on the other hand, show similar but weaker patterns of association with maternal behavior. Only two of the simple maternal behavior indices show associations with the conservation of length task score greater than .40: (a) the infrequency with which the mother attempts to motivate the child (Index #16) and (b) the frequency with which she physically intervenes by completing steps for the child (Index #30). The composite indices, however, are again the best predictors of the conservation of length task score (e.g., r = .49 with Composite Index K[#45]).

B. *The perspectives task.* The maternal behavior indices used in the present study seem incapable of predicting ability on the perspectives task. Undoubtedly, however, this task does tap specific abilities which are affected by other variables, as the perspectives task score has been shown to be responsive to subcultural group membership.

C. *The significance of Index #15.* Consistent relationships are observed between the mothers' frequency of reference to relationships and the child's rate of cognitive development as measured by the tasks.

6. DISCUSSION

Children's performance on the perspectives task is highly correlated with subculture, but not with maternal behavior. Performance on the conservation tasks is highly correlated with many features of maternal behavior, but not with subculture.

It is noteworthy that there are consistent and interpretable patterns of significant correlation between maternal behavior and conservation task score, in view of the fact that (a) the mother is not the only caretaker or teacher of the child (there are also siblings, fathers, aunts, etcetera); (b) caretakers and teachers are not the only environmental influences which might affect task performance; and (c) the maternal behaviors which have strong relationships with conservation task score do not involve specific training for conservation.

The major finding here is that subculture is not as closely associated with conservation skills in children as are certain features of maternal behavior. Interestingly, mothers who most frequently refer to relationships by use of specific referents, and who most frequently justify and explain, appear to produce children with greater conservation skill. This is consistent with later findings from Kenya (Kirk and Burton, 1976), where the mother's nonverbal communicative specificity in teaching interaction with the child is highly associated with the cognitive performance of the child. Coupled with the centrality of relational thinking to cognitive performance, the data would suggest that actual training in sensitivity to relationships may be a cross-culturally significant factor in cognitive development.

The present findings are consistent with the assertions that (a) conservation is essentially invariant from culture to culture and (b) good teaching facilitates its development.

NOTES

*The research on which this study was based was supported by a grant from the National Institute of Mental Health, Department of Health, Education and Welfare.

1. In rare cases Ga has not been mastered well, being replaced by English, for instance, in the suburban areas or by Twi or Ewe in the rural areas. Families not fluent in Ga were excluded from the sample.

2. The conservation of quantity and perspectives tasks were adapted from the unpublished test procedures written by Tuddenham for standardization among California school children.

3. In the rare instances in which this was not possible, many months were allowed to intervene between testing periods.

4. Testable children with respect to a given task are those who gave responses to all items of that task. A number of younger children were frightened or otherwise inhibited, sitting silently during the testing without responding to questions. A child might, however, be testable on some though not all of the three Piaget tasks. In these cases the children were dropped from the sample for computation of statistics for some tasks, although they were included in the sample for computation of statistics for other tasks.

5. Percentages of children in each age, sex, and environmental group for whom the concepts were lacking, transitional, or present are represented in bar graph form in a more extensive coverage of this data (Fitzgerald [Kirk], 1970).

6. It seems peculiar that old-town urban children show negligible improvement between eight and eleven years of age (Figure 9–1). This pattern may in part be

accounted for by the fact that old-town urban boys are sometimes taken by their more well-to-do relatives to less densely populated areas of Accra or to the suburbs, where they are given more educational opportunity. These boys would then no longer be among those sampled for this study, as they would be excluded from the old-town urban group on the basis of their present residence and from the suburban group on the basis of their residential histories. It is conceivable that a selection process takes place among boys between the ages of 6 and 12, increasing with age, and that the selection may be made on the basis of traits related to intelligence or school and task performance. Girls are also sometimes taken to other areas by well-to-do relatives, but in these cases they are usually taken as domestic help, and hence likely to be selected on the basis of other criteria. Some support is lent to the possibility of this kind of bias by the fact that on all three tasks the differential task score advantage shown by old-town boys over old-town girls at the 8-year level is either reversed or reduced at the 11-year level (see Fitzgerald [Kirk], 1970) for data on cross-sex differences in task score). This effect is by far most noticeable with the two conservation tasks (the only tasks to show an overall urban lack of improvement from the 8- to the 11-year level), where there is a sizeable reversal of male over female task score advantage on the conservation of quantity task and a marked reduction of the male advantage on the conservation of length task from the 8- to the 11-year level. It has not been determined whether this potential sampling bias problem in the old-town urban group can be held accountable for the drop-off effect of 11-year-old conservation scores, or whether the effects of this potential bias are insignificant.

7. Nonspurious indices are those whose relationships to Piaget task scores can be assumed to indicate that maternal behavior affects the cognitive growth of the child, rather than that the cognitive development of the child affects the maternal behavior. For a more elaborate discussion of this issue, see Chapter 5 of Fitzgerald [Kirk] (1970).

8. See Note 6.

REFERENCES

Adjei, K. (1977) Influence of specific maternal occupation and behavior on Piagetian cognitive development. This book.

Field, M. J. (1937) *Religion and medicine of the Ga people.* London: Oxford University Press.

———. (1940) *Social organization of the Ga people.* London: Crown Agents.

Fitzgerald, L. [Kirk] (1970) *Cognitive development among Ga Children: Environmental correlates of cognitive growth rate within the Ga tribe.* Ph.D. dissertation. Berkeley: University Microfilms, University of California.

Gil, B., Aryee, A. F., and Ghansah, D. K. (1964) *1960 population census of Ghana, special report E: Tribes in Ghana.* Accra: Census Office.

Goodnow, J. J. (1969a) Cultural variations in cognitive skills. In Price-Williams, D. R. (Ed.) *Cross-cultural studies.* Middlesex, England: Penguin.

————. (1969b) Problems in research on culture and thought. In D. Elkind and J. H. Flavell (Eds.), *Studies in cognitive development: Essays in honor of Jean Piaget*. New York: Oxford University Press.

Hudson, W. (1960) Pictorial depth perception in subcultural groups in Africa. *Journal of Social Psychology, 52*:183–208.

Huizinga, R. J. (1971) *The relationship of the Illinois Test of Psycholinguistic Abilities to the Stanford-Binet Form L–M and the Weschler Intelligence Scale for Children*. Unpublished Ph.D. dissertation, University of Arizona.

Kilson, M. (1966) *Urban tribesmen*. Unpublished Ph.D. dissertation, Harvard University.

Kirk, L. (1975) "Estimating the ages of children in non-literate populations: a field method." *Journal of Cross-Cultural Psychology, 6* (2): 238–249.

————. (1976) Cross-cultural measurement of maternal behavior in mother–child teaching interaction. *Quality and Quantity: European Journal of Methodology,* in press.

————. and Burton, M. (1976) Maternal kinesic behavior and cognitive development in the child. Presented at the New York Academy of Sciences Conference on Issues in Cross-cultural research, October, 1975. In *Annals of the New York Academy of Sciences*, in press.

Kirk, S. A., McCarthy, J. J., and Kirk, W. D. (1969) *The Illinois Test of Psycholinguistic Abilities*, (Rev. ed.) Urbana: University of Illinois Press.

Piaget, J. (1947) *The Psychology of Intelligence*. London: Routledge and Kegan Paul.

————. (1963) *The child's conception of space*. Translated by F. Langdon and J. Lunzer. London: Routledge and Kegan Paul.

————. and Inhelder, B. (1941) *Le développement des quantités chez l'enfant*. Neuchâtel: Delachaux et Niestlé.

————. Inhelder, B., and Szeminska, A. (1964) *The Child's Conception of Geometry*. Translated by E. A. Lunzer. Reprinted paperback from the original 1960 publication. London: Routledge and Kegan Paul.

Price-Williams, D., Gordon, W., and Ramirez III, M. (1969) Skill and conservation: a study of pottery-making children. *Developmental Psychology, 1* (6): 769.

Segall, M. H., Campbell, D. T., and Herskovits, M. J. (1965) *The influence of culture on visual perception*. Indianapolis: Bobbs Merrill.

Sellers, W. (1941) "The production of film for primitive people." *Overseas Education, 13*:221.

Tuddenham, R. (n.d) Mimeographed test protocols. Berkeley: University of California.

10
Kinship Concepts Among Rural Hawaiian Children

**DOUGLASS PRICE-WILLIAMS,
ORMOND W. HAMMOND, CEEL EDGERTON,
and MICHAEL WALKER**

Both psychologists and anthropologists have shown interest in the study of cognitive aspects of kinship relations. In the realm of psychology, the pioneer work of Jean Piaget (1926, 1928) which studied the way in which children develop concepts of family relations—that is to say, kinship—opened the way for developmental psychology. Piaget's work focused on the nuclear family and on the terminology associated with this type of kinship structure—in particular, the relationship of siblings. He attempted to tie the acquisition of kinship concepts to sequences of development of relational thought in children.

In the field of anthropology, the study of the cognitive aspect of kinship has lain with the specialist subdiscipline of cognitive anthropology (Tyler, 1969). Cognitive anthropologists have, on the whole, approached cognitive concerns from the standpoint of linguistics; their theoretical concerns are often associated with this other discipline. They appear to be at issue over whether organizational capacity calls for analysis of terminological usage purely through formal analysis, or whether it calls for a search for what they call psychological reality. As an example of the formal analysis approach, Robbins Burling's classic article (Burling, 1964) may be cited. A good example of the psychological reality approach would be Anthony Wallace (Wallace, 1965). Most, if not all, of the publications representing the psychological reality school describe methods not usually considered by psychologists—componential analysis, tree analysis, and applications of symbolic logic generally—although on occasion methods used by psychologists are also employed, such as the triads test and multidimensional scaling. On occasion, anthropologists use a formal experiment, as is the case in Sanday's (1971) study of concepts associated with the American kinship system.

It is difficult to relate the concern of cognitive anthropologists over the formal semantic organization of kinship terminological systems, and their possible psychological reality, with psychological researches which emphasize the development of a notion of kinship as part of a greater schema including the development of cognitive abilities. No doubt a rapprochement between the two disciplines is necessary, particularly inasmuch as they converge on a single substantive set of inquiry— kinship—but it would be outside the concerns of this paper to attempt this rapprochement.

Other psychological researches have taken up the Piagetian study of the development of notions of kinship in western societies where the nuclear family predominates, e.g., Danziger with the Australians (1957); Elkind (1962) and Haviland and Clark (1974) with the Americans. LeVine and Price-Williams (1974) reviewed the substantive and methodological problems which arose when other than nuclear families were studied with psychological concepts in mind. They then followed this discussion with their own, small-sample study of Hausa children who live in a northern Nigerian society where household compounds containing extended families are the norm. This study was one of the first to explore the concept of kinship in a non-Western society; consequently it was characterized partly as a methodological innovation.

In studying the Hausa, LeVine and Price-Williams had as their specific aims the discovery of the extent to which children's verbal reports concerning kinship would reveal developmental trends in three areas: relational thinking, informational accuracy, and the salience for the child of compound residents in certain relationships to him. The main thrust of the study focused on the use of ego-centered kin terms (terms used by the child for his kin) and other-centered kin terms (terms used between other pairs of the child's kin) to measure the gradual decentration in kinship concepts of the children and their acquisition of relational thinking, both as a function of increasing age and as a function of the type of family structure exemplified in Hausa society.

While the authors concluded that their findings in this non-Western society were in general agreement with the sequence of developmental stages posited by Piaget, they had several recommendations on specific points to which future researches among non-Western societies should pay attention.

It is clear that a literal equivalent of this type of study can seldom be carried out, as the nature of kinship structures differs across the world. In this as in other studies using a cross-cultural approach, all one can do is to strive for functional equivalence (Berry 1969). In doing this, we are following the notion of functional cognitive systems, which Cole and Scribner (1974, pp. 192–194) have advocated in cross-cultural work, following the psychological theories of Vygotsky and Luria. In terms of the present concern, with the growth of ideas of kinship, we need to pay attention to psychological processes that may differ functionally from one type of family structure to another; these may demand slightly different methodologies depending on the terminological universe of the samples, but one study relates to another because similar principles are involved.

With the present study, the main principle under review was the same as those studied in the LeVine and Price-Williams Hausa study, and indeed the same as with all psychological researches of family relationships that touch on the explanatory concepts originating with Piaget (e.g., Elkind, 1962; Danziger, 1957)—namely, the movement from an egocentric perspective to decentration. In this particular application, we gave special attention to the nature of the experience thought to influence the ability to adopt the perspective of another person. We had in mind Danziger's point made in his study of kinship terms (1957, p. 230) that "the level of conceptualization depends to a large extent on the child's experience in handling the different types of content."

SETTING

The study, which was carried out in a relatively remote fishing village in the Hawaiian Islands, was generated not only to contribute to the body of knowledge concerning the development of kinship concepts, but also because an entry into the cognitive realm of native Hawaiians was sought which did not depend upon performance in standardized achievement tests. The investigation was based on the general strategy of seeking domains of competence in which the population concerned has familiarity and interest. Preliminary ethnographic observation with the children of this locality established that children spend a good deal of time talking about family relationships, and indeed identifying friends in terms of how they are related. They were therefore ideal subjects for a study in which an index to the development of conceptual thought was sought through measurement of competence in handling relations in the kinship realm.

The village contains a population of approximately 130 regular residents, living in 20 households, who are supplemented in their number by visiting families, especially during the summer. The inhabitants all speak Pidgin English, a Hawaiian variant of Standard English, and send their children to the public schools. Despite the absence of electricity in the village, most have transistor radios and some even have television. The majority of the residents are of predominantly Hawaiian-Polynesian descent and continue to maintain a life-style which has been characterized as retaining many Polynesian features, even though the culture has undergone continuous change since the time of first contact.

Since family relationships form the topic under study in this paper, it is necessary to go in some depth into the pertinent background of the system of kin relations in the village in order to assess the terminological responses of our subjects in their relevant context. Relatively recent discussions of Hawaiian kinship in the literature include a fairly full treatment by Handy and Pukui (1972), and more limited discussion by Yamamura (1941), Kenn (1939), and Beaglehold (1937), as well as an unpublished paper by Heighton (n.d.). Despite this body of literature, there is lacking the kind of knowledge which is pertinent to such studies as the one on which we have embarked. What is required is not merely a schedule of kinship terms, but an understanding of the way in which such terms and their variants are actually used in social situations. Also, regional variations are apparent in the Islands, to the extent that in this study we have relied heavily on actual ongoing observations by ethnographers working in the particular fishing village of the study.

Present-day Hawaiian social life is divided between peer groups and family, with the family playing a central role as a unit of nurturance and responsibility. The unity of the family is an important value, and its continuity even more so; from a young age children are led to consider preparation for life as being preparation for raising families of their own (Heighton, n.d.). The kindred, a close-knit group of bilaterally-traced relatives, provides economic help in emergencies (Howard, 1971), homes to be shared for visits or actual residence, and a group to draw upon for solving serious family disputes or problems (Mays, 1973). The family and kindred rely on frequent family gatherings such as luaus to renew feelings of warmth, aloha, security, and dependence among relatives, which keep these groups functioning. In contrast, peer groups seem to be enjoyed as a respite from the responsibilities inherent in family life.

The domestic cycle might be described as starting at stage one with a nuclear family of parents and children. At stage two, the children are growing up and moving into consensual unions, having children, and eventually marrying. At this point, they may still live at home, or may have moved out if they are able. The original parents in the cycle have now become grandparents; and they may *hanai* (adopt) some of their grandchildren; still other grandchildren may join the household—with or without their parents, as need and circumstances dictate. Some grandparents may also be found living alone at this time. It should be noted that in most cases the grandparents own their own homes and therefore are considered to be at least the nominal heads of the household in which they live, although the families of adult children who may be living with them will form nuclear units within these extended households, having a separate sphere of nuclear associations and authority over their member children, except for any child *hanai*ed by the grandparent.

In this village, 11 of the 20 households contain only a nuclear family, one of which lacks a father. There is an additional family which might be considered nuclear in that the grandmother is not head of the household and has been living with the family only as a temporary measure while she disputes ownership of her own home with her husband.

Of the stage two types of households, there were three comprised of older couples living alone, one in which there was an older couple with older married daughter and spouse, one household of grandparents with hanaied grandchildren, and three families headed by grandparents—two of them by a grandmother alone—with married child, spouse, and children, other grandchildren, and some additional relatives and friends. Because several families from the nearby area were visiting in the village during the summer, our sample contained children from 17 different households, the visitor children all being from nuclear families.

It can be seen from this description that the majority of children living in the village are resident in nuclear households, and these households form their primary base of experience with kin relations. However, because of Hawaiian visiting patterns, children—with or without their parents—are likely to spend varying amounts of time with relatives. In another small village in Hawaii, Nanakuli, approximately 90% of the children surveyed had lived at some time with a relative who was more distant than mother, brother, or sister (Howard, 1971). At the time of our study, 1/3 of the children in our sample had one or more visitors in their household and 1/6 were themselves visitors to another household. There are also many inter-connections of close relationship between households in the village; the number of close links for households with children averaged 5.67 households, and this number would increase if households in the nearby area were included. It can therefore be seen that most children of the village receive a broad exposure to the full range of relatives, and this constitutes a secondary level of experiences with kin.

KINSHIP TERMINOLOGY

The system of kinship terminology presently in use among Hawaiians of this village is remarkably similar to that in use among English-speakers in mainland America, and shows only vestiges of the previous generational type of system.

As far as we can tell, the system of kin terms used in the home context does not differ from that used in the school context, although there are always more formal and less formal variations of terms according to social situation. In the following discussion, we will attempt to briefly summarize terms as they are used in this village, taking the viewpoint of an ego who is a child:

Grandparents are both addressed and referred to as "Grandma" and "Grandpa"; there is some use of the terms *tutu* and *tutuman* by the grandchildren, usually indicating warmth and affection.

Parents are most often referred to as "Mother" and "Father" or a variant such as "Mama" and "Daddy," and addressed as such.

As for *Siblings*: With occasional lapses to the use of "Sister" and "Brother" in reference either by parents or other siblings, siblings are called by their names or nicknames for both reference and address. The youngest sibling is often called "Baby." Among adults, "Sister" may be used as a form of address, affectionately a female speaker. "Brother" is a slang term used between men, usually without connotations of kinship.

Children are addressed by their names or nicknames; they are referred to as "Son" or "Daughter" but more often called by name.

Grandchildren are called by name. They are referred to either as "Grandson" or "Granddaughter," or *mo'opuna*, a Hawaiian term now meaning "grandchild."

Aunts and uncles: Aunts are addressed or referred to affectionately as "Aunty" especially when there is a warm caretaking relationship with a child; the use of the term "Aunty" plus a name indicates more respect. Uncles are referred to and addressed by the use of the term "Uncle" plus the name. When the aunt or uncle is not yet fully adult, or there is not much gap in age between aunt or uncle and nephew or niece, they may be addressed and referred to by name alone.

Cousin: Younger people address their cousins by name and usually use the name, not the term, to refer to them. Adults use the name for reference and address, but sometimes alternate this use with the term "Cuz" for address, and "Cousin" for reference. These villagers do not make divisions within the category of cousin; they extend the range of the term to cover any kin not covered by another term, no matter how remote the actual kinship link.

Husband and wife refer to each other as "my wife," "my old lady," "my husband," or "my old man," or use a name or nickname with close relatives and friends, but often use a variant of "Mother" and "Father" without the possessive pronoun when speaking of one another to the children. Some also address one another as "Mommy" and "Daddy," but more often couples use names or even terms of endearment. Typically no name is used at all by husbands in speaking to their wives who are waiting for their requests.

In-laws: The terms include mother-, father-, sister-, brother-, son- and daughter-in-law. There is not much data on usage; it would seem that for the most part names are used in address and reference, although the relationships are recognized. Some women may refer to a sister-in-law as *tiddah* (a term meaning "sister") or "Sister" or "Cuz," while referring to a brother-in-law by his name.

"Greats": Terms which have the prefix "great" are not used, nor are the categories apparently recognized, these categories being assimilated to the cousin category.

"Halves" and "steps": Reference to the fact that a person stands in a half or step relationship to ego is seldom made, although it will be noted when the situation calls for explaining a relationship explicitly. It is not used in address.

Hanais: Children who are *hanai*ed to another family usually adhere at least part of the time to the real biological situation in applying kin terms to their adopted families, except when they no longer have a competing real family of their own. The rest of the time they may use terms from the nuclear family unit for reference and address in their adoptive family, often prefixing the term *hanai* when making reference before someone who does not know the relationship. Use of nuclear terms versus real terms depends on the content. For instance, a 3-year-old *hanai* was heard to comment, "Here comes Grandma!" and as she got within hearing distance the child called out, "Mommy! Mommy!" Use of terms other than those for nuclear family relations is a trend away from the old system in which *hanai* set up a situation of dual parentage and dual kinship.

One quarter of the children in the village live *hanai*, almost all with at least one grandparent in residence, but most maintain contact—some quite closely—with their real families.

Fictional kinship: The kinship mode of social relations continues to be important to modern-day Hawaiians. Fictional kin terms are extended to many friends on the basis of sex and generational seniority. The latter is judged by factors such as relative age and whether or not the friend is married and has children. In the old days, there was a system of genealogical seniority differentiation. What remains is respect for elders; seniority now comes to mean age, not relative genealogical status. The use of terms and their reciprocals in address, and in reference, parallels that for real kin. The oldest generation is composed of "grandparents" a term used for both reference and address, alternating with *tutu* and *tutuman*. The next generation is "aunt" or "uncle," with the kin terms plus the name for reference and address; these terms may be used even by persons in the grandparent generation for persons in the parental generation. Persons in ego's own generation may be labeled "sisters" and "brothers" or else "cousin" for persons less close, if ego is an adult. Children use "cousin." These kin terms are for reference along with names, and names are usually used for address. The same is true for the reciprocals of all the terms given above.

Children presumably realize that there is a difference between a real relative and a fictional relative, since they are constantly being instructed by those around them to "treat so-and-so like a real aunty"—or whatever.

Honorary usages: So strong is the principle of genealogical seniority that it may on occasion override distinctions of generation based on actual genealogical linkings. These exceptions are made in terms of both address and reference, usually by younger children who are trained to elevate their adult cousins to "aunty" or "uncle." For instance, one child in our sample divided four sisters in a visiting family into two separate categories of kin. The two older married sisters were "aunties," while the younger sisters who were playmates were "cousins."

Although the terminology of the Hawaiian kinship system has been converging toward that of the mainland America system, similarities in the terms and their structural relations can be misleading and can conceal some real differences in kin behavior, attitudes, and associated social institutions.

A background of ethnographic knowledge about the village was gained through field work by a team of six graduate students in anthropology who, with the collaboration of a postdoctoral candidate in psychology, spent varying amounts of time off and on for a period of two years, collecting data under the supervision of senior researchers as part of a larger project on cognitive competence. Their observations included a study of children in the school setting, a census of the village taken at two different times, a genealogy of its residents, and observations of the children in natural settings. This preliminary work and the gathering of general ethnographic data developed into two long-term studies in the community, one of conflict resolution and the other of child caretaking patterns.

The availability of such data helped the researchers in this present study both in planning the design of their experiment and in evaluating their data. For instance, as a consequence of anthropological field work being carried out at the exact time of this kinship research, we were able to utilize very accurate kin charts for the family of each child investigated. This enabled us to know the stable family size for each child's family, and more importantly, allowed us to employ a criterion of correctness for the children's answers,—a step beyond merely invoking the use of kin terms, as in the Hausa study (LeVine and Price-Williams, 1974) and in a previous report on this same Hawaiian material (Price-Williams et al. 1974). Although some questions arose regarding the alignment of the children's kinship terms with that of the adult census, which will be discussed later, we nevertheless had a sufficient index with the latter to utilize it as a criterion of correctness. Our results, therefore, will be framed in that context.

Both from our own investigations and from those of other investigators, we have learned that psychological studies with Hawaiian children run into distinct methodological constraints, which we think it pertinent to outline here. First of all, it has been found that what is usually considered in psychological literature to be a testing or eliciting situation often serves to inhibit the mobilization of that type of behavior which must be manifested if we are to infer the presence of reasoning skills. This is reflected in behavior in various ways. First, Hawaiian children like to do things in groups. They are averse to being singled out by being taken aside. This may be related to the findings which Gallimore and his colleagues (1974) take to be indicative of an "affiliation motive." This makes any form of individual-in-isolation testing suspect, while the alternative of group testing often introduces a biasing element to the responses of individuals within the groups. Secondly, Boggs (1972) has reported that Hawaiian children tend not to verbalize when asked a direct question. A more successful strategy for eliciting verbalization is to "talk story"—to have free-flowing, congenial conversation organized to maintain sociability, with respondents. This clearly means that standardized procedures wherein precise formulation of the task is enunciated by an experimenter are not as effective as less structured means. This was shown to apply with pilot work in the present sample. Furthermore, verbalizing in the "talk story" mode is far more acceptable to these children than any form of written response. This has also been shown to be true for Hawaiian parents (Hammond, 1973). Third, although Hawaiian children, as with children in most cultures, like to play games and try hard to succeed at them, it was determined in pilot testing that they dislike a game when it has either an explicit or an implicit right-wrong answer element. This made it extremely difficult to design a game which would truly tap the skills of the children without invoking the negative affective element which confounds results. Lastly there is the matter of communication. Many of the implications of the methodological constraints on this score have been delineated by Labov (1971) and other sociolinguists working with U.S. minority group children. Specifically, Labov points out that children will "turn off" if an adult questioner commits any of a variety of misdeeds. Among these are: ordering the child to talk, asking questions with a tone implying that there is a morally "best" answer, talking down to the child, and confusing the child by asking him for information which he already knows the questioner knows. Following these caveats leads to a very free-form adult-child interchange much like the "talk story" method we have found to be most successful in Hawaii. The abject silence which meets seemingly friendly, but implicitly evaluative questioning, sometimes is called in Hawaii "being shamed." A classmate will speak up for a fellow who has been asked such a question and who is looking silently away, by informing the adult, "He shamed."

These constraints perhaps raise some questions concerning the validity of most standardized testing situations among Hawaiian children, even those performed outside of the school situation. An attempt was made here to assess the abilities of young Hawaiian children in reasoning and answering questions involving decentered kinship concepts, by avoiding the known methodological difficulties.

METHOD

Subjects and Setting

The subjects were 37 children, 21 male, 16 female, all of Hawaiian or part-Hawaiian background. The precise age range was from 4 years and 8 months to 14 years and 3 months at the time of testing. The degree of racial Hawaiianness was not determined; indeed it is almost impossible to determine this in modern Hawaii. Most residents of the islands who have some Hawaiian blood, even if it is not their major ethnic derivation, identify themselves as "part Hawaiian."

More importantly for the present purposes, these 37 children were being raised in an unusually homogeneous Hawaiian cultural background. All subjects resided at the time of the study in a remote fishing village. All were participants in a "Summer Fun" program conducted by certain village parents and members of a research team with whom the children had become familiar over a period of months. This Summer Fun program was generally a loosely structured set of recreational activities which were intended to serve the dual function of providing observational data to the researchers and worthwhile summer activities to the village residents, who were geographically isolated from other such programs conducted by the County of Hawaii. Activities were run each week day from 8 A.M. until noon. Participation was entirely voluntary, and parental consent was obtained. One of the goals of the research during this program was to pilot test various games and formats in order to determine their effectiveness as devices to tap cognitive abilities and interests. The program was run, and all data collected, in the natural setting of the home village. The data collectors were two male non-Hawaiian researchers known to the children on a first-name basis. These two researchers were considered nonthreatening to the children largely because they avoided assuming the teacher role in all dealings with the children.

Procedure

As part of the Summer Fun activities, the researchers played many games of various sorts with the children. One of these was called "The Family Game." The researcher would ask each willing child: (1) "Who lives in your house now?" Answers were recorded verbatim by the researcher on a work sheet. The researcher would say, "Any more?" or "Is that all?" until the list was complete to the child's satisfaction. The researcher then went down this original list, asking, for each person named by the child without any reference to kinship (i.e., "Jamie" instead of "Uncle Jamie"): (2) "Who is ———?" or "Who is ——— to you?" Next, the researcher took pairs of persons in the order listed, and asked the child: (3) "Who is ——— to ———?" or "——— is ———'s what?" This questioning was carried out in an informal atmosphere. The child was not physically removed from his group, and was in earshot of his playing comrades. The intent of the researchers' questions was to enable the child to answer fully if he could—that is, the attempt was made to standardize meaning rather than question-wording, within the constraints of the natural setting.

After the "family game," the child was asked several questions which it was hoped would reveal further knowledge about kinship concepts. The child was asked if he knew the meaning of two Hawaiian terms adapted for use in modern Hawaii (previously described, but now repeated): *tutu*, an affectionate term for grandparent—especially the grandmother—which is widely used today; and *hanai*, which is a word referring to traditional adoption practices, according to which a child simply goes to live in a different household. This practice amounts to adoption without going through legal channels (cf. Howard, Heighton, Gallimore, and Jordan, 1970).

Finally, the child was asked three questions involving the use of left and right to introduce a non-kinship measure of relational thinking: "Which is your right (or alternately, left) hand?", "Which is my right (left) hand?", and "Which side of me is ――― on?" This last question was carried out by having actual children lined up beside the investigator. All these questions followed in part those of the study by LeVine and Price-Williams (1974) for the kinship content, and Price-Williams and LeVine (1974) for the left-right questions, with certain minor modifications necessary for adapting to the cultural milieu.

RESULTS

Our first way of reporting results is to indicate the age at which the various variables tested were correctly attained. These are shown in Table 10–1.

Table 10–1
Percent of sample giving correct answers for both selected kin terms and left/right orientation in terms of age

Question	*Age ranges,* *mean percent*
Correct use of other-centered kin terms	4–6: 31.2% (n:5) 7–8: 73.3% (n:6) 9–14: 89.9% (n:21)
Correct kin term *tutu*	4–7: 33% (n:9) 8–14: 92.0% (n:25)
Reversibility of hands	4–8: 44.4% (n:9) 8.33–14: 87.0% (n:23)
Accuracy of hands reversal	4–9: 37.5% (n:16) 10–14: 87.5% (n:16)
Accuracy of person reversal	4–8: 20% (n:10) 9–14: 90.9% (n:22)
Correct use of ego-centered kin terms	Whole age range: 98.3% (n:35)

The various ages are indicated as thresholds, by showing—in terms of percentages for an age range—the proportion of children who have not attained the variable versus the proportion who have reached it. We set our thresholds at points at which there were substantial changes in the percentages of correctness. Since various percentages of correctness have been used in previous literature, this method of reporting results allows a comparison with different criteria previously used. The variables listed were taken from the questions previously described in the section on procedure. Thus the proportion of correct use of ego-centered kin terms stemmed from Question 2; the percentage of correct use of other-centered kin terms stemmed from Question 3 (we excluded from our count any duplicate use of terms for the same type of relationship); and the remainder of the variables came out of the analysis from the following questions about *tutu* and left-right orientations. Concerning the latter, we needed to make a distinction in responses to the left or right hand of the interviewer facing the child. A few children misapplied the terms "right" and "left" to their own hands but were correct in reversing the labels when asked about the hands of the interviewer; this group of children is called "reverse hands" in Tables 10–1 and 10–2. The group is distinguished from the larger group of children who correctly understood which was their right and their left hands, and went on to correctly reverse them in the case of the interviewer. This second group is labelled "Accuracy of hands reversal" in Tables 10–1 and 10–2. The question about the meaning of *hanai* proved to be fruitless, because it is a term undergoing transition. The adults still use *hanai* but the children use "adopt," and only one child in the sample could define the term. We therefore have not included this question in Table 10–1. The overwhelming success of the entire group (98.3%) for the correct utilization of ego-centered kin terms avoided the need for further analysis of this variable. It will be noticed in Table 10–1 that the sample numbers for each variable vary because of the fact that not all children answered each question uniformly.

We had previously stated that we were concerned with the factor of age and also with the factor of experience, as expressed here in terms of household size. We interpreted the role of the latter variable as providing a vehicle for indicating the extent of kin terms actually available to the child in his immediate environment. Through the use of partial correlations, controlling separately in each case for age and for household size, we analyzed the determining value of each component. The results are shown in Table 10–2. Also shown in the same table are the results of an intercorrelation matrix using the Pearson statistic, without the partial correlation aspect. We need to say something about the household size variable. We established the size of each household by using the ethnographic census information. In this we were able to ascertain the stable household size, avoiding fluctuations in the household due to the presence of visitors for the time period involved.

Table 10–2
Intercorrelation matrix of questions relating to kin terms and to left-right orientation

	(1) % correct Other- Centered Use	(2) Correct "tutu"	(3) Reverse hands	(4) Accuracy of hands reversal	(5) Correct person reversal
(1) % correct other-centered use		.6058**	.1553	.2008	.6267**
(2) Correct *tutu*			.2104	.2044	.4525*
(3) Reverse hands				.7454**	.2335
(4) Accuracy of hands reversal					.3133
(5) Correct person reversal					
Age	.738**	.534*	.235	.375#	.661**
Household Size	−.129	−.248	−.023	−.140	−.512*

p = .05
* p = .01   One-tailed; d.f. = 28
** p = .001

DISCUSSION OF MAIN RESULTS

The main thrust of our inquiry was aimed at the transition from ego-centered thinking to decentered thinking or the conceptual ability to put oneself in another's perspective. We pursued this in relation to kin terms and to left-right orientation. For the kin part of the inquiry we focused only on other-centered material about relations external to the ego, and not in relation to ego as Greenfield and Childs have done in Chapter 11 of this volume. A look at our Table 10–1 indicates that the big transition jump comes at the age range of 7–8, and that the ability to decenter in using kin terms is virtually completely attained from the age of 9 onwards. The figures for the age range 7–8 would therefore agree with Piaget's findings in this regard (Piaget 1928, p. 206), and are roughly consistent with the Greenfield and Child findings (see Chapter 11, Figure 11–5, center bar graph)—although the Hawaiian children appear to be slightly in advance of the Zinacantecan children. Likewise the percentages for the correctness of use of ego-centered kin terms in the two groups are also consistent, the Hawaiian children again appearing to be a little more advanced than the Zinacantecan children. We should not make too much of the differences in age attainment, however, as the age groupings in the two studies vary slightly and the sample in the Hawaiian case is relatively small. In summary we can say that with three remarkably diverse cultural populations— European, Mexican Indian, and Polynesian Hawaiian—a broad consistency in attainment of decentered thinking for a similar age range has been observed.

The concern with decentered thinking is further taken up in relation to left-right orientation. As has been demonstrated by Price-Williams and LeVine (1974) a comparison of left-right orientation studies by different writers is difficult to make, as different tasks were involved in the different cases. In the present Hawaiian sample, we have three indicators of left-right reversals. In those instances when the task was that of identifying left and right for the investigator's hands, we note that a substantial increase of accuracy takes place at the age of 10. If we ignore the fact that the child has originally got his left and right wrong but has got the idea of reversal firm (see the third item in Table 10–1), then the shift in decentration takes place at about the age of 8 years 4 months old. When we substitute actual people for the hands of the person standing opposite the child, then it is at the age of 9 years that the big transition is made. The range of ages for the various tasks is not unusual when one takes different tasks into consideration, as is seen in the paper by Price-Williams and LeVine (1974 pp. 359, second portion of Table 1). We can say, though, that the Hawaiian group developed reverse left-right orientation much later than the Hausa sample (who attained this at age 6 years) and this is more in keeping with previous European and North American populations.

It is clear from the partial correlations seen in Table 10–2 that age is the decisive factor, and that household size does not enter into the situation, except negatively with one criterion of left-right reversibility. It can also be seen from the intercorrelation matrix that the two kinship variables go together, but that there is only one criterion of the left-right orientation set that is linked with the kinship pair. It would have been more satisfactory if the results of the two tasks had been similar, but this just has not been found to be so. At any rate, by having correlation between at least one factor of left-right reversibility with the two kinship variables, especially that of the other-centered kinship question, we can feel more confident that the decentration noted is on firm footing, though established in two quite different domains.

Dealing with a small sample presents the investigator with both advantages and disadvantages. An intimate acquaintance with the circumstances of each individual in the sample and the ability to examine each question closely permits the researcher to check out quickly many alternative hypotheses, to attain certain insights, and to reject misleading surface appearances that mere sorting and counting might not avoid. In the final analysis, however, there will be many aspects of such a study about which the researcher can only speculate, finding suggestive evidence which may stimulate further research elsewhere but which lacks the convincing weight of numbers to give it authority. Because we believe that qualitative analyses of a small number of cases can often serve the function of stimulating thought, debate, and investigation, we want to attempt to discuss some of our results further.

One such qualitative analysis concerns a division of the sample into nuclear versus nonnuclear families. As we mentioned previously, most of the children in the sample live in a nuclear family, but some do not. The group of 12 children who live in nonnuclear families includes 6 children who were *hanai*ed (adopted). We might ask whether or not this difference in family type influenced at all the ability of the child to give correct answers regarding other-centered kin terms. To answer this more specifically in terms of age, we divided the children into those with nuclear families and those with nonnuclear families and compared their individual scores for correct use of other-centered kin terms by age levels according to the ability to use other centered kin terms from Table 10–1. The result of this analysis can be seen in Table 10–3.

Table 10–3
Effects of nuclear vs. nonnuclear family structure on response to other-centered questions

Age level*	N: nonnuclear households**	% correct use of other, centered kin terms	N: nuclear households	% correct use of other-centered kin terms
1. 4–6	2	41.5	3	24
2. 7–8	1	71	5	73.8
3. 9–14	8	88.6	13	91
All age levels combined	11	78.5	21	77.1

*Age levels used are those for ability to use other-centered kin terms from Table 10–1.
**Only 11 of the 12 children from nonnuclear families answered other-centered questions.

Although the numbers involved are too small for any real statistical significance, it would not appear that the children from nonnuclear families did significantly less well than children from nuclear families. There is also another way of looking at this matter. In a normal nuclear household with a full complement of members, there are 8 kin terms in use: mother, father, sister, brother, son, daughter, husband, and wife. Children who live in the nonnuclear households average 14.5 separate terms per household, therefore as regards the number of terms they must grasp (if this is important) these children should have had much more difficulty in answering other-centered question than did the children of nuclear families.

This result is also suprising in that there appeared to be a gradient of difficulty for all the children in applying terms to certain types of relationships—a matter which we will discuss in more detail later. Relationships of certain kinds—for example, relationships involving components of marriage and descent as opposed to siblingship—attracted a greater number of incorrect responses and were attained at a later age. These more difficult relationships tend to appear with a higher frequency in nonnuclear than in nuclear households.

There is an additional point to be made, namely, that *hanai* children are usually exposed to the full set of nuclear terms in their nonnuclear households, but primarily by hearing others use the terms. Where they themselves use nuclear terms for their adopted family, they also use alternative terms which correctly reflect the real biological situation. It would prove interesting to question these *hanai* children further about their definitions for various kin terms in order to check their accuracy as regards nuclear family terms and compare it with that of children who reside in nuclear families. For *hanai* children who use both sets of terms it might reveal what problems if any arise from the dual system of labeling. These children might also be asked about their real biological families. For *hanai* children who reserve nuclear terms for their real family, a comparison might show what role primary experience in the family plays in the learning of terms and whether or not the children gain mastery over various terms in the same order as do children in nuclear households. It would also be interesting to discover which terms are learned first in the child's adoptive family and whether or not these are structurally similar to those learned first in the nuclear family, and if so, how.

We turn now to the qualitative analysis of the term *tutu*. Most of the children asked to define *tutu* merely translated it into the English equivalent, which is "grandma." (In this village, the grandfather variant is *tutu-man*, and *tutu* does not appear to refer equally to either grandparent as has been suggested elsewhere in the literature.) Without further probes, it is difficult to know to what extent the children could give a full definition of the term *tutu*. However, it is instructive to examine the answers of the younger children.

Of the eight youngest children, aged 7 or under, three answered the *tutu* question correctly, three did not know the term, and two responded that it meant "old lady." The use of "old lady" to define this term might be considered an early use of concrete classes. Although "old lady" is a secondary definition of *tutu* in some parts of the islands, its use is rare if not nonexistent in this particular village. An additional example of concreteness in definition of kin terms at this age group was provided by a 7-year-old boy who was asked to define "grandfather." He first defined the term as "grampa," but when asked a further question about how "grampa" was related to the boy, announced: "He tell my father go fishing." There is an example from the Hausa (LeVine and Price-Williams, 1974) of a young girl doing very nearly the same thing—giving a particularistic action definition for a kin term. In fact, among the Hausa, the age at which there was a sharp rise in the number of children able to give some definition of *kaka* ("grandparent") fell at nearly the same point as among the Hawaiian children.

As we mentioned in the beginning of this chapter, nearly half of the children in the sample were either visiting or being visited. We might well ask to what extent other-centered term errors occurred in connection with being asked a relationship involving someone not regularly in the household of the child. There were a total of 33 such relationships involving non-householders; of these, 8 (or 24%) were incorrectly answered. The error rate for questions about relationships between householders runs 22%. Although the numbers involved are very small, the non-householder effect is most pronounced at age range 4–6 and still exists at age range 7–8; but by age range 9–14 it is nil; In fact, at age 9–14 the reverse occurs; these older children handle nonhouseholder relationships even better than householder ones. By age 12 or so, they are able to deal with most complexities of kinship which may arise, whether it be a stepfather who is "mother's second husband" or a pair of brothers-in-law.

Table 10–4
Response to visitor vs. non-visitor relationships

Age levels*	N correct answers/ N questions asked about visitors	% correct responses to visitor questions	% correct responses to nonvisitor questions	% correct responses to combined visitor nonvisitor questions**
Level 1 (4–6)	0/5	0	54	39
Level 2 (7–8)	1/3	33	70	75
Level 3 (9–14)	24/25	96	87	89.9

*Age levels correspond to those used for other-centered kin term use in Table 10–1.
**The percentages in this column are figured by taking the $\bar{X}$ of all responses and therefore differs from the figures in Table 10–1 which took the $\bar{X}$ of the percentages correct other-centered answers for children in each age group.

We will finish our minor analyses of the variables in Table 10–1 and Table 10–2 by reference to omissions made by children of various ages in naming members of their household and applying ego-centered terms to them, which we may compare with the Hausa study (LeVine and Price-Williams, 1974) and the Zinacantecan study in this volume (Greenfield and Childs, chapter 11).

In producing lists of household members, the youngest children, age 4–6, made many omissions; only one succeeded in naming all her household, and like the young Hausa children, several of these children included casual afternoon visitors in their enumeration and two included the family dogs. Past the age of 6, the children achieve a very high percentage of completeness of household lists, only 6 out of 30 failing to get 100%, even when households with visitors ranged up to a size of 20 persons. Most of the omissions did occur with these larger households.

The Hausa children tended to mention their mothers before their fathers; the Hawaiian children did so routinely. None of the Hawaiian children omitted a mother, but two forgot father—one girl and one boy. In Hausa, the father was frequently omitted, mostly by girls for whom the relationship was one of distance.

There was no other obvious patterning to the lists or their omissions, with one exception. Some of the households have taken in nonrelatives, usually older Filipino men who are friends of the family. In one such family, none of the children mentioned the "friend" as being resident in the household, although he was so at the time. In another family, two of the three youngest children did not mention the friend at all, while the older two did. It would appear that the concept of "living with" in a household applies most strongly to persons who can show either cognatic or agnatic connection. It is also likely that had the question been asked, "Who is in your family?" a different household list would have emerged, but it was not our interest to do so in the present experiment.

Among the Hausa, children of 7 and under frequently used kin terms as primary identifying labels. Yet many of the younger Hausa children, when asked what relationship someone had to them, did not use kin terms at all. In Hawaii, kin terms as primary labels were reserved only for certain persons—mother, father, grandmother, grandfather, and older aunts and uncles—and these labels were applied by all children of all ages. A few of the older children did list just kin categories when asked to name who was in their households. This phenomenon may have been due to their perception of what was wanted in the task, since it does not square with usual kin-term behavior in the village.

The children were also highly accurate in giving an ego-centered kin term for each person on their list. In only two cases did young children point or use perceptual attributes to describe ego-centered relationships. (One then provided kin terms after a probe, and the other, on an inadvertent re-test the next day, used the complete set of kin terms.) With these exceptions, none of the children failed to give kin terms, in contrast to the younger Hausa children.

FURTHER DISCUSSION

At this point we have finished our discussion of the variables mentioned in our first four tables and would like to move on to a discussion of another area of our study, namely patterns in the learning of different kin terms which we feel are also intimately related to Piagetian concepts of the growth of relational thought in children.

Our method in the study was to ask each child other-centered questions about the relationship—one to the other—of pairs of relatives living in this household. For this reason we did not get systematic data on the ability of each child to answer questions about the complete range of kin terms in use in the village. What data we did gather, however, seemed to point to the fact that the ability to use certain terms varies according to the age of the child, the kin term, and the relationship being described by the term. Although our data were scattered and our sample size small, we decided to pursue the matter further in the hope that an investigation of differences in the learning rate for various kin terms might say something about the process of learning kin relations in general. In order to do this, we borrowed from the other studies to supplement our own.

Piaget (1928) investigated only the sibling relationship, as did Elkind (1962) and Greenfield and Childs (Chapter 11). Danziger (1957) studied five different kin terms, as defined by a group of Australian children. He noted that each term moved at a different rate through the same developmental stages, but he did not separate them in his analysis. The Hausa paper by LeVine and Price-Williams (1974) suffers from the same problem. There is one study by Haviland and Clark (1974), however, which provides a rich source of data on this matter on children in California. We will need to delve deeply into this study in order to lay a base for further analysis of our own research.

In this paper Haviland and Clark investigate the ability of 30 children between the ages of 3;5 and 8;10 to define 15 of the basic consanguineal kin terms of the American kinship system. They propose that kin terms do differ in the ease with which various ones are learned. They first consider the possibility that the difficulty with which a term is learned may be tied to the complexity of its semantic components—the "semantic acquisition" hypothesis. They consider two different componential analyses of the American kinship system but point out that both share a problem—namely, that there is no way to measure complexity of terms when only components are considered because they cannot be metrically ordered, and that such a system lacks the feature of reciprocity implicit in all kin terms which is so important to Piagetian notions of the growth of relational thought. They decide instead to substitute a system which will dovetail with the component system, but which will allow for reciprocity and ordering. This system is one of relational components such as "X parent of Y" and the inverse "Y child of X." To this system can be added redundant features such as male/female, adult/child, and so on, which are so often a part of concrete categorical definitions and are often the basis upon which extensions of kin terms to nonrelatives are made in honorary usage.

Haviland and Clark suggest that a measure of relative complexity of relational components will predict which terms will be defined at the highest levels first. Mother, father, son, and daughter—all entries with one relational component—should be simplest and therefore be first. The next easiest group would be terms in which the same component is repeated: grandfather, grandmother, grandson, and granddaughter. Following this group would be brother and sister, which have two different types of relational components. The final group would contain aunt, uncle, niece, nephew, and cousin—with two different components plus recursive rules.

By Haviland's and Clark's statistical analysis, the relative ordering of kin terms according to mean level of definition for each age group does not change. Those terms which are hard for the young remain hard for the older children (Haviland and Clark, 1974, p. 35).:

> . . . a reasonable hypothesis is that less complex terms should be acquired before more complex ones. The less complex terms would therefore go through the three Piagetian stages earlier on in the acquisition process.

Relational complexity of terms appeared to account in large measure for the order in which the terms were learned. It was decided that the terms brother and sister, with two different components each, were perhaps easier than terms with recursive rules also containing two components, because recursive rules may represent a higher level of development of thought in children. By moving the brother and sister terms from third place to second in the complexity scale, Haviland and Clark managed to account for 65% of the variance in kin terms by their complexity hypothesis.

The relational complexity hypothesis would appear to have been resoundingly supported by the results of the analysis of variance. There remains a logical difficulty, however, which needs to be reconciled before this conclusion can be accepted without reservation. The "relational complexity" hypothesis, as we have said, is based upon the notion of learning to define terms by learning their relational components. Haviland and Clark themselves point out that the categorical stage of definition is characterized by attention to the perceptual attributes of classes; relational concepts would therefore not be likely to appear. Yet as mentioned previously, the kin-term learning pattern remains much the same throughout all the stages. How can this result be explained? There are at least three possible solutions which we put forth as suggestions. Both the semantic acquisition (for the categorical stage) and the relational complexity hypothesis (for the relational stage) may work with regard to kin term learning in a parallel fashion to bring a similarity of pattern in all stages. Alternatively, some outside factor such as a cultural emphasis on primary relationships may make learning the relationally simpler terms easier and may underlie the commonalities in patterning at various stages.

Perhaps the most serious and potentially troublesome explanation of the similarities in pattern would be that Haviland and Clark's grouping of the children of slightly differing levels of development within one age group, the youngest age group in particular, has produced a deceptive picture of the patterning of kin terms at the categorical level. Even for the youngest age group (age 3;5 to 5;11) there are children who are able to define some terms at the relational and even the reciprocal-relational levels. These children would weight the scores of these terms toward the higher end of the scale for mean level of definition, and the total higher score would be based on early relational definition of terms. The terms may or may not have also been the first to be defined at the categorical level. Unless a population is sampled in which the children are just beginning to be able to make categorical definitions, one cannot say with certainty which terms will be defined first at that particular stage nor with what speed other terms may move past them to be first at the next stage. While age groupings of children may be used successfully to indicate progressive ability to define kin terms according to age of the child, a study of the pattern of kin term acquisition should group together children of a similar level of ability.

We do not wish to try to choose between explanations at this point in our discussion, but would prefer to turn to an analysis of the data offered in Haviland and Clark's article (1974). We have regrouped the data slightly in order to bring out aspects of it which we feel would be interesting to discuss. In Table 10–5, we have rearranged their frequency counts of kin terms into one comparative table and will simply use the numbers descriptively, which seems reasonable given the relatively small numbers of children for each age level grouping.

Table 10–5
Level of kin-term definition by age group
(adapted from data from Haviland and Clark, 1974)

LEVEL OF DEFINITION

	Age Group 1 (3:5–5:11) N=10						Age Group 2 (6–6:9) N=10						Age Group 3 (7–8:10) N=10					
	P–C	C	R	R–R	R+ R–R	Total Def.	P–C	C	R	R–	R+ R–R	Total Def.	P–C	C	R	R–R	R+ R–R	Total Def.
Mother	1	6	3	0	3	8	1	3	6	0	6	9	0	3	6	1	7	10
Father	2	6	2	0	2	8	2	4	4	0	4	8	0	3	6	1	7	10
Sister	3	4	3	0	3	7	2	5	1	2	3	8	0	3	5	2	7	10
Brother	2	5	1	2	3	8	0	8	2	0	2	10	0	4	2	4	6	10
Daughter	4	4	2	0	2	6	2	6	1	1	2	8	1	3	2	4	6	9
Son	5	3	2	0	2	5	4	4	1	1	2	6	2	3	2	3	5	8
Grandmother	4	6	0	0	0	6	3	5	2	0	2	7	0	3	7	0	7	10
Grandfather	4	6	0	0	0	6	3	5	2	0	2	7	1	2	6	1	7	9
Aunt	7	3	0	0	0	3	4	4	2	0	2	6	4	1	5	0	5	6
Uncle	4	4	2	0	2	6	4	4	2	0	2	6	3	2	5	0	5	7
Granddaughter	7	1	0	2	2	3	5	4	0	1	1	5	3	1	0	6	6	7
Grandson	8	1	0	1	1	2	5	5	0	0	0	5	0	2	1	7	8	10
Niece	9	1	0	0	0	1	6	4	0	0	0	4	6	2	1	1	2	4
Nephew	8	1	1	0	1	2	8	1	1	0	1	2	8	0	1	1	2	2
Cousin	8	1	1	0	1	2	5	4	1	0	1	5	3	2	5	0	5	7
Total Definitions																		

P–C: Number of precategorical definitions given.
C: Number of categorical definitions given.
R: Number of relational definitions given.
R–R: Number of relational-reciprocal definitions given.
R+R–R: Total number of relational and relational-reciprocal definitions given.
Total Definitions: Total number of definitions given above the precategorical stage.

Each age group contains 10 children, each of whom defined the same 15 kin terms, the definitions then being assigned to one of four stages: Stage 1, does not know definition or gives an irrelevant answer; Stage 2, gives a categorical definition based on perceptual attributes of the category; Stage 3, gives a relational definition; Stage 4, gives a relational definition which shows recognition that all kin terms must have a reciprocal to exist as a relation. We have combined some of the stages and then separated them out again, in order to better be able to see where the bulk of answers lie for each term so that we may compare each term with similar terms and then, by separating the stages out again, judge which term is moving ahead first into a new stage.

Our second table, Table 10–6, divides the kin terms by the intersection of adult/child with male/female in a fashion similar to that of most children in the categorical stage of definition.

Table 10–6
Development of kin-term definition by category (Adapted from data from Haviland and Clark, 1974)

Kin term	Age Group 1 (3;5–5;11) N = 10			Age Group 2 (6–6;9) N = 10			Age Group 3 (7–8;10) N = 10			
	1	2	3	1	2	3	1	2	3	
Brother	50	10	20	80	20	0	40	20	40	
Son	30	20	0	40	10	10	30	20	30	
Grandson	10	0	10	50	0	0	20	10	70	Boy
Nephew	10	10	0	10	10	0	20	0	0	
Cousin*	10	10	0	40	10	0	20	50	0	
Sister	40	30	0	50	20	20	30	50	20	
Daughter	40	20	0	60	10	10	30	20	40	Girl
Granddaughter	10	0	20	40	10	10	10	0	60	
Niece	10	0	0	40	0	0	20	10	10	
Father	60	20	0	40	0	0	30	60	10	
Grandfather	60	0	0	50	0	0	20	60	10	Man
Uncle	40	20	0	40	0	0	20	50	0	
Mother	60	30	0	30	0	0	30	60	10	
Grandmother	60	0	0	50	0	0	30	70	0	Woman
Aunt	30	0	0	40	0	0	10	50	0	

Column header note: LEVEL OF DEFINITION

1. % of categorical definitions given for term
2. % of relational definitions given for term
3. % of relational-reciprocal definitions given for term

Kin-term categories within age group may not add to 100%, since precategorical definitions are omitted from consideration.

*A cousin is usually defined by children as a child; we have grouped the term with "boy" terms, arbitrarily.

In our discussion, we attempt to combine the notion that the nuclear family may be an important cultural factor underlying patterns of kin-term definition, with the Piagetian concept of decentration. We also draw ideas from examination of interview material presented by both Piaget (1928) and Danziger (1957) in their kin term studies and from the kin term counts of Haviland and Clark (1974) as well. While we may not refer to Tables 10–5 and 10–6 explicitly at all points in our discussion, our analysis is an attempt to offer explanations for some of the material in these tables and our presentation will follow the age groupings of these two tables. We will also argue that there are important changes in the pattern of kin term definition from one stage of definition to another.

Group Level 1 (age 3; 5–5; 11)

Most of the children of this age group should have started the Piagetian stage of categorical definition of kin terms. There are a few children who are ahead of the categorical stage in making definitions, and these children will be exempted from our remarks and better considered with Group Level 2 children who are leaving the categorical stage of definition and beginning to enter the stage of relational definition.

Children of the categorical stage of definition are said to take their own viewpoint on all matters and to be unable to enter the viewpoint of others. They therefore see kin labels as terms for classes in the absolute sense and offer definitions which are based on perceptual attributes of persons in the category rather than relationships between pairs of kin. These definitions in children of this age usually involve size (adult/child, big/little) and sex (male/female) and are matched to already existing terms for describing such persons—"boy," "girl," "man," "lady," and "baby."

The nuclear family being important in American society as a basic social unit which organizes a child's experience with kin and provides his closest and most important kin relationships, we would expect nuclear terms to be the first to be defined categorically, ahead of the nonnuclear terms. Because of the child's ego-centered view of the world, we would expect ego-centered kin terms to be the first ones to receive categorical definition while terms which are only used reciprocally toward children such as "son," "grandson," and "niece," would receive fewer definitions. The reason that they would receive fewer categorical definitions does not lie with the fact that they are terms which must be seen from the viewpoint of another in order to be defined, for at this stage such reckonings are not needed to make perceptual attribute definitions. We would propose instead that the terms are less salient in the experience of the child, and are heard and used less often than terms such as brother and sister since they do not clash in either usage of definition. It would be expected that of the reciprocals, those in the nuclear family would be most salient and would receive some categorical definitions, although these would not be as numerous as for "brother" and "sister". Brother and sister, if considered in their aspect of reciprocals, would fall under the same expectation, but being used more often than "son" or "daughter" would still be ahead of these other two nuclear family reciprocals.

The important thing to remember with the categorical stage of definition, as we said, is that children see kin labels as attached to individuals on the basis of perceptual attributes rather than relationships. Burling presents us with an illustration of how this works in the nuclear family with reciprocal terms when he discusses his young daughter's use of basic kin terms. His daughter was acquainted with all the basic ego-centered kin terms for the nuclear family and used them correctly. The reciprocals, "son" and "daughter," and the affinal terms, "husband and wife," were attached to their usual recipients, even though she was asked to do the labelling. Thus the child pointed to her mother when asked to point to her "wife" and pointed to her brother as her "son" (Burling, 1970, p. 17).

Group Level 2 (age 6–6; 9)

Children in this age group should be well into the stage of defining terms categorically. With some terms they will be starting to leave the stage of categorical definition; and with a few terms, beginning to make relational definitions.

We would like to suggest that the inception of the relational stage of kin term definition is not at first the result of the ability of the child to realize that there are viewpoints other than his own in the world, but rather arises out of the child's increasing refinement of his categorical-style definitions. At the beginning of the stage of categorical definitions, the child will state, when asked, that all boys are "brothers," all girls "sisters," and that the reverse also holds true. As the stage develops, however, the children seem to become aware of the fact that not all little boys are brothers nor all little girls sisters. There is some increased attention at this point to alternate terms for children (shown in the increase in categorical definitions for reciprocals and "cousin" which is not a pure reciprocal), and there is also increased attention to the fact that some children are not brothers or sisters at all! The children then seem to try to draw from examples and statements made by those around them, a better definition for "brother" or "sister." It seems only natural that the child will have been made aware of certain facts about the brothers that he knows—such as the fact that there are at least two of them, that they are in one family, or that they had the same mother who gave birth to them, or that they live together. The child will then use these facts or a variant version of them to make the kind of definition of brother which Piaget has called relational but not fully reciprocal. It is a definition which involves two persons but is not yet general in its application. Or it is not reciprocal in that only one of the two children involved in the relationship is considered to be a brother. Here is an example of such a definition from Piaget (1928, p. 105):

Hal. (age 9):—*When there is a boy and another boy; when there are two of them.* — Has your father got a brother? —*Yes.* —Why? —*Because he was born second.* — Then what is a brother? —*It is the second brother that comes.* —Then the first is not a brother? —*Oh, no. The second brother that comes is called brother.*

In like fashion, when the child is asked at this stage if a father can be an uncle he will, in the early categorical stage of definition, deny the possibility flatly (Danziger 1957, p. 225). Both terms refer to a male, but the child never applies them to the same male. When asked why father cannot also be an uncle, the child who still has an ego-centered view of the world does not see the possibility that his father could be an uncle in someone else's eyes. Instead he reverts to a statement such as the following when asked if a father can be an uncle (Danziger 1957, pp. 219–220):

Rod. (5;7) —*No.* —Why not? —*Because he's a father.*
Lyn. (6) —*No.* —Why not? —*Because they got children.*
Dia. (7;6) —*No.* —Why not? —*Because we can't have two fathers; we only have to have one. . . . Instead of being a father he's an uncle.*

Given the primacy of the parental roles in the child's life, it seems likely that the relationship between a mother and father and their children would be the first to be officially noticed and formulated in alternative definitions for brother and sister terms and in resolving the illogicalities arising from the fact that in the real world an uncle can be a father while by the child's rules of definition they cannot both be the same person.

Group Level 3 (age 7–8; 10)

In Piaget's sample, children of 8 were capable of taking other-centered points of view while children of 9 were also able to make correct relational and reciprocal definitions of terms. Not until the age of 10 however, were they able to take both someone else's point of view and their own simultaneously in order to view themselves as an object. Therefore we might judge that this group of children has probably just entered the stage of making relational definitions and is starting to make definitions which are both reciprocal and relational.

When the child comes to realize that a person viewed by another often has a different kin label, he is able to respond differently to the question of whether or not a father can be an uncle. He now may respond as these children did (Danziger, 1957, pp. 226–227):

Mar. (7;9) —How does a man come to be an uncle? —*He was someone's father and he was another little girl's uncle.*
Law. (7;6) —Can a father be an uncle? —*Yes.* —How is that? —*He could be an uncle to someone else.* —Is your father an uncle? —*Yes.* —Whose uncle? —*My cousin's.*

With this shift of viewpoint, we would expect that the child would begin to make relational definitions for his ego-centered kin, but that these definitions need not involve reciprocity.

There is a second area in which the ideas of the child seem to change. When children of the categorical stage of thought are asked whether or not their father is a brother, some of them will at first deny the possibility—even when a counterexample exists in their own families—and then finally admit the real facts under pressure, as in the following case (Piaget, 1928, p. 105):

Kan. (age 7;6) —*It's a boy.* —Are all boys brother? —*Yes.* —Is your father a brother? —*No.* —Why? —*Because he is a man.* —Isn't your father a brother? —*Yes.* —Why? —*Because he used to be the same as little boys.*

Others will say that their father is a brother but then admit that he has no sister or brother at present. In each case, the child seems to reason thus: A father is a man and a brother is a boy. Father was once a young boy, therefore father was once a brother, and this is the explanation for why it is said he is a brother, although he is not a brother now. Asked when father stopped being a brother, or mother stopped being a sister, children say it was when he or she got married (Danziger, 1957, p. 223). As the child achieves an other-centered viewpoint, however, he comes to realize how it is that fathers are still "brother"—as seen from the point of view of members of the father's nuclear family of orientation. The concept "brother" is now being freed of its total dependency on perceptual attributes for definition and coming to rely more on relational attributes.

One of the most noticeable characteristics of the definitions of these Group Level 3 children is the large increase in the number of definitions which are both reciprocal and relational. The other outstanding characteristic (as Haviland and Clark realize) is that these relational and reciprocal definitions are all associated with terms which are used reciprocally toward the child. In Group Level 1, the five relational-reciprocal definitions are of this sort, and in Group Level 2, the same is true. In Group Level 3, 29 out of the 31 definitions are thus. The other three relational-reciprocal definitions are of important ego-centered terms. We might suggest that these terms have started to follow along the path marked off by the reciprocal terms.

We would conclude that the association of relational-reciprocal definitions with reciprocal kin terms is connected to the child's newfound ability to take two viewpoints simultaneously and see himself as an object, and we would concur with Haviland and Clark that he may find this easier to do at first with roles and positions which he or other children hold. Haviland and Clark note that grandchildren terms receive a large number of reciprocal-relational definitions but only one purely relational one. Because other reciprocal terms receive many relational definitions, the grandchild terms are considered aberrant, but Haviland and Clark do not see a ready explanation. We would like to offer the suggestion that it may be the absence of alternative relational descriptions, alternatives which exist for other reciprocal pairs of terms, which force the child to make purely reciprocal definitions for these grandchild terms. For example, a daughter can be somebody's little girl or little child, but a granddaughter cannot be the child or little girl of her grandmother or grandfather. Even at the stage where a child produces definitions which are dependent upon linkages among kin terms, even where the child produces definitions dependent on facts of birth and marriage and which show a concept of linked nuclear families which interdigitate to form a kinship system, and even where the child is conversant with using the "primitive" terms of the system as Haviland and Clark call them—mother, father, sister, and brother, to define other terms, we would not expect to hear that a granddaughter was a "daughter's daughter." The referent point in common American definitional usage is not the other-centered term, but the ego-centered term. Thus a child conversant with the kin system may define a niece (Haviland and Clark, 1974, p. 38) by saying:

(56) Q. What's a niece?
A. A niece is like a mother had a sister, and I'd be her niece.

Niece and nephew terms seem to receive little attention from children at any level of definition. It would be interesting to see if, when they are defined, they go against Danziger's observation that all kin terms progress through all stages of definition without skipping to the level at which the child is presently operating, for it seems likely that children will be fairly sophisticated before they make relational types of definitions for these terms. We would suggest that a cultural factor explanation be sought for the relative lack of interest in these two terms.

Husband and wife terms should also become more important as the relational-reciprocal stage of definition progresses, because affinal terms are important in linking nuclear families together—as many of the statements the children make seem to implicitly recognize. They are also necessary for an appreciation of the finer points of the definition of aunts, uncles, and grandparents.

As the relational-reciprocal stage of definition progresses, we would expect to find increasing dependence of kin term definitions on relations among kin and genealogical linkage such that the children's definitional systems would begin to resemble systems held by other members of their society.

We will now attempt to quickly summarize the pattern which we think is revealed in kin term learning at the three age group levels, and express our feeling that it shows the interplay of factors such as child terms versus adult terms, nuclear family terms versus non-nuclear family terms, and ego-centered terms versus reciprocals.

At Group Level 1, ego-centered nuclear family terms lead in the number of categorical definitions given—counting the relational level of definition in with the categorical, since each relational definition implies a previous stage of categorical definition, according to Danziger (1957). (It cannot, of course, be said that these terms were the first to enter the categorical stage of definition.) The other ego-centered terms follow this first group and the reciprocals are behind—first those of the nuclear family and then the non-nuclear ones. The "aunt" term receives a very low frequency of definition and relative to it, the "uncle" term is quite high—a difference which it might prove interesting to explore. The tendency of terms to move in male/female pairs such as grandmother/grandfather, especially as children grow older, should also be noted. This tendency could be hypothesized to be traceable to a semantic acquisition factor or to a cultural one, given the close association of such pairs in American kinship thought.

At Group Level 2, much the same pattern prevails, but children have begun to work more on categorical definitions of children terms while adult categorical definition rates remain steady. Two of the adult terms, mother and father of the nuclear family, are surging ahead to be defined at the relational stage of definition. At this point, we might propose that these are the first two terms into the relational stage of definition.

In Group Level 3, several different patterns can be seen in the data, and it could be read in several different ways. Adult terms could be divided off from children terms, the former showing an increase in relational definitions generally and the latter an increase in reciprocal ones. The grandparent relational count and the grandchild reciprocal count might or might not be an instance of learning of a term and its reciprocal as a pair; certainly aunt/uncle and nephew/niece do not perform in this way, but judging from what little data are available on the matter in child interviews, children consider the aunt/uncle terms to be quite closely related to the cousin term and this connection may be the one being emphasized at this point in definitional learning. Looking solely at the relational definitions, parents and grandparents are ahead, with the aunt-uncle-cousin triad somewhat behind and the children terms further behind. Looking at the matter from the point of view of relational-reciprocal definitions, however, grandchildren are far ahead, with the nuclear family children terms behind them (all of these terms having a reciprocal component) but adult terms have almost no such definitions and niece and nephew as usual are virtually ignored. Cousin has no reciprocal definitions despite the fact that it is a reciprocal definition at this stage.

It is probable that several more interpretations of the data could be read from these tables, but we think that we have made our point that interpretation of the process of learning kin terms is a complex business in which hypotheses should still be subject to question and further investigation.

Some of our reservations about total reliance on a relational complexity hypothesis might be said to concern matter of "psychological reality." While an explanation need not have psychological reality in order to be a "good" one or in order to predict behavior, it could be argued that an assumption is being made here that relational components of various sorts differ in the ease with which they are combined in definitions and learned by children. In that case, it seems that it might be wise to discover just how these relational components seem to enter into definitional usage and whether they combine with other mechanisms of learning, such as the Piagetian concepts. Another idea would be to examine the way in which relational components are typically defined and used by children to see if there is a pattern. Greenfield and Childs (Chapter 11, this volume) have pointed out that a sibling relationship might be seen as two "child of" units, and we have also noted in the Danziger (1957) and Piaget (1928) interview data that children seem to view siblings as two similar units that arise from a similar act of birth from the same mother, rather than one relational component of parentage and another of birth.

We feel also, from our reading of interview material, that relational components may start to enter into kin term learning to a slight extent in the relational stage of definition and to a greater extent in the relational-reciprocal stage of definition, but that their impact varies from very little at the beginning of the relational-reciprocal stage—where Piagetian concepts of decentration seem to aid in the explanation of the kin term learning pattern (with cultural factors being a possible added item)—to a greater role as the child becomes more facile with kin-dependent definitions. It is also clear from interview material that kin-term learning is not a straightforward process, but consists of many small steps in which the child seems to be trying to separate out various of the terms on the basis of the examples to which they are applied in his everyday life, and to make sense of the combinations which they make when they meet at the nexus of one individual in the system. Two examples of this are the following taken from Haviland and Clark (1974, p. 38):

(54) Q. What's a father?
    A. An uncle's brother.

(55) Q. What's a son?
    A. A son is a father or a mother's boy.
    Q. Are you a son?
    A. Yes, a son is a brother of a daughter or of another brother.

And last but not least, it would be interesting to investigate what role the "primitives" of the kin term system—mother, father, sister, and brother—have in the comprehension, learning, storing, and production of kin terms in the American system.

Our first analysis of our sample of terms from Hawaiian children in which we sought to find a pattern in the usage of the various terms, relied on many of the same sorts of concepts which we discussed in our analysis of Haviland and Clark's data. We made a division of our terms in the following way. First we divided off the other-centered terms which are used in the same way that the child uses his own set of ego-centered terms (terms for relationships which the child's siblings hold towards others—since both the child and his sibling share the same set of terms for kin). Next we divided off reciprocal terms used toward the child's siblings which we considered might be more difficult, involving as they do the ability to view the self (or here, the sibling replacement) as object in a relationship. We also marked off other-centered usage of terms in which the child's own set of ego-centered terms for persons competed with the other-centered terms, on the theory that the conflict in labels for the same person would make such terms more difficult—especially for the younger children—both to learn as examples and to use. In addition, we divided off other-centered terms which the child does not use himself at this age,—except perhaps for occasional reference—and which are not reciprocals used toward him, such as "husband" and "wife" and other affinal terms. Our reason was that these terms would also compete with the child's ego-centered terms for such relationships, and hence make these terms more difficult for him to learn and use. Unfortunately, we did not have a really good distribution of cases in all of the categories and the numbers are somewhat small for a good comparison; but the table we made did seem to indicate some differences in the rate of correct usage for the various groups of terms. At this point, however, not too much weight should be assigned to our groupings without support from other sources.

Table 10–7
Other-centered term usage

	OTHER-CENTERED TERM USAGE			
Age group	1	2	3	4
1. (age 4–6)	57	*	20	*
2. (age 7–8)	77	*	*	40
3. (age 9–14)	100	89	78	75

1. Like terms: Percentage of correct use of other-centered terms when term was the same as the ego-centered term used by the child for that relation.
2. Unlike terms: Percentage of correct use of other-centered terms when term differed from ego-centered term used by the child for that relation.
3. Reciprocals: Percentage of correct use of other-centered terms when term used to name a relation was most often used reciprocally toward the child.
4. Affinal terms: Percentage of correct use of other-centered affinal terms by the child.
*$N < 5$

Turning now to the usage of terms by age group, and comparing our data with that for Haviland and Clark's groups (keeping in mind of course that usage and definition are different kinds of tasks and may vary in their level of performance by the same child) we found the following: For the youngest children who were able to produce accurate lists of ego-centered terms, some could not define *tutu*, even when a grandmother was resident in the household. This indicated that they could apply the term before they would attempt to define it categorically. This fact lends some support to Greenfield's and Childs's contention (Chapter 11) that their results "suggest that children learn kin terms as labels for specific relations before the labels themselves are organized into the conceptual components revealed in their errors of commission." In short, children use terms correctly before they can even begin to define them.

Children to about age 7—which is the age range where categorical definitions predominated in Haviland and Clark's study—all were able to say how their siblings were related to one another; and also managed to get a few of the other nuclear family relationships correct (although there was no pattern to these other successes); but they could not name relationships for persons not living in the household.

Children of 7 and 8—who if they matched Haviland and Clark's groups would increasingly be making definitions of a relational type—are scoring in the 70th percentile for correct use of other-centered terms. When their mistakes are analyzed, many of the errors seem to involve situations in which the child is being asked about a reciprocal relationship with one of his siblings. While technically it might be expected that the child should be able to place himself in the place of the "other" into generating a term for his sibling (who is, after all, not the child himself), the children appeared to find this task difficult. For example, one child (age 7;5) knew the relationship of his mother to his sister, but not that of his sister to his father, for which he replied simply, "Don't know." Another girl (8;4), when asked, "Theresa (sister) is your mother's ———?" responded, "Mother," in a reversal of the reciprocal pair terms. Children of this age had no trouble with other-centered relationships which did not involve use of a reciprocal term, even such relationships as that between a pair of uncles who were siblings. It would appear that a child asked about the relationship of his parent to his sibling more readily takes the view-point of his sibling, perhaps because the sibling is a child, too; but he is then unable to reverse his viewpoint to take the position of his parent.

By the age of 9—the age just beyond that of Haviland's and Clark's Group Level 3, which has started to make relational type definitions and is beginning to add reciprocal-relational definitions,—the children of our Hawaiian group were regularly attaining scores of 100% on their lists of other-centered kin terms. Their few mistakes, interestingly enough, continued to be with the use of reciprocal terms, but now they occurred mostly when the relationship involved a grandparent and the child's sibling, not parent and sibling. For example, one boy (age 10;6) stated that his father was his grandmother's "mother," in a repetition of the same kind of error which we described for a reciprocal relation in the stage before. Another girl considered her sister to be her grandmother's "daughter." By the age of 12½, however, as we have indicated before, the children were able to handle extremely complex relations with ease, and many of them were even able to explain fairly complex cousin relationships when called upon to do so. It is also at about this age—or earlier—that parents instruct the children on how various relatives are actually connected to them, rather than instructing the child merely to "behave toward so-and-so as an auntie."

One of the most interesting things about the responses made by children who were asked about the relationship between their parents was the variation in the answers. Such variation was not elicited by any of the consanguineal relationships. The youngest child in the sample could not make an answer to the question about this relationship but instead attempted to describe the role of his father as "father." This answer could be considered to show an egocentric viewpoint on the part of the child. Another boy of 8 applied the terms which he uses egocentrically toward his parents—"mommy" and "daddy"—to describe their relationship. So strong is the habit of viewing parents in this fashion, apparently, that a girl of 12½ who otherwise described accurately the extremely complex relationships in a household she visited, responded with "Mom" and "Dad." The fact that two terms are used in these answers seems indicative that a relationship between the two persons is recognized, but that the child's ego-centered kin labels intrude.

Other answers about the parents' affinal relationship also showed that the children were aware, at least from the age of 6, that the relationship between their parents was not of the same sort as that pertaining between consanguineal kin. Answers given with regards to the relationship between parents varied from "married" to citing the father's last name linked to the mother's maiden name (on at least two different occasions). Perhaps these responses are another indication of an early use of some concept of "family"; we also encounter this concept among the youngest children when analyzing the semantic components in their errors for naming other-centered kin. It was not until age 9 that children began to alternate use of the response "married" with the correct affinal terms.

It is interesting to note here that Haviland and Clark's Group Level 3 children (7–8;10) had a very high number of relational definitions for grandparent terms and relational-reciprocal definitions for the grandchild terms. Either the Hawaiian children are behind the mainland group in the development of the grandparent/grandchild concept, or, more importantly, it may be that use no longer lags behind definitional ability in the application of certain types of terms in the higher stages in kin term concept development.

A second point to make in regard to the errors of our older group of children (9–14;3), is that relational concepts such as "lineality" and "affinality" were maintained in errors. This finding lends support to Haviland's and Clark's hypothesis that relational components have a role in kin-term learning, although it should be pointed out that this group is an older group and the exact nature of the connection between relational components used as concepts, and relational components used to make up the definition of a term in the learning of kin terms, needs to be explored further.

As Greenfield and Childs point out in their article (Chapter 11), the analysis of terms which are incorrectly applied to a relationship may be a fruitful source of insights into the progress of development in the child's thinking about kin terms. It is not quite the same as asking the child for a definition, because the child might not have mentioned, and might not have been asked about, the particular kin relationship being labeled. For instance, children in our sample correctly apply the term "brother" to their siblings and even to siblings in other families. They also, on occasion, applied the "brother" term inappropriately as for a relationship between an uncle and a nephew who dwelt in the same household.

Almost 60% of the errors made by the Hawaiian children were errors of commission, as compared with only 11% among Greenfield and Childs' Zinacantecan sample. Children who answered incorrectly were just as likely as others to also answer "Don't know" to some of the questions. Therefore the difference between errors of commission and errors of omission does not seem to lie in a personality difference between individual children.

Greenfield and Childs noted that the first distinction to emerge among young Zinacantecan children in applying a kin term incorrectly was that of common parentage. Sex distinctions emerged slightly later, while relative age and remaining-within-the-reciprocal-pair were seldom retained at any age. They suggest that it may not be a categorical feature which emerges first in learning of a term, but the common feature which is the core of a set of terms. Common parents are common to all sibling terms.

Children in Hawaii perform very similarly to the Zinacantecan children, (although they always maintain correct sex in their usage), in that they maintain a rule of "common household" (rather than common parentage) which they follow in assigning terms. For example, persons who lived in the same household unit are labeled "brothers" and "sisters," while persons of two different household units are typically "cousins". Greenfield and Childs consider such use of "core features" of categories to be another instance pointing toward learning by examples.

It is also the case that Hawaiian children, like the Zinacantecan children who ignore the culturally important principle of relative age, ignore their own culturally relevant kinship principle of generational seniority. It may be that the influence of such cultural distinctions is not to be sought in the "natural" and perhaps universal types of definitions made by younger children, but only emerges later at the most sophisticated level of definition, when many other cultural rules in the kinship system also appear.

What is the role of individual experience in shaping the acquisition of kin-term definitions? Apparently very little with regard to which kin terms will be defined first. Despite the fact that Greenfield and Childs concluded that children seem to learn by example, and Danziger found evidence that the children he interviewed incorporated examples from their real world in their definitions (which nevertheless showed a remarkable similarity to each other), Haviland and Clark collected extensive data on the experience of each child in their sample with a range of relatives, and concluded that this experience in no way affected the child's performance with different kin terms. Our data also indicated no apparent difference in performance between children who live in nuclear families and those who live in nonnuclear families, even though approximately half of the latter did not have their real nuclear kin in residence. Piaget commented, with regard to the ability of only children to define sibling terms: "It is a remarkable thing that there is no noticeable difference between only children and others," (1928, p. 106). Apparently children can be aware of important kin relationships in their society whether or not they have direct firsthand experience with such relationships. We might hypothesize that there is a small but necessary amount of experience which children need in order to learn kin terms, but this experience does not seem to be difficult for most children to acquire in their natural settings, one way or another.

One case from our study, involving two girls living *hanai* in a complex family with their grandparents and many sister/cousins, brother/uncles, sister/aunts, brother/cousins, cohabiting "spouses," and their siblings, suggests that there may also be another basic requisite for learning kin terms from examples. These two girls both use many fictional terms for the relationships within their *hanai* family. The two of them, one age 7 and the other age 10;11, do quite poorly in applying other-centered terms to relationships and their mistakes cannot be reconciled with the system of fictional usages; it is also true that neither of these girls can even define *tutu*, although only two other children in our sample who are older than the 7-year-old fail to do so. It may therefore be the case that if children learn their culture's system of kin-term use through examples around them, they need to have the terms used in a consistent fashion—when they are applied to actual relatives—so that some pattern emerges that is comprehensible to the child.

In conclusion, we would like to suggest that many aspects of the Piagetian concept of the development of relational thinking in children remain to be explored as they apply to the learning of kin terms. The broad stages of kin-term learning have been established for both Western and non-Western cultures, by various studies. There is now need to investigate not only comprehension, but the definition and use of kinship terms—simultaneously. There is also a need to gather data on the whole range of terms—the affinal terms along with the consanguineal ones—since kin terms are part of a system and birth and marriage together form the building blocks of kinship systems in all societies. The investigative work should be done not only in Western societies, but in societies whose family structure and kin-term system differ radically from the Western pattern, so that ideas which have originated from examining Western data can be put to a cross-cultural test.

ACKNOWLEDGEMENTS

We wish to thank Ms. Jill Korbin and Mr. Frank Newton for their assistance in providing us with census and kinship terminology in the village studied. The research work upon which this article was based was supported mainly by a grant from the Carnegie Corporation of New York. It was also supported in part by PHS grant # HD 04612, NICHD, Mental Retardation Research Center; and by U.S. PHS-NIH # HD 00345.

REFERENCES

Beaglehole, E. (1937) *Some modern Hawaiians.* Honolulu: University of Hawaii
. Research Publications.
Berry, J. W. (1969) On cross-cultural comparability. *International Journal of Psychology, 4*, 119–128.
Boggs, S. (1972) The meaning of questions and narratives to Hawaiian children. *In* C. Cazden, D. Hymes, and V. John (Eds.), *Function of language in the classroom.* New York: Teachers College Press.
Burling, R. (1964) Cognition and componential analysis: God's truth or hocus-pocus? *American Anthropologist, 66*, 20–28.
Burling, R. (1970) American kinship terms once more. *Southwestern Journal of Anthropology, 26*, 15–24.
Cole, M. and Scribner, S. (1974) *Culture and thought: A psychological introduction.* New York: John Wiley and Sons, Inc.
Danziger, K. (1957) The child's understanding of kinship terms: a study in the development of relational concepts. *Journal of Genetic Psychology, 91*, 213–232.
Elkind, D. (1962) Children's conception of brother and sister: Piaget replication study V. *Journal of Genetic Psychology, 100*, 129–136.
Gallimore, R., Boggs, J. W., and Jordan, C. E. (1974) *Culture, behavior, and education.* Beverly Hills, California: Sage Publications.
Hammond, O. (1973) *Cultural learning and complex behavioral stimuli.* Unpublished doctoral disertation, University of Hawaii.
Handy, E. S. C., and Pukui, M. K. (1972) *The Polynesian family system in Ka-'u, Hawaii.* Tokyo: Charles E. Tuttle Company.
Haviland, S., and Clark, E. (1974) "This man's father is my father's son": a study of the acquisition of English kin terms. *Journal of Child Language, 1*, 23–47.
Heighton, R. H., Jr. (n.d.) *Some problems relating to the organization and disorganization of the Hawaiian domestic system* (Unpublished paper).
Howard, A. (1971) *Households, families and friends in a Hawaiian–American community.* Paper No. 19, working papers of the East-west Population Institution, Honolulu.
Kenn, C. W. (1939) Some Hawaiian relationship terms re-examined. *Social process in Hawaii, 5*, 46–50.

Labov, W. (1971) *Finding out about children's language*. Paper presented at annual meeting of Hawaii Council of Teachers of English, Honolulu.

LeVine, R. A., and Price-Williams, D. R. (1974) Children's kinship concepts: Cognitive development and early experience among the Hausa. *Ethnology, 13*, 25–44.

Mays, M. (1973) *Coming Together: A conflict resolution theme in Hawaiian–American families*. Report for the 299 Task Force, Honolulu. Unpublished paper.

Piaget, J. (1926) *The language and thought of the child*. London: Routledge and Kegan Paul.

Piaget, J. (1928) *Judgment and reasoning in the child*. London: Routledge and Kegan Paul.

Price-Williams, D. R., and LeVine, R. A. (1974) Left-right orientation among Hausa children: A methodological note. *Journal of Cross-Cultural Psychology, 5*, 356–363.

Price-Williams, D. R. Hammond, O. W., Walker, M., Edgerton, C., and Newton, F. (1974) *Kinship concepts and relational thinking among rural Hawaiian children*. American Psychological Association (Abstract).

Sanday, P. (1971) Analysis of the psychological reality of American–English kin terms in an urban poverty environment. *American Anthropologist, 73*, 555–570.

Tyler, S. A. (Ed.) (1969) *Cognitive anthropology*. New York: Holt, Rinehart and Winston.

Wallace, A. F. C. (1965) The problem of the psychological validity of componential analysis. *American Anthropologist, 67*, 229–248.

Yamamura, D. S. (1941) *A study of some of the factors in the education of the child of Hawaiian ancestry in Hana, Maui*. University of Hawaii. M.A. Thesis, Unpublished.

11
Understanding Sibling Concepts: A Devlopmental Study of Kin Terms in Zinacantan

PATRICIA MARKS GREENFIELD
and **CARLA P. CHILDS**

How do children acquire the semantic categories around which their social interaction is organized? What role is played by universal aspects of human development? How is this process influenced by specific cultural factors which vary from society to society? These questions were the focus of our study of the development of kinship terms among the Zinacantecos. We chose the conceptual domain of kinship because of its importance to the Zinacantecos, a Mayan group living in the highlands of southern Mexico. We wanted to avoid the ethnocentric bias inherent in studying conceptual development in a domain that is of importance in the investigator's own culture, but irrelevant to the people being studied.

We chose to study the development of comprehension rather than production or definition of kin terms because of its ontogenetic primacy (e.g. Fraser, Bellugi, and Brown, 1963). In this way, we hoped to maximize the performance of each child, thus approaching the child's underlying competence in the conceptual domain of kinship.

At the time of our data collection there existed four main strands of pertinent theory and research, two from psychology emphasizing universal processes of human development, and two from anthropology emphasizing cultural variation.

PIAGETIAN THEORY AND RESEARCH

Research on kinship concepts from the point of view of universal processes of human development stems from Piaget (1928). He questioned children about their families and about families in general, focusing particularly on the concept of "brother". Piaget sees this concept as requiring the logic of relations. A child who has not yet developed the logic of relations will see himself as having a brother X, but will not realize that he is also X's brother. According to Piaget's theoretical analysis, the child's difficulty in handling the logic of relations is a consequence of egocentrism: the child assumes his own point of view on the situation.

To understand a relation—that for instance of brother to brother—means thinking of at least two points of view at the same time, those of each of the brothers. Absolute notions like those of "boy," etc., presuppose only one point of view. The judgment "Paul is a boy" remains the same whatever may be the perspective adopted. (Piaget, 1928, pp. 91–92).

In Piaget's work, the development of a logic of relations which can be applied to sibling concepts is assessed through a number of different question sets. Each one reveals decentration, a movement away from egocentrism. Most similar to the questions we used is the set illustrated by the following excerpt from an interview with Raoul (age 4), who has one older brother, Gerald, age 7 (Piaget, 1928, p. 84):

— Raoul, have you any brothers?
— Gerald.
— And has Gerald a brother?
— No, only me has a brother.

Raoul cannot shift from his own point of view to answer the question about Gerald's brother. His answer is therefore an egocentric one. Piaget (1928, p. 103) comments that,

. . . in the case of his own family it is not enough for him to enter into the point of view of others, he must also look at *himself* from the point of view of others, which is twice as difficult [Italics added by authors.]

Piaget also says that children often show knowledge of reciprocal relations among siblings in another family before being able to answer the question that is so difficult for Raoul. From this one can infer that it would be easier to conceptualize a reciprocal relation between two siblings than between oneself and a sibling. Extrapolating from Piaget, we can formulate three *cumulative* stages in children's comprehension of sibling relations within their own family:

1. *Egocentrism*: Children understand kinship terms from their own perspective.

2. *Reciprocity*: Children's understanding of kinship terms reflects knowledge of the relationships between two of their siblings from both points of view.

3. *Reversibility*: Children's understanding of kin terms reflects knowledge of a relationship from two points of view even when they are part of it; they can now reverse their own perspective on a relationship.

Our study of the development of kinship concepts among the Zinacantecos tests the validity of these stages for a much more complex system of sibling terms existing in a completely different type of cultural milieu.

At the time we began to collect our data, Piaget's findings with Swiss children had been replicated in two other European cultures with the same basic kinship system as Piaget's Swiss sample—Australia (Danziger, 1957) and the United States (Elkind, 1962). Danziger also extended Piaget's developmental description beyond "brother" to other English kin terms like "aunt" and "uncle."

The first data on the development of kinship terms in an entirely different kind of culture were collected in Nigeria by LeVine and Price-Williams (1974) simultaneously with our data collection. Their interviews with Hausa children from 4 to 11 focused on kin relations existing in each child's compound, the Hausa's most salient unit of kin affiliation. Like Danziger, LeVine and Price-Williams did not limit themselves to sibling relations, but their questions were different. Children were asked to list the people in their compound. They were then asked "who is" each person on the list, and, if no kin term was given, "How is he related to you?" Responses to these questions were used as a measure of egocentric use of kin terms.[1] Next, children were asked, for each successive pair of people named, "How is this person related to that one?" Responses to this question were considered an index of other-centered use of kin terms. LeVine and Price-Williams found that ego-centered usage preceded other-centered, thus demonstrating in another way Piaget's process of decentration. Because the Hausa children were asked about each kin relation from only one point of view, however, this study does not yield direct information on the development of reciprocity or reversibility of kinship concepts. That is, a participant in their study would be asked "How is X related to Y?," but not "How is Y related to X?" and "How is X related to you?" but not "How are you related to X?"

Our study has two important points in common with that of LeVine and Price-Williams: (1) It asks children about kin relations in their own households. (2) It tests whether the acquisition of kin terms involves a decentration process. At the same time our study contrasts with theirs in several respects: (1) It focuses directly on reciprocity and reversibility. (2) Our procedure tests comprehension rather than production of kin terms. Whereas Hausa participants were asked to produce a kinship term ("How is X related to Y?"), Zinacanteco subjects were given a kinship term and asked to produce a name ("What is the name of X's brother?"). (3) Zinacanteco households are stable and generally limited to the nuclear family. Hence we were able to judge the accuracy with which sibling terms were understood. Hausa compounds, in contrast, have shifting membership and include extended family members, while kin terms are collaterally extended. LeVine and Price-Williams were therefore not able to judge the accuracy with which such sibling terms were used.

MEMORY

The second strand of psychological research indicates that the development of memory is a cognitive universal. Many studies show that the memory of American children increases with age (e.g., Hagen, 1972). Cross-cultural studies have made the same point for cultures as diverse as the Kpelle of Liberia (Cole, Gay, Glick, and Sharp, 1971) and rural Ladinos in Guatemala (Kagan et al., 1973). Cole et al. show, however, that memory development only shows up if the materials to be remembered are relevant to the people being tested. Kinship knowledge fits this criterion.

Because family size varies in Zinacantan and because larger families require the child to remember more relations, we were able to study the role of memory factors in our kinship task.

COMPONENTIAL ANALYSIS

The third strand of theory and research, componential analysis, comes from anthropology. It emphasizes variable cultural factors, in focusing on linguistic sources of variation in kinship terms. Componential analysis is a technique from cognitive anthropology which attempts to reveal the conceptual relations within a semantic domain by analyzing its terminology into dimensional components. Cross-cultural analysis of a given domain like kinship shows that different terminological systems involve different conceptual dimensions. From a psychological point of view, one can then ask whether these conceptual dimensions have psychological reality for the people who speak the language.[2] If so, then one would expect them to come into play in the development process by which children learn kinship terms. One of the goals of our study was to see whether or not this would be the case.

Our article focuses on sibling terms because, from the point of view of componential analysis, they constitute a particularly interesting subset of Zinacanteco kinship terms. At the outset of our study, two componential analyses of Zinacanteco sibling terms had been worked out by J. Collier (1969). One analysis is presented in Figure 11–1.

	SIBLING			
	OLDER		YOUNGER	
	THAN REFERENCE POINT			
	FEMALE	MALE	FEMALE	MALE
FEMALE REFERENCE POINT **MALE**	**VISH** (girl's or boy's older sister)	**SHIBNEL** (girl's older brother) **BANKIL** (boy's older brother)	**MUK** (girl's younger sibling) **ISHLEL** (boy's younger sister)	**IZ'IN** (boy's younger brother)

Figure 11–1. Componential analysis of Zinacanteco system of sibling terms of reference

It is based on three dimensions, sex of reference point, sex of sibling, and age of sibling relative to reference point. That is to say, a Zinacanteco speaker would use a different word to describe a sibling depending upon whether the speaker is male or female, and whether the sibling is male or female, and younger or older. Distinctions in two of these semantic components or dimensions are, however, incompletely realized, as Figure 11–1 shows. Sex of reference point is not distinguished in the term for older sister, which is the same for both male and female reference points. Sex of sibling is not distinguished in naming a female's younger sibling; the basic term *muk* applies to younger siblings, both boys and girls. It can, however, be modified to specify sex by the addition of *kreb* (boy) or *zeb* (girl). If these semantic components or dimensions guide the acquisition process, then one might expect the child's comprehension of the terms at different stages to reflect the gradual acquisition of the three semantic components.

A second possible way in which semantic components might be

reflected in the acquisition process would be that componentially more complex terms would be learned before componentially simpler ones. For instance, *bankil* (boy's older brother) and *shibnel* (girl's older brother) are componentially more complex than *vish* (older sister), which does not involve the component, sex of reference point.

The other componential analysis (Collier, 1969) is present in Figure . 11–2.

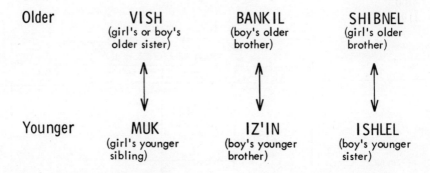

← → indicates a reciprocal pair of terms: e.g., if you are my SHIBNEL, I am your ISHLEL.

Figure 11–2. Componential analysis of Zinacanteco sibling terms based on two dimensions

This one is based on reciprocity and relative age. The relative age dimension is the same as in the three dimensional analysis of Figure 11–1 but the two sex dimensions have been replaced by a reciprocity component. Two terms, p and q, are in a reciprocal relation to each other, if, where A and B are two people, the proposition *A's p is B* is the inverse *B's q is A*. Here is an example from English sibling terms:

$$A = Sarah$$
$$B = Jeremy$$
$$p = brother$$
$$q = sister$$

A's (Sarah's) p (brother) is B (Jeremy) B's (Jeremy's) q (sister) is A (Sarah). Hence "brother" and "sister" are a reciprocal pair of terms.

This model substitutes one relational component, reciprocity, for two categorical components, sex of ego and sex of sibling. Since all terms now have the same number of components, this model reduces all to the same componential complexity. Hence, our prediction from this model would be that all terms would develop at the same rate. This prediction differs from that derived from the first model.

Another issue in the relation of lexicon to psychological use of terms relates to the status of descriptive terms. We included two descriptive terms: *muk kreb* "girl's younger brother") and *muk zeb* ("girl's younger sister"). Brown and Lenneberg's (1954) codability argument says that shorter terms are more codable and therefore easier to retrieve and use. If a concept can be expressed in a single word, in a particular language it is thought to be more salient in that particular culture than another concept which must be expressed by a phrase. Extending the codability argument to acquisition, one would predict that a compound term like *muk kreb* ("girl's younger brother") would be harder to learn than a simple term like *iz'in* ("boy's younger brother").

On the other hand, we conceived of arguments which would lead to the opposite prediction. *Muk kreb* includes the term *kreb*, "boy," which makes explicit the fact that the referent is a boy. This explicitness about the sex of referent component could make such a term easier to learn and to use. The inclusion of two descriptive terms *muk kreb* ("girl's younger brother") and *muk zeb* ("girl's younger sister") allowed us to study the effect of compound terms on the acquisition of kinship terminology.

After our data were collected, a third type of componential analysis was suggested as a model of children's development of English kin terms by Haviland and Clark (1974). They tested the psychological validity of a system of componential analysis (developed by Bierwisch) for describing the development of children's definitions of English kin terms. Their system makes fairly good predictions about the relative developmental difficulty of different terms (e.g., mother, aunt) and about stages in the acquisition of particular terms. Applying their system to Zinacanteco kin terms, we emerge with the following componential analysis: we first represent X's relationship to Y.

vish: [Y child of A & B] (A & B parents of X] [X older than Y] [female X]

Two inverse rules are necessary to derive the reciprocal term:

[W parent of Z] ⇔ [Z child of W]
[U younger than V] ⇔ [V older than U]

Applying these rules, we get Y's relationship to X:

muk: [X child of A & B] [A & B parents of Y] [Y younger than X]
    [female X]

Other pairs can be similarly defined.

bankil: [Y child of A & B] [A & B parents of X] [X older than Y] [male
    X] [male Y]

Again, the application of the two inverse rules yields the reciprocal term,
Iz'in (boy's younger brother).

iz'in: [X child of A & B] [A & B parents of Y] [Y younger than X] [male
    X] [male Y]

The last pair of Zinacanteco sibling terms *shibnel* ("girl's older brother")
and *ishlel* ("boy's younger sister") would look like this:

shibnel: [Y child of A & B] [A & B parents of X] [X older than Y] [male
    X] [female Y]

Applying the two inverse rules, we get:

ishlel: [X child of A & B] [A & B parents of Y] [Y younger than X] [male
    X] [female Y]

This analysis combines all the features of the other two into a single system.
It also includes relational features indicating that siblings must have
common parents. (Although Haviland and Clark put their definitions in
terms of a single parent, siblings are actually defined in terms of two
parents, and this fact is recognized in our definitions above.) Predictions
about the relative complexity of terms would be exactly the same as those
derived from the first componential analysis shown in Figure 11–1. That is,
the terms *vish* ("girl's or boy's older sister") and *muk* ("girl's younger
sibling") would be the least complex; each one has one sex feature while the
other terms have two each.

    Of particular value for our data analysis was Haviland's and Clark's
(1974) realization that componential analyses involve the same conceptual
features as Piaget discusses, sex and reciprocity for example. This
connection allows us to make developmental predictions not possible from
componential analysis alone. Because, according to Piaget (1928)
relational concepts are more difficult than categorical (absolute) ones, the
two sex components should precede the two relational components,

younger/older and parent/child. If we consider the sibling terms alone, it seems that the parent/child components in Haviland and Clark's (1974) model could be simplified from [A & B parents of Y] [X child of A & B] to [A & B parents of X] [A & B parents of Y]. It would not be necessary to conceive of the parent-child relation as a reciprocal one. The application of the inverse parent-child rule (p. 29) is not necessary to derive reciprocal sibling terms. Thus the number of rules is reduced from two to one. As Haviland and Clark (1974) point out, a one-way relation is easier than a reciprocal one. Therefore, one might expect the parent/child component to develop before the necessarily reciprocal relation older-younger.

We used our data to see whether the development of sibling kin terms reflects the development of semantic components and, if so, which of the three models makes the most accurate predictions about the psychological facts of comprehension.

ETHNOGRAPHIC INFORMATION

The last strand of theory and research, ethnography, comes from anthropology and also emphasizes sources of cultural variation. Knowledge of the culture itself has led to hypotheses about the development of Zinacanteco kin terms lies in the culture itself. Vogt (1969) in his comprehensive ethnography about the Zinacantecos comments on the great importance of the older-younger contrast throughout the Zinacanteco culture. The contrastive terms *bankilal*, the property of being older, and *iz'inal*, the property of being younger, derive from the words for "boy's older brother" and "boy's younger brother," but they can be used to distinguish pairs of hills, crosses, shamans, fireworks, and so forth. Vogt states that the age-ranking principle symbolized by these terms is a way of comparing two things in terms of relative power or status, with the older being the more dominant of the two. If cultural importance is a factor in the development of kinship terminology, then one might predict that the pair *bankil* ("boy's older brother") and *iz'in* ("boy's younger brother") would be acquired earlier. Another possibility is that the terms for older siblings might be more salient and therefore easier to learn. If, as Vogt (1969) suggests, "age is of overriding importance" (p. 230) in the Zinacanteco sibling terms, then this fact might be reflected in the early acquisition of the older-younger semantic component relative to the semantic components of sex. Note that this hypothesis runs counter to the prediction from Piagetian theory, which predicts the opposite order. The actual result will enable us to compare the utility of Piaget's developmental theory with that of ethnographic material for understanding the acquisition of sibling terms by Zinacanteco children.

METHOD

Procedure

Before asking our subjects any question, we elicited family trees from their mothers which gave the names of all the household members and showed the kinship relationships between them. We used these family trees to compose a personal set of questions for each subject. Because we wanted to test comprehension rather than production of kinship terms, we phrased our questions so that they included the kinship terms and required one or more proper names for an answer.

Our questions using Zinacanteco sibling terms were of two types: "ego-centered" and "other-centered". Ego-centered questions concerned the relationship of an individual subject to his siblings. These questions were given in the following form where "p" stands for his kinship terms such as "older brother" and "younger sister":

Tzotzil:	*K'usi sbi la p?*
English (literal):	What his-name the–your–p
English (free):	What is the name of your p?

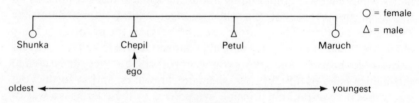

Figure 11–3.

For the sample family tree in Figure 11–3, we would compose three such ego-centered questions for the boy Chepil

1. Q: What is the name of your older sister?
   A: Shunka.
2. Q: What is the name of your younger brother?
   A. Petul
3. Q: What is the name of your younger sister?
   A: Maruch.

Other-centered questions concerned a given sibling's relationship to *his* siblings. They were given in the following form, where "A" stands for a proper name, and "p" and "q" stands for kinship terms:

Tzotzil:	*A*	*la p A,*	*k'usi sbi*	*lis q?*
English (literal):	As for	the-your-p A,	what his-name	the-his-q?
English (free):	As for	your p A,	what is the name of his q?	

For the same sample family tree we would address seven such other-centered questions to Chepil, using each of his three siblings in turn as the reference point:

    1. Q: As for your older sister Shunka, what is the name of her younger brother?

    A: Chepil, Petul.

    2. Q: As for your older sister Shunka, what is the name of her younger sister?

    A: Maruch.

    3. Q: As for your younger brother Petul, what is the name of his older sister?

    A: Shunka.

    4. Q: As for your younger brother Petul, what is the name of his older brother?

    A: Chepil.

    5. Q: As for your younger brother Petul, what is the name of his younger sister?

    A: Maruch.

    6. Q: As for your younger sister Maruch, what is the name of her older sister?

    A: Shunka.

    7. Q: As for your younger sister Maruch, what is the name of her older brother?

    A: Chepil, Petul.

We asked all of the questions in the singular form, even when a complete correct answer included more than one person. (e.g. questions 1 and 7, above) After each response, we asked the subjects:

Tzotzil:	*Mi*	*oy*	*to*	*s p?*
English (literal):	?	there is	still	his-p
English (free):	Does he have any more p's?			

We repeated this question until the subject had told us that there were no more. We also addressed questions to each subject concerning his parents, both ego-centered (e.g. "What is the name of your father?") and other-centered (e.g. "As for your mother, what is the name of her child?") This paper, however, deals only with sibling terms.

Sample and Analysis

Our data was collected in the Zinacantèco hamlet of Nabencauk in the summers of 1969 and 1970. Our sample consisted of 66 subjects, who can be classified on three dimensions: age, sex, and schooling.

Table 11–1
Distribution of participants and questions
by age, sex, and schooling*

	4–5 YEARS		8–10 YEARS		13–18 YEARS	
	Girls	Boys	Girls	Boys	Girls	Boys
unschooled	7	6	12	7	8	5
	(66)	(51)	(141)	(82)	(97)	(48)
schooled	—	—	5	9	1	6
			(55)	(120)	(7)	(76)

*The total number of questions asked each group is given in parentheses.

There were no schooled children in the youngest age group because children in Nabencauk do not go to school until age 6. The virtual absence of a group of schooled girls in the 13- to 18-year-old age group is explained by the fact that Zinacantecos had only recently began to send their girls to school.

Because each participant had a set of questions based on his or her place in a specific family configuration, very few received exactly the same set of questions. For this reason, our unit of analysis is the question rather than the person. Although not all participants would of course have been asked to answer the same number of a particular type of questions, this strategy of analysis allows us to consider homogeneous groups of questions a necessary requirement if we are to draw conclusions about the acquisition process. While the question seemed the most logical unit of analysis, it prevented us from using inferential statistics because of the unequal contributions of each participant to the data pool. Our data analysis has therefore relied entirely on descriptive statistics, and we have been very conservative in presenting only the most clearcut and consistent results.

Another analytic problem was the fact that a given question would vary in the number of required answers depending on the family configuration and size. Take the question, "What is the name of your younger sister?"; the required answer would vary depending upon how many younger sisters the participant had. Variation in the number of required answers—that is, the size of the answer category—was thought to affect the participants' ability to answer in itself, and this needed to be taken account of in the analysis. Because the most frequent size of the answer category was one, we based most of our analysis on these questions alone, thus holding the size of answer categories constant and minimizing the effect of memory skills. Unless otherwise noted in the "findings" section, results are based entirely on questions having an answer category of one. In separate analyses, we looked at the effects of category size per se on the ability to answer kinship questions.

FINDINGS

Decentration

A basic (and also obvious) finding is that the ability to demonstrate comprehension of sibling kin terms in our interview situation increases with age. This is shown by the graph in Figure 11–4. Whereas the 4- and 5-year-olds answer 47% of the questions correctly, the 13- through 18-year-olds correctly answered 94% of them.

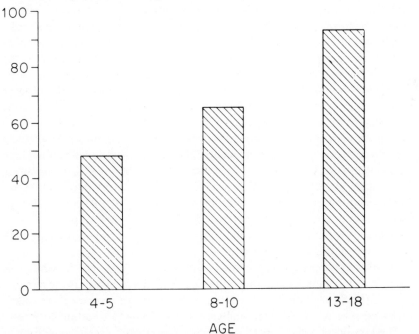

Figure 11–4. Percentage of questions answered correctly at different ages

We found no differences between boys and girls in the development of sibling terms, and so have combined sexes in all analyses. The absence of a sex difference would seem to indicate that kinship is of equal importance to males and females in Zinacantan.

Figure 11–4 also combines data for schooled and unschooled participants, as they did not differ from each other. Since Zinacantecos do not learn about kinship in the Spanish-language Mexican schools, we would not have expected school to make a difference on that basis. It was possible, however, that the *form* of our questions or the questioning situation itself involved skills foreign to the Zinacanteco culture, but native to the culture of the school. The absence of a schooling effect indicates that this was not the case and that we were successful in our attempt to tap a culturally-relevant domain of knowledge. Because of the general absence of schooling effects, we combined data from schooled and unschooled participants in the findings to be presented below.

A difference between the schooled and unschooled participants appeared in only one subset of questions, to be noted, where the unschooled subjects do better.

If we divide the questions into two types, ego-centered and other-centered, we can see that a decentration process is one of the factors involved in this developmental change. Recall that ego-centered questions are of the form "What is the name of your older brother?": they ask about a relation relative to the child. In other words, an ego-centered question takes the child's perspective. Other-centered questions, in contrast, are of the form "As for your younger brother X, what is the name of his older brother?" An other-centered question does not take the child who is being questioned as its reference point; it takes the perspective of someone external to the child. Consequently, a correct answer to an other-centered question demands, in principle, relatively greater cognitive decentering than a correct answer to an ego-centered question. Figure 11–5 shows how skill in answering ego-centered questions develops before skill in answering other-centered questions. We can also see that, at every age level, other-centered questions are more difficult than ego-centered questions, although the gap becomes extremely narrow for the oldest age group.

These graphs provide strong evidence of decentration as a component in the development of kin terms.

Other-centered questions are in fact of two types, one in which the answer is the name of a sibling and one in which the answer is the name of the child being questioned. The latter type demands a reversal of the child's own perspective. It is functionally similar to Piaget's question to Raoul. "Has Gerald a brother?" in that a correct response requires a recognition of self as someone else's sibling. For the 4- and 5-year-olds particularly, this

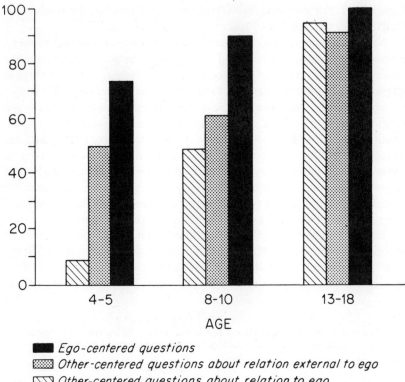

Ego-centered questions
Other-centered questions about relation external to ego
Other-centered questions about relation to ego

Figure 11–5. Percentage of different types of question answered correctly at different ages

is the hardest type of question, as Figure 11–5 shows.[3] Among the youngest children we have a situation where the child can name, for example, her older brother (see Figure 11–5, ego-centered questions), but cannot name herself as her older brother's younger sister (see Figure 11–5, other-centered questions about relation to ego). One might think that the child lacks the ability to comprehend reciprocal relations, but this is not the case. We must turn to the other-centered questions whose answers require the name of a sibling. Figure 11–5 shows that, while the ability to answer these questions increases with age, even the younger children are able to answer a considerable number. These also are composed of a set of reciprocal pairs: e.g., to a boy, "As for your older sister X, what is the name of her older brother?" Answer: "Y." "As for your older brother Y, what is the name of his younger sister?" Answer: "X." Each reciprocal pair of questions involves comprehending a reciprocal pair of sibling terms, as shown in

Figure 11–2. For instance, the example just given involves the pair *shibnel* ("girl's older brother") and *ishlel* ("boy's younger sister").

Now let us examine the other-centered questions about sibling relations external to the child pair by pair. For the child who does not yet have the concept of reciprocity, the reciprocal relation between a pair of siblings might make it harder to answer both questions concerning such a pair correctly. For the child who does have this concept and who can derive one relation from its reciprocal by applying the inverse rule, a reciprocal relation between siblings should make it easier to answer both questions. Table 11–2 shows the results of an analysis of responses to pairs of reciprocal questions. (Only those pairs where *both* questions had but a single answer could be included in this analysis.) The table compares the actual rates for answering pairs of reciprocal questions, with the expected rates assuming that each question is answered independently.

If children were learning about relations independently, as a series of specific one-way relationships, the actual distribution of rates should be the same as the expected one. If the absence of the concept of reciprocity were making the question pairs more difficult, there should be a heavier-than-

Table 11–2
Expected and actual rates for answering pairs of reciprocal questions about sibling relations external to self

| | AGE 4–5 | | Age 8–10 | | Age 13–18 | |
	expected	actual	expected	actual	expected	actual
Neither member of question pair correctly answered	25%	37.5%	1%	0%	0%	0%
One member of question pair correctly answered	50%	25%	20%	22%	0%	0%
Both members of question pair correctly answered	25%	37.5%	79%	78%	100%	100%
Total number of question pairs		8		9		11

Note: The expected rates were generated by calculating binomial distributions based on the overall rate of correct answers in each group. The 13- 18-year-olds are, of course, the limiting case of a 100% rate of correct answers.

expected concentration of answers in the category "One member of question pair correctly answered", and a lighter-than-expected concentration in the category "Both members of question pair correctly answered". This is never the case. The only noticeable difference between expected and actual distributions occurs in the youngest group, where the actual rate of answering only one member of a question pair correctly is less than the expected rate, thus demonstrating that the existence of reciprocal pairs of relations among the other-centered questions is not an interfering factor for the youngest children.

The middle age-group correctly answers most pairs of reciprocally related questions, and the distribution of their answers is exactly what you would expect if each question were being answered independently. If these children were using an inverse rule (see Haviland's and Clark's model) to derive a relation from its reciprocal, one would predict the actual rate of correctly answering both members of a question pair to be greater than the expected rate, and the actual rate of correctly answering only one member of a question pair to be less than the expected rate, since the knowledge of either relation in a pair would be sufficient to derive the other one. But inspection of the data from the 8- to 10-year-old group shows that this is not the case. The children seem to be learning reciprocal pairs of relations by treating each member of a question pair as an independent one-way relation rather than as part of a reciprocal relation.

Our results thus far confirm Piaget's view of the process of development. If we take 60% correct as our criterion for having a given skill, we emerge with the following developmental sequence:

Age 4–5:   Egocentrism.
            Can answer ego-centered questions
Age 8–10:   Reciprocity.
            Can answer other-centered questions about sibling relations
            external to self, including reciprocal pairs.
Age 13–18: Reversibility.
            Can answer other-centered questions about relations involving
            ego.

Thus, we have found exactly the same sequence of stages which we extrapolated from Piaget's description of his findings with Swiss children answering questions about brothers and sisters.

Memory

Another non-culture-specific developmental factor is quantitative

for each term.) Hence, componential complexity did not relate in any way to psychological complexity. Nor were descriptive terms more or less difficult than basic terms. Furthermore, the terms for boy's older brother and boy's younger brother are not less difficult for their cultural importance. Similarly, the terms for older siblings were not easier than the terms for younger siblings, although older could be considered more salient in Zinacanteco culture than younger.

Now let us look at the effects of the specific components. If sex of reference point were problematical in the learning of kin terms, we would expect other-centered questions that involve a reference point of a different sex from the child to be more difficult than other-centered questions involving a reference point of the same sex, for the child must learn terms different from those he uses in talking about his own siblings. But questions involving a reference point of a different sex were no harder. That is to say, a girl was as likely to answer a question correctly about a *boy's* older brother as one about a girl's older brother.

Thus far we have only considered whether children answered questions correctly or not, and have not dealt with the nature of their incorrect answers. These can be divided into two categories: errors of omission (omitted answers) and commission (wrong answers). Errors of commission were relatively infrequent—only a total of 89 out of 835 errors (counting all required answers on multiple-answer questions). Thus, only 11% of all errors were errors of commission, a fact which indicates that there was very little guessing in response to our questions. But errors of commission are of particular interest because they can be used to see whether the participants of various ages have analyzed sibling terms into various components. A pattern in errors of commission reveal the existence of a concept, as opposed to knowledge of specific examples. Table 11-3 organizes errors of

Table 11-3
Errors of commission
at different ages*

	Maintain common parentage	Maintain right sex	Maintain relative age	Stays within reciprocal pair	Number of questions
Age 4–5	75%	46%	38%	23%	20
Age 8–10	94%	80%	16%	30%	55
Age 13–18	100%	79%	21%	14%	14
					89

*The percentages do not add up to 100 because each one represents a binary split of the complete data for a particular age group. The small number of errors that referred to people outside the sibling group were not included on the age, sex, and reciprocity analyses, because we sometimes did not know who they were.

commission according to which semantic component is maintained. The semantic components refer to the componential analyses described in the introduction. If the experimenter asks a boy "What is your older brother's name?" and he responds by naming a younger brother, his answer maintains the sex (male) of the correct answer and stays within the same reciprocal pair (older brother/younger brother). If he had responded by naming his older sister, he would have maintained the relative age of the correct answer (older) but not sex and reciprocal pair.

The only semantic component consistently maintained by the youngest children is common parentages; that is, they infrequently name people outside their sibling group in answer to sibling questions. The middle and oldest groups maintain the attribute of sex as well. Relative age and reciprocal pairs are not maintained by any age groups. Thus, in terms of psychological validity, none of the three models of componential analysis (two by Collier and one by Haviland and Clark) is completely supported by the results; relative age and/or reciprocity would be needed to complete any of the three analyses. The fact that common parentage is the first feature to be maintained in errors of commission disagrees with both Piaget (1928) and Haviland and Clark (1974), who state that categorical features—sex in this case—should appear first. But common parents are common to *all* sibling terms, and it could be that the core is the first aspect of a concept to be learned. The fact that only sex and parentage are maintained in errors of commission shows that kin terms can be learned through actual examples without the child analyzing a term into its semantic components. Understanding of all the terms in ego-centered usage is possible as early as age 4 or 5 before any semantic component except common parentage stands out in errors of commission. Applying a term in a comprehension situation evidently does not require the awareness of semantic features necessary for definition (Piaget, 1928; Haviland and Clark, 1974).

DISCUSSION

Our results confirm Piaget's theory of the development of kin concepts very strongly, for we have found evidence of decentration and the corresponding development of reciprocity and reversibility as Zinacanteco children acquire skill in applying sibling terms. This result is particularly interesting because the Zinacantecos have system of sibling terminology totally different from the French system on which Piaget's original research was based. Thus, decentration is central to the development of kin concepts for the Zinacantecos of Mexico, just as it is for the Hausa of Nigeria (LeVine and Price-Williams. 1974). Price-Williams, Hammond, Edgerton and Walker (in this volume), using a method similar to that of LeVine and Price-Williams (1974), report a similar pattern of development.

The development of memory was another important and independent factor in the ability to answer questions. The results of this study lead to the conclusion that Piagetian concepts and other notions of general developmental processes can be demonstrated cross-culturally when they are tested in a realm that is meaningful for members of a particular culture.

On the other hand, the results did not support the validity of any single componential analysis nor reveal the influence of any culture-specific factors.

Danziger (1957) and Haviland and Clark (1974) have found an early stage in definition of kin terms—before semantic components appear—when the child can name examples of terms but cannot define them. In essence our task required naming rather than definition. Our results suggest that children learn kin terms as labels for specific relations before the labels themselves are organized into the conceptual components revealed in their errors of commission.

We found that children could construct reciprocal pairs of relations between people without utilizing the concept of reciprocity. The kind of reciprocity identified by Piaget (1928), Danziger (1957), Elkind (1962), and Haviland and Clark (1974) in the reciprocal stage of children's definitions (e.g., "To have a sibling you must be one") is a very conscious and aware use of a reciprocal relationship. The development outlined in our paper demonstrates a progression in children's use of terms in their daily life which can form the basis for the later acquisition of reciprocity and reversibility on a more conscious plane.

Development in the application of kin terms differs in other respects from definitional development. Whereas very young children will define brother as "boy" (Piaget, 1928), our results for errors of commission show that they will not think that a brother can be any boy whatsoever. Nelson (1973) has found that a new word is first used to refer to something in a particular functional relationship to the child, but that generalization to new instances will first occur on the basis of perceptual attributes. If we consider definition a form of generalization, then this would account for Piaget's (1928) and Haviland and Clark's (1974) findings that the earliest definitions of kin terms refer to perceptual attributes like sex (e.g., defining brother as a boy). However, earliest comprehension involves referents that are of functional importance to the child.

It is interesting and somewhat surprising that our results manifest clearly the influence of supposedly universal processes, like decentration and memory development, but do not show any effect of the distinctive features of the Zinacanteco environment—either the three dimensions in their system of kinship terms or the cultural emphasis on the older/younger distinction. Perhaps the lack of influence of culture-specific factors relates in some way to the universal importance of kinship as the basis for all human societies.

NOTES

1. LeVine and Price-Williams actually speak of "ego-centered kin terms" and "other-centered kin terms." This, however, is incorrect, as they are really talking about a single set of kin terms used in two different kinds of situation. Therefore, it would have been more accurate to contrast ego-centered and other-centered *use* of kin terms.

2. As Price-Williams, Hammond, Edgerton and Walker point out elsewhere in this volume, whether or not componential analysis *should* have psychological reality has been a matter of controversy within cognitive anthropology. While anthropologists like Wallace have made psychological claims, others like Burling have seen it as a purely formal tool.

3. For those other-centered questions involving a reversal of the child's own perspective, the unschooled 8- to 10-year-olds do better than the school children of the same age—67% correct vs. 29% correct. It is not clear why this isolated difference in favor of Zinacanteco traditional education should have occurred, although kinship is, of course, important in the traditional process of socialization.

REFERENCES

Brown, R. and Lenneberg, E. H. (1954) A study of language and cognition. *Journal of Abnormal and Social Psychology, 49,* 454–462.

Cole, M., Gay, J., Glick, J., and Sharp, D. W. (1971) *The cultural context of learning and thinking: An exploration in experimental anthropology.* New York: Basic Books.

Collier, J. F. (1969) *Changing kinship terminology in a Tzotzil Maya community.* Unpublished paper.

Danziger, K. (1957) The child's understanding of kinship terms: A study in the development of relational concepts. *Journal of Genetic Psychology, 91,* 213–232.

Elkind, D. (1962) Children's conception of brother and sister: Piaget replication study V. *Journal of Genetic Psychology, 100,* 129–136.

Fraser, C., Bellugi, U., and Brown, R. (1963) Control of grammar in imitation, comprehension, and production. *Journal of Verbal Learning and Verbal Behavior, 2,* 121–135.

Hagen, J. (1972) Attention and mediation in children's memory. In W. W. Hartup (Ed.), *The Young Child: Reviews of Research* (Vol. 2). Washington, D. C.: National Association for the Education of Young Children. Pp. 112–131.

Haviland, S. E., and Clark, E. V. (1974) "This man's father is my father's son": A study of the acquisition of English kin terms. *Journal of Child Language, 1*.

Kagan, J., Klein, R. E., Haith, M. M. Morrison, F. J. (1973) Memory and meaning in two cultures. *Child Development, 44,* 221–223.

LeVine, R. A., and Price-Williams, D. R. (1974) Children's kinship concepts: Cognitive development and early experience among the Hausa. *Ethnology, 13,* 25–44.

Nelson, K. (1973) Some evidence for the cognitive primacy of categorization and its functional basis. *Merrill-Palmer Quarterly, 19,* 21–39.

Piaget, J. (1928) *Judgment and reasoning in the child.* New York: Harcourt, Brace.

Price-Williams, D., Hammond, O. W., Edgerton, C. and Walker, M. (1977) *Kinship concepts among rural Hawaiian children.* Chapter 10 in this book.

Vogt, E. Z. (1969) *Zinacantan: A Maya community in the highlands of Chiapas.* Cambridge, Mass.: Belknap Press of Harvard University Press.

12
Caveat Interventor

GAVIN N. SEAGRIM

I regretfully state in conclusion that no other will have a chance of seeing again what I have here described.

—Herbert Basedow,
Knights of the Boomerang (1935)

I first applied the warning which forms the title of this article in concluding a paper I read to a conference held in Canberra during 1974 (Seagrim and Lendon, 1976). Leonard Doob (1976) was a speaker at the conference and had been telling us about the contact-group techniques he had been applying at various trouble spots around the world. The fact that the troubles seemed to increase shortly after his interventions surely had nothing to do *with* his interventions! It could be argued, indeed, that they would have occurred in any case and that they would have been more severe if he had not practiced his intervention. Besides, no one could possibly argue that the effort was not worthwhile: if the intervention worked out successfully, everyone would agree that it had been justified.

Doob was disappointed with my antiinterventionist stand, and as a result we had a useful discussion of the whole question. As can be imagined, the discussion was largely concerned with moral, ethical, and political considerations. However, the problems it raised are equally relevant in other areas and have a particular cogency in cross-cultural contexts.

I will be concerned mainly with cross-cultural intervention in the cognitive domain, but will preface that discussion with examples taken from other more obviously contentional areas in order to heighten the reader's awareness of the issues involved.

The question arises in perhaps its ultimate form in regard to genetics, and particularly in regard to genetical engineering. Earle Hackett (1969) has warned against the reduction of genetical diversity, a warning which scientists are beginning to take seriously but one which they may find it impossible to heed. The possibility of applying a eugenics policy for the eradication of some of the world's ills is—extreme forms of genocide apart—still within the bounds of possibility. Quite recently, for example, it was seriously considered as a possible solution to the Kuru problem which forms the basis of my next example. At this time it was thought that the disease had a genetic origin and the intention needs to be assessed within that context. I quote: "This genetic theory [of the origins of Kuru] was rather hastily accepted by the government of Papua New Guinea. A eugenic policy was considered, with the intention of placing the entire Fore tribe under quarantine, prohibiting migration of tribal members from their own ethnic area, and returning to their homeland all those Fore men who had been recruited as laborers elsewhere (Dobzhansky, 1960). This, some believed, would impede the spread of the lethal kuru gene. Fortunately this scheme has never been enforced." (Zigas, 1975, p. 484).

In a medical cross-cultural context we thus have this interesting and bizarre case of the disease of Kuru, a form of viral infection causing a progressive and slow degeneration of the nervous system and always resulting in death. It was first reported by an anthropologist in the mid-fifties and is now fully documented in the medical literature, commencing with reports by Zigas, who describes the people and the events as follows:

The Fore are a linguistic and cultural group numbering approximately 18,000 members. They occupy a mountain-dissected region of the Eastern Highlands of the Australian Trust Territory of New Guinea. Physically, Fore are quite similar to other Eastern Highlands people. Though noticeably shorter in stature than most Europeans, their bodies are very well proportioned, and their muscular development is outstanding. Fore society belongs to what we may call the primitive world in transition. Direct contact with whites did not begin until the late 1947s when the first governmental patrol entered the Fore region. In 1949, a Lutheran mission was established, and later in 1952, the first government patrol post was set up. Today, almost all Fore are nominal Christians. The younger people are becoming literate and knowledge of the outside is beginning to expand. Much of the traditional way of life is breaking down, becoming lost to memory, however, neither government nor mission has taken any stand against the central beliefs in the Fore traditional religion. The Fore still hold to most of the religious beliefs which they developed before their first contact with Europeans. Apart from ritual cannibalism, which was stamped out by "Pax Australiana", they continue to practice most of the customs which go with their beliefs.

Kuru

In early 1956, while I was District Medical Officer in the Eastern Highlands, I encountered many cases of a strange syndrome and found it to be the principal cause of death among Fore people and a few neighboring groups. I brought this unusual phenomenon, this plague, to the attention of several scientific observers who, disappointingly showed very little interest in this unique and extraordinary disease. In early 1957, Dr. D. C. Gajdusek of the National Institutes of Health, U.S.A., joined me, and through his vision, sincere interest and dynamic energy, we made the first medical description and epidemiological study of the disease. This dreadful scourge has since then attracted the wonder, curiosity, sympathy and imagination of the lay and scientific world. Kuru was causing more than half of the mortality after infancy of a whole people, and became a matter of immense theoretical importance to social and medical science. Unfortunately, apart from a few investigators, Kuru and the Fore people became just another "private enterprise" serving as a source for publicity among lay people and for degrees and recognition among the academic world. The press went so far as to sensationalize Kuru to the point of calling it "the laughing death." [Zigas, 1972, p. 689.]

An exciting piece of scientific detective work seemed finally to pin the blame on a practice of the women and children of the Fore people of eating their deceased adult female relatives (but see Zigas, 1975, for an apparent reopening of the case).

The adult males did not "catch" the habit, nor the disease. At its height in 1955, the disease accounted for 50% of deaths among women and children while the murders and tortures in retribution for the supposed sorcery leading to these deaths accounted for 20% of adult male deaths (Burnet, 1971).

This case is fairly straightforward. The particular practice of cannibalism is thought to have started circa 1910 (Burnet, 1971) so no very ancient practices needed to be interfered with in order to eradicate the disease. The investigators could not be accused of unjustified or impudent interest in the subjects of their study: While the discoveries were of great scientific interest and could only have arisen in a cross-cultural context, the need for them to be undertaken would not be denied by anyone. And for the interventionists who followed, the case was almost equally good: If the indigenes would only stop eating each other, they would stop suffering from this dread disease. In fact, of course, this advice is now followed and appears to be taking effect, and no doubt the disease will eventually disappear except as an exotic exhibit in medical primate laboratories, where it has been transmitted successfully to chimpanzees (King, 1975). If any doubt were entertained about the wisdom of the intervention, it might have been argued that, at worst, the consequent self-denial would have no more than a transitory and minor effect on ceremonial life and on the structure of the society—and none, perhaps, on nutrition. Minor adjustments in notions of what were proper sex roles might be required and no doubt the resulting increase in population would have consequences less unpleasant than those of the disease.

However, it must be conceded that such comfortable thoughts are based on a naive and short-term view of the consequences of intervention in the affairs of any well-integrated society. Just because our particular form of society is extraordinarily adaptive to changes forced upon it (perhaps a reflection of its lack of integration) we should not assume that this is the case in better integrated societies. This point is made with great clarity by Shantzis and Behrens (1973). Their paper is entitled *Population control mechanisms in a primitive agricultural society*, and their concern is with the development of a theoretical model which will describe the dynamics of such situations. Their paper is an exercise in prediction, not an account of the effects of intervention of various sorts.

The group whose behavior they took as an example is the Tsembaga, another New Guinea population. They obtained their information mainly from an anthropological study by R. A. Rappaport, entitled *Pigs for the Ancestors* (1968).

The Tsembaga are described as follows:

They are a subset of a group of clans that speaks one particular dialect, called Maring.

The Maring-speaking peoples number about 7,000. They are aggregated into approximately twenty clans, each within its own subterritory of the region. Because the New Guinea highland region is a very rough country, there is a fair degree of isolation between the Maring-speaking peoples and other people of New Guinea, including the Australian government. The Maring practice a primitive form of slash-and-burn agriculture for subsistence. Only a portion of their total acreage is used for cultivation at any given time. This area is cleared of forest and burned over. Burning clears away the underbrush for planting, produces a nutrient ash residue, and improves the soil fertility, probably by catalyzing certain chemical reactions in the upper inches of topsoil. The land is planted with root crops for one or two years until the nutrient store in the soil begins to be depleted and the land's fertility decreases, as indicated by decreasing yields. The people then move on to a new area of land and repeat the procedure, leaving the old land to fallow. The fallowed land is quickly covered by secondary tropical rain forest. In fifteen to twenty years the forest is sufficiently regenerated that the procedure can be repeated.

It should be obvious that this process requires either a very large amount of land or, given limited total available land, a controlled population. The latter is the case for most slash-and-burn agricultural societies. The particular subclan of the Maring under study, the Tsembaga, possesses about 1,350 acres of available land, with about 350 acres in virgin forest and the rest under secondary forest. They are surrounded by dense forest and mountainous terrain, making further expansion opportunities highly limited. Under these circumstances, it is critical to the survival of the population that its natural tendency toward growth be controlled. The Tsembaga accomplish this control through an elaborate automatic societal mechanism that triggers intermittent wars with neighboring populations at intervals of twelve to fifteen years. The triggering device, which sends them to war frequently enough to contain their population, is controlled by a very complex ecological symbiosis between the Tsembaga and their domesticated pig herd. The Maring peoples herd pigs, but not solely for their nutritional value. Although pigs are occasionally eaten, they represent a net energy loss (or at least a comparatively unfavourable return). The Tsembaga unconsciously use the pig herd as both an information monitor and a homeostat in a complex, automatic population control system. [Shantzis and Behrens, 1973, p. 260.]

The dynamics of the situation are that when the pig population reaches a triggering point (when the food situation becomes precarious) the community decides to hold a pig feast to which neighboring tribes are invited. The pig population is then decimated by slaughter and by gift giving. However, this involves elaborate rituals in which an associated event is the uprooting of a particular tuber, the *rumbin*, which has been planted at the cessation of the previous pig feast, ten or fifteen years before. Its planting then placed a truce on warfare but did not, of course, bury with it unsettled grudges. Its uprooting removes the embargo on fighting and war breaks out almost immediately. The fighting may continue intermittently for a few weeks or months and up to 10% of the population (presumably male) may be killed. The tuber is then replanted and outward calm prevails once more even if the score of dead is unequal on the various sides.

The system dynamics model applied to these events predicts accurately that the population's fluctuations will be kept indefinitely within safe limits.

Of interest to us, however, is that the model predicts disaster if certain likely interventions occur. For example, if warfare is discouraged, if medical intervention increases life expectancy or if agriculturists of the colonial power controlling the situation persuade the tribes to increase the size of their pig herds—all these events are extremely likely to be introduced in the name of progress or of humanity.

Once more on the basis of our own society, it may be argued that the Tsembaga should be able to adapt to the changed circumstances. This, however, is totally unrealistic because it is based, as usual, on a model of society whose institutions are as closely integrated as are those of more "primitive" societies: you cannot alter one element of such an integrated society without disturbing the equilibrium of the whole. There are plenty of examples in the world's recent colonial history of the predicted disaster, not least amongst the Australian aborigines. The outcomes are nearly always disasters of one sort or another but, fortunately for the peace of mind of their initiators, they tend to be delayed and often to be of a less lurid nature than the "ills" they replaced.

Perhaps the problems are not as great in the area of cognitive studies. Here, where the introduction of literacy and other scholastic benefits is involved, surely there can be less cavil at what we are doing? In these cases, cross-cultural inquiries are of inestimable worth. At the same time they are becoming more difficult to carry out because, on the one hand, the contrasting cultures are disappearing at an increasing rate, and on the other, those remaining are becoming increasingly disenchanted with being investigated.

There can be no doubt at all of their scientific value. This derives from the fact that it is almost impossible to identify the major variables which contribute to the formation of our own styles of thinking, let alone to uncover the processes through which that contribution takes effect in our own children. There is a weakening confidence, first, that our ways of seeing the world are universal and/or the best possible; and, second, that we will soon understand those ways and the factors that affect their development: recent educational interventions in our own society can hardly be claimed to have met with resounding success. This loss of confidence is accentuated by the parallel loss of confidence in the contribution to our understanding to be expected from animal studies, particularly those of lower animals. Unfortunately the higher animals which, like the divergent cultures, have a contribution to make, are becoming extinct or otherwise inaccessible in appropriate forms (of natural living).

It is thus being borne in upon us increasingly that it is very difficult—impossible, some think—for us to examine and to describe our own ways of thinking when we are restricted to observing ourselves with those instruments of thought. Like the fish, we shall be the last to discover the water in which we swim; its nature will only become apparent to us when we have been removed from it, hopefully not for a fatal length of time. The present publication, and others like it, bears testimony to the urgency with which present-day workers are attempting to make good the neglect of their predecessors: the urgency is great, the pace furious, and the insights, if sometimes unconvincing and meagre, at least challenging.

Let us take a case in point, one which will not have been included in this volume and one which is apparently neutral in tone. It concerns the old question of what different people, in this case peoples, see in the pictorial constructions they indulge in.

I refer here to a study by yet another anthropologist (Forge, 1970) who sought his intellectual fortune and enjoyment in the exotic highlands of New Guinea. After describing the unusual—to us—use of color terms by the Abelam, Forge goes on to observe:

The association between colour and ritual significance can also be seen in Abelam reactions to European importations. Coloured magazines sometimes find their way into the villages, and occasionally pages torn from them are attached to the matting at the base of the ceremonial house facade. In all such cases I have seen, the pages selected were brightly coloured, usually food advertisements of the Spam and sweet corn, and honey-baked ham type. Inquiries revealed that the Abelam had no idea of what was represented but thought that with their bright colours and incomprehensibility the selected pages were likely to be European tambarans and therefore powerful. Similarly, younger artists, encouraged to innovate while painting on paper, included as new elements the hilt of the sword that forms part of the 'Dettol' trademark, copied from a large tin of the antisceptic with whose medical use they were familiar, and the Christian cross, believing both to be powerful tambaran-like design elements.

The inability of people in cultures not used to them to see photographs is of course well known (cf. Segall, Campbell & Herskovits, 1966), and the comparison of inabilities is a difficult task for which I have no systematic material. Nevertheless, the Abelam's lack of understanding of photographs after more than twenty years of contact remains almost absolute, and provides possible support for my hypothesis that they have very definite and limited expectations about what they will see on any two-dimensional surface made to be looked at. In other words, their vision has been socialized in a way that makes photographs especially incomprehensible, just as ours is socialized to see photographs and indeed to regard them as in some sense more truthful than what the eye sees.

Photography has been known to the Abelam since the first contacts with Europeans in 1937. Nowadays, when all young men go away for at least a two-year stint of labour on the coast, they bring back photographs of themselves in all their modern finery, usually taken by Chinese photographers. The subjects stand rigidly at attention facing the camera, either singly or in groups, against a background of either a white sheet or a wall. No Abelam have any difficulty today in 'seeing' such a photograph and in recognizing and naming the individual concerned if they know him. But when shown photographs of themselves in action, or of any pose other than face or full figure looking directly at the camera, they cease to be able to 'see' the photograph at all. Even people from other villages who came specially because they knew I had taken a photograph of a relative who had subsequently died, and were often pathetically keen to see his features, were initially unable to see him at all, turning the photograph in all directions. Even when the figure dominated (to my eyes) the photograph I sometimes had to draw a thick line round it before it could be identified, and in some cases I had the impression that they willed themselves to see it rather than actually saw it in the way we do. Photographs of ceremonial houses and objects were easier, although in black and white people could identify a house as a ceremonial house rather than say which house it was. With colour they were happier, partly because they looked into a viewer, which itself was three-dimensional, instead of staring at a flat sheet, but they could rarely identify individuals and had a tendency to regard any brightly coloured photograph with no outstanding form as a tambaran display. Since I needed identifications from photographs of yam exchanges, brawls, ceremonies, and debates, I trained a few boys to see photographs; they learnt to do this after a few hours of concentrated looking and discussion on both sides. [Forge, 1970, pp. 286–8.]

While art historians such as Gombrich have for long been aware of some of these problems and while some attempts have been made to collect evidence on these questions, by the relativists of perception, who are well represented in this volume, it seems to the present author that the phenomena observed are usually not related to general and well-developed theories of representation. Perhaps Piaget (1969), Neisser (1967), and, of course, Forge are exceptions.

The fact of the matter is that it is extremely difficult for us to imagine what it would be like to see the world differently from the way we see it and it is therefore difficult to describe how it could come about that we see it the way we do. Only cross-cultural evidence will sufficiently shake us out of our complacency to make us undertake the hard work that will be required to build the proper conceptual structures to handle the data.

So cross-cultural studies in cognition may have an admirable effect, and if we feel a little guilty at using other people in order to further our scientific understanding rather than to "help" them, we can at least make a justifiable show of claiming ourselves to have been intellectually enriched and perhaps even to have acquired new tastes in art form, etc. It is not likely that Forge's attempts to instruct the indigenes in the subtleties of photographic interpretation will seriously have affected their art form or ceremonial lives. They may, of course, now buy cameras themselves, but the use to which they are likely to put the photographs will be assimilative to their present artistic techniques, as Forge has shown. It is doubtful, I would think, that they would even use the technique of portrayal thus offered for purposes of retributive sorcery, if they go in for such a thing.

So what is all the fuss about? Perhaps there need not be any, where the study of art forms is involved, although there are examples from the bad old days where attempts were made to reform the indigenes from their wicked—if unconscious—ways by destroying or locking up their artistic productions. No one wants to do that nowadays.

I am still not convinced, and perhaps an account of my own studies will show why this is so.

My work on the intellectual development of some Australian aboriginal children (in which I was assisted by Robin Lendon), and that of my colleagues de Lemos (1969) and Dasen (1974), has been centered on a relatively large and tribally homogeneous group of aborigines, numbering about 800, living on a Lutheran mission settlement at Hermannsburg. This is located about 90 miles due west of Alice Springs, in Central Australia. The mission settlement has been in existence for nearly 100 years and the present inhabitants derive from one section of the Aranda people and from a section of the Loritja people. Before "coming in" to the mission they were hunter-gatherers and occupied very large tracts of land on the fringes of the Western Desert. Like many hunter-gatherer people, they did without the encumbrances of clothing or material possessions and practiced a very complete form of sharing, the rules of which were based on kinship ties. There were no "rulers" in our sense of the term, but the most influential people were those elders possessing the most detailed knowledge of the myths and rituals which, like the kinship systems, were very rich and complicated.

The Aranda, who form the bulk of the present population at Hermannsburg, had a very high standing among neighboring nations. They are tall people and serious, as befits people whose ritual life and magic are powerful.

As they were progressively deprived of access to their traditional lands by white grazing interests, they settled more and more in and around Hermannsburg. The mission provided for their spiritual, physical, and intellectual needs after the manner of their kind.

The situation when I first encountered it in 1969 was not inspiring. The atmosphere was depressing and the people seemed to be somewhat unfriendly. This is not surprising, as they could see no hope for the future either in regard to the recovery of their lands or in regard to occupational opportunities: they would have to remain the recipients of inconsistent and vacillating white man's charity and the cynosures of his weekly or more frequent tourist excursion groups. The children went to school regularly and were there subjected to the very devoted attentions of white teachers, but seemed to make very little progress.

It is a pleasure to be able to paint a less gloomy picture of the present scene and I would like to do this, even though it is not entirely relevant to the present discussion. A transformation of great interest and hope has occurred in Hermannsburg during the last two or three years. Its causes are complex and will undoubtedly be described in due course by those best able to do so. I will therefore restrict myself to reporting my immediate impression of the situation without speculating on its causes or on its probable consequences.

In effect, a great exodus has occurred: Almost all the Aborigines have left Hermannsburg and, in family groups of various size, have established themselves in out-stations located geographically as near as possible to their original family group territory. Traditional leadership, submerged but not lost, is reemerging; they live in makeshift shelters, are planting gardens, and appear to be much happier. They are said to be healthier and the behavior of the young children certainly seems to be more controlled. They obtain their supplies and medical care from the settlement, and teachers visit the groups and teach the children under the trees rather than in classrooms. Tourists are not welcome. While it is far from the Garden of Eden and many enormous problems remain, the recovery of identity and its accompanying dignity augurs well for the next phase of interaction with the dominant white group. It is to be noted that in all of these events the aboriginal population has received the full and largely nondirective assistance and support of the mission.

In 1970, the rationale of my study was as follows:

Taking a group of aboriginal children living in a stable community, "enjoying" reasonably modern educational opportunities, not suffering from obvious malnutrition, and apparently receiving adequate parental encouragement in their schooling (or, perhaps, not encountering parental hostility to their schooling) was it possible to account for the apparent complete lack of advantage taken of the opportunities offered? Why was it that the children seemed to make no scholastic progress, no matter how that was assessed?

The advantages in taking such a group were:

(a) that they were clearly subject to quite different forces than our children, in respect of scholastic matters;

(b) that the scale of the differences were such that the chances of locating some comparable group which had begun to move towards our norms would be considerable;

(c) that in the present climate of political and material change surrounding them, the chances that some changes would occur were high, and the changes might be observed in a longitudinal study;

(d) that the changes, if they occurred, would give us some insights into forces which may be operating in our own society but which, because of the homogeneity of our experience, are unidentifiable except by an extraordinary stroke of serendipity.

All these considerations were properly scientific and noninterventional: I was simply going to observe a process which was going on and which was beyond my control. All I needed to do was to carry out periodic tests[1] of a nonscholastic nature which I hoped (fortunately justifiably) would reflect changes that occurred in the real, as opposed to the experimental, dependent variable: educational progress. If I was not pretending to do any good, at least I was confident that I was not doing any harm.

But it was not as easy as that, even before I started. And it became more and more difficult as I went on.

To start with I had to get a grant. This proved relatively easy. Researchers associated with me had previously done some studies on the same groups, so we knew how to go about the work. We also knew that it could be done. But one of the requirements to be met was that the outcome of my studies would have educational relevance. In the flush of my early enthusiasm that was easy enough; I have outlined the justification above. But educational relevance for whom? In either case I should have been given pause to consider. If the relevance is for members of our own culture, then what happens if I find that some identifiable and manipulable factor affects the age at which, say, conservations are achieved—and if I show also that conservation test performance reflects scholastic progress? Surely then—no matter what Piaget has said and most evidence notwith-standing—the pressure is going to be on, from fond if ambitious parents and enthusiastic educators, to do something about it? If not, why have the conservation tests found their way into curricula? Well, perhaps it does not matter in our own society, providing the changes required are not too radical in nature. The consequences for the observed groups of aborigines would be similar. Unless the changes required should turn out to be more radical in their case. We shall return to this shortly. In any case, surely it is unexceptionable, incontrovertible that solutions to educational problems are "good"?

Having got my grant, I had to obtain permission to carry out the necessary studies. Here again I encountered the same requirement, but more specifically this time: Could I make a case that my findings would be of use to the people who were trying to school the children? In other words, I was now being asked by the local authorities to justify my research on the grounds of its immediate and local usefulness. Well, in a general way and without actually making false claims, it is not too difficult to persuade nonspecialists that any advances in knowledge regarding educational matters will be useful. As I myself am far from convinced of this, I have at times refused to make this claim. The consequences are surprising: Instead of being refused permission to do the research, my interlocutors have rather chided me for my reserve and have tried to coerce me into "coming clean": they want help and are determined to get it!

This particular problem arose afresh in the present case when it recently became necessary for researchers to obtain the permission of the leaders of the groups under scrutiny to conduct the studies. This is by no means a pushover with the so-called uneducated aborigines, but the outcome is much more capricious: It is very difficult to know on what grounds studies are accepted and others rejected, but I doubt very much if anyone who said that he could see no reasonable or desirable advantage for the group in the possible findings of the study would receive permission to carry it out. It is at this stage that the first real test of one's integrity occurs, and it is up to each researcher to examine his own conscience. I regret, in retrospect, that mine is not too clear.

One of the questions asked me by the meeting of the school council at Hermannsburg was: "Will this kind of research help our children to become better at their school work?" My reply was that it might identify some of the reasons for their present lack of progress in such matters as arithmetic; and as this seemed to satisfy them, I presume it can be accepted that I had met the requirement increasingly imposed on cross-cultural researchers that the groups they wish to observe should be agreeable, or even keen that the work should be done. However, it is singularly naive to assume that the people in question can assess the implications of possible research findings. In fact, by definition, those groups that will be most valuable to us are the least likely to have the conceptual framework required for making such an assessment. So even in those cases where one's "help" is positively sought by groups or governments, there is a burden of responsibility placed upon us.

The trouble is,-of course, that very often we ourselves cannot predict what sort of results we will come up with, let alone their long-term implications. A brief account of the results of my own research will illustrate these matters.

As more detailed accounts of the findings have appeared elsewhere and are to be followed by further accounts (Dasen, de Lacey, and Seagrim, 1973; Seagrim and Lendon, 1976) a summary will suffice at this stage.

As already pointed out, aboriginal children from Central Australia living on settlements seem to take little advantage of the scholastic training offered to them: they go to school more or less regularly, are attentive and on the whole cooperative, but the results are, for the teachers, very disappointing. This is reflected in the test results. On the other hand, aboriginal children who have been adopted into, fostered with, or in some other way brought up in white households make considerable, even admirable progress, by our standards, in all matters scholastic. This, too, is reflected in our test results. The most unexpected findings are obtained with aboriginal children who come from the Central Australian area and who attend a boarding institution, St. Mary's, a church-run community at which they stay either permanently, if orphaned, or for a few months at a stretch, and at which they are attached in small groups to one cottage and in the care of one housemother of European descent. These children, too, make considerable advances after a relatively short stay at the village. It can be seen in Figure 12–1 that the changes are not of the order which

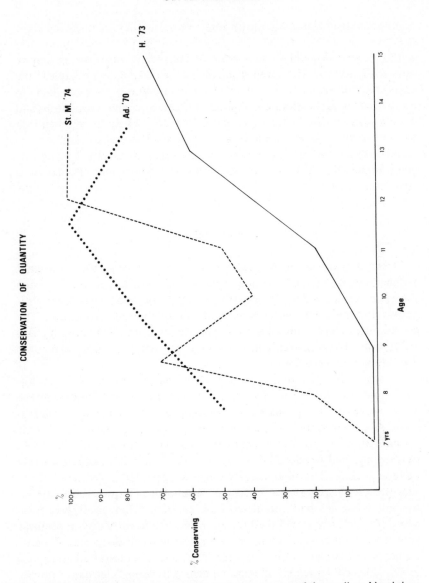

Figure 12–1. Conservation of quantity in three groups of Australian Aborigines.
Ad. '70   Adelaide adopted and fostered children (Dasen *et al.*, 1973)
H. '73   Hermannsburg Mission station
St.M '74   St. Mary's boarding institution

require a statistical microscope for their detection: they are massive by any criteria.[2]

Now, what? Should we have done the research at all? If yes, should we publish the results? (Our grant requires that we make them available to the government instrumentality involved and future grants are more likely to be obtained if publications are obtained.) If yes, with what precautions and warnings should we hedge them about? Are they likely to be taken into account in any way at all and, if so, are we likely to regret that?

Let us survey some of the uses to which they may be put. This may be done under the headings of Government, Aboriginal, Public, and Academic.

GOVERNMENT

The government of Australia has what is called "the aboriginal problem" on its hands. It is not a problem unique to Australia but is none the less a very considerable one. It need not be outlined here, being well-known, but one aspect of it is what to do about aboriginal education. The expenditure of large sums of revenue calls for justification in terms of quick results and what is emerging from the very considerable educational effort is no apparent success at all.

In such cases governments and their administrators tend to develop straw-snatching tendencies: they seek for some unique and simple solution to their very complex problems. For example, most aboriginal children do badly at school; some are undernourished; it has been proved (sic) that malnourishment leads to brain damage; so feed them up and all will be well (see Seagrim and Lendon, 1973). What sorts of snatchable straws will our findings suggest? The mind boggles at the prospect, but it *has* already been suggested, in the report of a government committe of inquiry (Gibb, 1971), written before we had conducted our research, "that an experimental boarding school be established for aborigines at an early age on pastoral properties with a curriculum including both traditional and Western elements and designed to encourage a process of cultural adaptation." (p. 76) Innocent enough, but what happens if it works? Our data from St. Mary's suggest that it *would* work and at least one mission settlement, Santa Teresa, again near to Alice Springs and recruiting from another section of the Aranda people, adopts that policy for its brighter students: They are sent away to boarding school, "interstate" (in the Australian parlance), but not yet at an early age. I understand that on the single criterion of cultural adaptation, some—perhaps most—of them do well. But at what other cost?

ABORIGINES

As everyone knows, the present policy of the Australian government in regard to the aborigines is "self-determination". They should and will decide for themselves what they want to be. I think it is even just possible under our present regime (September, 1975) that a decision on their part to dispense with our educational efforts would be respected. But, of course, such a decision is most unlikely to be adopted even if they (the aborigines) read, understand, and accept the accuracy and validity of findings like ours.

There is undoubtedly a perfectly rational and objective understanding among aboriginal leaders that the white culture is here to stay and that they must learn how to master it if they are to maintain their integrity—their existence as a separate culture. To do this they must master our skills. The problem is, what skills and how to master them? And what will the mastering do to rather than for them?

The tendency to snatch at straws is probably as prevalent amongst aborigines when dealing with the white community as it is among that community when dealing with them, but with more justification because of the difficulty they (the aborigines) have in detecting any continuous strand of motive running through our vacillating and unpredictable policy decisions concerning them. In their case, the straw snatching sometimes has some of the attributes of cargo cult about it. As one aboriginal said to a school-teacher in the Northern Territory: "We want our children to learn English, not the kind of English you teach them at school, but your secret English. *We* don't understand it but we want our children to do so".

In a very real sense, it seems to me, our results indicate that he was making a penetrating and insightful remark: We do have a secret English, secret in the sense that to understand the thought that lies behind apparently straightforward verbal utterances you need to think like an English-speaking person. And you learn to do that at your mother's knee, in the bosom of the family, where you learn to interpret and to adopt the value system to which the verbal utterances give expression. What he may not realize—and I do not see how he could if he does not understand the secret English—is what he is letting himself in for, because, of course, you cannot "have" that English without also having the attitudes that go with it: the Western materialism, the "property" mentality, the restricted-extent territoriality, the estimation of monetary as opposed to spiritual wealth. These are incompatible with the maintenance of the aboriginality which he may also like to preserve. My concern is not that he might decide to surrender his children to our particular kind of child-buyer, because I do not think for a moment that he—or nis wife, anyway— would countenance it, but rather that having seen that success *is* possible he may insist on it even more energetically on the unformulated assumption that it does not carry consequences which he may later regret. And, of course, one of the conditions imposed on me when I obtained permission to carry out the work was that I would tell the people whose children I was studying what I discovered! How on earth am I going to do that?

THE PUBLIC

By this I mean the Australian taxpayer who made my studies possible. The extent of the derogation of aborigines in the white Australian community is well-documented and extremely prevalent, if widely denied. Our results, while not supporting the notion of important racial differences in innate abilities—a notion widely espoused both by the uneducated and by too many of the educated—do lend support to another widely held opinion that an aboriginal will never make "good" (become like us!) if he stays with his kith and kin. As this is undoubtedly true in most cases and in Central Australia, at the present time, our results, insofar as they become known, can only strengthen the belief. Unfortunately it is quite another problem, and strictly speaking not mine, to persuade people, first, that our way of living is not necessarily "good", second, that it may not be "best" for the aborigines and third, that aborigines when deviating from our norms may in fact have a lot of useful lessons to teach us—may indeed have vital lessons to teach us. It is a hopeless task, of course, and perhaps the only regret one should have is that his findings will make it even more hopeless.

In fact, the "public" would not be likely to hear about our findings if it were not for—

THE ACADEMICS

There is not the least doubt that the relevant academics will hear about our findings and that some of them, perhaps many and certainly those most given to public pronouncements, will use the results to bolster arguments they wish to put forward—"These results can be interpreted to mean that . . ." Since the results are related to emotionally charged issues there is a danger that versions of them—contextless extracts from them—will find their way into public scientific publications. There, insofar as they confirm existing or developing beliefs, they will be remembered; insofar as they go counter to those beliefs, they will be either forgotten, distorted, or reviled.

On the positive side, of course, the picture is not so gloomy. Our findings are of moderate scientific interest; they confirm what, with the wisdom of hindsight, we should have been able to predict. They pose interesting questions about the causes of the events but do not answer them; they suggest that we should take a closer look at the same events in our own culture. It is unlikely that the potency of the forces apparently operating would have been suspected had studies such as the present one (that is, cross-cultural and developmental) not been conducted.

I do not wish to exaggerate the possible effects of the publication of our findings. They may well be ignored, quickly forgotten, or shown to be irrelevant. And there lies the rub: Either I have failed as a scientist or I may wish I had not succeeded, for an intellectual homogenization of mankind, on the Western model, is taking place at an exponential rate which, in my opinion, is as unmitigated a disaster as would be the genetical one against which Earle Hackett warned us. And the researcher is the pathfinder, the scout sent out to probe for the weak points in the enemy's defences. One is not exonerated by not having seen himself in that role nor in the often expressed but pious hope that one day soon "they" will be in a position to turn the tables or the spyglass on us, to come and peer at us and to investigate, scientifically, our odd ways—because, by then and by definition, they will have ceased to be unlike us in most important respects.

NOTES

1. The research reported here was made possible by a grant from the Department of Education of the Australian government. The tests used all derive from Piagetian models and were administered in a Piagetian manner. Two concerned conservation (of liquid quantity and of weight). Two concerned classification (a matrix test and a test of reclassification). A fifth test was of seriation and the final one was of abstraction (Piaget's test of inclined liquid containers).

2. The adopted children were tested in 1970, in South Australia. They all came from Central Australian stock. Only 35 of such children could be located for testing (Dasen, de Lacey and Seagrim, 1973). The number of children at St. Mary's is also small, 33, and all were tested. At Hermannsberg, 10 per age group were tested. The small size of samples should be remembered when interpreting Figure 12–1. Aboriginal children attending an urban primary school also show some advance over their peers living on settlements. However, as the interpretation of these differences, which are less than those reported above, is complex, it will not be gone into here.

3. I have selected only the test for conservation of liquid quantity here because it is so well-known and widely described in the literature. The findings with the other tests used were very similar in broad outline and will, of course, be published in due course.

REFERENCES

H. Basedow (1935) *Knights of the Boomerang*. Sydney: Endeavour Press.

Burnet, F. M. (1971) Reflections on Kuru. *Human Biology, Oceania, 1*, 3–10.

Dasen, P. R. (1974) The influence of ecology, culture and European contact on cognitive development in Australian aborigines. In J. W. Berry and P. R. Dasen (Eds.), *Culture and cognition: Readings in cross-cultural psychology*. London: Methuen Pp. 381–408.

————. de Lacey, P. R., and Seagrim, G. N. (1973) Reasoning ability in adopted and fostered aboriginal children. In G. E. Kearney, P. R. de Lacey, and G. R. Davidson (Eds.), *The psychology of aboriginal Australians*. Sydney: Wiley. Pp. 97–104.

de Lemos, M. M. (1969) The development of conservation in aboriginal children. *International Journal of Psychology, 4*, 255–269.

Dobzhansky, T. (1960) Eugenics in New Guinea. *Science, 132*, 377.

Doob, L. (1976) Evaluating intervention: an instance of academic anarchy. In G. E. Kearney and D. W. McElwain (Eds.), *Aboriginal cognition: Retrospect and prospect*. Canberra: Australian Institute of Aboriginal Studies.

Forge, A. (1970) Learning to see in New Guinea. In P. Mayer (Ed.), *Socialization: The approach from social anthropology*. London: Tavistock. Pp. 269–291.

Gibb, C. A. (1971) *The report of the committee to review the situation of aborigines on pastoral properties in the Northern Territory*. Canberra: Commonwealth of Australia.

Hackett, E. (1969) Disease and diversity. In R. O. Slayter, *Man and the new biology*. Canberra: Australian National University Press. Pp. 35–49.

King, H. O. M. (1975) Kuru: epidemiological developments. *The Lancet*, October 18, 1975, 761–763.

Rappaport, R. A. (1968) *Pigs for the ancestors*. New Haven: Yale University Press.

Seagrim, G. N., and Lendon, Robin. (1973) Malnutrition and intellectual development in aboriginal children. *Medical Journal of Australia, 2*, 46.

————. and Lendon, Robin. (1976) The settlement child and school: intellectual assimilation and accommodation. In G. E. Kearney and D. W. McElwain (Eds.), *Aboriginal cognition: Retrospect and prospect*. Canberra: Australian Institute of Aboriginal Studies.

Segall, M. H., Campbell, D. T., and Herskovits, M. J. (1966) *The Influence of culture on visual perception*. New York: Bobbs-Merrill.

Shantzis, S. B., and Behrens, W. W. III, (1973) Population control mechanisms in a primitive agricultural society. In D. L. Meadows and D. H. Meadows, (Eds.), *Toward global equilibrium: Collected papers*. Cambridge, Mass.: Wright-Allen Press.

Zigas, V. (1972) A study of attitudes towards pains, disease, and death among the Fore people. *Social Science in Medicine, 6*, 689–95.

————. (1975) Kuru: A critical review. *The Medical Journal of Australia, 2*, 483–486.

Index